FLORIDA STATE
UNIVERSITY LIBRARIES

MAY 29 1998

TALLAHASSEE, FLORIDA

JESSIE McBRIDE

AUSTRALIAN ABORIGINAL ANTHROPOLOGY

AUSTRALIAN ABORIGINAL ANTHROPOLOGY

Modern Studies in the Social Anthropology
of the Australian Aborigines

edited by
RONALD M. BERNDT

PUBLISHED FOR THE AUSTRALIAN INSTITUTE OF ABORIGINAL STUDIES
BY THE UNIVERSITY OF WESTERN AUSTRALIA PRESS

First published in 1970
for the Australian Institute of Aboriginal Studies
by the University of Western Australia Press, Nedlands
Western Australia
Registered in Australia for transmission by post as a book

This book is copyright. Apart from any fair dealing for the purposes of private study, research, criticism or review, as permitted under the Copyright Act, no part may be reproduced by any process without written permission. Enquiries should be made to the publisher.

© Australian Institute of Aboriginal Studies, 1970

Set 'Monophoto' in Baskerville and printed in Western Australia
by Alpha Print Pty Ltd, Perth, Western Australia
and bound by Stanley Owen and Sons Pty Ltd
Alexandria, New South Wales

National Library of Australia Card Service Number
and Standard Book Number 85564 044 8
Library of Congress Catalog Card Number 74-138971

Contents

INTRODUCTION, *Ronald M. Berndt*   1
    The Purpose   2
    The Theme   4
    The Contributions   7

BEFORE IT IS TOO LATE, *A. P. Elkin*   19
    A Recurrent Challenge   19
    To Our Notebooks, Before It Is Too Late   22
    Use and Value of the Old Field Books   23

PROLEGOMENA TO A STUDY OF GENEALOGIES IN NORTH-EASTERN ARNHEM LAND, *Catherine H. Berndt*   29
    Circumstances of Recording   29
    Overview of Content   33
        Personal Names   35
        Formal Affiliations   37
        Betrothal and Marriage   39
    Appendix   43

LOCAL EXOGAMY AND THE WIFE'S MOTHER IN ABORIGINAL AUSTRALIA, *Warren Shapiro*   51

DEMOGRAPHIC FACTORS IN PITJANDJARA SOCIAL
ORGANIZATION, *Aram A. Yengoyan*   70
    Contemporary Setting   71
    Population Characteristics   72
    Social Organization   79
    Conclusions   90

GEOGRAPHY AND THE TOTEMIC LANDSCAPE IN CENTRAL
AUSTRALIA: A FUNCTIONAL STUDY, *T. G. H. Strehlow*   92
    Totemism in Central Australia Based on Geography   92
    Totemism and Exploitation of Natural Resources:
       Tribal Links   93
    The Great Ceremonial Centres   95
    Totemism and Social Organization   97
    Totemism: Religious Functions, Initiation and
       Iŋkŭra Festivals   102
    Geographically Based Totemism and the Problem of
       Authority   105
    Authority in the Western Desert Area   107
    Authority in the Aranda-speaking Area   110
    Capital Punishment in the Aranda-speaking Area:
       Historical Examples   112
    Capital Punishment Outside the Aranda-speaking
       Area   119
    Protection for Authority of Elders   121
    Asylum   122
    Punishment of Ceremonial Chiefs and Elders for
       Sacrilege   123
    Summary: Geographical and Religious Foundations
       of Aboriginal Authority   128

THE TRANSFORMATION OF SUBJECTS INTO OBJECTS IN
WALBIRI AND PITJANTJATJARA MYTH, *Nancy D. Munn*   141
    The Structure of Walbiri and Pitjantjatjara
       Transformations   142
    Land Claims and Local Ancestral Ties   145

The Content of Transformations	148
Transformation and Inter-generational Transmission	151
Transformation and Birth	154
Summary and Conclusion	156

A DECISION AS NARRATIVE, *Marie Reay* — 164

MYTHS OF THE ACQUISITION OF FIRE IN NORTHERN AND EASTERN AUSTRALIA, *Kenneth Maddock* — 174

BULUWANDI: A CENTRAL AUSTRALIAN CEREMONY FOR THE RESOLUTION OF CONFLICT, *Nicolas Peterson*	200
The Walbiri Fire Ceremonies	200
The *Buluwandi*	202
The Ceremony	203
The Pattern of Interaction in the Buluwandi	209
The Pattern of Co-operation: ZD Exchange as an Explanatory Model	211
Conclusion	213

TRADITIONAL MORALITY AS EXPRESSED THROUGH THE MEDIUM OF AN AUSTRALIAN ABORIGINAL RELIGION, *Ronald M. Berndt*	216
The Problem	216
The Dingari as a Moral System	221
The Overall Conception of the Dingari	232
Conclusion	243

STABILITY AND CHANGE: PRESENT-DAY HISTORIC ASPECTS AMONG AUSTRALIAN ABORIGINES, *Helmut Petri and Gisela Petri-Odermann*	248
Introduction	248
The Survival of Aboriginal Tradition	250

The Rise of a New Cult Perspective	253
The Revelation of Jinimin	258
The Introduction of the Worgaia	260
The Preliminary Ngaru-ngaru	263
The Migrations	267
The Dominance of Desert People	270
Conclusion	272

ABORIGINAL DREAM-SPIRIT BELIEFS IN A CONTACT SITUATION: JIGALONG, WESTERN AUSTRALIA, *Robert Tonkinson* — 277

Introduction	277
The Setting	278
The Dream-Spirit Concept	280
The Dream-Spirit in Curative Magic	281
The Dream-Spirit in Ritual	283
The Role of Dream-Spirit Beliefs at Jigalong	287

POLYGYNY, ACCULTURATION AND CONTACT: ASPECTS OF ABORIGINAL MARRIAGE IN CENTRAL AUSTRALIA, *Jeremy Long* — 292

THE IMPACT OF URBANIZATION ON ABORIGINAL MARRIAGE PATTERNS, *Fay Gale* — 305

THE CONTRIBUTORS — 327

INDEX — 335

Figures

GENEALOGIES, *Catherine H. Berndt*

1	Betrothal arrangement		40
2	Wrong and acceptable unions		42
3	A (i)	Blocked betrothal	45
	A (ii)	Blocked betrothal	45
	A (iii)	Blocked betrothal	46
	B	By 1968	47

MOTHER-IN-LAW BESTOWAL, *Warren Shapiro*

1	Aranda semi-moiety system	52
2	North-east Arnhem Land semi-moiety system	52

FIRE MYTHS, *Kenneth Maddock*

1	Location of myths	175

RITUAL CONFLICT-RESOLUTION, *Nicolas Peterson*

1	Ground plan until the penultimate day	204
2	Ground plan on the final night	207
3	Ceremonial interaction between workers and owners	209

MORALITY AND MYTH, *Ronald M. Berndt*

  1 Ethical universe of Desert people   234
  2 Three-sided discourse between man-man, man-god and man-natural environment   246

DREAM-SPIRIT BELIEFS, *Robert Tonkinson*

  1 North central area of Western Australia   279

URBANIZATION AND MARRIAGE, *Fay Gale*

  1 Age pyramids of the Aboriginal and non-Aboriginal population, Adelaide, 1966   309
  2 A comparison of the marital status of Aborigines and non-Aborigines, Adelaide, 1966   312
  3 A comparison of Aboriginal male and female marriage choices in Adelaide   317
  4 Regional origins of Adelaide Aborigines   319
  5 Marriage choices of Aborigines on the basis of group identification   321

Tables

MOTHER-IN-LAW BESTOWAL, *Warren Shapiro*

1	Age factors in marriage	61

DEMOGRAPHIC FACTORS, *Aram A. Yengoyan*

1	Population pyramid, Amaṭa, January 1967	73
2	Pitjandjara births, Amaṭa	74
3	Pitjandjara deaths, Amaṭa	75
4	Population pyramid, Ernabella, 1963 census	76
5	Ernabella, 1957 census	77
6	Pitjandjara births, Ernabella	78
7	Pitjandjara deaths, Ernabella	79
8	Age-specific deaths	80
9	Infant death rates	81
10	Pitjandjara crude death rates, Ernabella	81
11	All existing marriages	87
12	Bush marriages and all actual marriages with a duration of twenty or more years	88
13	Recent marriages in contact situation	88
14	Total adherence to marriage rules	88
15	Wives/married man ratio	89

RITUAL CONFLICT-RESOLUTION, *Nicolas Peterson*

1	Subsection grouping in ritual	202

MORALITY AND MYTH, *Ronald M. Berndt*

1	Relationship between Dingari myth and ritual	236-7
2	Dingari incidents seen in moral-immoral terms	240-2

ACCULTURATION AND MARRIAGE, *Jeremy Long*

1	Polygyny and monogamy in some Aboriginal populations, I	293-4
2	Polygyny and monogamy in some Aboriginal populations, II	296-7
3	Adult sex ratios in some Northern Territory Aboriginal populations (1956)	301
4	Polygyny and monogamy in some Arnhem Land populations, 1966	302-3

Acknowledgements

The Editor takes this opportunity to acknowledge with appreciation the assistance provided by the Australian Institute of Aboriginal Studies —not only its financial aid, in terms of a subsidy, but also, and in particular, the encouragement of Mr F. D. McCarthy, Principal, and Professor N. W. G. Macintosh, Chairman, of the Institute, as well as its former Secretary, Mr S. J. Boydell.

In the Introduction to this volume, I have mentioned the debt I owe my wife (Dr Catherine Berndt). Without her active help in various editorial tasks, this volume would have been considerably delayed. Mrs B. Craig, Bibliographer at the Australian Institute of Aboriginal Studies, has prepared the index.

Finally, I should mention the Board of the University of Western Australian Press, which has readily co-operated in this venture, and especially the good offices of Mr John O'Brien, Executive Officer of the Press, and the energetic and helpful editorial advice of Mrs N. Zeffertt, who has seen this work through the press.

Ronald M. Berndt

Abbreviations

English Kin Terms

B	brother	O	older
D	daughter	S	son
F	father	W	wife
H	husband	Y	younger
M	mother	Z	sister

Introduction

This volume is a result of a symposium on Social Anthropology held in Canberra in May 1968 as part of the programme arranged for the General Meeting of the Australian Institute of Aboriginal Studies. The contributors were all social anthropologists and/or Australianists who had carried out fieldwork in Aboriginal Australia. Some who could not be present at that meeting presented summarized statements *in absentia*. Among these were Professors A. P. Elkin, Helmut Petri and A. A. Yengoyan; Drs Nancy Munn, M. J. C. Calley and R. Gould; and R. Tonkinson. Professor Petri has contributed in conjunction with his wife (Dr Gisela Petri-Odermann), while Dr Gould's paper fell more within the sphere of Archaeology than Social Anthropology. Dr Calley's submission was a sketch of the present state of social anthropological fieldwork in Queensland, and consequently fell outside the scope of this volume.

Actual participants included Professors W. R. Geddes and F. G. G. Rose; Drs J. Beckett, L. Hiatt, Marie Reay, Fay Gale and K. J. Maddock; and T. G. H. Strehlow, N. Peterson, J. Long and W. Shapiro (now Dr Shapiro). The editor and his wife (Professor R. M. Berndt and Dr Catherine H. Berndt) also contributed. Except for Professors Rose and Geddes, and Drs Beckett and Hiatt, all prepared papers which now appear in this volume. In the actual symposium, summarized versions only were submitted, spoken to and discussed. At that time, no paper was in its final state ready for publication. Since then, the contributors have reconstructed their papers. Some have changed or modified their themes. Others have submitted new ones. In other words, since 1968 a great deal of energy has gone into the preparation of the papers presented here, and I would like to take this opportunity of thanking all who have participated in this venture. Especially, I acknowledge the help of my wife in preparing this manuscript for the printer. I should add that the last of this collection (not the final paper in the volume) was received early in 1970. So, although the 1968 symposium served as a base line for what we had in mind, it was really only the beginning of two years of writing and editing.

The Purpose

Those familiar with the anthropology of the Australian Aborigines will know that at the first conference on Aboriginal Studies, in 1961, a decision was taken to establish an Australian Institute of Aboriginal Studies, which was eventually centred in Canberra. This was made possible by a Commonwealth government grant, which has generously been maintained. Also following the 1961 conference, the various papers and discussions were assembled in the form of a volume on Aboriginal Studies. This was intended to provide an overview of information on all aspects of Aboriginal life—traditionally, and in regard to changes stemming from contact with others. It also pointed up gaps in that information and indicated lines for further investigation. Conference participants emphasized the importance of recording as much as possible of the fast-disappearing traditional Aboriginal cultures. But they acknowledged also that research into *all* facets of the situations in which people of Aboriginal descent find themselves today was an essential part of the Institute's activities. The volume finally appeared in 1963, under the title of *Australian Aboriginal Studies*. Its publication was a landmark in Australian Anthropology.

The present volume has no pretensions in this direction. For one thing, its coverage is not as wide: it centres on one particular field of Aboriginal-oriented Anthropology, Social Anthropology. In the 1963 Institute volume, this field was certainly taken into account. But since the time of the 1961 conference, much social anthropological research has been carried out on the Australian Aborigines, under the auspices of the Institute and of various other research bodies, including Australian and overseas universities and other institutions. The Institute, however, has borne the main brunt of this task, and in so doing has stimulated others to do likewise. A number of us therefore, including the editor of the present volume, felt that it would be useful to present a range of material which reflects both the interests of our discipline, and what Australianists are doing in the field. In a way, then, the contributors are saying, 'This is the kind of thing we are working on now, ten years after that first conference: these are the problems which concern us.' Of course, this is only a glimpse into what social anthropologists are doing in this country. It would not be possible to reflect all the problems they are working on, or interested in, even in relation to this one region, Aboriginal Australia. But I think it is fair to say that what we have here carries further some of the basic issues brought up at the 1961 conference.

We are not making an assessment of what has been accomplished in these last ten years. That would be a formidable and also a very different task. What is more, only a fraction of what has been collected on the field has been analysed and processed for publication. In one sense, what we are doing now is displaying some of our commodities in a metaphorical shop window—recognizing, and trusting others too will recognize, that there is much more 'inside': more in our field notebooks, and very much more to be obtained from people of Aboriginal descent themselves.

The 'shop window' analogy is deliberate. In 1967 (*Oceania*, Vol. XXXVII, No. 4:241-59) I commented on the interest in Australian Aboriginal material shown by the external world—external to Australia—the external world of anthropologists. I suggested that such interest was then very slight indeed, despite a few outstanding exceptions: and that these included special outcrops, so to speak, focused on the abstract building of models, often on the basis of secondhand source materials and not necessarily recent sources at that, relevant, for example, to kinship. In some cases, such model building was transmuted, and became in the process something that belonged primarily to the realm of aesthetics, where pattern is of paramount significance—or something not unlike a Rorschach design, which perhaps tells us more about the anthropologist involved than about the ethnographic material itself.

But putting it like this does less than justice to the most famous and also the most controversial of these exceptions—the flourishing phantasmogoric world of Lévi-Strauss, the world of myth and totemism, with its new dialectic—even though it has all too often meant a juggling with Aboriginal data. This inspiration has been so tremendously fructifying that it has given rise to numerous progeny, legitimate and otherwise. Some recent contributions on myth and totemism tread with conspicuous reverence in the footsteps of the master, endeavouring to demonstrate essential 'truths'. Others, approaching the problems in more or less the same style, try to show the essential falsity of Lévi-Strauss's approach. And others again, still working within the same broad framework, fall somewhere between the two extremes. Be this as it may, Lévi-Strauss's work has a special relevance to Australian Anthropology. Like Émile Durkheim in an age now chronologically past but in some respects perennially present, Lévi-Strauss has inked-in an Aboriginal outline which as far as overseas Anthropology is concerned was becoming slightly faded. It is too early yet to see his influence in perspective, although this is apparent in some of the contributions to this volume. The point I am making here is that Lévi-Strauss's writing has to some extent resurrected Australian Aboriginal material as far as *non*-Australian anthropologists are concerned—even though he has not always used contemporary sources.

To return to the local scene, the stimulation provided by the establishment of the Australian Institute of Aboriginal Studies has been manifested in a greatly increased volume of research. I do not propose to answer such questions as, How far have we progressed within recent years since, for instance, the 1961 conference? Are we saying more today, or are we saying things today so differently that they could not have been said in the same way a decade ago? Or, are we engrossed today in problems so very different from those which preoccupied us then? Personally, I do not think we are—but this is not the place to assess and evaluate. But it *is* the place to raise these questions, since they constitute part of our reason for producing such a book. In one sense, it is unfair to make the comparison between the Institute's volume of 1963 and the present one. In the first, as I have said, the terms of reference were different. It concentrated on ethnographic assessment and delineation of gaps in our information. The second, this one, takes up specific social anthropological problems. Our contribution is much more specific and particular and its ethnographic coverage is not so diffuse—except in regard to the implications arising from that material.

But this does not make the present contributions essentially different from those of the immediate past. One of the primary strengths of this volume would appear to be that it is genealogically linked with what has gone before. We are *not* faced with a range of spontaneous growths, a series of 'virgin births'. We have before us logical developments within a common frame of reference—attempts to carry the argument or arguments a little further and, in doing so, indicating (in some cases) what might lie ahead.

Another primary strength rests in our presentation of ethnographic material. As social anthropologists, we are interested in general theoretical issues, but this has not been at the expense of concern with basic empirical data. We have a primary commitment to our discipline, irrespective of ethnographic specialization, but most of us contributing here have a research focus on Aboriginal Australia. We are interested, for instance, in exploring such issues as what makes one particular Aboriginal society tick, what makes it meaningful to the people concerned, how they themselves conceptualize it and how they actually live and behave within it. In looking at the topics dealt with in these chapters, that broader framework should be kept in mind.

The Theme

The title of this volume is a straightforward statement of its overall *raison d'être*, comprising as it does a series of modern social anthropological studies on the Australian Aborigines. But within this are two interrelated themes, or dimensions. One is the sphere of social relations: the patterning of relationships between persons and groups, providing both substance and context for behaviour and belief. The other, equally pervasive, is the sphere of religious values and practice. In spite of cumulative influences from non-Aboriginal sources, the 'old way', as it is sometimes called, has proved remarkably resilient.

A decade ago, both T. G. H. Strehlow and I predicted that by now, or almost by now, 'Aboriginal traditional life as a functional reality and as a major emphasis will have virtually disappeared from the face of this continent' (*Australian Aboriginal Studies*: 394). Happily, our prediction was not fulfilled, nor does it seem likely to be within the immediate future. In recent years, a number of interesting things have been happening. In more than one area there has been a gradual but nonetheless perceptible strengthening of traditional Aboriginal ways, a resistance to assimilatory pressures. On this last point, official assimilation policies have been modified to include explicit provision for individual choice. Also, more opportunities are available now for retaining traditional elements, even though the context in which they were previously set has been changed. And public interest in Aboriginal affairs has increased considerably. Almost all people of Aboriginal descent are accessible to these influences, which purport to encourage and sustain traditional features in one form or another.

These influences, and others, have contributed to a superficial appearance of traditional vitality. But the tide seems to be turning again. The plethora of interest in this direction may in fact have the opposite effect. The drive for socio-economic viability for Aborigines, increased educational opportunities and so forth—all essential and long overdue in this respect—can only mean the widening of the gap between traditional life and that which is available to them in the wider society. And with this has come an upsurge of emphasis on Aboriginality. Many people of Aboriginal descent living in the southern and eastern cities are rediscovering themselves—attempting to establish a special identity and, in so doing, seeking to link themselves in various ways with those Aborigines who still retain a traditional or part-traditional orientation. This is a further factor of some importance contributing to a breakdown of traditional life, where it does survive within a meaningful framework. Other influences are at work, too, especially in Arnhem Land, the Western Desert and the Kimberleys. Ten years ago these areas were virtually protected. But not today. Along with exploitation of natural resources goes exploitation of human resources—not least, Aboriginal human and natural resources. In one way, then, our 1961 prediction is not really so far out!

Despite all this, Aboriginal conservatism—the persistence of traditional themes, often religious ones—is still something to be reckoned with. From the Kimberleys to the Western Desert, from Central Australia to Arnhem Land, even in a highly industrialized city like Adelaide, the survival of the past is significant in the present. In northern outback areas, many features of Aboriginal traditional life continue more or less in their time-honoured way, and their adherents include not only old and middle-aged Aborigines but also many of the younger ones. The traditional life we see today is very different from what it was even twenty years ago, and very far removed from pre-contact times. It has been drastically modified. Nevertheless, the contributions in this volume show that it still has considerable vitality. Traditional life is not being discarded lock, stock and barrel: the continuing linkage with traditional systems of belief and values is one of the major points emphasized here. We are dealing with things alive, not with things dead or about to die. But they *are* changing, and changing quite radically—much more rapidly than ever before.

A further pervading theme, and one that is actually a pivotal factor in Aboriginal religion, has political as well as economic implications for the present. This concerns Aboriginal ties with the land. In several of these contributions, land looms large—as a primary focus, reinforced and expressed in terms of social relations and social groupings. Land is a heritage from the great spirit beings of the past, a past that is always relevant to the present and, indeed, to the future; and it is not conceptualized simply as a source of material benefits but is regarded as having spiritual substance, with ramifications that are personal as well as social.

Unlike their southern 'brothers', many northern Aborigines were not, in the immediate past, faced *directly* with the prospect of complete deprivation of land and sacred sites. It is true that much of the north was taken up for pastoral and other purposes and pockets of Aborigines were left stranded within a context that was alien to them. Also, from a European point of view Aborigines had no legal rights in that land—even though they themselves had no doubts about their traditional rights to it. In the northern, central and other outback areas, large tracts of land were declared Aboriginal reserves—giving Aborigines the impression that this was Aboriginal land, land which they could use and which they were entitled to legally. But events have proved otherwise. Large tracts have been excised from such reserves for mining and other enterprises, and Aborigines have been powerless to prevent this erosion of their property.

It is not my intention, in a book of this kind, to follow this problem further. I mention it because land was overwhelmingly important to Aborigines, and it remains so today. Aboriginal religion, as some of the writers here have demonstrated, rests firmly on the land which inspired and stimulated it. Deprivation of land has brought them not just material poverty, because in basic terms this was and is their only substantial wealth, but socio-cultural impoverishment too.

The Contributions

Emeritus Professor A. P. Elkin, who retired from the Chair of Anthropology in the University of Sydney in 1956, introduces the series with a hinge chapter bridging the gap between *Australian Aboriginal Studies* (1963) and the present volume. As the most senior anthropologist represented, it is right that he should point up historic linkages, tracing out our Australian disciplinary (in fact, genealogical) connections. One major point that he makes draws attention to the tremendous backlog of unpublished material some of us have, especially those who have worked for many years in the Aboriginal field. It is certainly time we went back to this, not only because of its intrinsic value, anthropologically. Not only because the data collected, sometimes twenty to thirty years or more ago, differ from what fieldworkers can obtain today—certainly more 'traditional', certainly less influenced by pressures from the non-Aboriginal world. But, in Elkin's words, 'to see what light it throws on the reports and the interpretations of recent workers'. Of course, this poses problems of comparability: but it does, or could, provide us with more information on changing patterns in the realms of actual and purely verbal (construct, ideal) behaviour.

Dr Catherine H. Berndt's paper reports on genealogical material collected over a period of nearly twenty-four years. Although primarily methodological in orientation, it is intended as a preliminary statement on the kinds of data available on this topic in her notebooks. It underlines the vital issue of variability in social relations, specifically genealogical relationships; and this is not just a function of change through time, but an indication of flexibility in choice and in action. There is also a further consideration. North-eastern Arnhem Land is well known anthropologically through the misnamed 'Murngin' people, and has been the subject of some controversy. Many who have no first-hand knowledge of these Aboriginal people have had what they regard as the final say, on the kinship system, or sub-system, of social relationships. Dr Berndt's study is not one of kinship, but it does imply that such material must be seen in context. One of the obvious points emerging here is the difference both in material and in interpretation, when compared with the following contribution by Dr Shapiro, especially in the sphere of betrothal and marriage.

Dr Warren Shapiro's paper is based on material collected at Elcho Island, within the north-eastern Arnhem Land cultural bloc. It would be inappropriate here for me to take up various aspects of Shapiro's discussion where our data or interpretations diverge. The matter of terminology, however, requires comment. The identification of semi-moieties, unnamed in north-eastern Arnhem Land (but named in western Arnhem Land), is straightforward; they can be separated out from the formal kinship system itself, or correlated with the subsection system, which was introduced into this area between 1926-29 and 1946. Shapiro uses the term 'sib' for Warner's clan/language/people (phratry) and our (Berndts') *mada* (language or dialect unit) -*mala* ('clan'): the equation of different usages poses a problem. There is also the question of what the north-eastern Arnhem Landers should most conveniently be called. Warner used the term 'Murngin': Shapiro uses 'Miwuyt'. Miwaidj or Miwoidj (as we have preferred to spell it) is a collective name for all the *mada*, used occasionally by the people themselves. Those farther west, such as the Gunwinggu, also call them Malag (referring to their *mala*, clan, organization).

In Shapiro's paper, Professor Elkin comes in for some criticism in his identification of patrilineal cross-cousins as kinds of siblings: certainly they are not in Miwoidj thinking, although the content of behavioural pattern between these relatives (DUWEI-GALEI) could be said to make them appear to be more like brothers in an ideal sense than actual brothers. But the Miwoidj case does not necessarily rule out Elkin's contention, although that probably requires modification. Also, it is true that there was traditionally, in this particular area, a marked emphasis on gerontocracy. But in formal terms, (*a*) males in a man's own patriline married women of their own or senior alternate generation levels; (*b*) females in a man's own patriline married men of their own or junior alternate generation levels. With this 'balance', as it were, gerontocratic aspects were less clear-cut. One point on which disagreement will undoubtedly arise concerns Shapiro's 'mother-in-law bestowal'. It is taken up briefly by Catherine Berndt and need not be considered here in more detail. But I should note that the information we have does not support the emphasis on 'bestowal' *as such*, of a mother-in-law, whether a child or an adult. The ritual mentioned by Shapiro is similar to the one I have referred to earlier (R. M. Berndt, in M. F. Nimkoff, ed., *Comparative Family Systems*, 1965:84) and, in translation, is the 'promise' meeting when a betrothal is ratified. In our understanding of the case, it is not the mother-in-law who is being bestowed but the issue of her womb. It is true that, even today, a small boy may be told, 'There's your mother-in-law, she will provide you with a wife', and the person in question may be a very small girl: but the weighting is on what she is expected to produce. One of the difficulties here is that Shapiro is dealing with retrospective material, since the ritual to which he refers is rarely carried out these days. But even when it was operative a decade or so ago, from what we have seen it referred to direct betrothals. It is certainly an interesting thought that wives may be a by-product of mother-in-law bestowals: but more evidence is needed.

Still within the dimension of social structure and organization, Professor Aram A. Yengoyan turns to questions of demography. As he observes, social anthropologists have rarely concerned themselves with purely demographic problems. Yet, many of us have worked in regions where alien pressures have been minimal—especially those anthropologists who carried out field research in outback areas up to, say, 1945. Ooldea in 1941 contained a large proportion of Desert people who had only recently (at that time) come into the mission settlement there: and during the period we worked there others were coming in and were having their first experience of aliens and their ways. The area to the north was hardly touched by Europeans. The Bidjandjara (Pitjandjara) with whom Yengoyan worked, as a dialect unit, belong to a wider population which, under different dialect names, spread across the whole of the Western Desert (see R. M. Berndt, *Oceania*, 1959:82-107). Yengoyan rightly points out the significance of spheres of interaction focused on specific areas. This means that in most of the Desert, with the probable exception of the Aranda, actual territories were defined flexibly and that even in traditional times interactory spheres were of major importance. The population figures presented by Yengoyan are revealing, but one point should be noted in this connection. It is doubtful whether female infanticide was as prevalent, traditionally, as has been suggested in the early literature and by missionaries. The implications of population *vis-à-vis* ritual are noteworthy. Yengoyan suggests that acceptance of a European diet and economy makes it possible for large groups to meet for ritual purposes. In the pre-contact period, he says, a large ritual meeting would have been rare. This is probably quite true, and was certainly the case in bad to middling seasons—but in good seasons it was another matter.

As Yengoyan notes, the traditional pattern of local organization (among the Bidjandjara) is no longer operative; but in the western sectors of the Desert region, at least to some extent, the local descent group is still significant. What Yengoyan is saying is not at variance with this: the organizational scene (the aspect of 'process') is changing radically. Claims may be made to local sites, sacred or otherwise, which have economic potentialities from a European standpoint (in regard to mining, etc.), and these claims may be based on fairly tenuous kin linkages. But this is quite in order, traditionally. Stanner's and Hiatt's discussions on the nature of the local group and on residence patterns are not really very appropriate in this context; the picture of Desert local group organization is well known in a traditional sense and poses few problems. Here, as elsewhere, expressed perhaps in different ways, we are faced with two sorts of unit, or group—the local descent group and the food-collecting and hunting unit, sometimes called the horde or band, each serving different but associated functions, and each different in composition but recruited from the same range of persons. This distinction is important to Yengoyan's analysis. With all this, Bidjandjara ties with their land emerge clearly and significantly—even in the light of substantial alterations in the traditional organization.

T. G. H. Strehlow's contribution provides us with an intimate view of Central Australian totemism or religious perspective in relation to the land. It is the totemic landscape with which he is concerned, and he sees this as a clue to understanding socio-cultural life among the Aranda and Desert peoples. This article is a follow-up of one which appeared in *Aboriginal Man in Australia* (R. M. and C. H. Berndt, eds, 1965).

One point in this context which needs to be looked at again, not necessarily by Strehlow, is the labelling of Western Desert organization as being *looser* and more fluid than that of the Aranda. This is certainly a plausible suggestion in regard to the dialect unit as such, but it is not necessarily so because they traditionally lacked a subsection or land-based class system. Over and above this question, Aranda social life certainly appears to have been more formalized than that of their neighbours. From Yengoyan's perspective Desert life *was* relatively fluid (at the time of his fieldwork): Bidjandjara traditional social organization has been considerably modified within the last couple of decades. But traditionally the Desert local group was quite decidedly land based—and in many parts of the Desert remains so. In some cases this is an indirect connection, as Tonkinson has shown for the people at Jigalong who cherish a belief in the possibility of dream-visits to sacred sites. Moreover, the traditional Desert local group was a kin-based group as well. Especially in Strehlow's detailed consideration of the religious functions of Aranda local groups, I can see many striking parallels to Western Desert belief and practice.

One of the outstanding features of Strehlow's paper is his discussion of authority and social control. He takes up a number of points that I have touched on elsewhere in *Aboriginal Man in Australia* (Chapter 7) and in *The World of the First Australians* (Chapter X), and particularly the fact that we cannot dismiss the importance of Aboriginal leadership. This is substantiated by material from the Western Desert as from the Aranda, where his data are more expansive. Strehlow takes up the views of some anthropologists (for example, Meggitt and Hiatt) who hold that certain Aboriginal groups were leaderless and had no governmental institutions. Strehlow sees the totemic landscape as forming a basis for religion, for social order and for established authority.

Dr Nancy Munn, continuing the religious theme, deals with mythical transformations among the Bidjandjara (Pitjantjatjara) and the Wailbri (Walbiri). She takes up the point that the term for Dreaming (that is, the label often used in anthropological writing to refer to the sacred past, the creative period, and the sacred spirit beings) also means 'dream', and she follows the implications of this, especially among the Wailbri. As she is probably aware, though she does not go into this facet of the question, ordinary dreams are usually distinguished from this particular (mythical) time-perspective, and among the majority of the Desert groups the demarcation between the two concepts is relatively clear cut. What emerges plainly from her contribution is Aboriginal identification with the land, in what is basically a three-fold relationship between land-spirit being-person. Supporting this is Dr Munn's reference to the belief that a spirit being is metamorphosed as a permanent feature of the countryside: the word used, *burga-ri* (or *bugari*) is not equated with dying—the spirit being *becomes* the country, or a particular piece of country. In other areas, the terms used, in translation, mean 'turned into', 'changing shape', 'becoming'. The theme is continued: generations of dead are successively transformed into country: and they maintain a perpetual claim upon it. For the living, claim to land is ratified not only through mythic charter but through their immediate dead—who, in fact, enter the mythic stream.

Dr Marie Reay has chosen, in her contribution, an acculturated situation where traditional mythic material is used in a non-traditional way and where the investigator herself is used as one of the pawns in the game of social living. The material relates to Aboriginal women and their own ritual cycle, the *jawalju* (*yawalyu*), which is widely distributed and which has been discussed elsewhere by Dr Catherine Berndt.

Dr Kenneth Maddock takes up Lévi-Strauss's myth analysis in considering Aboriginal myths relevant to the acquisition of fire. In doing this, he covers a wide range of material and has had to be, necessarily, selective. Some of the myths he considers have several versions or are segments of long sacred cycles. For instance, the Dalabon (Dangbon?) myth appears among Gunwinggu at Oenpelli. Myth, of course, lends itself to different interpretations. And as Maddock points out, Aborigines, when asked about the origin of things, usually place the responsibility on the broad shoulders of their mythic beings: 'They did this, we must follow', 'We do this because the ancestors did', and so on: explanations are found in the Dreaming. But the question of whether this is intended to deny their own *human* responsibility and creativeness is another matter. In view of what others have said, another interpretation could be put forward. For instance, with the close identification of human and spirit beings, it could be said that such statements enhance their own position: the mythic beings are not seen as essentially separate or distinct from their living counterparts.

The bringing of fire is an interesting theme, the subject of numerous myths throughout the continent. The Nagugur (or Maddock, Nagorgo) are major characters in Gunwinggu Kunapipi mythology: teaching men to use firesticks was one small item in their wanderings over a large stretch of country, including Dangbon territory. The summarized account quoted from Mountford, of the Crocodile and Plover myth from Oenpelli, actually exists in a much larger version and contains some interesting side-issues. The essential thing about such myths is that they are not fantastic even though they may deal with shape-changing creatures. It is not Plover as a bird who manipulates firesticks, but Plover in human shape. The same is the case with a 'Murngin' myth, a fragment of a sacred cycle, in which Crocodile burns his 'arms'. One version of the Kakadu myth recorded by Spencer, on women's secreting of fire in their vaginas, was told to me at Oenpelli but said to be of Amurag origin. Maddock postulates a super-myth on fire, made up of segments which have been scattered over a wide area. He suggests that, for instance, all Arnhem Land fire myths fit together, forming a larger explanatory narrative. This opens up some intriguing lines for speculation, and involves the problem of separating myth-segments from the context of other issues—since mostly an explanation of the origin of fire is embedded in a wide range of other mythic incidents not necessarily related to fire at all.

The Kunmanggur myth from Stanner bears comparison with the Chickenhawk one from the same Daly River area, although Stanner's was Murinbata and mine Ngulugwongga. This raises the question of the 'cooked and the raw', so apparent in the Wawalag myth of north-eastern Arnhem Land and so relevant to Lévi-Strauss's framework. The question of fire (and its possession) being mythically linked with life and death is an interesting proposition that Maddock puts forward, in terms of the takers and the losers. To clinch this, or perhaps give it a different twist, an analysis of myths concerning how death came into the world would be useful.

Nicolas Peterson writes on the 'Fire Ceremony' witnessed by Spencer and Gillen in 1901. In their case it involved the Waramunga (Warramunga): in Peterson's, the Wailbri (Walbiri). I should probably mention that my wife and I observed such a ritual at Wave Hill in 1944 (with Mudbara, Gurindji and Wailbri participants), although the mythological background differed. In Peterson's case, it is the myth of Yaripiri. (This has been the subject of a volume by C. P. Mountford, entitled *Winbaraku and the myth of Jarapiri*, 1968. T. G. H. Strehlow has a great deal of material on this mythological constellation.) In the Balgo region of the southern Kimberleys, people influenced by the Wailbri (especially Gogadja/Mandjildjara) have a similar fire ritual, but in that case ritual action is substantiated by a mythical fire. (See R. M. Berndt's contribution in this volume.)

Peterson's analysis is in social terms, and depends on the patterning of co-operation (which in this context is limited) between members of different subsections. A focal point is the stylization of aggressive tendencies, which he sees as a reflection of sister's daughter exchange.

My own contribution brings in a number of aspects already referred to in other papers. For example, the significance of religion in varying contexts of social living, its basic connection with the land, the transformation of mythic beings and symbolic elements associated with them, along with the three-fold relationship with Aboriginal man. The main burden of the analysis rests on the meaning of mythology within a local area which can be classified as Western Desert in orientation. This analysis owes little to Lévi-Strauss, although the general statements made are directly relevant to his scheme. The focus is predominantly inward-looking, concerned with meaning for the people themselves. Essentially, too, the contention is that myth is reflective of contemporary problems. In this instance, the problems dealt with in myth are those facing all traditionally oriented Aborigines—even those influenced by external pressures. These problems refer to relationships between interdependent entities—man, land/nature, spirits; and problems concerning action and decision against a system of values. In both cases, an explanatory model is used to view this as an integrated configuration articulated on the basis of moral-immoral issues.

Professor Helmut Petri and his wife (Dr Gisela Petri-Odermann) have approached the problem of changing ritual perspective from a strategically positioned area, the Catholic mission settlement at La Grange. There, an indigenous population nucleus, subjected to intensive contact over many years, has been augmented by Desert Aborigines who have come in to the station from time to time and in the process have formed a new community, structurally different from the traditional style. From the perspective of La Grange and neighbouring areas, the Western Desert *looks* different. One would expect this to be so, since looking out and over to another area is bound to provide a view unlike that other's own view of itself and the outside world—even though contacts exist between them. This is certainly the case as far as the La Grange view of Jigalong and Balgo is concerned. Obviously, in the process of Desert removal (migration) from their home areas, these people have undergone marked changes. These are to be expected, but are not necessarily recognized by themselves. The influence of varying Christian ideology, together with pressures derived from the McLeod activities in the Pindan district, has apparently produced a fascinating admixture of syncretistic belief and ritual, still embedded in traditional roots. In other words, the degree of cultural alteration is not so far advanced as to obliterate essentially traditional elements. And this has led the Petris to emphasize the conservative nature of Aboriginal life in this particular area. The influence of the McLeod group is an interesting factor here. It is one which J. and K. Wilson studied in some detail in 1958-61 (see for instance, in *Aborigines Now*, M. Reay, ed., 1964:133-42, 151-66; but mainly in their two Master's theses). Another area of influence for the La Grange people was Jigalong. Here again we have R. Tonkinson's material (see his contribution in this volume, and his Master's thesis). A third area is that of Derby, where M. Robinson has been working. And a fourth is Balgo, where my wife and I have carried out field research at intervals over several years. These are all impinging influences, and all are mentioned in this contribution. However, from no one of these have we reports of syncretistic cults as described by the Petris. Certainly, in each, Christian influences are at work—but they have not crystallized in the way they have at La Grange. This, then, provides us with a very interesting problem, in the transmutation of ideas and Aboriginal attribution of features which are projected into situations which they think they know by virtue of having come from them in the immediate past or by means of direct or indirect communication. It also raises a further question of the compartmentalization of belief and action, since interaction does take place between La Grange and these other areas— at least from time to time: it is not a case of separation.

Several issues here require extended discussion. One is the millenarian aspect, especially in comparison with *An Adjustment Movement in Arnhem Land* (R. M. Berndt 1962), which did not take on this guise although it was partially syncretistic. And there are other examples. Another interesting point, from the perspective of the La Grange people, is the placing of the source of all traditional knowledge firmly in the Western Desert. The revelation of Jinimin (Jesus) took place, it is said, among the Woneiga (or Wonajagu). The Woneiga are closely associated with the Wailbri (Walbiri), and some were present at Birrundudu (near Gordon Downs on the Northern Territory side) in 1944-45. However, at Balgo a distinction was sometimes made between Woneiga and Wailbri. As the Petris rightly point out, the collective term Julbari-dja (as used at La Grange) means 'south, *julbara* [or *julbre*], from'. Birrundudu people called the Wailbri Juwalbri or Julbre; Tindale's distinction is incorrect, and it is highly probable that the term Wailbri is derived from the word Julbari-dja. From Balgo perspective, the Wailbri were (as noted) sometimes distinguished from the Woneiga; but close links existed between the Wailbri and the Gogadja and Ngadi who, in turn, were considered 'true' Western Desert people. The Walmadjeri, on the other hand, were located around old Balgo station, and a little way down the Canning Stock Route: but their territory abutted on the Djaru (not too far from Sturt Creek) and into Billiluna, roughly fringing southern Kimberley pastoral stations. Intervening between them and Christmas Creek were Gunia, with Djiwalin (Djualin) at Christmas Creek. In spite of Meggitt's reference to the Worgaia as a tribal name, it is doubtful if this is more than a reference term suggesting that people in a certain direction have the *worgaia* ritual. Tindale's reference to Gogadja as having abandoned their hunting grounds to travel as far south-east as Eyre's Peninsula in South Australia is romantic speculation. The Kukatja, as mentioned by T. G. H. Strehlow in this volume, were not the same people as the Gogadja near Balgo, although it is apparent that they were culturally of the Western Desert.

The contribution of the Petris rests on the problem of the amalgamation of ritual elements seen in terms of cultural revival. Certainly a crucial aspect in this connection is the sustaining force of tradition, actually supported by external elements but also through intelligent adaptation to contemporary pressures of a politico-religious nature. In migratory terms, the so-called Julbari-dja have played an important role in stimulating cult activity at La Grange. A parallel can be drawn with the situation at Ernabella in the middle 1940s when 'bush people' served to bolster ritual life which, through mission and pastoral pressures, was rapidly losing ground. Not just vitality (emotional or psychological stimulus) but *content* or substance was communicated, bending the balance toward the traditional in Aboriginal terms. But even then the reservoir was gradually drying up, and the indication was that, once the influx ceased, the process of de-traditionalization would continue on unhindered. However, within the last few years there has been an upsurge of cult activity throughout the Central Ranges region, especially in regard to the Red Ochre ritual. How long this will persist is another matter. At La Grange, the Walmadjeri did not have far to move. Like the Djualin, they were directly exposed to European influences; but they were bolstered by the Gogadja who, in turn (from a Balgo perspective), did not have to exert much pressure to force Walmadjeri movement. The Balgo-Yuendumu axis (in terms of Gogadja-Wailbri cultures) is crucial in this whole question of traditional influences; and intermediaries carrying these far afield (relatively speaking) owe their strength to this. How long it will remain as an inspiration to linked peoples territorially removed from the axis is open to question. But once it is weakened or disappears, there are no further cultural resources of a purely traditional nature to rely on. The implications of this, in the Petri article, are especially interesting.

Robert Tonkinson shows that even though Jigalong Aborigines live a long way from their home territories, they are not psychologically separated from them. One way of maintaining contact is through dream-spirits: native doctors and others travel, in their dreams, over a wide area. The spirits themselves are Dreaming and belong to the eternal stream, and in this context they are manifested through dreams. They and their ritual and magical expressions have a vital place in the lives of Jigalong people. Significantly, they underwrite land ownership and intimate association with the country, often far-distant country, for people living away from it without much hope of physically revisiting it. Here we have, as it were, a staking of claim which is fully substantiated by traditional usage. They show no intention of relinquishing their land. The fact that they no longer occupy it physically does not signify; in their view it *is* occupied, spiritually. This is simply an extension of the different functions of the local descent group and the food-collecting and hunting unit, in a situation where mixed social and economic pressures had forced them away from their traditional territories: from the estate and domain; from the sacred sites on one hand and, on the other, from the country over which they previously hunted. Coming to Jigalong they formed a new community—a mixed one, as at La Grange. In the circumstances, it has been virtually impossible for them to maintain the former shape and content of the food-collecting and hunting unit, or the on-the-site ritual obligations of the local descent group. But traditional precedent has enabled them to sustain these connections at the level of 'real' *spiritual* action, manifested through stylized dreams. On this basis they can claim, for instance, that they have not relinquished their responsibility toward their sacred sites. One precedent for such action is to be found at Balgo, where some spirit beings in the *dingari* mythology mounted their sacred boards and flew through the air. A direct parallel there, as in the Jigalong situation, is with the vehicles used by native doctors.

The strengthening of traditional belief at Jigalong (which reinforces the Petris' statements regarding conservatism) has direct implications for the present. As Tonkinson notes, the Jigalong people are attempting to dissociate themselves from outside influences which, in their view, might weaken their traditional perspective.

Jeremy Long takes up the incidence of polygyny primarily in three Desert areas, making comparisons with other Aboriginal populations. This material links up with several other contributions in this volume, and is especially significant in testing propositions put forward by F. G. G. Rose (for Groote Eylandt) and M. Meggitt (for the Wailbri). Decline in polygyny *seems* to be correlated with degree of acculturation—

but this is not the whole story, as Long points out. In his discussion, it is fairly clear that traditional and near-traditional demographic factors are important. Moreover, in Desert areas the incidence of polygyny was traditionally lower than in other regions—but even here, there is variation.

As the final contributor, Dr Fay Gale considers Aboriginal marriage patterns in the face of urban pressures. Her study focuses on Adelaide, and on people of Aboriginal descent who are usually regarded as having little of their traditional life left to rely on: people who are to all intents and purposes oriented in Australian-European terms. As Dr Gale points out, in rural areas up to the last decade or so it was possible, mainly because of their comparative isolation, for people of Aboriginal descent to retain socio-cultural features which marked them off distinctively from the wider society. In recent years, with their movement into the city and the spread of urban influences into rural areas, this is less evident. But even with this increased mobility, the 'old ways' are not as yet entirely eradicated.

As editor, I have found it impossible to resist the impulse to comment on the various contributions offered here. On one hand, my wife and I have worked in or near most of the areas dealt with in these articles: and it can, at times, be useful to have one of the 'older' anthropologists look at these from his own standpoint—in terms of 'What has he got to say about the things I'm discussing?' (But I would hasten to add that I do not consider myself an anthropologist of the 'older generation' but simply, to use Elkin's words, one 'of the generation not so old'.) On the other hand, the commentary is intended to serve a dual purpose—that of providing an inter-connected summary *and* a demonstration of basic threads and themes.

In a way, then, looking again at the overall scope of this volume, we have here a cross-section of varying Aboriginal situations. For the most part, these studies have concentrated on regions where traditional life is still a dominant force: in the Western Desert, in the southern Kimberleys, in Arnhem Land. Even at La Grange, cultural revivalism is a factor of considerable importance: even among the Aranda, and even among those women at Borroloola. Except for the last two contributions in this series, the significance of religion is still an overriding aspect, which must be taken into account. And there is sufficient evidence to suggest that claims to land on one hand and the development of self-identification on the other could become even more salient issues. Aborigines are seeking ways in which their aspirations in these directions can be tangibly expressed, and one way of doing so is through avenues that are conceived of as being traditionally Aboriginal. I shall not attempt to predict what will happen in the immediate future. Moreover, we must be sure we do not read too much into these particular instances, when so many other influences are at work. One thing is certain: whatever in the way of traditional elements survives in the immediate future will be considerably modified to fit changing circumstances.

This volume, then, is not only a contribution to anthropological theory, in the various issues which are considered within it. It is a document which provides us with an overall assessment of Aboriginal sociocultural life, on the basis of a number of specific regions and topics. Naturally, it is selective; naturally, there are numerous gaps; it is not possible to review all Aboriginal situations found in this continent today. There are many variations on the circumstances dealt with here. It does not claim to provide a full-scale view of Aborigines in Australia. But it does present a picture of contemporary Aboriginal life, concerning quite a large number of people of Aboriginal descent. It is a life in which the majority (except for those living in cities or in immediate country areas), even though they are in varying ways under pressure to change and adapt, are still very much concerned with Aboriginal traditional features. And a corollary to this is, to put it generally, the need to understand such factors if we are at all concerned with their social welfare and advancement.

Ronald M. Berndt
Department of Anthropology
University of Western Australia

A. P. ELKIN

Before It Is Too Late

A RECURRENT CHALLENGE

'Before it is too late' has been a recurrent challenge to research in Australian Aboriginal Anthropology. Faced by the sure and certain dying out of the tribes and by the even quicker breakdown of their culture, George Taplin, R. Brough Smyth, E. M. Curr, A. W. Howitt and R. H. Mathews recognized and responded to the challenge. With the help of correspondents near and far, they observed, gleaned and garnered what and where they could. Like Baldwin Spencer, the forerunner of scientific and intensive field research in the Australian region, they knew that opportunity was passing fast. As Spencer wrote (1921: lix): 'It is only those who have worked in the field, both amongst natives in their natural state and amongst others who have been in more or less close contact with settlements, who can realize how rapidly, under the latter conditions, their genuine and primitive customs become modified or even lost.'

In my paper presented to the 1961 Conference on Aboriginal Studies (Elkin 1963:3-28) I summarized what I termed a compiling and collating phase of Aboriginal enquiry, and a phase of individual, fortuitous projects into which it shaded. In both phases, however, the dominant aim was one of salvage or at best of recording before it was too late. 'The old order quickly changes', wrote Dr E. C. Stirling in the Anthropology section of the *Report of the Horn Scientific Expedition to Central Australia*, 1894 (published 1896). 'Through the heart of the continent from Adelaide to Port Darwin (as well as from Newcastle Waters to the Gulf of Carpentaria) the telegraph line, in its construction and maintenance' had brought the Aborigines into contact, and sometimes into clash, with the 'white' man. In addition, pastoral settlement had already been effected east and west of the line 'for a considerable distance and for some years'. No wonder that Baldwin Spencer introduced the epoch-making *Native Tribes of Central Australia* (1899) by F. J. Gillen and himself, with the words, 'The time in which it will be possible to investigate the Australian native tribes is rapidly drawing to a close', and their second book, *The Northern Tribes of Central Australia* (1904), with the explanation that the research for it was undertaken (in 1901-2) 'to learn more of the customs and beliefs of the aborigines before it is too late to study them'. Thus, time was already running out at the turn of the century, even among the Aborigines of Melville Island and of Oenpelli in the far north, whom Spencer studied in 1912 (Spencer 1914) with the help of a well-established settler in each case.

A valuable contribution in this 'individual and fortuitous phase' was made by Pastor Carl Strehlow on the Western Aranda and the neighbouring Loritja—tribes whose culture he was working to change. As for the other workers during this phase, such as A. W. Howitt and R. H. Mathews, who belong also to the preceding phase, Mrs Langloh Parker, H. Basedow, John Mathew, H. Klaatsch and A. R. Brown, a trained and experienced professional anthropologist: these were all engaged in salvaging information and studying aspects of Aboriginal social organization and culture while tribal remnants remained. Apart from Basedow on a few, brief occasions,[1] they had no experience of a pulsating Aboriginal social structure and culture not yet broken down by contact with white settlement. But they did what they could before it was too late, according to their own and current anthropological interests.[2]

To do more required organized systematic plans of research, supported by adequate finance and carried out by trained personnel. This was to come in the third decade of this century. It was led up to by a recommendation of the Australian Meeting in 1914 of the British Association for the Advancement of Science, and more definitely by a resolution of the meeting in Melbourne and Sydney of the Second Pan-Pacific Science Congress in 1923. The Australian National Research Council carried on from there. As the result of its representations, a Department of Anthropology was established in the University of Sydney in 1925 to be financed by grants from the Australian federal and state governments. In addition, the Council obtained substantial grants from the Rockefeller Foundation which enabled research to be planned and carried out from 1926 to 1938. I have summarized the progress of this phase of research and what followed in *Mankind* (Elkin 1958:225-42; 1959:321-33), and referred to it in my contribution to the 1961 Conference. In that, too, I referred to the important research projects carried out in collaboration with the Research Council or independently by workers from other institutions.

I only refer to this phase here because inherent in the challenge to the Australian National Research Council and in the Council's representations to governments and foundations was the theme that the research must be done very soon, or it would be too late. Thanks mainly to Commonwealth research grants to universities, and to some private grants, fieldwork went on after World War II, but usually on inadequate budgets. Then, once again the 'before it is too late' challenge rang out, and the Australian Institute of Aboriginal Studies was established. As a result we can look on the decade of the 1960s with a sense of achievement. A great deal has been done in the several branches of Anthropology. There has been much bustling, much going to and fro both in fieldwork and in administration, while committees, plans and reports have demanded almost all the time and energy of senior members of the Institute—at least, it has seemed at times to be like that.

On the other side, the list of projects undertaken is formidable and the list of publications put out by the Institute or supported by it very praiseworthy, and indeed, comforting, for Australia can rightly demand worthwhile results in return for the large expenditure involved.[3] Before long, an overall picture should be prepared of the field research undertaken, accomplished, and made available through publication. It would show the gaps filled in wholly or in part, the geographical regions of research 'occupied' and the subjects and problems tackled, together with an evaluation of results.

As with search in the mineral and oil fields, so, too, the Institute is observing, surveying, probing, sounding, drilling and extracting. The dividends will be high, though probably not in every project. Some fields are poor. Some individuals are just not good fieldworkers. Moreover, many are apprentices, usually with no master nearby—a situation which the Institute recognizes. The individual using the field opportunity to gather material to write up for a first or even second postgraduate degree may not only lack training, and of course field experience, but also may feel the strain of working for an examination—a degree. He must get material, and it must be good. He probably thinks it is. The temptation of the apprentice, the postgraduate student thesis gatherer, is to think that what he sees, records and interprets is the correct version, and it may be so. Others who preceded him in earlier years, and reported or interpreted something differently, were, in his opinion, possibly wrong; in any case they are out of date, not 'with it'.

This attitude and this criticism may seem naïve to the seasoned fieldworker, who has 'some grey hair', as the Aborigines would say, and is not under thesis strain. But I would not discourage it. Such criticism is good for the earlier and older workers. It challenges their versions and interpretations, which could be at fault. It should drive them back, not into memories so much as into their own field notebooks and to their studies based on these.

To Our Notebooks, Before It Is Too Late

So I come to my use here and now of the oft-repeated challenge: 'before it is too late'. It is not for field research with its glamour and difficulties, and which the older we are, the more we enjoy, for the field is peopled with old friends and reveals ever deepening knowledge. The challenge is for research into one's own field notebooks, reports and publications. And this really is urgent and important. A linguist hastens a few hundred miles to catch the only surviving speaker of a language before he dies. A social anthropologist hurries hither and thither to piece together the last shreds of a tribe's culture. Or our film makers take their equipment many hundreds of miles to visit a group who may still be able to perform a certain dance or ritual or re-enact old-time daily activities.

It is just as important, perhaps more so in some cases, to persuade all those anthropologists of the older generation, and of the generation not so old, who have worked in the field, to revalue their material, to see what light it throws on the reports and interpretations of recent workers, and particularly to make available all the material they gathered. The Institute has tried to obtain from such persons an inventory of the contents of their field records, but much of the latter is a closed book except to the individual fieldworker.

I am not saying anything original. The Institute's Council has said it. The former Australian National Research Council said it. But I am saying it as part of the 'before it is too late' challenge: the 'BIITL' challenge.

Of course, the call is primarily to myself. With the best will in the world, I cannot allow, on statistical grounds, years and years for me to work up my unpublished field material or to rework the basic data on which my publications were based. Other workers, members of the Institute or not, not so old as I, who have been in the Aboriginal field from ten to forty years ago, should also re-examine their notebooks searching for treasures new and old. For who can set the term of his working life, whatever be his age? I must not mention names lest bone-pointing be suspected, but I guess there are boxes and drawers and files full of primary research material, still unmined, and much more which should be reworked.

We all have good reasons for not having published more: running a university department or other institution, working for the welfare of native races, serving the Research Council or the Australian Institute of Aboriginal Studies, or just living. But whether our priorities were correct or wise is another matter. It is too late to argue about that. The relevant question is: what remains in our notebooks and working files?

Speaking for myself, much of value is so hidden. Its value lies not only in the quality and range of the data, but in the periods of fieldwork. Thus the scores of Kimberley genealogies and related data, of which only a bare summary has been published, were obtained in 1927-28, a base line for changes which have occurred; similarly my material for northern and western South Australia and the Laverton district of Western Australia dates from 1930; for the north coast of New South Wales and south-eastern Queensland from 1931-36 and 1944; for Delissaville (Darwin region) and the upper Roper, Beswick Creek and Mainoru, roughly south-western and central Arnhem Land, from 1946 to 1953; and for the northern Arnhem Land coast from 1946. Since changes have occurred, drastic in some cases, in all these regions, this basic material, if lost, could not be obtained again. 'Memory culture' salvaged from survivors is seldom unmodified by the experience of the informants and by what has happened during the intervening years. Of course, we older workers have published much; for myself: totemism and some ritual in the Kimberleys; kinship and totemism in South Australia; music and ritual in Arnhem Land, and so on. Moreover, my full kinship and other material from the Forrest River and East Kimberley, and from the Karadjeri (La Grange) was made available long ago to Phyllis Kaberry and Ralph Piddington as a basis for their own fieldwork. In addition, my lectures in the University of Sydney and at the Australian School of Pacific Administration have been based largely on my unpublished material.

I have no doubt that the fieldworkers of the late 1920s and the 1930s and 1940s could give a similar, and possibly better account of themselves.

Use and Value of the Old Field Books

So much for the challenge and appeal to those of us with unpublished material. Let me illustrate its use.

In a review of the first edition of *The Australian Aborigines: How to Understand Them*, 1938, Father E. Worms, a comparatively recent arrival in Beagle Bay in Nyul-Nyul tribal territory, said I erred in stating that the Bard tribe, the next tribe to the north, lacked sections. But sections were not recorded in any of my fifty-four Bard genealogies, and in addition the term for mother's mother's brother's son was 'wife's father' and not 'father' as was usual when kinship terms were correlated with a section system. The point was that my recording was for early 1928. By the time Father Worms was established the section system was spreading northward to the Bard. This was confirmed by Dr Capell. Whether or not the term for mother's male cross-cousins had become adjusted to the sections was not reported. I witnessed in 1930 the spreading of section systems to the Mt Margaret region, and in 1946 of the subsection system to Yirrkalla.

Similarly, when the Djauan subsection table I had prepared for fieldworkers was queried, reference to the genealogy books for the Djauan and its neighbour the Ngalgbun as well as to Baldwin Spencer's table resolved the matter. Likewise, when my genealogies for the Mangarai on the Roper suggested that Spencer wrongly attributed subsection totemism to this tribe, further examination of them and enquiry showed he was right, and that the totemic names appearing in more than one subsection were Dreamings, symbols of membership of patrilineal cult-lodges.

A few years ago Rodney Needham, when debating with F. B. Livingstone on prescriptive alliance (marriage) systems in Australia, wrote asking whether any further Ungarinyin material was available. After consulting my notebooks and genealogies I sent data which included the following: marriage is always with the daughter of a *waiiŋi* man, but variation appears on the wife's mother's side; thus in most cases wife's mother's mother and wife's mother's brother's wife are classified with *mariŋi*, wife; half that number are *ŋadji*, mother; a few are *maleŋi*, sister's daughter; or father's sister's daughter; and fewer still are *wuniŋi*, sister's husband's sister. Further, wife's mother's father and wife's mother's brother may be *noliŋi*, brother, or *idje*, father, and wife's mother can be, and occasionally is, *amalŋi*, father's sister, or *laliŋi*, sister, provided these persons are 'distant' relatives. I noted eleven cases of marriage with distant brother's daughter's daughter or distant father's daughter's daughter. In two cases wife's mother's father was *kaiiŋi*, which is mother's mother's brother, but the latter was not Ego's own mother's mother's brother, although he did belong to the same clan country.

These statements, bewildering to hear, show, first, that the Ungarinyin were very human and, second, that I should make available all the data I possess so that theorists can pursue their goals. I fear that the Ungarinyin can no longer pursue theirs within their former social structure; reduced in number, they now live out of their own territory in the Derby district. However, I am checking some details through Howard Coate, who is in Derby and who has mastered the Ungarinyin language, but I realize that 'memory culture' may be unreliable in details. Thus, in my genealogies of 1928 *mamiŋi* denotes mother's father only twice; every other time the term is *kandiŋi*, which is mother's brother and in all my material is also mother's brother's son. But Rose and Jolly, after questioning hospital patients in Broome in 1939-40, said it was not used for the latter nor for mother's father; these two were always *mamiŋi*. Coate's aged informant in Derby also says *mamiŋi* is mother's father and mother's brother's son. However, in both cases the enquiries were of an abstract nature, whereas my genealogies record terms applied between actual persons. However, changes were no doubt occurring in the direction of indicating alternate generation levels in the mother's brother's patrilineal clan; certainly, these were distinguished in a person's own clan back in 1928.[4]

Another interesting case which could perhaps be settled from early notebooks, and elaborated, if possible, by further fieldwork, is that of the so-called 'Murngin'. J. Barnes (1967) has conducted an inquest on this. But his is not the final inquest. Among many others, Pin-Hsiung Lin contributed, in late 1967, a 'Note' on the system with the promise of a paper to follow. However, it is likely that W. L. Warner must have in his genealogy books—since these were fashionable in the late 1920s—actual details of many marriages along with relevant information on descent, clans, subsections and moieties. Be this as it may, we do know quite definitely that R. M. and C. H. Berndt have a considerable amount of unpublished material on these scores. If this were published in some form, our coroners would be in possession of a substantial amount of evidence which would enable them to reopen the case and perhaps come up with a judgement.[5]

We would like to know the percentage of marriages between (1) a man and his actual mother's brother's daughter; (2) a man and his second degree cross-cousin who is classified with the former, and is in the same subsection; (3) a man and a member of the alternate subsection which is related to his mother's brother's daughter's subsection (the norm) as daughter's daughter, woman speaking; in this a man finds his father's mother and mother's father's sister (who may be the same person with matrilateral cross-cousin marriage). This latter eventuality means that a man and his father's father may marry into the same subsection and same clan. This is not uncommon in Australia, and among the 'Murngin' is an alternate marriage and quite straight or orthodox. The difference between marriage of, say, a man of subsection A^1 with a woman of B^1 or B^2 is that one is the norm, or preference. Both are straight because the children in either case belong to the same ritual moiety as the father. Through preceding alternate marriages, of course, the mother's brother's daughter may be in the case of a man of A^1, in B^2, and so justify to some extent Warner's treatment of the 'Murngin' scheme as one of four sections. But more empirical material is needed.

Consideration of the 'Murngin' leads naturally to the Karadjeri. I have no space to examine it here, but my genealogies of forty years ago show that although the kinship system is structured around matrilateral cross-cousin marriage and the prohibition of marriage with father's sister's daughter, the former hardly ever occurs. A fieldworker who followed me among the Karadjeri calculated that unilateral cross-cousin marriage could not be correlated with the (four) section system which that tribe possessed. He based his calculations on the false assumption that every man actually married his mother's brother's daughter, which would preclude exchange of sisters in every case. But this was not so. Clearly, however, I must examine my Karadjeri material for the various structural and other factors associated with its system of marriage and kinship.

If space permitted, other examples could be given, such as data showing the different 'uses' or versions of the one ritual (e.g. Kunapipi or Yabuduruwa, according to the region and the headman of the particular performance). Light, too, could be thrown on such topics as the authority of the elders, 'gerontocracy' in marriage in F. G. G. Rose's use of the term; and local organization. My own material and that of others recorded in nearly 'uncontacted' situations should help. What we 'early' workers saw and experienced is useful, if not irrefutable, evidence.

Enough has been said to urge the older and not so old fieldworkers to re-examine their data, and also to make these available, before it is too late.

Notes

1. As an example of this, see H. Basedow's journal of an expedition to the north-west in 1903 which took him into the Everard, Musgrave, Mann, Tomkinson ranges and to Mts Olga and Connor and Ayer's Rock, and his expedition to north-western Australia in 1916. (See Basedow 1915, 1918.)

2. A. W. Howitt did see something of the life of Cooper's Creek natives but as an explorer rather than as a student of anthropology. Most of his data for the region came from the missionaries Otto Siebert and J. G. Reuther. His Kurnai material was obtained from individual survivors of that tribe, and his interesting account of a New South Wales south coast initiation was an example of a 'revived' performance of a ritual at his instigation. This is paralleled by the performances of some Aboriginal activities today, secular and sacred, to enable the Institute to obtain permanent records.

3. Full references to the work of the Australian Institute of Aboriginal Studies can be obtained direct from its Canberra office. But it is best seen in the wide range of monographs and other publications it has published, along with bibliographies and archival lists, and in its *Newsletter*.

4. See also P. Lucich (1968).

5. R. M. and C. H. Berndt have a large range of unpublished material on the Arnhem Land region from 1946 up to the present time. This concerns both north-eastern and western Arnhem Land, including the area which has come to be known in anthropological literature as 'Murngin'. See, e.g., Catherine Berndt's article in this volume (also W. Shapiro's article relating to a part of that area). Further published material can be got from R. M. Berndt 1965, 1970; Berndt and Berndt 1970. (Editor.)

References

BARNES, J. A. 1967 Inquest on the Murngin. *Royal Anthropological Institute Occasional Paper* No. 26.

BASEDOW, H. 1915 Journal of the Government North-West Expedition (1903), *Royal Geographical Society of Australasia*, South Australian Branch: Proceedings, Session 1913-14, Vol. XV.

——— 1918 Narrative of an Expedition of Exploration in North-Western Australia, *Royal Geographical Society of Australasia*, South Australian Branch: Proceedings, Session 1916-17, Vol. XVIII.

——— 1925 *The Australian Aboriginal*. Preece, Adelaide.

BERNDT, R. M. 1965 Marriage and the Family in North-eastern Arnhem Land. In *Comparative Family Systems* (M. F. Nimkoff, ed.). Houghton Mifflin, Boston.

——— 1970 Social Relationships in two Australian Aboriginal Societies of Arnhem Land: Gunwinggu and 'Murngin'. In *Kinship and Culture* (F. L. K. Hsu, ed.). Aldine Publishing Co., Chicago.

BERNDT, R. M. and C. H. 1970 *Man, Land and Myth in North Australia: the Gunwinggu People*. Ure Smith, Sydney.

BROWN, A. R. See under Radcliffe-Brown, A. R.

CURR, E. M. 1886-7 *The Australian Race*. (4 vols), Government Printer, Melbourne; Trübner, London.

ELKIN, A. P. 1938 *The Australian Aborigines: How to understand them*. Angus and Robertson, Sydney. (4th edition, 1964.)

——— 1958 Anthropology in Australia: one chapter, *Mankind*, Vol. 5.

——— 1959 A Darwin centenary and highlights of field-work in Australia, *Mankind*, Vol. 5.

——— 1963 The Development of Scientific Knowledge of the Aborigines. In *Australian Aboriginal Studies* (H. Sheils, ed.), Australian Institute of Aboriginal Studies: Oxford University Press, London.

HOWITT, A. W. 1904 *The Native Tribes of South-East Australia*. Macmillan, London.

KLAATSCH, H. 1907 Schlussbericht über meine Reise nach Australien, *Zeitschrift für Ethnologie*, Vol. 39.

LUCICH, P. 1968 The Development of Omaha Kinship Terminologies in Three Australian Aboriginal Tribes of the Kimberley Division, Western Australia, Australian Institute of Aboriginal Studies, *Monographs in Social Anthropology*, No. 15, Canberra.

MATHEW, J. 1899 *Eaglehawk and crow: a study of the Australian Aborigines*. Nutt, London; Mullen and Slade, Melbourne.

MATHEWS, R. H. 1897 The totemistic divisions of Australian Tribes, *Journal of the Royal Society of New South Wales*, Vol. 31.

——— 1898 Australian divisional systems, *Journal of Royal Society of New South Wales*, Vol. 32.

——— 1899 Divisions of north Australian tribes, *Proceedings of the American Philosophical Society*, Vol. 38.

——— 1900 The origins, organization and ceremonies of the Australian Aborigines, *Proceedings of the American Philosophical Society*, Vol. 39.

PARKER, K. L. 1905 *The Euahlayi Tribe*. Constable, London.

RADCLIFFE-BROWN, A. R. 1913 Three tribes of Western Australia, *Journal of the Royal Anthropological Institute*, Vol. 43.

——— 1918 and 1923 Notes on the social organization of Australian tribes, *Journal of the Royal Anthropological Institute*, Vols 48 and 53.

ROSE, F. G. G. 1960 *Classification of Kin, Age Structure and Marriage Amongst the Groote Eylandt Aborigines*. Akademie-Verlag, Berlin.

SMYTH, R. BROUGH 1878 *The Aborigines of Victoria*. (2 vols), Government Printer, Melbourne.

SPENCER, W. B. 1914 *Native Tribes of the Northern Territory of Australia*. Macmillan, London.

——— 1921 Presidential address to the Australasian Association for the Advancement of Science, *Report of the Fifteenth Meeting*.

Spencer, W. B. and F. J. Gillen 1899 *The Native Tribes of Central Australia*. Macmillan, London.
——— 1904 *The Northern Tribes of Central Australia*. Macmillan, London.
Stirling, E. C. 1896 *Report on the work of the Horn Scientific Expedition to Central Australia*, Part IV, Anthropology. Dulau, London; Mullen and Slade, Melbourne.
Strehlow, C. and M. von Leonhardi 1907-21 *Die Aranda- und Loritja-Stämme in Zentral Australien* . . . Veröffentlichungen des Frankfurter Museums für Völkerkunde, Frankfurt.
Taplin, G. 1873 *The Narrinyeri*. Wigg, Adelaide.
Warner, W. L. 1937/58 *A Black Civilization*. Harper, New York.

CATHERINE H. BERNDT

*Prolegomena to a Study of Genealogies
in North-eastern Arnhem Land*

To begin with, I have to repeat the remarks I made in speaking to the Social Anthropology section at the Institute's 1968 meeting: '... These notes are not a summary of a paper that is already completed, but a preliminary account of a paper I have begun to prepare: and that paper will be a compressed version of a larger study. The larger study will be a joint one, involving my husband as well. The subject matter in both cases is genealogical and census material from north-eastern Arnhem Land.'

Two remarks are pertinent here. One: unfortunately, in the time available it has not proved possible to finalize this preliminary statement in the form in which I had planned to present it. Two, and directly connected with the first point: although my original plan was to prepare two separate papers on the basis of this material, one utilizing only my own data collected from women and the other including my husband's data collected from men, that plan had conceptual as well as practical disadvantages. For example, parts of the second paper would have had to be devoted to commenting or elaborating on items contained in the first. Readers might well have asked, 'Why wasn't all of this published together in the first place?' The benefits of combining the two in a single study are in fact obvious, and outweigh the extra delay involved.

Circumstances of Recording

We first began to collect census and genealogical material in north-eastern Arnhem Land in 1946, concentrating on the Yirrkalla area, and have been building on it at intervals since then—most recently in 1968. Initially, it was one kind of practical information that helped us to identify the persons we met and observed interacting with one another. This was very much like, in a figurative sense, what we were doing at the same time in a literal sense—learning the language (starting with one dialect each). In both respects, at that stage of our fieldwork, acquiring such information was predominantly a means to an end rather than an end in itself, a means of communicating with people in more than superficial terms and making sense of what we saw as well as what we heard. We had met a few eastern Arnhem Landers in Darwin and on the Army settlements just before the end of World War II, mainly from the Milingimbi region, but had attempted no systematic research where they were concerned. It was, however, those earlier contacts with them (and with western Arnhem Landers from the Oenpelli area) that first stimulated us to carry out research in Arnhem Land itself.

Later we were deflected by other tasks from writing up this material. As it happened, this was probably all to the good, because one of its interesting features now is the time span it covers. A period of more than twenty years offers some scope for analysis, particularly in regard to the changes that have been taking place in a number of aspects, demographic and otherwise.

The 'population explosion' among the Arnhem Landers was just beginning. Several women had borne between six and ten surviving children each, but the local emphasis on fertility was countered to some extent by what seems to have been a fairly high rate of infant mortality. Also, missionaries—and visitors—were much fewer in number. There had been an Air Force Base in the Yirrkalla area, abandoned shortly before we arrived; its all-weather airstrip was for a very long time the only one of its kind in Arnhem Land. But for much of our stay in that area, the Methodist mission there was represented by one Fijian minister and, for part of the time, his family. The contrast between 'then' and 'now' is both dramatic and drastic. Even the now vastly enlarged mission staff, augmented by Welfare and educational personnel, pales beside the mining and other developments at Gove, with the current construction of a township not far from the main mission station, and the explorations of various kinds that are being pursued over a large part of the Arnhem Land Reserve.

In this statement, I assume that readers have some familiarity with north-eastern Arnhem Land ethnography and know enough about the relevant sources to be able to put my remarks in context. This is not the place to provide even an outline of the sociocultural situation there, or of the Arnhem Landers' contacts with the outside world. Enough written material is available on both those scores, so that references to them here will be minimal. (See, for example, R. M. Berndt 1962, 1964, 1965, 1970; Berndt and Berndt 1964, e.g. pp. 62-7; and Warner 1937/58.)

Nor shall I list or discuss here the mass of material, mostly on a 'second-hand' basis, that has been accumulating around the topic of social relations, especially kinship relations, in this region. Some of it, notably the attempts to articulate 'the Murngin system' in the form of graphic and other models (for example in the journal *L'Homme*), is both ingenious and provocative. Much of it, however, is equally instructive in a very different sense—for students of the Sociology of Knowledge, or the Sociology of the Social Sciences, or Metasociology. What has become known as the Murngin Controversy has developed a life of its own—but the unreal life of a 'double', a 'Doppelgänger', resembling in certain attributes the empirical system it is supposed to represent but quite divergent from it in others, like an image seen in a series of distorting mirrors. The controversy has culminated, if that is the right word, in an Inquest (Barnes 1967). The label is pertinent, in that it is an enquiry focused on a corpse—but (to stay with the metaphor) the corpse is that of the Doppelgänger; it is not an enquiry into the still living, although changing, organism that is the 'Murngin' system itself.

The population of eastern Arnhem Land in 1946-47 was, on the whole, more mobile than it is now. People drew upon mission goods and services as it suited them. Not the least of these services was the appearance, and to a large extent the actuality, of physical protection that they afforded. In general terms, a mission station was a zone of safety: *miringu* 'war' parties would not normally venture within its boundaries, although there are reports of isolated alarms at Milingimbi, especially, in its earlier days. In personal terms, a mission station provided a refuge for eloping couples or those who had contracted unions that were traditionally regarded as unreservedly wrong, for example between members of the same moiety. Sporadic violence continued over a long period, in fact until quite recently, on as well as outside the stations, as part of the long-established feuding complex, so that this physical safety was not absolutely assured; but, generally speaking, in the course of any such attack a station-dweller was likely to be wounded or frightened rather than deliberately killed—reflecting the change in social control that has now extended to the entire region.

In 1946-47, then, with a few individual exceptions, the people we met on eastern Arnhem Land mission stations gave the impression of being interested but essentially uncommitted. Even for those few, the core of mission supporters, there was not the same range or quantity of interlocking incentives as now. Such tangible inducements as tobacco, sugar, flour and tea, though highly valued, were fitted into the overall pattern of hunting, fishing and collecting as desirable additions to it, not (as now) the other way round. Movements in and out of the stations were not only voluntary, except for the use of 'expulsion' or 'exile' as a punishment for offences against mission discipline. But, also, there were fewer pressures discouraging or inhibiting such movements; and the hinterland of the settlements was still very much as it had been, still unoccupied by non-Aborigines apart from isolated crocodile-shooters and other intruders.

'Village'-style living was beginning to develop, as something more deliberate than a mere by-product of mission endeavour. For example, the Fijian missionary at Yirrkalla planned and supervised the building of the first quasi-permanent corrugated-iron huts in 1947, during our visit, to replace some of the rough shelters and windbreaks that people habitually used there. But the small groups that moved irregularly into and away from the settlements seem to have been closer to their traditional counterparts than those that do so today on 'holidays', or those that now form the nuclei of the small mission-established out-stations at various points in (for example) the Arnhem Bay, English Company Islands, and Caledon Bay areas. In the former case, the initial attraction of the mission stations and later of the Gove Air Force Base possibly paralleled the earlier 'pull' of the Indonesian traders, which must have had some influence on land-occupancy and (e.g.) on movement between coastal and inland sites.

In the current situation, in contrast, the total context is utterly different. The greater part of the population is 'anchored' at specific points, and this in itself affects the range and nature of interaction, both between social units (themselves considerably modified) and between persons. Their movements, commitments, and interests now radiate well outside the traditional system, embracing not only visits to Darwin and to southern cities—Brisbane, Sydney, Melbourne, Adelaide, Perth—but longer periods of employment in some of these places, and even quasi-permanent settlement.

Over and above sheer growth in numbers (in the Yirrkalla case, from a little over 200 in 1946-47 to approximately 900 today; in the Elcho case the rise is even steeper), then, figures for the Aboriginal population centring on any of these mission stations connote something different from what they do now. Of the 200-odd adults and children who came and went in the Yirrkalla area while we were there, only a very small proportion had actually settled more or less permanently at the mission station itself—taking 'permanently' to mean living there for most of the time with absences only on daily or other brief hunting trips or on 'holidays'. For the majority, Yirrkalla was only one site (although perhaps the most consistently important site in that region) in a still semi-nomadic existence.

Once they had been established, the mission stations served as foci of population and population movements, drawing in people from relatively wide areas. For example, Yirrkalla was a focus for people from Arnhem Bay and the English Company Islands as well as from Caledon Bay and Blue Mud Bay and, to a lesser extent, from Rose River and Groote

Eylandt; but Arnhem Bay and English Company Island people also moved between Elcho Island and Milingimbi. The shifting of the Methodist mission station from Elcho to Milingimbi and later back to Elcho possibly reinforced this link. An individual example: Bangaliwi, who had close associations with Milingimbi in Warner's day (see Warner 1937/58: e.g. 85-6), was based at Yirrkalla when we were there, but has been for some years now domiciled at Elcho. Our genealogies actually extend westward to Cape Stewart and beyond, linking up with others that we obtained from the perspective of Oenpelli and Goulburn Islands before Maningrida was established, and since; but for the Cape Stewart area and recently for Milingimbi these rest almost wholly on verbal information and not on first-hand observations of most of the people concerned. On the other hand, a number of the people we knew at Yirrkalla in 1946-47 had moved to Rose River and toward the Roper by 1958, and most of them do not seem to have returned.

The initial problem in this respect, therefore, was the rather obvious one of what population should be taken as the main unit of analysis, aside from appendixes or footnote references to other material that seemed to offer interesting side-problems or side-issues. Our larger study therefore begins with a statement of who was at Yirrkalla during the time we initially worked there, with some reference to individual and group mobility; this extends to Elcho Island and, to a lesser extent, Milingimbi; also, who was at these places during our subsequent visits, the most recent being to Yirrkalla and Elcho in 1968.

Overview of Content

The minimum of information we recorded for each individual person covers formal affiliations in terms of *mada* (dialect or 'tongue'), *mala* (which we translate as 'clan'), and, of course, moiety; 'country'; personal names, including nicknames (and, these days especially, English names), and their meanings. The earlier material on subsection affiliations is patchy (see below), especially for older people in the Yirrkalla region. In regard to social relationships, the minimum includes information on current or betrothed spouses and on any previous unions (where possible, on extra-marital and pre-marital unions as well), and on offspring; but, except on the very periphery, there are no instances where this is all the information we have. There are always other linkages in terms of kinship, consanguineally traceable or imputed. Genealogies tend to overlap. Within a certain range, some of the same persons reappear from different angles, but from the perspective of middle-aged and older people genealogical depth is small; we could rarely go further back than the grandparents' generation (rarely: there are exceptions).

Looking back *now*, from the present, over the period to 1946, we have quite extensive information on genealogical linkages. (From 1946 backward, of course, where the material could not be checked by observation, it is much less complete.) This information is useful, especially, in regard to transactions where kinship plays an important part—as in betrothal arrangements. For example, for children who are not already betrothed, I have made a practice of asking some such question as, 'Where will he/she look for a spouse?', 'Who will give him/her a spouse?', 'Why is he/she not betrothed yet?' Apart from distinguishing between first and subsequent unions, I have also found it helpful to distinguish, where possible, between unions arranged solely or mainly by other people (that is, other than the marital pair themselves) and those where responsibility rests solely or largely with either or both of them (for example, in elopements). This information is not as complete as I would like; but I do have a fair amount of it. And it is relevant in looking at the relation between ideal and actual—at how far actuality and ideals coincide, especially in connection with changes over time.

The information I have obtained in these respects and in regard to genealogical information generally is, on the whole, quite consistent. I have made a point of asking much the same questions to and/or about the same people at intervals; and although some discrepancies have emerged, my impression at the moment is that the majority are relatively slight. A couple of examples are somewhat puzzling: for example, differing information on the names and affiliations of close relatives in the grandparents' generation; earlier acknowledgement of part-'Macassan' mixture in one case does not entirely account for divergent statements in that particular genealogy. There are discrepancies between male and female versions in a few instances, including the interesting problem of disputed paternity evidenced in disagreement on *mada* and *mala* affiliation. Also, there are a few discrepancies between what people say about themselves and what other people say about them—which points up the need to take both kinds of source into account. As one would expect, such divergence is most evident on sensitive issues such as extra-marital liaisons and 'wrong' unions. I had thought of setting out, here, examples of several types of discrepancy, but to do so effectively would involve bringing in too much small detail in what is intended to be simply a brief statement.

In a tentative sorting out of this material some time ago, I drafted out two genealogies as exercises for fourth year students in Anthropology in the University of Western Australia. One had as central figure a woman now living at Elcho whose connections extend to the Cape Stewart area and Maningrida, with some distant Gunwinggu ties. The other, in two parts, was from the perspective of a woman born at Elcho who had spent some time at Milingimbi (where her parents died a few years ago). Her first husband resided at both of these places (he died recently at Elcho); but she eloped to Yirrkalla where she still lives with her second husband—and this second husband's genealogy, from her angle, comprised the second part of this second genealogy. In both cases, I simplified the data (for the purpose of the exercise) to the extent of omitting a number of less central cross-linkages, and cutting off the lateral spread rather arbitrarily to make the task more manageable. Nevertheless, even in that truncated form (covering, all told, a little under 500 names), these two genealogies alone showed up some interesting points—for example, the (small) proportion of *actual* cross-cousin marriages, the incidence of polygynous unions, and the inheritance of widows; and geographically they covered quite a wide span.

One kind of data I did not collect systematically in survey style was a record of what *everyone* in a given area called *everyone* else in that area, and why—although I have recorded a great deal of such material from women in the course of conversations and discussions as well as genealogical enquiry, and my husband has a fairly wide coverage from the points of view of a large number of men. This is not to underestimate the potential usefulness of a total survey. I first attempted one in the Victoria River District, in 1945; but it seemed to me then that it could not be used to maximum advantage without a corresponding genealogical coverage. After all, one of the most fascinating aspects of the study of genealogies, and of kinship generally, is the interplay between the biological and the social—the ways in which, for instance, consanguineal relationships are modified and translated in the social dimension, in the sphere of action. In the recording of genealogies in north-eastern Arnhem Land, it is this interplay with which I have been especially concerned.

Personal Names

Every adult has at least two personal names, often more, over and above nicknames, category names (individual, like 'Blind' or 'Wrinkled'; or on a *mada-mala* basis, like 'Crocodile'), and European names. As a rule, and allowing for exceptions, only one is in general use at a given time; one may be temporarily set aside on the death of someone bearing that name, another may have been simply a childhood name, and so on. However, people in different areas may continue to refer to a person by different names. This can be just as much of a trap in genealogy-taking as the existence of two or more separate persons known by the same name—and not only a trap to 'outsiders', or to young adults. Some of the confusion and disagreement involved in retrospective discussion at Elcho Island and recently at Yirrkalla centred on the question of individual identification, especially in regard to siblings: 'Was this one woman [man] with two names, or were they two sisters [brothers] with separate names?' Identification-through-offspring helps to individualize the dead in retrospect—but only up to a point.

During our earlier work in the region, personal names of the dead were not mentioned freely or consistently—except insofar as they appeared in songs or were borne by living persons. Apart from song-allusions, they were, and are, remembered and handed on by and to appropriate relatives—for example, 'given' to a girl by her father's sister or by her mother's mother. Specifically, they are incorporated in particular song-cycles shared among various *mada* and *mala*, and refer to the creatures (etc.) and sites that are commemorated in these. More broadly, they can be recognized as belonging to one or other of the two moieties: a person bearing a '*dua* name' is thus identified as a '*dua* person', even by someone who may not be clear about his/her other affiliations.

As usual, I did not ask for names of the dead (or, for that matter, of relatives whose names were tabu to the persons I was speaking with), but noted them when they were volunteered or mentioned in other (for example, song) contexts. A few names of individual dead, even of persons fairly recently dead, were uttered at Yirrkalla in 1946-47, but rarely their 'bigger' or more important names. Mostly the reference was to nicknames, or to the less person-specific names used to single out members of particular *mada* and *mala*, or to the sites where they had died. (The recording of sites provided a further check on this kind of information. In addition to mythical associations, it normally included material on 'local history', such as deaths that had taken place there— especially, violent deaths.) Such clues are important when one is trying to establish individual relationships—for example, to discriminate between siblings. In this respect, Elcho Island has an advantage where genealogy-recording is concerned. As one consequence of the Adjustment Movement there in the late 1950s (see R. M. Berndt 1962), in most instances people utter names of the dead fairly freely after a short interval, although where strong emotional ties are involved the time span is longer. The position is changing even at Yirrkalla. Also, right through the region there are interesting developments in this respect in regard to deciding, as they have been asked to do, on names that can serve the same purposes as Australian-European surnames.

The endeavour to fill in separate name-slots for every person, wherever possible, confirmed one impression that perhaps does not need such support. It demonstrated quite clearly that, in reckoning social relationships in this situation, genealogical links yield ground over a fairly short time-span to category-based links—that is, references to *mada* and *mala* as such and not to their individual members. The shallowness of genealogies and the absence of distinctive terms for kin in the great-grandparents' generation (descendant or 'junior' terms are used) are further pointers in that direction. The same thing applies to distance in space. The farther one gets from the territory-based 'core', the greater the predominance of criteria based on category alone (moiety, *mada*, *mala*, subsections). Consanguineal linkages are regarded as highly significant only within a fairly limited span, even though they serve as a model for most other relationships outside it.

Formal Affiliations

In regard to *mada* and *mala*, information derived from census and genealogies enables us to make an estimate of 'who belongs to what', or is affiliated or identified with what. This complements other information that is not included in this particular study, on 'who acts as a member of what' in other contexts: for example, in ritual/ceremonial contexts, who sings or dances or performs in his/her capacity as a member of a specific *mada-mala* combination. Information on the meaning and transmission of personal names is also relevant in these connections.

Paternity queries, traditionally rare, formerly involved only married women but now extend to children born to unmarried girls (also, still rare). These aside, however, recording individual *mada-mala* affiliations presents no difficulty, since each person belongs through patrilineal descent to one *mada-mala* pair. Conventional signals are used, in large gatherings, to attract the attention of people having maternal or other links with specified *mada* and/or *mala*. For example, '*Delingin* Mararba!', those with mothers and mothers' brothers of the Mararba *mada* (*delingin*, 'breast'); '*Waiari* Mararba!', those with *mari* (mother's mother, mother's mother's brother) of that *mada*.

It is true that in 1946-47 we were told that certain *mala* names had been changed (exchanged), as between at least two *jiridja* moiety *mada*, and even that there had been a change in one *dua* moiety *mada*. (That is, that the Galbu *mada* 'now', in 1946-47, was the type of speech labelled '*ngangadang*' which had formerly been characteristic of the Riradjingu *mada*.) But these represent only label-changes, not complications in individual alignments. So do changing preferences for certain *mala* names. To take one example, the Djabu *mada*, traditionally located to the east and south-east of Yirrkalla. Even at Yirrkalla, the *mala* name most often mentioned in connection with this *mada* is Wulamba, or occasionally Balamumu. In 1946-47, 'Wulamba' had a less restricted application, and the specific *mala* associated with the Djabu included Damalamiri (in effect, 'stingray-eaters'), and Dagobabwi or Bilgana — a distinction between coastal and upstream groups. These names are still known, within a certain regional span, but not used in the same way—for example, not volunteered so often as a first-level response.

What *is* complex, and to some extent difficult, is delineating the relationships between and among the various *mada* and *mala*. Between certain of these within the same moiety there are very close links, even to the point of partial identification. The main areas of interconnection and differentiation are territorial affiliations, and ownership of and participation in myths, rites and songs, with associated emblems. A few years ago, people frequently spoke of ideal intermarrying relationships on this *mada-mala* basis, but this preference seems to have lapsed.

One very noticeable change has to do with subsections. As we have noted elsewhere, when we first worked at Yirrkalla older men and women refused to acknowledge any subsection affiliation, both for themselves and in general terms. Younger people, on the other hand, took the opposite stand. For at least some of them, the system provided a new and exciting sport, of superimposing the new pattern to produce a double set of kin terms and relationships—turning a wider range of persons into ostensibly eligible spouses or sweethearts, and nullifying traditional interpersonal tabus and restraints. At that time, because traditional norms still carried much weight, the subsection-based pattern of relationships was referred to as 'inside' or quasi-private or quasi-secret, in contrast to the 'outside', public, socially accepted pattern. By 1958, however, the subsection system was apparently completely accepted; and the impression now, especially at Elcho (where subsections were introduced much earlier, via Milingimbi) but also at Yirrkalla, is that they could hardly be more strongly entrenched. However, there are some intriguing examples of open subsection-changing (as against informal 'turning one's skin' for sweetheart purposes), to satisfy the appearance of correctness in marital unions where other, for example moiety, criteria are in order.

In this connection, it would be interesting to know more about the approximate ages at which children learn, or remember, subsection and moiety and *mada* and *mala* affiliations, specifically their own. I have not looked into this seriously. But I have quite often asked children for information on these, and on their personal names; and in almost every case those of, say, about ten years old and younger did not know their *mala* affiliation although they could answer on the other scores. Differences in age and in ability count here, of course, but it seems that children are not expected to learn about *mala* at the same time as they learn about *mada*, their own or other people's. (And, as one might expect, their general knowledge of genealogies and of name-meanings is mostly rather slight.)

[I include here a not entirely frivolous postscript that I appended to my remarks at the Conference. In this I drew attention to what might be seen as a shortcoming in the study: 'I regret to say that I do not have a complete coverage of dogs—their personal names, subsections, *mada* and *mala* affiliations, and their relationships with other dogs and with people. For example, a Wonguri *mada* dog is said, at least half seriously, to have a distinctively different bark from a Dalwongu *mada* dog, although both are of the *jiridja* moiety. This might be a convenient introductory project for a dog-loving student (an English one, perhaps?)—with individual photographs, of course; and for someone a little shy with people, or less interested in people, the exercise could be personally absorbing as well as catering for a somewhat more general interest.']

Betrothal and Marriage

Our larger study is, needless to say, directly concerned with marriage and betrothal patterns, in reference both to kinship and to *mada* and *mala*—with subsections, significant as they undoubtedly are, playing a minor role. Those patterns are actually the central core of the study, and even in this preliminary statement a great deal could be said about them. All I shall do here, however, is to emphasize a few points that are in danger of being overlooked.

(i) In the system of kin-based marriage preferences, a man's matri-cross-cousin is an ideal spouse: it is to her parents that he, or rather his sponsors, look in their efforts to arrange his betrothal. This is not always possible. There are numerous cases in which a young man has waited in vain for his mother's actual brother(s) to give him a daughter as wife. The genealogies show a fair sprinkling of *actual* cross-cousin betrothals and, a little less frequent, marriages, but (or so it appears at this juncture) they are certainly in a minority.

(ii) Other types of union, however, are also acceptable, even if they do not conform with the ideal. One in particular is the 'patriate', as R. M. Berndt (1965:89-90) has called it, where a man may take over a woman who has been married to his father, or marry his father's widow(s) provided she is not his own mother. In other instances, once a betrothal has been ratified, the potential husband apparently has (or had) sufficient jurisdiction over his wife to pass her on almost immediately to one of his brothers—to 'give' her on his own initiative with a minimum of discussion with her own parents, although presumably (in the cases known to me) with at least their tacit consent. Another 'acceptable' union is illustrated in Figure 1.

(iii) Some men, of whom only a few are still living, had the reputation of being 'rich' in women and usually, in consequence, in sons and daughters. They tended to be 'big' men in other ways as well; and one procedure through which they could, and often did, obtain wives was

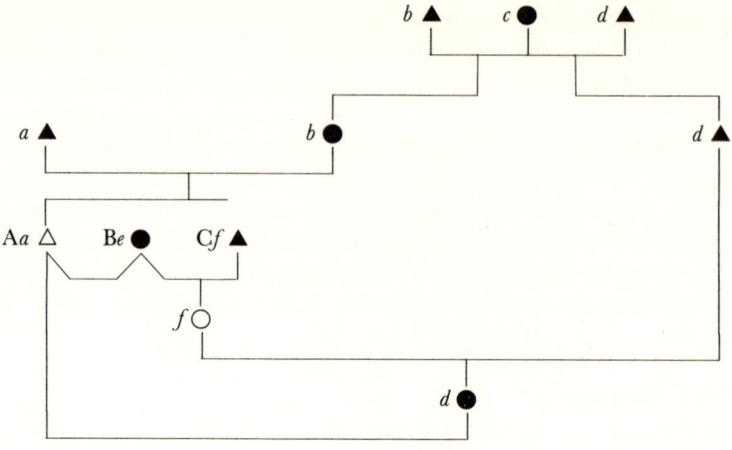

Fig. 1 Betrothal arrangement

Key

(1) Symbols used: ○   female, living   ●   female, now dead
                    △   male, living   ▲   male, now dead
                    └─┘ marriage link   └─┐ descent link

(2) Specific notes:
  a Wonguri *mada*, Mandjigai *mala*.
  b Djambarbingu *mada*, Durili *mala*.
  c Gobubingu *mada*, Lialanmiri *mala*.
  d Maragulu *mada*, Durili *mala*.
  e Marangu *mada*, Durili *mala*.
  f Dalwongu *mada*, Nargala *mala*.
  C was killed by A, who then married B. A's betrothed wife was his MMSD, the actual DD of B and C.

through the use of force. A number of older women's genealogies show a pattern of passing from one husband to the man who had killed him (either to obtain her or for some other reason), and case histories indicate that this sequence was a very real possibility.

(iv) Betrothals rested almost as much on the convention of payment in goods and services as on formally correct kinship. Similarly, a system of payments and indemnities was an intrinsic part of the feuding-and-warfare complex. These two spheres overlapped in instances where a betrothal was blocked because the potential husband or his kin had not made the appropriate gifts, or made the appropriate restitution. Among the cases I know of personally, of blocking or threatened blocking on these grounds (there are others), the main mover in three of them was the girl's father. (See Figure 3, in Appendix to this paper.)

(v) In other words, the combination of economic considerations, and physical force and threat, as a 'given' in this situation, militated against conformity with the ideal of cross-cousin marriage. As outside contact intensified, and especially in the last few years with the mixing of boys and girls in mission schools, other influences have also served as pressures against it. Some parents, discouraged by all this, have asserted that any attempts to betroth their children are doomed to certain failure and that it would be better to yield to circumstances. Recent decisions by mission Aboriginal councils not only discourage child betrothals but anticipate banning them entirely.

(vi) Marriages that are regarded as unequivocally wrong are not, of course, a post-1946 development. In part, they are connected with the practice of marriage-through-force—but only in part. In what was perhaps the most notorious case, in the late 1950s, a woman left her husband and was reputedly cohabiting with her mother's half brother from the same father, a union terminated only on his death: but it was claimed that she herself had taken the initiative in this. Another case of an extra-marital intra-moiety union (no close kin connection) dates from the late 1940s and now appears to have been 'legitimized'. There are other examples too, although the trend seems to have been, in formally wrong but not 'incestuous' unions, to bring the situation to an appearance of normality by betrothing any offspring who survive, in the conventionally most correct way—that is, to the appropriate cross-cousins.

Figure 2 illustrates a wrong union and two acceptable ones. (Other genealogical interconnections are not shown; but none of the marital partners were actual cross-cousins.)

This was one of the cases cited on several occasions at Yirrkalla, in 1946-47, as evidence that such unions were outside the pale and would not be tolerated. Allowing for a considerable measure of bias here, and the relatively short span within which dependable data are available, there may be something in this claim. Intra-moiety unions that have escaped punishment (apart from short-term escapades, which were normally not punishment free) seem to have been not only rare but also recent. Traditional sanctions other than sorcery are no longer available now. It is very doubtful whether the mother's brother-sister's daughter liaison would have been permitted to endure had it been attempted, say, thirty years ago. Marriageable women being a sought-after commodity, this alone would have provided an incentive for men in the appropriate moiety to break up the union. In such circumstances, women were more often taken as spouses (as in Figure 2, below) than killed, though there are a few examples (for example, where the woman was pregnant). On the other hand, the 'mother's brother' concerned had a reputation for aggressiveness, which he shared with his brothers and their father; and it is just possible that, if they had formed a solidary front on his behalf, he would have got away with it. And this kind of behaviour, though not usually in this context of intra-moiety unions, was (as Warner's material also demonstrates) just as typical of north-eastern Arnhem Land as the verbal emphasis on the ideal of cross-cousin marriage.

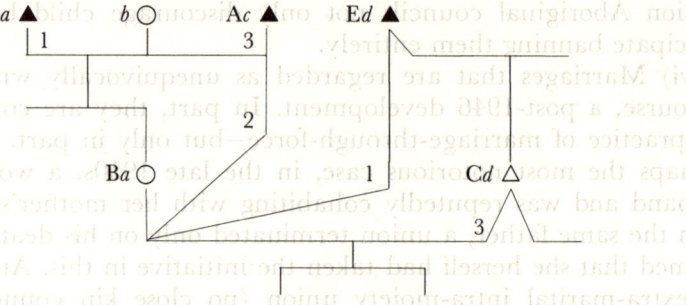

Fig. 2 Wrong and acceptable unions

Key
(1) As in Figure 1.
(2) Specific notes:
    a Galbu *mada*, Gawur (or Malawur) *mala*.
    b Dalwongu *mada*, Nungbulula *mala*.
    c Ngeimil *mada*, Kapin *mala*.
    d Gumaidj *mada*, Raiung *mala*.
    1, first husband; 2, second husband; 3, third husband.

A was allegedly killed and 'cut to pieces' by a *miringu* (fighting, vengeance) party on account of his marriage to B, and B's small child from him was allegedly killed by C (because it was the child of an intra-moiety union), who then married B. Her first husband, E, had been much older than herself; like his son, C, he was a 'wife-collector', the centre of a large polygynous family. C's mother was one of the few women noted in 1946-47 as having no previous kin, linguistic, or other ties in north-eastern Arnhem Land. They had allegedly been brought ('kidnapped') by Macassan traders from regions farther south, around and beyond the Roper River.

(vii) In so far as one can speak of conventionalized expectations and norms in regard to the economic and social aspects of betrothal and marriage, including the giving or bestowing of wives, it is a mistake to see this as centring only on that particular ideal (of cross-cousin marriage). It needs to be considered in the context of the *total* system of norms and ideals, contradictory and inconsistent as these may sometimes appear to be. A tidy conceptual pattern that does not do this may represent an interesting intellectual exercise but has very limited utility as a statement about the local situation.

This paper has outlined the nature of the material which is being processed as the basis of a larger study. Apart from verbal description and discussion, two kinds of procedure are involved. One is the straightforward sorting and assessment of various types of marital and (to a lesser extent) extra-marital unions, together with supporting material. The other entails the sorting of a great quantity of genealogical material, which is far too unwieldy and complex to be treated by one or two persons but appears to be an ideal task, or an ideal game, for a computer. The next step is to work out an appropriate programme for this particular facet of the study.

APPENDIX

A Blocked Betrothal (see Betrothal and Marriage, iv, in main text). A young Elcho Island girl of the Galbu *mada*, Malawur *mala* (No. 23, below), was betrothed to a middle-aged Yirrkalla man of the Gumaidj *mada*, Raiung *mala* (No. 12, below). By the end of 1946 she was said to be old enough to marry him, and to be personally agreeable to the match. Her father, however (No. 17, below), would not allow her to join him at Yirrkalla until compensation was forthcoming for three deaths, for which he (but in conjunction with others, also Gumaidj-Raiung, specifically the brothers of No. 3, below) was allegedly responsible. Among the statements made on the case in 1947, by persons with and without a direct interest in it, one received special emphasis: that is, unless a satisfactory 'payment' was made to balance the death-debt, the betrothal would be cancelled and the girl would be given to another potential husband, of the Waramiri *mada*. And that is what happened: her father 'gave' her to No. 59, below—and acquired No. 59's half-sister as an additional wife for himself.

Comment. I shall not discuss the various links noted in these outlines, since they are plain enough as they stand. They would be plainer still had it been possible to expand on them—for instance, noting all the wives of Nos 11, 17, 22 and 27 (who died recently), because these are very pertinent to the relationships set out and implied here; or all the spouses of the women in this Figure (for example, No. 73 was first married to No. 74). The son and daughter of Nos 1 and 2 both married Galbu-Malawur spouses; the son's wife, whose mother was Waramiri-Bralbral, later married No. 27, who had as wives her three sisters as well as No. 15. Or, for instance, the mother of Nos 8 and 13 was Djambarbingu-Durili, while the mother of Nos 19, 20 and 21 was Riradjingu-Miliwurur— and in both cases these lead into further interlocking relationships. Or, both Nos 36 and 37 were first promised to No. 48, but eventually to No. 16, with whom No. 37 had 'already slept' (*bili ngura*); but by 1968 No. 37 had married No. 48, while No. 36 had married a new husband. Nos 31 and 42 were married 'wrongly': they first called each other *ngati/gominjar*, distant 'mother's father'/'daughter's daughter'; and No. 42 was No. 13's third husband, in an elopement match.

Because of the divergences in chronological age and also in generation levels, I have not tried to keep strictly to these in setting out names. Also, I have deliberately omitted kin terms and subsection labels and the 'inheritance' of personal names, since they would complicate the picture too much. These should be regarded simply as small selections

(to p. 48)

FIGURE 3

To facilitate reading, this is divided into two parts (A and B), the first being in three sections (i, ii, and iii), retaining sufficient detail to indicate a few of the cross-linkages involved, as part of the social context of the case. The four main protagonists are shown thus: ⊗ (female), ▲ (male).

Key

(1) As in Figure 1, *except* that: ○, △, indicate male and female, respectively, still living in 1947, for Ai, ii, and iii, in 1968 for B (although No. 13 died during 1947); .... indicates betrothal; and – – – – a close but putative or not easily demonstrated relationship. (1), (2), etc. indicate first, second (etc.) husband(s). No. 11, below, is noted as 'E' in Figure 2, and No. 22 as 'C'.

(2) Specific notes:
    a Waramiri *mada*, Bralbral *mala*.
    b Galbu *mada*, Malawur *mala*.
    c Gumaidj *mada*, Raiung *mala*.
    d Gudji'un *mada*, Miliwurur *mala*.
    e Djambarbingu *mada*, Gwiula *mala*.
    f Gumaidj *mada*, Jarwila *mala*.
    g From another region; see Figure 2. (Later, at Elcho, classified as 'must be Djabu *mada*, Wulamba *mala*'.)
    h Riradjingu *mada*, Miliwurur *mala*.
    i Dalwongu *mada*, Nargala (or Nungbulula) *mala*.
    j Galbu *mada*, Gawur *mala*.
    k Ngeimil *mada*, Kapin *mala*.
    l Djabu *mada*, Dagobabwi *mala*.
    m Djambarbingu *mada*, Ngaladar *mala*. (Or *e*.)

N.B. b and *j* are frequently identified, and in such cases the difference is said to be merely a matter of preference for one *mala* name rather than the other. I am not going into the matter of alternative *mala* names.

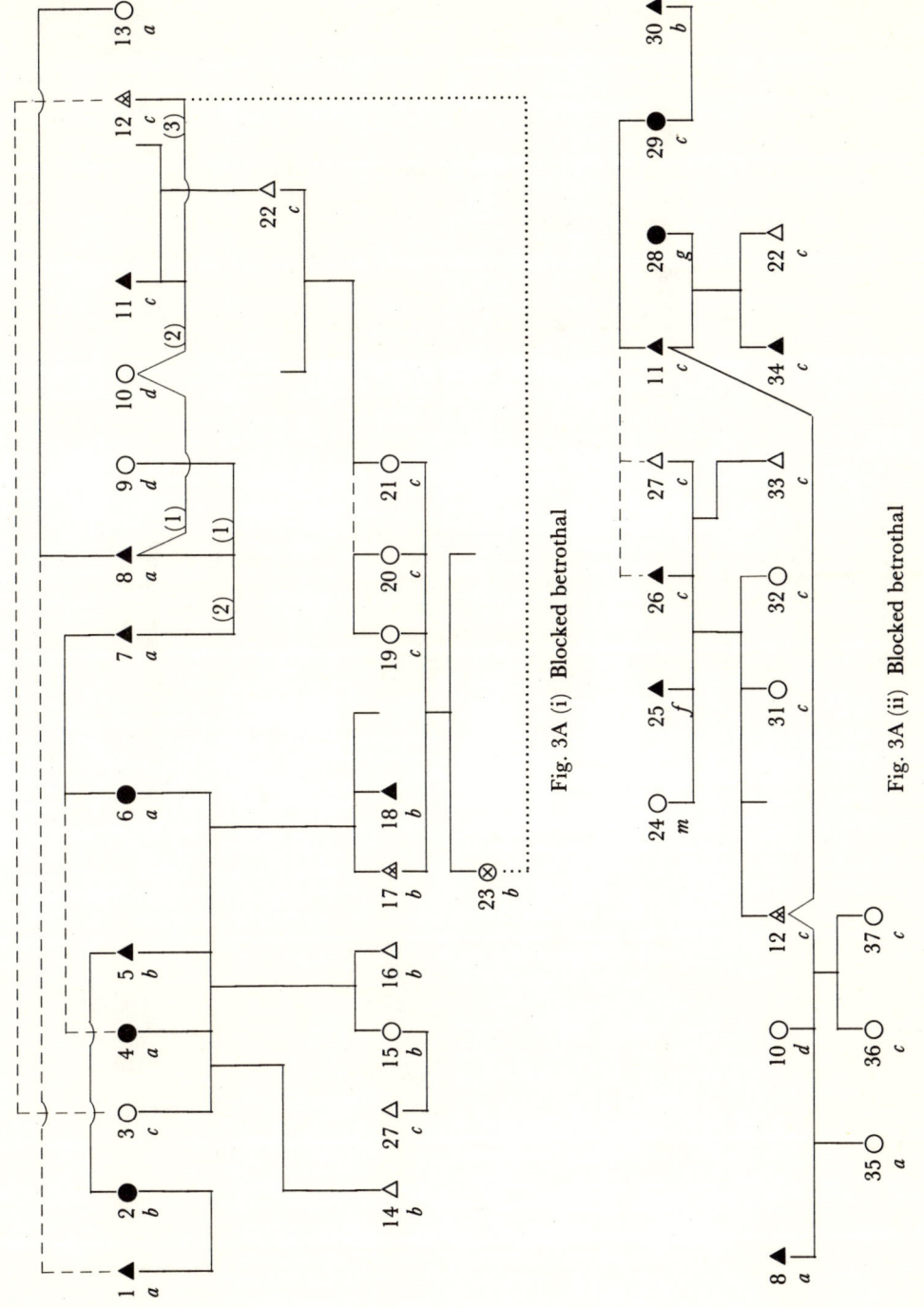

Fig. 3A (i) Blocked betrothal

Fig. 3A (ii) Blocked betrothal

Fig. 3A(iii) Blocked betrothal

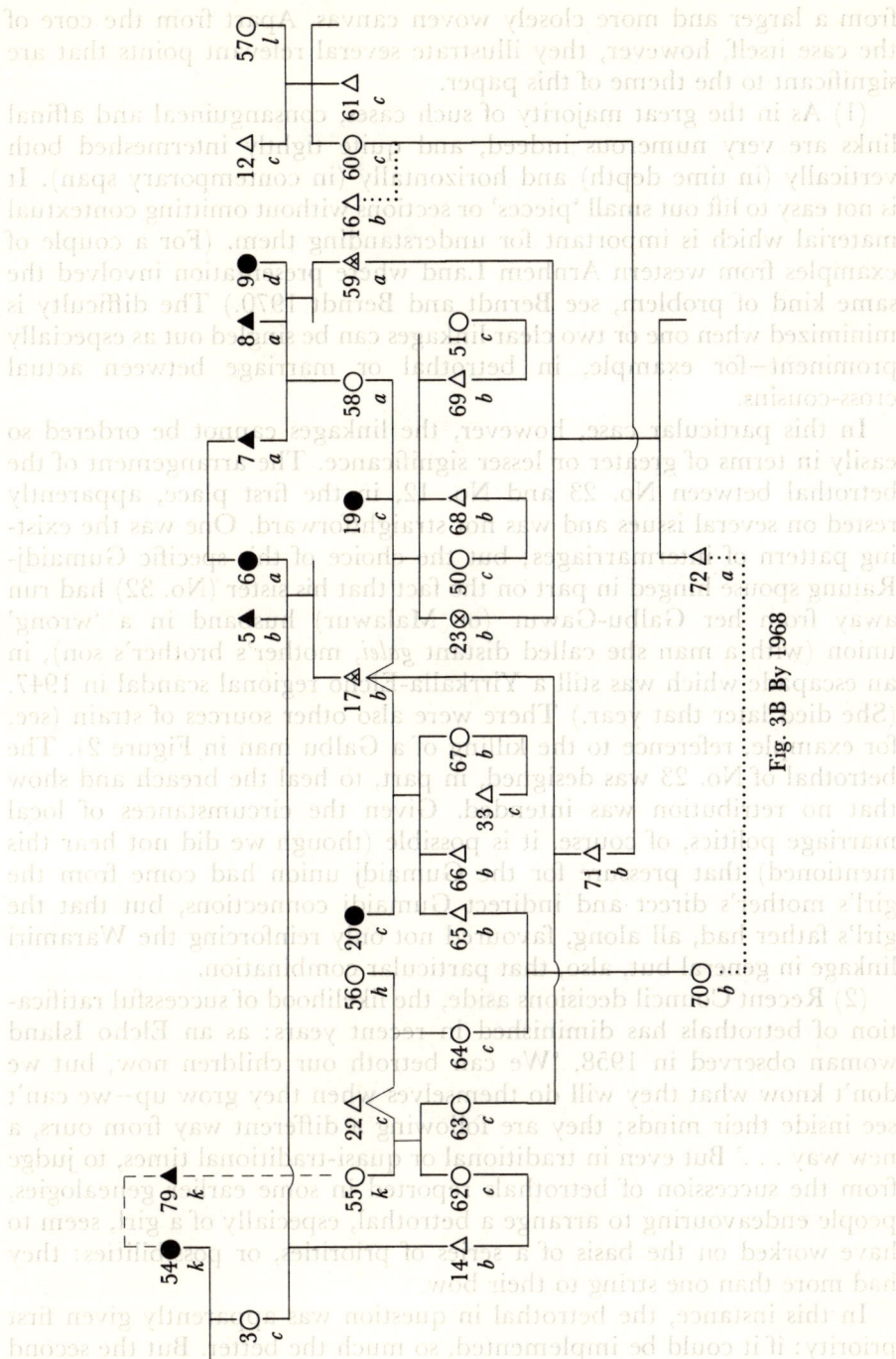

Fig. 3B By 1968

from a larger and more closely woven canvas. Apart from the core of the case itself, however, they illustrate several relevant points that are significant to the theme of this paper.

(1) As in the great majority of such cases, consanguineal and affinal links are very numerous indeed, and quite tightly intermeshed both vertically (in time depth) and horizontally (in contemporary span). It is not easy to lift out small 'pieces' or sections without omitting contextual material which is important for understanding them. (For a couple of examples from western Arnhem Land where presentation involved the same kind of problem, see Berndt and Berndt 1970.) The difficulty is minimized when one or two clear linkages can be singled out as especially prominent—for example, in betrothal or marriage between actual cross-cousins.

In this particular case, however, the linkages cannot be ordered so easily in terms of greater or lesser significance. The arrangement of the betrothal between No. 23 and No. 12, in the first place, apparently rested on several issues and was not straightforward. One was the existing pattern of intermarriages; but the choice of this specific Gumaidj-Raiung spouse hinged in part on the fact that his sister (No. 32) had run away from her Galbu-Gawur (or Malawur) husband in a 'wrong' union (with a man she called distant *galei*, mother's brother's son), in an escapade which was still a Yirrkalla-Elcho regional scandal in 1947. (She died later that year.) There were also other sources of strain (see, for example, reference to the killing of a Galbu man in Figure 2). The betrothal of No. 23 was designed, in part, to heal the breach and show that no retribution was intended. Given the circumstances of local marriage politics, of course, it is possible (though we did not hear this mentioned) that pressure for the Gumaidj union had come from the girl's mother's direct and indirect Gumaidj connections, but that the girl's father had, all along, favoured not only reinforcing the Waramiri linkage in general but, also, that particular combination.

(2) Recent Council decisions aside, the likelihood of successful ratification of betrothals has diminished in recent years: as an Elcho Island woman observed in 1958, 'We can betroth our children now, but we don't know what they will do themselves when they grow up—we can't see inside their minds; they are following a different way from ours, a new way . . .' But even in traditional or quasi-traditional times, to judge from the succession of betrothals reported in some earlier genealogies, people endeavouring to arrange a betrothal, especially of a girl, seem to have worked on the basis of a series of priorities, or possibilities: they had more than one string to their bow.

In this instance, the betrothal in question was apparently given first priority: if it could be implemented, so much the better. But the second priority was noted at the same time, perhaps with the purpose of suggesting an incentive or a threat: if that plan fell through, 'she might go to a Waramiri husband'. And that was what she eventually did.

(3) The girl's father is a 'wife-collector' of long standing, with a wide scattering of 'promises' as well as a large number of current and ex-wives; but in the last fifteen or so years he has suffered a number of set-backs, being publicly rejected by several girls when the time came for him to claim them. Figure 3B shows one of his current marriages, to the half-sister of his daughter's husband.

As noted in the main text, the balancing and exchange of wives is as much a part of the system as is the ideal of (from a male viewpoint) matri-cross-cousin marriage: the two are not parallel, but interdependent. (I shall not, at this juncture, comment on the false dichotomy that has developed between 'alliance theory' and 'descent theory'.) The presence of successful wife-collectors has added a third factor to be taken into account—since each completed marriage, even if it turns out to be of limited duration, adds a further 'growing point' or a further linkage, which is incorporated into the system on a basis of *de facto* equality in this sense, as a transaction which must lead to other (potential) transactions. The 'right and authority to give and to withhold' (as in the case that is the core of this Figure) could traditionally be overridden by the 'power to take' (but only so far: see Figure 2). The first has survived well into the current situation, whereas the second has not, or not in the same sense. The checks and sanctions that limit or block the power to take are not only more multi-faceted now but also much more effective.

This factor (the presence of more or less successful wife-collectors), then, weighted the system more heavily in favour of active male decision-making in betrothal arrangements, at the expense of females, however relevant those females might be in ideal (kinship) terms (a girl's mother, father's sister, mother's mother and father's mother).

Maybe I should spell this out. I am not saying that women play no part in such arrangements. I know personally of numbers of cases in which they have played a major part, and not only in the present altered circumstances. But, now that the element of acquiring wives through violence or threat of violence is no longer a factor to be contended with, it is easy to overlook the conditions under which it operated. This third factor, of forcible wife-collecting, rested predominantly on decisions made by men, usually on their own behalf. And to underline this is not to discount the role of individual women who are reported to have taken the initiative in elopements, or in becoming involved in 'wrong' unions, whether these were 'wrong' in the formal kinship (etc.) sense or in the sense of not having been arranged by appropriate kin.

References

BARNES, J. A. 1967 Inquest on the Murngin. *Royal Anthropological Institute Occasional Paper*, No. 26.

BERNDT, R. M. 1962 *An Adjustment Movement in Arnhem Land*. Cahiers de l'Homme. Mouton, Paris and The Hague.

—— 1964 The Gove Dispute: the question of Australian Aboriginal land and the preservation of sacred sites, *Anthropological Forum*, Vol. 1, No. 2.

—— 1965 Marriage and the Family in North-eastern Arnhem Land. In *Comparative Family Systems* (M. F. Nimkoff, ed.). Houghton Mifflin, Boston.

—— 1970 Social Relationships in two Australian Aboriginal Societies of Arnhem Land: Gunwinggu and 'Murngin'. In *Kinship and Culture* (F. L. K. Hsu, ed.). Aldine Publishing Co., Chicago.

BERNDT, R. M. and C. H. 1964 *The World of the First Australians*. Ure Smith, Sydney. (Paperback edition, 1968.)

—— 1970 *Man, Land and Myth in North Australia: the Gunwinggu People*. Ure Smith, Sydney.

WARNER, W. L. 1937/58 *A Black Civilization*. Harper, New York.

WARREN SHAPIRO

Local Exogamy and the Wife's Mother in Aboriginal Australia[1]

The theme of the present paper is an old one in the history of Anthropology: the explanation of systems of social classification by reference to behavioural norms. The explanatory factor suggested is even older: local exogamy. I shall address myself to a relatively esoteric problem in the study of Australian Aboriginal social classification, but my solution to it will, I hope, be of interest to all those concerned with the foundations of human society.

I

The classificatory scheme to be explained is one found in probably the vast majority of Aboriginal societies. It consists of a division of the social universe into what are, or at least look like, patrilineal moieties (see Shapiro 1967*b*), both of which are subdivided into two actually or apparently patrilineal categories which may be called semi-moieties (Shapiro 1967*d*). These moieties and semi-moieties are sometimes given explicit cultural recognition, such as by having specific or generic names, though in other cases they are only implicit in the structure of subsection systems or relationship terminologies (Radcliffe-Brown 1931).

The most common system of this kind appears to be the one exemplified by the Aranda (Spencer and Gillen 1927), in which, in consecutive generations, each semi-moiety is related by symmetric marriage to a different semi-moiety of the opposite moiety. The system, from the standpoint of Ego's semi-moiety, may be represented as in Figure 1.

A comparable, though apparently less common, system is one in which each semi-moiety is related by asymmetric marriage to both semi-moieties of the opposite moiety, and this pattern is repeated in every generation. My own fieldwork revealed the existence of such a system in north-east Arnhem Land (Shapiro 1967*c*, n.d.: Chapter 8), and elsewhere (Shapiro 1967*d*, 1969) I have suggested it is also found

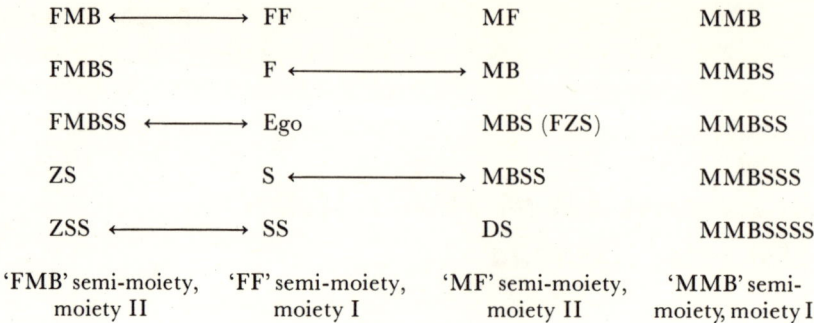

Fig. 1 Aranda semi-moiety system

among the Karadjeri and Yir-Yoront. It may be represented as in Figure 2.

The two systems differ in the relationship between intermarrying semi-moieties in any one generation (symmetric in one system, asymmetric in the other), in the connubial positions of consecutive generations of the same semi-moiety, and in the distribution of kin-types between the two semi-moieties of the opposite moiety. They are identical, however, in the distribution of kin-types between the two semi-moieties of *one's own* moiety—i.e. in the separation of the patri-category ('patriline') of Ego and his FF from that of his MMB and the latter's agnatic descendants. A unitary explanation of these systems is therefore largely an explanation of this distinction.

Before proceeding, I shall have to redesignate the phenomenon under consideration in terms of something other than genealogical specifications, which, though they may facilitate a kind of comprehension for Western minds, do not necessarily reflect Aboriginal thought. Since the other categories represented in Figures 1 and 2 by genealogical notation

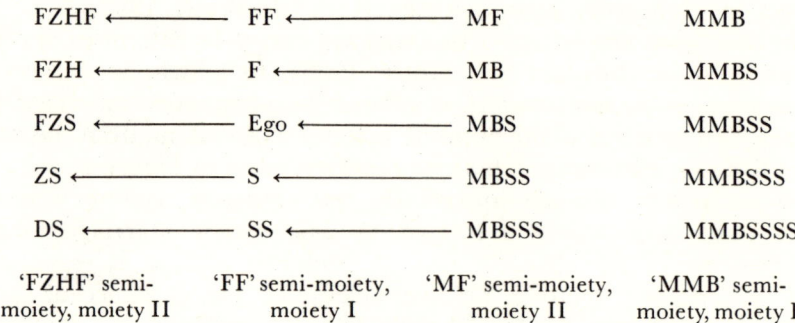

Fig. 2 North-east Arnhem Land semi-moiety system

seem to have something to do with the bestowal and acquisition of females as wives, it would not appear unwarranted to ask: What significance of this sort do the 'MMB' semi-moiety and its sub-categories have?

Unlike the ideologies of many other societies, Aboriginal marriage norms are concerned not only with the categorical relationships between husband and wife, and between son-in-law and father-in-law, but those between son-in-law and mother-in-law as well. Thus in all societies with classificatory schemes of the kind noted above, the wife's mother (who, it should be noted, must be of one's own moiety) is supposed to be of the 'MMB' semi-moiety, regardless of whether or not she is or may be also the genealogical MMBD. In the same semi-moiety, *ipso facto*, are WMB and WMF, whose importance in the arrangement and idiomization of marriages in Aboriginal societies has been stressed by Elkin (1964:124-6), Hiatt (1967), Goodale (1962), myself (Shapiro 1969), and numerous others. These three affinal statuses—WM, WMB, WMF—or rather, the native categories including their normatively possible occupants, seem usually or always to be the only ones found in the 'MMB' semi-moiety.

This being the case, the distinction with which we are concerned—that between the two semi-moieties of one's own patri-moiety—may be rephrased as a distinction between 'own people' and—the justification for this label will become obvious later—'mother-in-law people'. The problem at hand, then, is to explain why 'mother-in-law people' are differentiated from 'own people'.

I shall proceed with a type of assumption which, though frequently made by students of Aboriginal social organization, has yet to be supported by quantitative ethnographic report: I shall assume that the semi-moieties in some sense correspond to local patrilineal groups. This does not necessarily mean that there are four such groups, no more and no less, in any society, or that the male members of each group reside together. All it implies is (1) that every individual has, on the basis that some other individual is his recognized *genitor* or *pater*, some kind of symbolic association with a locality[2]—a characteristic which was probably universal in Aboriginal Australia; (2) that the number of local patrilineal groups is *at least* four; and (3) that there is in native theory some notion of articulation between the semi-moieties and the local patrilineal groups, such that each group is *ideally* correlated with one and only one semi-moiety. With this assumption, I may reformulate the problem under consideration as: Why is it that in at least most Aboriginal societies, there is some scheme of social classification expressing the norm that a man's mother-in-law should not be a member of his own local patrilineal group?

II

I shall first consider some relevant material from my own fieldwork in north-east Arnhem Land.³ In this area, marriage is prohibited with a female of the relationship category including the genealogical FZD, and a man's mother-in-law may not be a member of the category including the genealogical FZ; instead, marriage is prescribed with a female of the category including the genealogical MBD and MMBDD, who is normally the daughter of a woman of the category including the genealogical MMBD. In the relationship terminology, the FZ and MMBD categories are located on separate patri-sequences ('patrilines'), but, largely because the relationship term Ego applies to Alter is much more frequently determined by the term Ego applies to Alter's mother than by the one he employs for Alter's father, there is not perfect congruence between patri-sequence and local patrilineal group⁴ (cf. Warner 1937: 26-7). Females of the MMBD category are sometimes found in one's own sib, and since there is no prescription concerning the mother-in-law other than relationship category,⁵ it is therefore possible to marry a girl whose mother is in fact a member of one's own local patrilineal group.

Though rare, such marriages actually occur. Of 264 marriages in one of my samples,⁶ I recorded the relationship term the husband applies to the wife's mother in 224 cases; this term is *mukul rumaru* (MMBD) in 193 of these latter cases (86 per cent), not counting several instances in which the wife's mother is now *mukul rumaru* but was formerly in another category (see note 5). In only eighteen of these 193 cases (8 per cent of the 224 cases), however, are son-in-law and mother-in-law members of the same sib.⁷ I have information on the arrangement of ten of these eighteen marriages: three involved 'stealing' (*djawyunaray*) the wife from the man to whom she had been promised, but the other seven were effected by legitimate means. Perhaps the most important consideration, for present purposes, is that I have no evidence whatever that any of these seven marriages are regarded as improper in any way or liable to stigmatization.

These considerations aside, certain schemes of social classification in north-east Arnhem Land do seem to be predicated upon the notion that the sib of a man's mother-in-law is not also his own sib. Thus the sibs of each moiety are divided into two sociocentric categories, and the mothers-in-law of the men of any category are supposed to be of the other category of the same moiety (Shapiro 1967c, n.d.: Chapter 8). Further, the wife's mother is ideally a sibmate of the maternal grandmother, and the sib of the latter is symbolically distinguished from one's own sib: own totems are called *gulukulunga*, which appears to mean something like 'our very own'; whereas totems of the maternal grandmother's sib are called by the relationship term *mari* (MM/MMB), and also by a term, *bun milmarra*, signifying the wife's mother and certain other affinal statuses and prestations owed to occupants of these statuses (Shapiro n.d.: Chapters 5 and 7; cf. Thomson 1949:43). It is worth noting that members of the MMBD, MMBS and MMB relationship categories, even if they are not actual affines, may be referred to as *bun milmarra* if they are sibmates of the maternal grandmother—a fact which indicates the close association in Miwuyt thought between the maternal grandmother's sib and the wife's mother and her agnates.

What is involved here, I suspect, is something like the phenomena psychiatrists call 'repression' and 'functional autonomy' (see e.g. English and English 1958:56, 458). Specifically, I would suggest that in northeast Arnhem Land, as elsewhere in Aboriginal Australia, the idea of marrying a girl whose mother is a member of one's own local patrilineal group is for some reason psychologically unacceptable, and that this attitude is repressed and projected in the form of socially shared symbols, such as those described in the preceding paragraph. But these symbols must co-exist with other cultural facts, such as the dominance, noted above, of matri-determination in the application of relationship terms. The requirement of some kind of integration between these partially conflicting norms can and sometimes does lead to behaviour which is in violation of the repressed material, i.e. which is functionally autonomous. One would like to know what the impact of this violation is upon the Miwuyt mind, but I am not prepared to deal with this here.

That the unacceptability of marriage with a girl whose mother is of one's own sib is repressed accounts for the fact that the Miwuyt seem unable explicitly to verbalize this attitude. I am well aware that, other than this, my hypothesis has, like most psychoanalytic propositions, few or none of the characteristics of a scientific explanation, and I do not offer it as such. I ask only that the proposition be accepted that there is in the Miwuyt case evidence for a negative attitude toward marriage of the kind mentioned—this despite the fact that such unions do occur without criticism. If this is granted, we are led back to our original question: Why should there be such an attitude in the first place?

III

On various occasions A. P. Elkin has concerned himself with precisely this problem, though regrettably in genealogical terms. Thus he attempts to account for the prohibition of FZD marriage among the Karadjeri in terms of:

> the complete avoidance of the wife's mother which prevails in Australia, and . . . the strong desire to maintain the solidarity of the father's (that is, one's own) local horde. In other words, a man desires to be as free of each member of that horde, including his own father's sister, as he is of his father. But if a man makes this woman his wife's mother, he may no longer see nor have any social intercourse with her . . .
>
> There is another factor . . . namely, the desire, as it was put to me, to be free not only of one's father's . . . country, but also of one's father's mother's country. Now if a man married his father's sister's daughter, then his father's mother would become wife's mother's mother, and . . . he would be obliged to observe a taboo towards her almost as severe as the mother-in-law taboo. Moreover, her husband, that is, his own father's father, would also become subject to the same taboo . . .
>
> . . . Marriage with mother's brother's daughter means that father's mother may actually be mother's father's sister . . . that is, she may belong to . . . the local horde which includes mother's father, mother, mother's brother . . . and so on . . . But as no taboo associated with the mother-in-law is imposed on the mother and others mentioned, a man shrinks from making any member of that horde his wife's mother's mother and so breaking up the solidarity of the horde so far as his relations with it are concerned (1932: 302-3).

It is not clear to me what the evidential basis is of the statement that relations within the local patrilineal group ('horde') are normally unrestrained. Elkin (1964: 127-8) himself has pointed out the wide distribution of sister-avoidance in Aboriginal Australia. Further, in some areas, such as north-east Arnhem Land, sib brothers are expected to behave with circumspection toward each other (see also Beckett 1967). An avoidance relationship with the father's sister would not seem, therefore, to entail the inconsistencies Elkin implies.

As for the mother's local patrilineal group—toward whose members, according to Elkin, one acts without restraint—there is frequently a restricted, if not avoidant, relationship with the mother's brother, especially where he may be at the same time wife's father but also otherwise. Elkin (1964: 128) himself has noted this for Aboriginal Australia generally, and it is true, by the way, for north-east Arnhem Land in particular. Neither, therefore, would an avoidance relationship with MFZ entail inconsistencies in behaviour.

Underlying Elkin's explanation is his view that Aboriginal societies tend to attempt to separate consanguineal and affinal relationships. Thus he has maintained that

> the growth of the prohibition first of marriage with the father's sister's daughter and then with second cousins is associated with

the desire to find a mother-in-law outside one's close kith and kin ... (1938:433).

And, with reference to certain tribes of eastern South Australia:

> the ... custom of seeking a mother-in-law outside one's own close relations ... must be correlated with an urge to maintain the solidarity of both the father's and father's mother's hordes ... by avoiding affinal ties which would entail avoidance between a person and any members of these hordes (Elkin 1940:381).

Elkin (1964:72) employs analogous reasoning to explain the prohibition of marriage with the genealogical MBD:

> There is ... also a rule of restricted social intercourse between a man and his wife's father. ... I have just shown how the mother-in-law avoidance seems to lie at the heart of the prohibition of marriage with father's sister's daughter. In the same way the taboo on wife's father is closely connected with the prohibition of marriage with the other cross-cousin ... for a man does not desire to avoid one so closely related to himself by the tie of blood as his own mother's brother ...

Leach (1961:123) has pointed out that in some societies with unilineal descent groups, marriages tend to be widely scattered so that 'a complex scheme of individuation' results, while in others there is regular connubium. While we have little detailed information on connubial relations between local patrilineal groups in Aboriginal Australia, facts such as those to which Elkin has called attention do suggest that the tendency is toward 'a complex scheme of individuation'. This is an important point, because the structure of most Aboriginal relationship terminologies is such that they can easily be, and have been, mistaken for aggregates of patrilineal groups which regularly intermarry.

There is, however, a definite class of Aboriginal societies characterized by regular connubium among local patrilineal groups. Thus in northeast Arnhem Land, as noted above (section II), the sib of a man's mother-in-law is ideally that of his maternal grandmother, while his wife's sib is preferably also his mother's. Something like this seems also to prevail among the Wikmunkan and Yir-Yoront, and in north-central Arnhem Land (McConnel 1934; Sharp 1934; Hiatt 1965:38). Particularly for these and similar societies must the explanation of the prohibition of FZD marriage be sought elsewhere.

In his *The Australian Aborigines*, Elkin (1964:71) states:

> we can understand why a man would prefer not to make his father's sister, mother-in-law. She belongs to his own and his father's local group, even though she marries . . . into another group. Her spirit belongs where his does, and therefore no barriers to social intercourse should be set up between them.

It is not clear what the ethnographic or theoretical basis is of the principle that behavioural freedom holds between persons whose spirits 'belong to' the same place. In any case, this is contradicted by sister-avoidance, noted above.

Later in the same work we learn that

> in the Karadjeri and Murngin tribes . . . father's sister is called father, with the result that her children are included in the range of the sentiment which attaches to father and children; they are like brothers and sisters, with the result that there can be no thought of marriage between a man and his father's sister's daughter, even though the actual term used towards her is not the one for sister . . . this sentiment is associated with the tribal prohibition of patrilateral cross-cousin marriage (1964:128).

I cannot speak for the Karadjeri case, but the relevant facts from north-east Arnhem Land are these: (1) the native relationship category including the genealogical father is *bapa*; (2) the one including the genealogical father's sister is *mukul bapa*, sometimes given as *bapa mukul*; (3) individuals of the latter category are sometimes referred to as *bapa miyalk*, lit. 'female father'.[8]

All this would seem to support Elkin. In fact, however, his argument is both logically fallacious and ethnographically unsound. Thus in north-east Arnhem Land and among the Karadjeri, a man may marry his genealogical MBD, in which case a woman marries her genealogical FZS, who according to Elkin's logic is a sort of 'brother'. Further, I have no evidence of any kind that in Miwuyt society patrilateral cross-cousins are regarded as in any sense siblings. Their mother, to be sure, is a 'female father', but to be able to deduce what Elkin does from this requires that the mother-child tie be seen as similar to the father-child bond; this is not only not the case in north-east Arnhem Land (Shapiro n.d.:Chapter 3), but, as Elkin (1964:90) himself has pointed out, it is foreign to Aboriginal thought generally.

It can be seen, I think, that Elkin's 'explanations' of the phenomenon under consideration are little more than *ad hoc* predications of it; they fit where they fit, and they don't fit where they don't fit. That there are several of them violates the principle of Occam's Razor; that they are based upon factors which are presumably pan-Aboriginal means that they have little or no predictive value. They are, in short, not explanations at all in a scientific sense.

IV

Although it does not deal specifically with why marriage is disliked with a girl whose mother is of one's own local patrilineal group, the work of Rose (1960, 1965) on the influence of 'gerontocracy' upon Aboriginal marriage suggests a further explanation. Rose (1960:6) defines 'gerontocracy' as a situation in which 'most young girls married men considerably older than themselves . . .' In such a situation, Ego's MB will normally marry much later than Ego's mother, with the usual result that Ego will be rather older than his MBD and may therefore 'gerontocratically' take her as his wife. On the other hand, FZ marries much earlier than father, with the result that FZD will be disposed of in marriage before Ego is of mature age or perhaps even before he is born. Under 'gerontocracy', then, a man may marry his genealogical MBD but not his genealogical FZD.

Analysis of some of Rose's data by Josselin de Jong (1962) and Needham (1966) suggests that these conclusions will not regularly hold if one substitutes for the genealogical MBD and FZD simply any female of their relationship categories. But suppose one takes a middle road—not only these genealogical specifications on the one hand or the entire membership of relationship categories on the other, but, say, (*a*) any female of the MBD category who is a member of the local patrilineal group of Ego's mother, and (*b*) any female of the FZD category whose mother is a member of Ego's own local patrilineal group. Do the members of class (*a*) tend to be younger than Ego and those of class (*b*) older? Rose's tabulations (1960) do not provide the data by which these questions could be answered, but my own field material from north-east Arnhem Land does.[9]

During the course of my fieldwork I carried out a project inspired by Rose's work and very similar to it. Specifically, I photographed approximately 285 Aboriginal men and women living on the Elcho Island Methodist Mission Station—about four-fifths of the island's adult population. These 285 photographs, together with the names of about sixty other individuals from Elcho Island and other parts of the Miwuyt area, were shown or spoken to each of roughly sixty male informants, who was asked to give his relationship term for each individual thus identified. The (more or less) 345 responses of each informant were entered upon a separate form. (For further details on this project, see Appendix A.) I also obtained genealogies from most of the men thus employed, as well as other data which are not relevant here.

Since Miwuyt marriage is markedly 'gerontocratic' (Shapiro n.d.: Chapter 6), data collected by these means may be used to test the validity of Rose's ideas for north-east Arnhem Land. To this end I have more or less arbitrarily selected the photo- and name-identification forms of twenty informants. Each form has been examined for females of the MBD and FZD categories, who have been classed according to the following typology:

(1) genealogical FZDs and other females of the FZD category whose mothers are Ego's sibmates—class (b) above (hereafter abbreviated as FZD);
(2) all other females of the FZD category ('FZD');
(3) genealogical MBDs and other females of the MBD category who are sibmates of Ego's mother—class (a) above (MBD);
(4) all other females of the MBD category ('MBD').

Every female in each of these four taxons has been classified as 'older than' (O) or 'younger than' (Y) Ego. An O female is one who is chronologically older, or less than ten years younger, than Ego; a Y female is one who is ten or more years younger than Ego. This arbitrary weighting of ten years in favour of the female stems from (a) the need to make a relative age-judgement in cases where, by all indications, both parties seem to be of about the same age, and (b) the social fact that in north-east Arnhem Land females are ready for marriage at about age twelve, males not until their early twenties. (Criteria used to judge relative age in this way, and to select informants' forms for this purpose, are set forth in Appendix A.)

The results are given in Table 1. As might be expected from the weighting just mentioned, O females outnumber Y females in all four taxons; what is significant, however, is the O:Y ratio in each case. Thus, in support of Rose, there are five times as many O FZDs as Y FZDs, but only about half again as many O MBDs as Y MBDs. More surprising is that propositions derived from Rose's ideas seem to hold even for the 'FZD'-'MBD' sphere, though not as strongly as for the FZD-MBD domain. Thus there are over two and a half times as many O 'FZDs' as Y 'FZDs', but only about 1·7 times as many O 'MBDs' as Y 'MBDs'.[10] (Tests of statistical significance are not used here, since the sample is not random.)

The Miwuyt data thus seem to fit Rose's hypothesis even better than his own material from Groote Eylandt does. Have we here, then, an adequate explanation of why there is a negative attitude toward marriage with a girl whose mother is a member of one's own local patrilineal group? Can we say that such an attitude exists because females of this type[11] are usually older than Ego and must therefore, under 'gerontocracy', be bestowed as wives before he is ready for marriage, or perhaps even before his birth? Even assuming that something like the distribution given in Table 1 is general in Aboriginal Australia (cf. Rose 1960; Goodale 1962; Meggitt 1965), I think these questions must be answered negatively, for the following reasons:

First, Rose's and derivative arguments fail to distinguish between statistical tendencies on the one hand and cultural symbols and rules on the other, a point already made by Leach (1965). Thus, in north-east Arnhem Land, it is not simply that females of the MBD category are more frequently available for marriage than are those of the FZD class; there is also a rule *prescribing* marriage with the former and prohibiting it with the latter.

Second, although I am not as unsympathetic toward it as Leach is in the paper referred to, the assumption that statistical tendencies equal cultural rules and symbols is too inconsistent with certain facts of Aboriginal ethnography to be allowed to pass unquestioned. Thus if it is the case, as Rose (1960:168) contends, that the 'matrilateral' tendencies inherent, with 'gerontocratic' marriage, in Kariera-type systems find cultural expression in systems like Karadjeri, 'Murngin', and Yir-Yoront, then why are these latter apparently so rare? Why are the same tendencies in Aranda-type systems never, so far as we know, manifested in symbolic form? Elsewhere (Shapiro 1967d), I have stressed the fact that there is no modern description and analysis of a fully-functioning system quite like the one Radcliffe-Brown (1913) reported for the Kariera, but the existence of orthodox Aranda-type systems has been demonstrated beyond reasonable doubt (see e.g. Meggitt 1962; Hiatt 1965; Reay 1962). Since these appear to be by far the most common variety found in Aboriginal Australia, we can hardly dismiss them, as Rose (1960: 169-70) seems to do, as products of misconception on the part of anthropologists.

Third, Rose-type arguments place great weight upon the very tenuous proposition that only primary marriages can influence social

TABLE 1

AGE FACTORS IN MARRIAGE

	O	Y	Total
FZD	21	4	25
'FZD'	78	30	108
MBD	43	26	69
'MBD'	138	82	220
Total	280	142	422

institutions and cultural symbols (see Shapiro 1966). Even under 'gerontocracy', FZD marriage can occur regularly as a secondary union for the wife, a fact which Rose (1960:123) himself appreciates.

V

I would suggest that a more adequate explanation is founded upon a fact noted thirty years ago by Elkin (1938:432), viz., that 'The tendency amongst the Australian Aborigines is to select the mother-in-law rather than the wife...'

It is regrettable that Elkin has yet to enlarge upon this remark with reference to any particular society he has studied. Its first substantiation in the literature seems to be the account by Spencer and Gillen (1927: 469-71) of the *tualtja mura* institution among the Aranda. By this institution, an unmarried girl is bestowed as a mother-in-law upon a boy, who thus acquires conjugal rights to the daughters she will eventually bear. The only other description, in a scholarly publication, of similar practices is to be found in Jane Goodale's paper on Tiwi marriage contracts (1962).

Mother-in-law bestowal is, however, also practised in north-east Arnhem Land. Though uncommon nowadays, it seems formerly to have been inevitable in a woman's life-experience. It may involve only a verbal agreement between the recipient and those who have rights of bestowal (see below) — this is the form it appears invariably to take nowadays — or it may be more highly formalized. In the latter case, the relevant ceremony, briefly described by the missionary Chaseling (1957) in a popular book, is called *yinipi* by the eastern Miwuyt, *munyuk* by groups further west.

Four classes of persons are involved, directly or indirectly, in a *munyuk* performance: the girl to be bestowed (who is still a child), the boy or man upon whom she is to be bestowed, the girl's father, and the girl's matrikin (her mother, MB, MM, and MMB). The last-named have rights of bestowal over the girl but, apparently because they are ideally in avoidance categories with respect to the recipient, they do not take an active part in the ceremony. The girl herself *must* be in the MMBD category, her father *should* be (and usually is) in the MMB category, with respect to the latter, and they are, as noted (section II above), preferably sibmates of his maternal grandmother.

I myself have never seen a *munyuk* performance; its ideal form, as related by informants, appears to be as follows:

The girl is made to sit in an area which is in full public view. Her father holds her, beckoning to the recipient, who waits in the wings: *Gu, gutarra, munyukmirriangu!* ('Come forth, sister's daughter's son, and perform *munyuk!*'). The latter comes forward and sits near the girl, facing her. With his right thumb he removes some facial oil (sebum) from the area immediately above his right nostril, places it directly upon the girl's abdomen a few inches above her navel, and proceeds to move it downward to the navel itself. This concludes the minimal requirements of the ceremony, though the movement to the navel may be repeated for emphasis.

This act formally signifies the creation of a *bun milmarra* relationship (section II above) between the recipient on the one hand and the girl, her father and brothers, and her matrikin on the other. The performance of *munyuk* is the last direct contact the recipient will ever have with his mother-in-law; henceforward their relationship is characterized by the most extreme avoidance behaviour. The former assumes the obligation of providing, throughout life, various gifts and services for the girl; she in turn is expected to deliver to him as wives all daughters she will eventually bear. The father of these daughters will, according to native theory, be a member of the MB category with respect to their husband and a sibmate of his mother, but whether or not this is in fact so does not alter the rights and obligations of the *bun milmarra* relationship.[12]

The foregoing, it will be noted, does not square with what Warner and Berndt have written about the arrangement of marriages in northeast Arnhem Land: both imply, though not unambiguously, that girls are bestowed as wives by their fathers (Warner 1937:93; Berndt 1965), and both idiomize the ideal union as MBD marriage, thus placing undue emphasis upon the wife's father.[13] Similarly, Hart and Pilling, who have also studied the Tiwi, seem to have missed mother-in-law bestowal; thus they report (Hart and Pilling 1960:14-15) that fathers have rights of bestowal over their daughters as wives, a notion quite at variance with Goodale's findings.

It is relevant to note here that Mrs Annette Hamilton has found evidence of mother-in-law bestowal among the Gidjingali, first studied by Hiatt (1965). Hiatt himself notes that 'A woman and her brothers had a joint right to bestow her daughters in marriage' (1965:41), but he makes no mention of the wife's mother herself being bestowed. Yet he spent twenty months in north-central Arnhem Land, and his monograph deals especially with marriage rights! We have here, I suspect, still another case of mother-in-law bestowal eluding a competent ethnographer, though for a substantiation of the Gidjingali situation we must await the results of further fieldwork by Mrs Hamilton.

These considerations suggest that mother-in-law bestowal is rather more widely found in Aboriginal Australia than the ethnographic literature would indicate; in fact I would hazard the guess that it is general, though perhaps not quite universal.

Now it seems in line with ethnographic facts and anthropological conceptions to say that in some societies, marriage is part of a transaction between groups, acting either as corporations or as representatives of cultural categories; and that in these societies exogamy is an expression of the norm that such transactions must take place. In most societies which use marriage to express alliance, the salient object of the transaction is a wife; hence both native and anthropological conceptions of exogamy pertain only to the husband-wife dyad. But in Aboriginal Australia, if my hunch is correct, wives are frequently no more than by-products of the bestowal of mothers-in-law. Might we not, therefore, expect that Aboriginal conceptions of exogamy will be broader?

I submit that *in societies in which the wife's mother is herself bestowed, a situation in which mother-in-law and son-in-law are members of the same local patrilineal group is seen as a violation of the exogamy of that group and is therefore unacceptable.*

It should be noted that none of the foregoing is intended to imply adherence to a Tylorian or any other view of the causes of exogamy. All I assume is what I believe to be an ethnographic fact: that, for whatever reasons—and I am not concerned here with what these might be—exogamy of the local patrilineal group is something in which Australian Aborigines have a very high psychological investment.

VI

My argument has been based on an extentionist premise: not, to be sure, that Aboriginal schemes of social classification are essentially genealogical distinctions, but that they, or rather some of them, have basically to do with distinctions among local patrilineal groups for purposes of alliance. This is not a new thought and I do not think it is the key to all classificatory schemes in Aboriginal Australia; but it does, I believe, provide realistic definitions of the kind of structures I have called semi-moieties. The Aranda and Miwuyt systems may be taken as illustrative:

Aranda
'FF' semi-moiety = Ego's own local patrilineal group, plus local patrilineal groups which are totemically allied with Ego's;
'MMB' semi-moiety = local patrilineal groups which supply Ego's group with mothers-in-law, and which Ego's group in turn supplies with mothers-in-law, in every generation;
'MF' semi-moiety = local patrilineal groups which supply wives for the men of Ego's group of his father's and son's categorical generation;

'FMB' semi-moiety = local patrilineal groups which supply wives for the men of Ego's group of his own categorical generation.

Miwuyt

'FF' semi-moiety = same as Aranda;
'MMB' semi-moiety = same as Aranda;
'MF' semi-moiety = local patrilineal groups which supply wives for Ego's group in every generation;
'FZHF' semi-moiety = local patrilineal groups to which females of Ego's group go as wives in every generation.

I shall conclude by enumerating what I believe are the advantages of my explanation, particularly in contrast to the one derived from Rose's ideas:

First, my explanation does not confound statistical tendencies with cultural rules and symbols; instead, it explains particular rules and symbols in terms of another cultural form.

Second, acceptance of Rose's ideas forces us to regard both Kariera- and Aranda-type systems as cultural fictions, or as products of the anthropologist's imagination—this despite the fact that the latter systems are probably more common in Aboriginal Australia than those of all other types taken together. My own explanation, by contrast, sees nothing abnormal in the Aranda model, making as it does the expected categorical distinction $FZ \neq WM$; I do, however, regard orthodox Kariera-type systems as anomalous. If my explanation is to hold for the entire continent, then either systems of this kind must not exist, or—I think this is more likely—they must be associated with the absence of mother-in-law bestowal.

Third, my explanation does not rely upon the already exploded hypothesis that only primary marriages influence social institutions and cultural symbols.

Appendix A

Collection and Analysis of Age and Kin-term Data

Photo- and name-identification project. The choice of individuals to be photographed was entirely haphazard: I simply photographed every adult I came across, stopping only when the cost of the inevitable duplication of subjects seemed to outweigh the advantages of a larger sample. The selection of the sixty additional names was rather more deliberate, emphasizing as it did parents of individuals photographed who were themselves unphotographed but still living. The reason for this emphasis is that the Miwuyt recognize two fundamental principles in the application of relationship terms—patri-determination and matri-determination—and I was (and am) concerned with the development of a statistical model of the relationship terminology. The selection of informants for this project was made mostly on the simple bases of availability and willingness, though, particularly for genealogical purposes, I successfully attempted to employ at least one man from each of the larger sibs. My informants varied in age from youths of perhaps sixteen to ritual headmen in their sixties and seventies.

Selection of informants' forms for data summarized in Table 1. Table 1 would be quite meaningless if there were only a handful of FZDs and MBDs; hence I attempted to select only the forms of informants who had photographed representatives of these taxons.

Judgement of relative age. Since the Elcho Island Mission Station was established in 1942, it has kept a record of all births in areas under its jurisdiction. It has also made official estimates of the ages of individuals born before 1942; obviously, in the cases of persons born considerably earlier, such estimates can only be very approximate. For want of a better technique, however, I relied exclusively upon mission records and estimates, except in those cases where the latter were patently in error (e.g. where a woman's date of birth was given as two years prior to that of her eldest daughter). I might mention that mission estimates of the relative ages of siblings agree substantially with data I obtained in genealogies.

Appendix B

Analysis of Marriages in which Mother-in-law and Son-in-law are Sibmates

As noted in the main text (section II), there are in my sample eighteen such marriages, the method of arrangement of ten of which is recorded in my field notes. The ten marriages may be broken down as follows: (1) three involved 'stealing' the girl from the man to whom she had been promised; (2) two involved a transfer, on the part of bestowers, of a promise originally made to another man; (3) one was the result of an exchange of wives between two men; and (4) four are the result of mother-in-law bestowals.

It thus sometimes happens that a girl is bestowed as a mother-in-law upon a man of her own sib, i.e. that a mother-in-law bestowal is endogamous with respect to the local patrilineal group. A wife, by contrast, can *never* be a sibmate of her husband. This greater insistence on patrilineal group exogamy with respect to the wife is, I suspect, found throughout Aboriginal Australia.

NOTES

1. I am indebted to Professors J. A. Barnes and F. G. G. Rose, and to Dr A. L. Epstein, for their comments on earlier versions of this paper.

2. I suspect some anthropologists would object to my using 'patrilineal' here, on the grounds that what is involved is not descent but filiation, or a kind of locality-tie expressed in terms of the father-child relationship (see e.g. Dunning 1959:77; Service 1962:129). At a purely scholastic level I would acknowledge this criticism, though I cannot help wondering whether these distinctions have any relevance for a realistic comprehension of Aboriginal thought. I hope to expand upon this elsewhere.

3. I have spent sixteen months in north-east Arnhem Land—from November 1965 to September 1966, and then from May to November 1967. My research was financed by the Institute of Advanced Studies of the Australian National University. As has frequently been pointed out, the Aborigines of north-east Arnhem Land have no ethnic or tribal name for themselves, though they have been called 'Murngin' and 'Wulamba' in the literature. I shall refer to them as 'Miwuyt', a term applied to them by peoples to their west (cf. Berndt and Berndt 1964:63).

4. The 'local patrilineal group' in north-east Arnhem Land appears to be more or less equivalent to Warner's 'clan' (1937) and Berndt's '*mada-mala* combination' (1965: 84). I shall from now onward refer to it as a 'sib', for reasons which have been given elsewhere (Shapiro 1967*a*).

5. In Miwuyt theory, the wife's mother is a member of the MMBD category; when a man marries a girl whose mother is a member of another category, his mother-in-law is sometimes, though by no means always, incorporated into the proper class. Following what I take to be Maybury-Lewis's logic (1965), I would therefore regard *mukul rumaru* (MMBD) as a category which is, in a sense, intermediate between 'preferred' and 'prescribed', though for present purposes it may be unequivocally classed as 'prescribed'.

6. This sample is, I believe, a nearly exhaustive one of the effective marriages (as of November 1965) in the areas I visited. For further details, see Shapiro (n.d.: Chapters 1 and 6).

7. There are several other cases in which the two are sibmates, but the mother-in-law is not a member of the MMBD category. Such marriages are on this count regarded as improper; and the conceptualization of, and behavioural norms toward, the wife's mother in a situation of this kind are entirely different from those that prevail when she is a *mukul rumaru* (Shapiro n.d.: Chapter 7). I have therefore excluded these marriages from present consideration.

8. For reasons beyond the scope of the present paper, I believe 'father' is the basic meaning of the relationship category *bapa*.

9. In their present form, the questions are applicable only to Groote Eylandt, north-east Arnhem Land, and the few other parts of Aboriginal Australia where FZD is categorically distinguished from MBD. It would not be difficult, however, to rephrase these questions for other areas (see Goodale 1962; Meggitt 1965).

10. It will also be noted that the number of MBDs-'MBDs' is more than twice the number of FZDs-'FZDs'. I am not certain why this should be so, but in any case it is not relevant to the present inquiry.

11. That is, of this type and also of a 'cross-cousin' relationship category. It is taken

for granted here that a man cannot marry his genealogical ZD or any other female of the same relationship category, since such 'adjacent generation' marriages are prohibited in the vast majority of Aboriginal societies.

12. The foregoing is intended only as an outline of bestowal procedures, affinal obligations, etc.; for further detail, see Shapiro (n.d.: Chapters 5 and 7).

13. These divergences of findings among Warner, Berndt, and myself are discussed in greater detail in Shapiro (n.d.: Chapter 5). It may be noted here that Donald Thomson seems to have some idea of the pre-eminent position of the mother-in-law in northeast Arnhem Land, though his slender volume pays little attention to this subject (Thomson 1949:42-5, 51n).

References

BECKETT, J. 1967 Marriage, circumcision, and avoidance among the Maljangaba of north-west New South Wales, *Mankind*, Vol. 6:456-64.

BERNDT, R. M. 1965 Marriage and the family in north-eastern Arnhem Land. In *Comparative Family Systems* (M. F. Nimkoff, ed.). Houghton Mifflin, Boston.

BERNDT, R. M. and C. H. 1964 *The World of the First Australians*. University of Chicago Press, Chicago.

CHASELING, W. S. 1957 *Yulengor: Nomads of Arnhem Land*. Epworth Press, London.

DUNNING, R. W. 1959 *Social and Economic Change among the Northern Ojibwa*. University of Toronto Press, Toronto.

ELKIN, A. P. 1932 Social organisation in the Kimberley Division, north-western Australia, *Oceania*, Vol. 2:296-333.

—— 1938 Kinship in South Australia (Part I), *Oceania*, Vol. 8:419-52.

—— 1940 Ibid. (Part V), *Oceania*, Vol. 10:369-88.

—— 1964 *The Australian Aborigines*. Doubleday, New York.

ENGLISH, H. B. and Ava C. 1958 *A Comprehensive Dictionary of Psychological and Psychoanalytic Terms*. Longmans Green, New York.

GOODALE, Jane C. 1962 Marriage contracts among the Tiwi, *Ethnology*, Vol. 1:452-66.

HART, C. W. M. and A. PILLING 1960 *The Tiwi of North Australia*. Holt, Rinehart and Winston, New York.

HIATT, L. R. 1965 *Kinship and Conflict: a study of an Aboriginal community in northern Arnhem Land*. Australian National University, Canberra.

—— 1967 Authority and reciprocity in Australian Aboriginal marriage arrangements, *Mankind*, Vol. 6:468-75.

JOSSELIN DE JONG, P. E. de 1962 A new approach to kinship studies, *Bijdragen tot de Taal-, Land- en Volkenkunde*, No. 118:42-67.

LEACH, E. R. 1961 *Rethinking Anthropology*. Athlone Press, London.

—— 1965 Unilateral cross-cousin marriage, *Man*, Vol. 65, No. 12.

McCONNEL, Ursula M. 1934 The Wik-Munkan and allied tribes of Cape York Peninsula, *Oceania*, Vol. 4:310-56.

MAYBURY-LEWIS, D. H. P. 1965 Prescriptive marriage systems, *Southwestern Journal of Anthropology*, Vol. 21:207-30.

MEGGITT, M. J. 1962 *Desert People: A Study of the Walbiri Aborigines of Central Australia*. Angus and Robertson, Sydney.

—— 1965 Marriage among the Walbiri of central Australia: a statistical examination. In *Aboriginal Man in Australia* (R. M. and C. H. Berndt, eds). Angus and Robertson, Sydney.

NEEDHAM, R. 1966 Age, category, and descent, *Bijdragen tot de Taal-, Land- en Volkenkunde*, No. 122:1-35.

RADCLIFFE-BROWN, A. R. 1913 Three tribes of Western Australia, *Journal of the Royal Anthropological Institute*, Vol. 43: 143-94.

——— 1931 The social organization of Australian tribes. *Oceania Monographs* No. 1.

REAY, Marie 1962 Subsections at Borroloola, *Oceania*, Vol. 33: 90-115.

ROSE, F. G. G. 1960 *Classification of Kin, Age Structure, and Marriage amongst the Groote Eylandt Aborigines*. Akademie-Verlag, Berlin.

——— 1965 Unilateral cross-cousin marriage, *Man*, Vol. 65: No. 11.

SERVICE, E. R. 1962 *Primitive Social Organization: An Evolutionary Perspective*. Random House, New York.

SHAPIRO, W. 1966 Secondary unions and kinship terminology: the case of avuncular marriage, *Bijdragen tot de Taal-, Land- en Volkenkunde*, No. 122: 82-9.

——— 1967a Preliminary report on field work in northeastern Arnhem Land, *American Anthropologist*, Vol. 69: 353-5.

——— 1967b Relational affiliation in 'unilineal' descent systems, *Man*, Vol. 2: 461-3.

——— 1967c Semi-moiety organization in northeast Arnhem Land. Paper presented at a meeting of the Association of Social Anthropologists, Australia and New Zealand branch. Sydney.

——— 1967d Semi-moiety organization: some moot points in the literature, *Mankind*, Vol. 6: 465-7.

——— 1969 Asymmetric marriage in Australia and Southeast Asia, *Bijdragen tot de Taal-, Land- en Volkenkunde*, No. 125.

——— n.d. Miwuyt marriage: social structural aspects of the bestowal of females in northeast Arnhem Land. Ph.D. thesis, Department of Anthropology and Sociology, Australian National University (in process).

SHARP, L. 1934 The social organisation of the Yir-Yoront tribe, Cape York Peninsula, *Oceania*, Vol. 4: 404-31.

SPENCER, B. and F. J. GILLEN 1927 *The Arunta*. Macmillan, London.

THOMSON, D. F. 1949 *Economic Structure and the Ceremonial Exchange Cycle in Arnhem Land*. Macmillan, Melbourne.

WARNER, W. L. 1937 *A Black Civilization: A Social Study of an Australian Tribe*. Harper, New York.

ARAM A. YENGOYAN

Demographic Factors in Pitjandjara Social Organization

Systematic demographic studies of Aboriginal populations in Australia have been rare or virtually non-existent except for F. G. G. Rose's (1960) analysis of kinship and age structure among the Aborigines of Groote Eylandt. The factors leading to the absence of demographic interests among anthropologists can be traced to at least two reasons. First, Aboriginal societies described by social anthropologists were usually (although there were exceptions) in the contact situation which meant that population characteristics of various groups had been affected by European diseases, famine and population disruption and dispersion on to settlements, homesteads, towns and missions. These conditions are still present among most of the central Australian groups though the more drastic changes have been modified. Second, social anthropologists in general avoid quantification of field information. Exceptions to this are Meggitt, Hiatt, Rose, etc. Or, if observations and interpretations are quantified, the published works in most cases do not provide the quantification which is needed to explain and compare social phenomena. The overriding concern with structure, models and rules has hindered attempts to determine intragroup and intertribal variation and how such variation might influence the operation of the social structure.

Structural analysis of social phenomena does not completely explain how rules and conceptions of social behaviour operate under varying non-structural conditions. The analysis of social phenomena as symbolic constructs (in the minds of either the people or the ethnographer) provides us with a means of determining the degree of variation between what occurs in reality and the ideal conceptions of how things should operate. But the understanding of phenomena must utilize demographic, ecological, economic and historical/processual factors as possible explanations as to 'why the structure is as it is' and how the structure works as part of the real world. This paper is an attempt to deal with variations in Pitjandjara marriage rates as they are influenced by demographic factors.

The Pitjandjara represent one of the most viable present-day Aboriginal populations in central and western Australia, thus a descriptive demographic study could be done with certain limitations which will be discussed later. Furthermore, the Pitjandjara are known to the Social Anthropology of the Australian Aboriginal through the early observations of Basedow and more definitive accounts by Elkin, Berndt, Tindale and Mountford. My own fieldwork among these people was done at Amaṭa (Musgrave Park), Mulga Park and Ernabella from May 1966 to June 1967.[1] The original objectives of the fieldwork were (1) to ascertain the nature of pre-contact social organization and broader socio-geographic units, and (2) to determine the demographic structure of the present population and to analyse its influence on certain aspects of social organization.

This paper is primarily descriptive in that basic demographic parameters are analysed and their relationship to population fluctuation, marital arrangements and other aspects of social organization are discussed.

Contemporary Setting

The Pitjandjara belong to a wider population unit which covers an area from Ernabella (east) to the Warburton Ranges Mission, Western Australia (west), and from Areyonga on the north to Ooldea on the south. Within this large network, one finds different spheres of interaction which allow one to demarcate certain networks, where the interaction is much more intense, from other comparable networks. Thus, one of these intensive units of interaction is a region covering Ernabella Mission, Mulga Park, and Amaṭa (Musgrave Park). The populations in these three centres are related to one another, have had a long period of intensive interaction, and still commonly change residence for different reasons. To the north of this area, the major population cluster is at Areyonga with smaller settlements at Curtin Springs, Angas Downs, and Mt Ebenezer. On the east, Everard and Kenmore Park have communication with Ernabella. To the south and west, one finds stretches of depopulated areas; thus Ooldea was and Yalata is an important southern settlement while Warburton was at the time of my fieldwork the major population cluster west of Amaṭa. Network boundaries are not hard and fast demarcations since rates of interaction between networks vary due to the occurrence of ceremonies and climatic factors.

The area of the Ernabella-Mulga Park-Amaṭa network is about 200-250 miles across and 80-100 miles wide, or roughly the whole of the Musgrave-Mann-Tomkinson ranges including Mulga Park. Ernabella, at the eastern fringes of the Musgrave Ranges, is a Presbyterian mission founded in 1937. In 1961 an out-station to decentralize the sheep raising industry and provide additional labour for Pitjandjara men was established at Fregon, 40 miles south of Ernabella Mission. Mulga Park, a small homestead, is north-west of Ernabella and provides for the meeting of roads to Ernabella, Amaṭa and north to Curtin Springs and Ayers Rock. Amaṭa is a government settlement on the Northwest Reserve and is located about 100 miles due west of Ernabella. The settlement was started in 1961 though the 27,000 square mile reserve had been designated as a reserve at a much earlier time.

In each locality the Pitjandjara are settled in camps and commonly work for wages either in construction jobs or as shepherds, livestock keepers, fencers or in other jobs. But as the drought ended in 1966-67 and game increased, the local populations moved off the settlements and lived off the land through the hunting of game, the collecting of wild foods, and the hunting of young dingoes ('pupping') for a bounty. However, the scattered population clusters had to be occasionally provisioned with tea, sugar, flour and canned goods from either Ernabella or Amaṭa.

Within this network, the Pitjandjara population ranged from 600 to 800 people during 1966-67 though marked variance from this range took place when a Red Ochre ritual group came through from the south. Furthermore, the few vehicles owned by Aborigines provide a more rapid and intensive movement of population, that is, when the vehicles are operating. The stable population in this network can be divided as follows:

Location	Population Range
Ernabella	350–450
Amaṭa	150–250
Mulga Park	50–75

Although the economic organization of the Pitjandjara in this area has changed through adaptation to and reliance on a European diet, the socio-ceremonial structure of Pitjandjara society has not been severely affected and in some cases it may be claimed to have reached new levels of intensity and output (Yengoyan 1968b).

Population Characteristics

The Pitjandjara population at Amaṭa ranged from 150 to 300 during 1966-67 though some 300-400 people had gathered for major ceremonial activities. In January 1967 the first good census was made since the local population was more sedentary during the warm summer months. The total population at this time was 264, though another twenty to thirty individuals had temporarily left the reserve. Table 1 presents the total population by age and sex.

TABLE 1

POPULATION PYRAMID, AMAṬA, JANUARY 1967

Age Brackets	Male	Female	Total
80–84	1	0	1
75–79	0	0	0
70–74	1	0	1
65–69	2	0	2
60–64	1	2	3
55–59	1	4	5
50–54	7	1	8
45–49	3	2	5
40–44	9	10	19
35–39	11	17	28
30–34	14	9	23
25–29	13	24	37
20–24	7	6	13
15–19	13	12	25
10–14	8	15	23
5–9	12	10	22
0–4	23	26	49
Total	126	138	264
Percentage	47·7	52·3	100

The difference of nearly 10 per cent between male and female children (i.e. up to fifteen years of age) is due to differential infant mortality as well as the reduction of female infanticide which only occurs among those who have recently come in from the bush.

Out of sixty-three males over the age of twenty-five, fifty-two were married, while the remaining eleven were either widowers or unmarried. Sixty-three females out of seventy-five over the age of twenty were married, while seven were widowed and five unmarried. Three females in the age bracket fifteen to nineteen were married. The average number of living children for the sixty-three married females was 2·79 with a range of one to eight per couple. Average family size ranges from 4·7 to 5·1 persons.

Table 2 lists births by sex for a six-year period (1961-66). The increasing number of births per year is due to in-migration after 1961 and has nothing to do with the intrinsic rate of population growth. A male/female sex ratio of 94·7 among all births during the six-year interval

TABLE 2

PITJANDJARA BIRTHS, AMAṬA

Year	Approximate Amaṭa Pop.	Total No. of Births	Male	Female	Crude Birth Rate
1961	150	5	2	3	33·3
1962	150	5	1	4	33·3
1963	200	11	7	4	55·0
1964	250	14	4	10	56·0
1965	300	23	15	8	76·7
1966	300	16	7	9	53·3
Total		74	36	38	51·3 (six-year av.)

is not significantly different from the 91·3 male/female sex ratio characterizing the total Amaṭa population. As will be seen, this variable is different from male/female ratios at Ernabella. Crude birth rates should not be accepted at face value since the total Amaṭa population for each of the six years (except 1966) is estimated from census materials. But each year indicates the increasing viability of the Pitjandjara population.

As indicated by Table 3, infant mortality is exceedingly high during the first year of life. From 1961 to 1965, thirteen of fourteen infant deaths occurred before the age of one year.

Although the crude death rate has dropped over the past twenty years, due to increasing control of disease and sickness, and a more ample diet, the crude death rate is still higher than the Commonwealth (minus Aborigines) rate of 9·7. Infant mortality is high, but the contemporary rate is significantly lower than what was determined for the pre-contact population through genealogical information.

The computing of the Amaṭa population through more refined demographic rates and ratios is most difficult since the data are adequate for only one year and no historical evidence on population characteristics is available. A good discussion of historical changes among an Aboriginal population is found in Jones' (1963) demographic analysis of the Tiwi. Furthermore, the assessment of age in populations where age is unknown can be done only through estimates on relative age and the sequence of births. My estimates in most cases were wrong, but later in the study I was able to determine the rate and direction of my error in age analysis. For males in their thirties my estimates were usually lower than what would be the case, but age assessments for males in their forties and fifties were commonly overestimates. For females, the problems of age assessment were more difficult. Although girls marry between fifteen and twenty years of age, the number of living children is not always an adequate criterion of age. High infant mortality, infanticide, miscarriages, etc., may skew one's estimate. One means of assigning ages is to list all siblings of an individual and to find out their rank order from eldest to youngest. If we assume that the reproductive period per female is twenty to twenty-five years, then ages may be roughly established within five-year intervals. Yet this is also difficult, since deceased siblings are quickly forgotten. Most enquiries into deceased kinsmen result in short answers such as 'gone' or 'finish'. This abhorrence of talking about the dead was also noted among the Angas Downs Pitjandjara by F. Rose. However, one may partially surmount this obstacle by asking relatively distant relatives about other persons.

While the Amaṭa population presents limitations for a more complete

TABLE 3

PITJANDJARA DEATHS, AMAṬA

Year	Total Deaths	Deaths (0–6 months)	Deaths (6 mths–1 year)	Deaths (1-2 years)	Males	Females
1961	2	0	2	0	1	1
1962	3	2	1	0	1	2
1963	2	0	1	1	2	0
1964	2	1	1	0	0	2
1965	5	3	2	0	4	1
Total	14	6	7	1	8	6

Year	Infant Death Rates (per 1,000)
1961	400·0
1962	600·0
1963	90·9
1964	142·9
1965	217·4
Five Year Average	290·24

Year	Total Deaths	Crude Death Rate (per 1,000)
1961	5	33·3
1962	7	46·7
1963	6	30·0
1964	4	16·0
1965	10	33·3
1966	4	13·3
Total	36	28·7
Rate of natural increase per 1,000		22·6

analysis, the Pitjandjara at Ernabella Mission have been enumerated in at least two recent censuses with some population information going back to the early 1940s. In 1963 the Ernabella population totalled 416 with a male/female sex ratio of 102·9. This increase in the masculinity rate when compared to the Amaṭa rate of 91·3 may be due to the more sedentary economic pursuits of Ernabella Mission, where most Aboriginal men are working on a wage income. The population pyramid for the 1963 Ernabella population is presented in Table 4.

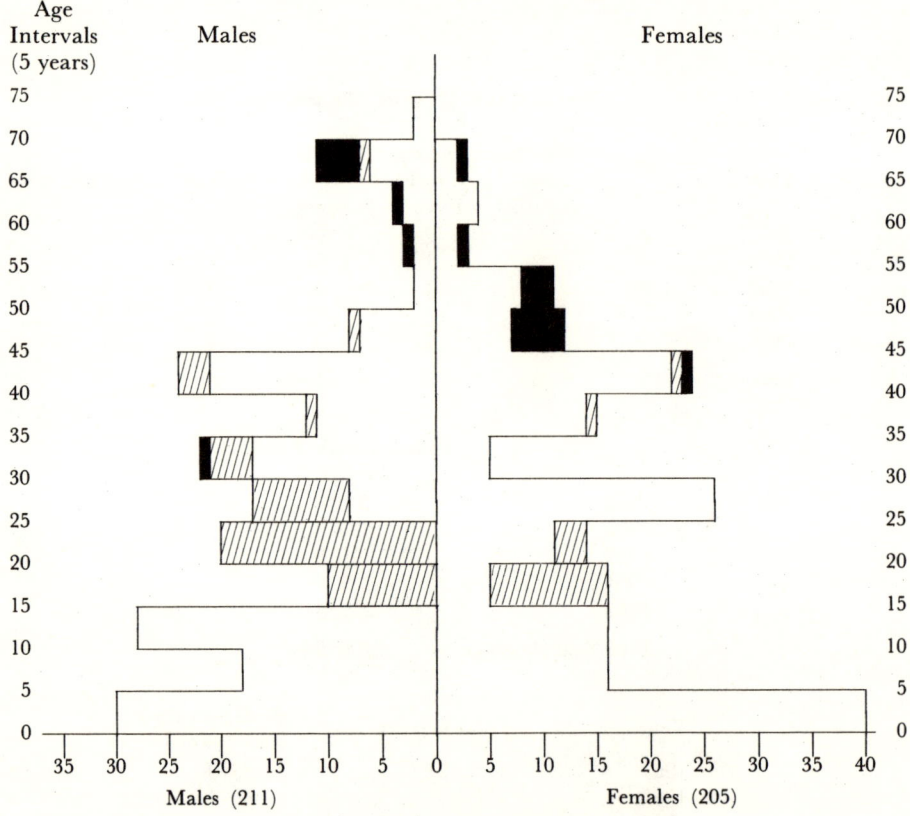

TABLE 4

POPULATION PYRAMID—ERNABELLA, 1963 CENSUS. TOTAL OF 416

▨ = Unmarried.   * All individuals under 15 are unmarried.   ■ = Widows/widowers.

An earlier census in 1957 listed the Ernabella Pitjandjara population at about 541. Age-specific data were not available from this census, but a population breakdown by tribal affiliation, sex ratio, marital status by sex, and groupings by age and social differentiation is given in Table 5.

Table 5
Ernabella, 1957 Census

Tribal Affiliation

	Total	Percentage
Pitjandjara	487	91·7
Jankunjatjara	38	7·2
Ngatadajara	6	1·1
Total	531	100·0

Sex Ratio

	Total	Percentage
Males	271	50·1
Females	270	49·9
Total	541	100·0

Marital Status by Sex

	Single	Married	Total
Males	140	131	271
Females	108	162	270
Total	248	293	541

Percentages

	Per cent
Single males	25·9
Single females	24·2
Married males	20·0
Married females	29·9

Sex Distribution by Age Groupings and Social Differentiation

Category	Males	Females	Total	Percentage of Total
Pre-school	14	18	32	11·1
School children	24	28	52	18·1
Adolescent boys	7	—	7	2·4
Nursing mothers	—	45	45	15·7
Working individuals	68	44	112	39·0
Old people	22	17	39	13·6
Total	135	152	287	99·9

In 1966-67, the number of living children for ninety-one females was 2·25, but the number of children (living and dead) for nineteen females whose reproductive years were completed was 4·12. Average family size among the Ernabella group falls within the range presented for the Amaṭa Pitjandjara.

A list of births from 1941 to 1966 is presented in Table 6. While births have risen in Ernabella due to increasing in-migration, the crude birth rate is difficult to estimate since yearly total population figures for Ernabella are not available. Except for 1957 and 1961-66, no other population approximations were utilized.

TABLE 6

PITJANDJARA BIRTHS, ERNABELLA

Year	Approx. Population	Total No. of Births	Male	Female	Crude Birth Rate
1941	—	6	4	2	—
1942	—	12	2	10	—
1943	—	14	7	7	—
1944	—	7	4	3	—
1945	—	11	6	5	—
1946	—	5	2	3	—
1947	—	7	3	4	—
1948	—	9	3	6	—
1949	—	13	7	6	—
1950	—	18	9	9	—
1951	—	16	7	9	—
1952	—	18	11	7	—
1953	—	23	13	10	—
1954	—	20	7	13	—
1955	—	20	8	12	—
1956	—	29	16	13	—
1957	541	20	8	12	37·0
1958	—	28	15	13	—
1959	—	23	8	15	—
1960	—	22	9	13	—
1961	425	28	13	15	65·9
1962	425	22	7	15	51·8
1963	416	28	17	11	67·3
1964	450	31	12	19	68·9
1965	450	28	16	12	62·2
1966	450	16	8	8	35·6
Total		474	222	252	64·8

(seven-year av.)

Death records at Ernabella go back to 1941; however, age-specific death figures are recorded from 1948 onward though not always complete. The infant death rate of 1948 and 1949 was due to a measles epidemic which spread through the mission and other settlements in the Western Desert. Table 7 lists all recorded deaths while Table 8 presents age-specific deaths from the available data.

Infant death rates and the crude death rates from Ernabella are presented in Tables 9 and 10.

From the demographic data collected at Amaṭa and Ernabella, one readily notes that the Pitjandjara are an increasing population whose rate of natural increase compares favourably with the Commonwealth average and the Walbiri (see Meggitt 1962:30-3). Although infant death rates are still high, the yearly fluctuations indicate a gradual reduction. The severe infant death rate of the late 1940s was due to a measles epidemic; however, in all probability deaths of this magnitude will not occur as long as an active vaccination programme is maintained.

TABLE 7

PITJANDJARA DEATHS, ERNABELLA

Year	Male	Female	Total
1941	–	–	–
1942	1	3	4
1943	2	–	2
1944	0	1	1
1945	1	1	2
1946	0	1	1
1947	1	1	2
1948	1	3	4
1949	4	2	6
1950	0	2	2
1951	2	5	7
1952	3	3	6
1953	3	6	9
1954	2	5	7
1955	4	7	11
1956	9	6	15
1957	2	2	4
1958	3	5	8
1959	3	1	4
1960	3	2	5
1961	1	5	6
1962	3	4	7
1963	5	5	10
1964	3	2	5
1965	8	4	12
1966	5	1	6
Total	69	77	146

SOCIAL ORGANIZATION

The viability of the Pitjandjara population has important implications for the analysis of social organization. The frequency with which marriages, ceremonies and local group activities follow ideal structural rules depends on demographic, economic and ecological factors. The increasing sedentarization of the contemporary population coupled with the adaptation to a Western diet and increasing population are important in explaining how the cognized system operates in reality.

In this discussion I will discuss local organization and marriage regulations only in regard to their ideal composition and how, in reality, non-structural factors regulate the operation of social phenomena.

The reconstruction of pre-contact local organization was the most

TABLE 8

AGE-SPECIFIC DEATHS

Year	Total Deaths	0 to 6 months	Deaths 6 months to 1 year	1 to 2 years	Males	Females
1948	4	3	1	0	1	3
1949	6	5	1	0	4	2
1950	2	1	1	0	0	2
1951	7	5	0	0	2	3
		(other 2 not age-specific)				
1952	6	1	0	0	1	0
		(other 5 not age-specific)				
1953	9	1	0	0	0	1
		(other 8 not age-specific)				
1954	7	(No age-specific data)				
1955	11	1	0	3	2	2
		(other 7 not age-specific)				
1956	15	0	0	2	1	1
		(other 13 not age-specific)				
1957	4	1	0	0	1	0
		(other 3 not age-specific)				
1958	8	0	1	1	2	0
		(another female died at age 3, rest unknown)				
1959	4	1	1	0	2	0
		(another female died at 22)				
1960	5	1	0	1	1	1
		(male at 2½, male at 7, female at 78)				
1961	6	1	2	1	0	4
		(male at 40, female at 69)				
1962	7	1	2	2	3	2
		(female at 35, female at 60)				
1963	10	0	3	2	3	2
		(male at 33, male at 43, female at 60, female at 65, female at 40)				
1964	5	2	0	0	1	1
		(male at 29, male at 47, female at 41)				
1965	12	3	2	1	3	3
		(male at 13, male at 82, male at 45, male at 15, female at 26, one unknown)				
1966	6	1	2	0	2	1
		(male at 50, male at 75, male at 55)				
Total	134	28	16	13	29	28

Table 9
Infant Death Rates (per 1,000)

Year	Births	Deaths	Infant Death Rate
1948	9	4	444·44
1949	13	6	461·53
1950	18	2	111·11
1951	16	5	312·50
1952	18	Incomplete data	—
1953	23	Incomplete data	—
1954	20	Incomplete data	—
1955	20	Incomplete data	—
1956	29	Incomplete data	—
1957	20	Incomplete data	—
1958	28	Incomplete data	—
1959	23	2	86·95
1960	22	1	45·45
1961	28	3	107·14
1962	22	3	136·36
1963	28	3	107·14
1964	31	2	64·51
1965	28	5	178·57
1966	16	3	187·50
Twelve-year average			186·93 (per 1,000)

frustrating phase of the overall study. Since local organization, as manifest prior to European contact, is no longer functioning, data on this aspect were collected from the living memory of tribal elders.[2] The exact composition of local groups could not be determined; however,

Table 10
Pitjandjara Crude Death Rates, Ernabella

Year	Approximate Population	Total Deaths	Crude Death Rate (per 1,000)
1957	541	4	7·39
1958–60	Incomplete data	—	—
1961	425	6	14·11
1962	425	7	16·47
1963	416	10	24·03
1964	450	5	11·11
1965	450	12	26·66
1966	450	6	13·33
Total		50	16·16 (seven-year av.)
Rate of natural increase per 1,000			48·64

most informants tend to stress an 'ideological' patrilineal bias. Furthermore, the criterion of local group exogamy appears to be crucial in defining the characteristics of a local group.

In reality, the picture is more confusing and flexible. In over half of the recorded cases, matrilineal kinsmen and affines were listed as members of a particular residence group. However, it should be stressed that the duration of time in which kinsmen were part of a group, besides where they 'ideally' should have been, varied greatly. When a number of local groups met for initiations or other collective activities, the local population would tend to redistribute themselves within different local groups. An individual would attach himself to another group where 'close' kin ties could be genealogically traced. Commonly, unmarried males would join different groups for varying periods of time. The latter point was stressed by older informants, and is also evident from the wide geographic knowledge which tribal males possess of different areas which are not normally considered as their own country.

Although males attached themselves to different local groups, each man was fully aware of his 'own' local group. Furthermore, each local group had a 'core' of patrilineally linked married males; thus most men would commonly return to their ancestral group and area. The geographical knowledge among most males is vast, but differences are readily observable when one takes into account the time duration spent in a particular country. This breadth of information concerning surface waters, soaks, availability of food resources, etc., is mostly limited to older males since younger generations no longer need this type of cultural 'baggage'.

The other frequently used terms referring to particular people and areas are *mob* and *country*. Both terms are utilized at two different levels of abstraction. Mob refers to the people who inhabit a particular geographic area or country. On one level, the whole Pitjandjara 'network' from Ernabella to Warburton is viewed as being 'my country' as opposed to other countries, i.e. Aranda country, etc. In this usage, country denotes larger socio-linguistic boundaries which set off one tribe from another. Country also refers to a particular geographic area within the larger Pitjandjara network. Thus, one's birth place and local group compose his or her country, such as the Mt Davies country, etc. However, in most cases, people state that they belong to the Mt Davies mob, namely the local groups which inhabited the Mt Davies area. In general, mob and country are roughly equivalent when utilized in this manner and both terms are interchangeable. There are from seven to ten different mobs, referring to geographical areas such as Warburton, Blackstone, the Rawlinsons, the Petermanns, Mt Davies, Amaṭa, Ernabella, Areyonga, etc. Within these larger areas, each individual belonged to a particular smaller unit which was probably the local group.

Local group areas were mapped with limited success. In the Petermann and Rawlinson ranges the resident group was always small in size, ranging from twenty to seventy people. Larger clusters of small groups seldom occurred except in cases of initiation, where two or three bands would meet for three or four days at the longest. The long initiation ritual and other ceremonies which characterized the Aranda and other central Australian groups were absent. Although the drought had ended in 1966 and the environment in the Petermanns was 'lush', local groups of 200-300 individuals could never be stabilized in any given locality for extended periods of time. It may be hypothesized that the contemporary interest and manifestation of ceremonial life is a function of the acceptance of a European diet and economy which may support large groups of individuals over many weeks. During the pre-contact period, the formation of large ceremonial groupings was probably rare and occurred only in selected environmentally rich areas.

The resident group was loosely organized and flexible as regards membership. Yet in each case a patrilineal core of kinsmen was recognized. It was this core which possessed and transmitted a detailed knowledge of the traditional area of exploitation for each group. Although knowledge of geographical particulars was patrilineally transmitted, a broader knowledge of certain key water sources and areas of permanent foods was always known to different resident groups. Thus, in cases of extreme economic hardship, various groups would expand or contract to certain key waters where they would ride out the drought.

Local group exogamy was the most important characteristic of resident groups. After initiation, males would serially link up with various resident groups and in turn would acquaint themselves with different areas. After marriage, a male might continue to reside in his wife's resident group but at some time in the near future would return to his own patrilineal core group.

Although the whole pattern of local organization is no longer operative, the idea of group membership and personal claims to different 'countries' is not fully dead. The latter was dramatically brought forth in late 1966 when the mining of chrysoprase (Australian jade) started at Mt Davies, 128 miles west of the native settlement at Amaṭa. Usually five to six men are taken to the Mt Davies area to mine chrysoprase for periods of ten to fourteen days. Since mining has brought about a fast, if not easy income, many of the local people at Amaṭa are anxious to 'have a go'. The Mt Davies mob elders have been ambivalent about the mining since its inception. One of the factors is that the Mt Davies country belongs to only those individuals who can claim either one of the following factors:

1. born in the Mt Davies area
2. have a *malupiti* (Kangaroo) 'dreamtime'
3. kinship relations with one who is from the area.

The third factor and its interpretation is most interesting. Many of those who claim kinship ties base their case on matrilineal or affinal linkages. Some of these claims are valid, others are somewhat slim. Distant consanguines or affines from the area are 'discovered' and a case is made. The Mt Davies elders view matrilineal and affinal ties as quasi-acceptable, but some of the more distant 'creations' are regarded as dubious at best. The flexibility by which kin ties are arranged with the Mt Davies mob is not a new phenomenon. In general, one is permitted a set of varied means by which access to the area is gained. Kinship relations also affect the 'Dreamtime'. In one case, a man who was from the Deering Hills area, which is south of Mt Davies, with a *tjurki* (owl) 'dreamtime', gained access to the chrysoprase mining. The *tjurki* is supposed to be related to the *malupiti*; however, many people were not clear what the relationship was, if one did exist.

How does this analysis relate to the current discussion on Aboriginal local organization? While Hiatt (1962, 1965, 1966), Stanner (1965), and more recently Birdsell (1970) have posed the major arguments, I think the polarization of ideas in their discussions has obscured the fundamental difference between ideological conceptions of residence groups and the reality of the situation. The Pitjandjara recognize a patrilineal core as the basis of every residence group. Through adjacent generations of related males, important and vital environmental knowledge is transmitted. Although local groups were also ideally exogamous, at no time did one find any local group which conformed to the ideal patrilineal, patrilocal unit. The constant movement of unmarried males from one residence group to another through consanguineal and affinal relationships permitted individuals to acquire a vast amount of information about different places and micro-environments. This all-important information was the basis of survival, since all local groups were constantly in fluctuation through contracting and expanding into different areas due to the presence of droughts. Population movements throughout the Western Desert are not new and post-contact only. All my information on local group movements indicates that most males had a broad but qualitatively differentiated amount of knowledge of various localities as far apart as from Ernabella to Warburton and north to Lake McDonald. Water sources which may be permanent, quasi-permanent, temporary or highly unreliable are all noted, and when a drought is in full process, each male in every local group has a fine knowledge of where to move for water and for how long particular and potential water sources can support 'X' numbers of people.

The Pitjandjara themselves also accepted the fact that ideal conceptions of residence arrangement do not occur with any degree of frequency. In my recording of residence cases and in questioning about the exceptions to the rules, the Pitjandjara made no attempt to 'correct' things as they do for other aspects of socio-ceremonial life. No one was concerned that cognized residential arrangements were seldom realized. I would interpret this response as perfectly expectable, since ecological and demographic factors are critical enough to create a system of residence arrangements which is highly flexible. This flexibility in local organization as regards the structure of residence groups and their relationships to land is probably the only means by which these highly mobile, scattered populations could survive. Residential flexibility maintains the delicate balance in man-land ratios as they vary with each macro- and micro-environmental change.

Furthermore, flexibility is a safety valve to equalize micro-differences in population and resources. Differential population size which may put pressure on available resources is levelled through population movements between adjacent local groups. The combining and re-combining of different individuals into various local groups would obscure any ideal conception of residence. Yet the survival of the population depended on the ability to acquire a broad knowledge of resources and environment, to maintain contacts between adjacent and extra-adjacent groups, and to level population differences between groups.

Much of my data on the formal aspects of Pitjandjara family structure, kinship terminology, kin groupings, totemic units and marriage arrangements is not new to the social anthropology of the Pitjandjara. Elkin's (1931, 1938-40) and the Berndts' (1945) papers on kinship and social organization provide an excellent account of the formal properties of the social structure which characterize the Pitjandjara and other related groups in the Western Desert.

The emphasis in kinship and social organization has been to ascertain the operations of the formal structure 'on the ground'. Through genealogical materials, one may note the number of cases which fit 'ideal' norms of behaviour and structure. In most cases, the stated marriage arrangement is with one who is a very distant matrilateral cross-cousin; however, distant patrilateral cross-cousin marriage is also regarded as acceptable. Distance is primarily established in the four section system which appears to be prevalent within the area, although everyone is aware that certain individuals are 'too close' even though they are in corresponding correct sections. The section terms are as follows:

                Panaka = Taruru
                Purungu = Kayrimara

It is also claimed that sections (skin groups) are absent at Ernabella. The Ernabella Pitjandjara population originates in the western areas where the four section system is widespread. Furthermore, section terms are not utilized in interaction between closely related kinsmen, but are important when dealing with distant relatives and/or non-relatives. 'Skin' groups are usually the first basis for reckoning relationships. When a person's 'skin' is established and his local country or mob is known, then finer kinship connections are determined if possible. The use of section terms in the above manner is recognized by elders at Amaṭa. From a limited empirical base, it is hypothesized that the use of section terms and groups in establishing relationships co-varies with the mobility of a population. As semi-nomadic groups become sedentary, such as the Pitjandjara were in the recent past, the network of kin relationships may be determined through genealogical connections. Thus, sections lose their importance.

Case studies on 'wrong marriages' and subsequent alterations in kinship terminology were obtained. 'Wrong marriages' are commonly due to a man's not marrying into his corresponding group, the lack of 'correct' partners on account of population factors, and males marrying at an early age and not completing the male initiation cycle. Certain features are common in each circumstance. In each case, couples run off from any period up to two years, and at times permanently. Most 'wrong' marriages stem from a couple eloping prior to the male's having completed the initiation ceremonies. Not only are initiations 'dragged out', but the Red Ochre ceremony, which is the last and most important one, is commonly avoided. However, the most important feature is that male initiation starts much later in comparison with other central Australian groups. At times, boys who are nearly twenty have yet to be circumcised. Tribal violations and elopement rates are related to the relatively late start of male initiation. At present, tribal elders are aware of this factor and are pushing circumcision at a much earlier age. Correspondingly, ages of marriage for females are becoming progressively earlier. Further data and enquiry are needed on this subject before any possible co-variation between such factors may be determined.

Contrary to my first impression, and after further investigation, the six section system is present in the Musgrave-Mann-Tomkinson area but it is undergoing a gradual transformation into a classic section system. The theoretical workings of the six section system are basically similar to Elkin's findings in the Mt Margaret area to the west. In the

Musgraves and neighbouring areas the population is from the west and the old tribal divisions are no longer operative. The transformation is briefly as follows. Ibarga combines with Panaka and can marry only Taruru, thus excluding Kayrimara as a possible marriage category. Milangka combines with Kayrimara and marries only into Purungu, thus excluding Panaka as a possible marriage category. Old men who are really Ibarga call themselves Panaka, but after a number of genealogies were analysed this inconsistency became apparent. Later the elders noted that Ibarga and Panaka are one. Furthermore, none of the elders who were Ibarga or Milangka would agree that they could marry a Kayrimara or Panaka respectively. Probably the major reason for this conversion is the absence of old tribal divisions. Work is now in process to determine generational differences and the conversion to a section system.

Marriage data are presented in the following manner. Tables 11, 12 and 13 consist of observed marriages which are divided into three analytical categories. Marriages which are considered 'correct' are with a distant 'MMBDD' and sometimes with a very distant 'FFZSD'. 'Optional' marriages are with a 'MBD' and sometimes with a 'ZSD'. The latter marriage arrangement is debatable. Many elders, who have acquired younger wives, regard 'ZSD' as acceptable; however, younger males were not sure if 'ZSD' marriages were correct or optional unions. Prohibited unions are with any female in adjacent generations as well as with a 'MM', 'Z', 'DD', etc. Terminologically, 'ZSD' and 'DD' are separated by tribal elders but are occasionally merged by younger people.

Table 11 presents the overall breakdown for 108 marriages which existed during the period of 1966-67. Table 12 consists of sixty-six cases involving marriages among those who have recently come in from the bush and/or elders who have been married for twenty years or more.

TABLE 11

ALL EXISTING MARRIAGES

	Cases	Per cent
'Correct'	91	84·26
'Optional'	12	11·11
'Prohibited'	5	4·63
Total	108	100·00

Of all cases 86·36 per cent adhere to the preferred marriage rule. In Table 13 we have forty-two recorded cases of marriages of less than twenty years and/or those who have had contact with missions and homesteads. 'Correct' marriages account for 80·95 per cent of all cases. The total adherence to marriage rules from actual marriages and marriages abstracted from genealogical materials is presented in Table 14.

In Table 12, a total of nine cases is listed as optional and prohibited. Six of these cases involve two males. One man has four wives and two of the marriages consist of a prohibited partner. The other individual has two wives, both of whom are 'MBD'. Furthermore, both men are recently in from the bush south of the Blackstone Ranges in Western Australia. These cases may have been due to a lack of eligible females, which is a function of a small and declining population size.

TABLE 12

BUSH MARRIAGES AND ALL ACTUAL MARRIAGES WITH A DURATION OF TWENTY OR MORE YEARS

	Cases	Per cent
'Correct'	57	86·36
'Optional'	6	9·09
'Prohibited'	3	4·55
Total	66	100·00

One might expect that adherence to marriage rules would be relatively low in Table 13. Although elopements and marriage violations take place among younger men and women, violations in general are a result of breaking or short-circuiting the initiation cycle. The Pitjandjara in this area have not gone through the destructive processes which many other Aboriginal groups have suffered. Most homesteads are to the north-east and east, and Ernabella Mission has acted as a buffer between

TABLE 13

RECENT MARRIAGES IN CONTACT SITUATION

	Cases	Per cent
'Correct'	34	80·95
'Optional'	6	14·29
'Prohibited'	2	4·76
Total	42	100·00

TABLE 14

TOTAL ADHERENCE TO MARRIAGE RULES

	Cases	Per cent
'Correct'	339	80·9
'Optional'	61	14·6
'Prohibited'	19	4·5
Total	419	100·0

the western Aboriginal population and the homesteads to the east. Furthermore, 'large' population clusters such as Finke and Alice Springs are quite distant from the western areas of the Musgrave Ranges. Finke is about 250 miles distant and Alice Springs is 330 miles to the north-east.

The average age of marriage for males is from twenty-five to twenty-nine. The 1963 census listed only eight married males out of 144 between the ages of nought and twenty-nine. All of the married males were over twenty-five years of age. However, in some cases, marriages occur in the early thirties due in part to the delaying of male initiation ceremonies. Marriage ages among females are generally late when compared to northern groups such as the Tiwi, Walbiri and Wanindiljaugwa. Females commonly marry in their late teens and early twenties. Although this variation may be partly due to European and mission contact, I do not think this is the full factor. From recorded genealogies, most female marriages are later than expected even in cases where the groups involved were recently 'bush' Aborigines. Furthermore, among older females who married prior to mission contact, similar results emerge. This pattern may be connected in some way with the relatively late ages in which males start and finish initiation rites.

Polygyny is not very common and at present may represent 25 per cent of all recorded marriages. Undoubtedly, the contact situation has reduced the rate of polygyny, which at one time was presumed to be much higher. However, even among tribal elders the presence of numerous cases of monogamy may indicate that polygyny was never as widespread as among northern groups. The decline in female economic importance is also another factor in reducing rates of polygynous marriages.

Table 15 lists the observed number of wives per married man. Genealogically recorded families have not yet been analysed.

TABLE 15

WIVES/MARRIED MAN RATIO

	Number of wives				Total Men	Total Wives	Mean Wives per Husband
	1	2	3	4			
Cases	48	15	0	1	64	82	1·28

$$\frac{\text{No. of polygynous families}}{\text{No. of total families}} = 25 \text{ per cent}$$

It should be noted that of the sixteen composite families, thirteen of the males involved were forty years of age or over. Relatively few young men have acquired a second wife. The economic incentive behind polygynous unions has markedly decreased.

Conclusions

Pitjandjara social organization in terms of marriage arrangements and kin groupings is probably more viable now in contrast to the early contact period in its statistical adherence to cognized rules. With an overall natural rate of increase of 35·6 per 1,000 and a gradual decline in infant mortality, the Pitjandjara population is numerically expanding. Population increase will put pressure on contemporary Aboriginal settlements and missions, not only in educational facilities, but in the more fundamental issue of finding employment for young men. Also, migration rates will increase as various segments of the young population move between settlements in the search for work. But as long as tribal lore and marriage structures are maintained through male initiation ceremonies such as Red Ochre, we should expect a resurgence in adherence to ideological rules of behaviour.

Demographically, the Pitjandjara with 600 to 800 people are above the predicted value of 530, which is an operational value in which section systems will numerically conform to statistical marriage rules (Yengoyan 1968a). Thus the 80-85 per cent confirmation of marriage rules among both the Amaṭa and Ernabella groups is expected, given the number of individuals and eligible mates in the system. Meggitt's (1962:86) data on Walbiri adherence to a preferred union with classificatory matrilineal second cross-cousins are 91·6 per cent. The Walbiri numbered 1,400 in 1954 and in 1967 were up to 1,700. The confirmation of ideal cognized rules depends on a population which is large enough to provide eligible mates for most marriages. A full analysis of differential population size and section systems is presented elsewhere (Yengoyan 1968a:185-99).

However, Meggitt (1968:180) notes that among fifteen central Australian groups with subsections, population size varies from 1,570 to fifty-four with a mean of 343 and thus 'intertribal demographic differences have no discernible effects on the presence or absence of subsection systems'. This might be true, but only one or two of the fifteen populations could statistically confirm ideal marriage rules. Subsections are present as the summary expression of cognized marriage rules, but only the Walbiri could adhere in reality to the ideal norm. The presence or absence of subsections should not be confused with the more basic question of how these systems work as either ceremonial, social or intertribal mechanisms, and what is required to make subsections operative. The working of any socio-ceremonial rules and/or groups is a function of a viable population size as indicated by the Pitjandjara and Walbiri. For Aboriginal societies to survive and flourish as a quasi-complete way of life, population growth with minimal infant mortality is imperative.

Notes

1. I wish to express my appreciation and thanks to the Australian Institute of Aboriginal Studies and to the Horace Rackham School of Graduate Studies, University of Michigan, for their financial support in carrying out this fieldwork.

2. During the 1930s and earlier, the Pitjandjara traditionally occupied the area west of Opparina Creek and Mt Caroline. The eastern area was occupied by the Jankuntjatara, who during the 1930s accounted for about 90 per cent of the Ernabella population. At present, the Pitjandjara cover the whole area and the Jankuntjatara have been reduced to about five to ten individuals at Ernabella, and have moved south.

References

BERNDT, R. M. and C. H. 1945 *A Preliminary Report of Field Work in the Ooldea Region, Western South Australia.* Reprinted from *Oceania*, Sydney.

BIRDSELL, J. B. 1969 Ecology, spacing mechanisms and adaptive behaviour in Australian Aboriginal land tenure. In *Land Tenure in the South Pacific* (R. Crocombe ed.). Oxford University Press.

——— 1970 Local Group Composition among the Australian Aborigines: A Critique of the Evidence from Fieldwork Conducted Since 1930, *Current Anthropology*, Vol. 11, No. 2.

ELKIN, A. P. 1931 The Social Organization of South Australian Tribes, *Oceania*, Vol. 2:44-73.

——— 1938-40 Kinship in South Australia, *Oceania*, Vol. 8:419-52, Vol. 9:41-78, Vol. 10:196-234, 295-349, 369-88.

HIATT, L. R. 1962 Local Organization among Australian Aborigines, *Oceania*, Vol. 32:267-86.

——— 1965 *Kinship and Conflict: A Study of an Aboriginal Community in Northern Arnhem Land.* Australian National University, Canberra.

——— 1966 The Lost Horde, *Oceania*, Vol. 37:81-92.

JONES, F. L. 1963 A Demographic Survey of the Aboriginal Population of the Northern Territory, With Special Reference to Bathurst Island Mission, *Occasional Papers in Aboriginal Studies* No. 1. Australian Institute of Aboriginal Studies, Canberra.

MEGGITT, M. J. 1962 *Desert People.* Angus and Robertson, Sydney.

——— 1968 'Marriage Classes' and Demography in Central Australia. In *Man the Hunter* (R. Lee and I. DeVore, eds). Aldine, Chicago.

ROSE, F. G. G. 1960 *Classification of Kinship, Age Structure and Marriage Amongst the Groote Eylandt Aborigines.* Akademie-Verlag, Berlin.

——— 1965 *The Wind of Change in Central Australia: the Aborigines at Angas Downs.* Akademie-Verlag, Berlin.

STANNER, W. E. H. 1965 Aboriginal Territorial Organization: Estate, Range, Domain, and Regime, *Oceania*, Vol. 36:1-26.

YENGOYAN, A. A. 1968a Demographic and Ecological Influences on Aboriginal Australian Marriage Sections. In *Man the Hunter* (R. Lee and I. DeVore, eds). Aldine, Chicago.

——— 1968b Demography, Social Structure and Ritual in Central Australia. Paper read at the American Anthropological Association meetings, Seattle (November 1968).

T. G. H. STREHLOW

Geography and the Totemic Landscape in Central Australia: a Functional Study

The influence of geography on human societies and human institutions is apparent at a glance in all human cultures and populations. Topographic features such as mountains or rivers often provide convenient boundaries between populations divided by language differences. Climatic conditions determine economic activities at all levels of technological advancement. Even in the sophisticated areas of the world, urban and country communities tend to differ structurally in many significant respects; and the divergent economic interests of such communities are sometimes used—as has happened recently in South Australia—to gain political advantages for the ruling élite. In short, the fortunes of human communities as coherent political and economic units have always been influenced by geographic factors as well as cultural considerations.

Totemism in Central Australia Based on Geography

Aboriginal Australia in the pre-European era was no exception to this general rule. Though it may at first seem paradoxical to us, the fact that the Aboriginal inhabitants did not live in towns, villages, or even fixed dwellings, did not turn them into aimlessly wandering bands of nomads who continually clashed with one another over disputed natural food supplies. For in Australia the operation of the concept of the totemic landscape ensured that such things as the stability of tribal boundaries and of linguistic groups, the distribution of interlocking and intermarrying subgroups, and even the firm establishment of authority—and hence of the agencies of social control, and of law and order—were all based on the geographic environment. It is hence all the more surprising that, on the whole, so little attention has been given in the past to the plotting of accurate maps giving the Aboriginal tribal boundaries and listing the Aboriginal place-names, accompanied by detailed notes of the totemic significance of the latter.

Totemism and Exploitation of Natural Resources: Tribal Links

I shall now attempt to make these general remarks clearer with illustrations drawn from Central Australia. A convenient starting point for this discussion can be found in the generally accepted, and indeed obvious, observation that tribal units living in well-watered country were able to enjoy a more stable and settled way of life than those that were living in so-called desert areas where most waters are unreliable in drought seasons. In a paper published in *Aboriginal Man in Australia* (1965), I have already pointed this out in some detail when discussing the differences in point of culture, social structure, and environment between the Western Desert tribes and the Aranda-speaking people. In my present paper I do not intend to repeat these earlier comments, but to pursue the remarks there expressed into new fields of thought.

How effectively social and religious links could be used to ensure economic survival in an area completely devoid of permanent waters can be illustrated best from a consideration of the original habitat of the Waŋkaŋuru tribe. Two of my 1967 informants at Port Augusta—Mick McLean Ĕrinjĕli (an elderly Waŋkaŋuru man) and Tom Bagot Injŏla (an aged Lower Southern Aranda man who had worked for years on stations in south-western Queensland)—stated that the Waŋkaŋuru country bordered upon the Kallakoopah Creek in the south, stopped short of the Warburton-Diamantina in the east (the Diamantina being in Waŋkatjaka country), terminated in the north-east about ten miles short of Kătițări (Annandale Station) in Queensland (Kătițări being in Waŋkamala territory), continued from there roughly along the northern extremity of the Simpson Desert as far as the entry point of the Plenty River, and finally touched, in the west, the Eastern and Lower Southern Aranda borders at Aljŏa (on the Hale River) and Ilbŏṛa (on the lower Finke River). There seems no reason for doubting this definition of the Waŋkaŋuru tribal area, even though it places the whole of it within the confines of the Simpson Desert. The Waŋkaŋuru, accordingly, in the pre-European days, were dependent for their water supplies on the great clay-bottomed freshwater lakes shown on recent aerial maps as being located in the south-eastern part of their sandhill country, and on numerous large swamps elsewhere. Ĕrinjĕli had been given the names of the larger freshwater lakes by his male relatives, who had left this area only about the turn of the century.[1] At least two of them—Pŭḷawĭni and Păŋalŭṇa—had been considered permanent freshwater lakes up to this time. The Waŋkaŋuru had been able to live in their tribal homeland with a feeling of complete security. Had their swamps and lakes dried out in long droughts, they would have had the right to retreat temporarily to the permanent waters situated in the lands of their neighbours, with all of whom they had close social ties through intermarriage and through the sharing of sacred traditions. For the Simpson Desert was criss-crossed from south to north and from east to west by the myths of travelling totemic ancestors and ancestresses; and these mythical travel routes provided lawful points of social contact between the totemic clans and local groups joined by them. Thus, the Waŋkaŋuru rain clan of Părapăra was linked with the Eastern Aranda rain clan of Aljôa and the Lower Southern Aranda rain clan of Ilbôṛa; the Waŋkaŋuru carpet snake tradition which went through Pănti on the Macumba Creek, close to its junction with the Kallakoopah, continued north-westward to Apŏtanaṭăra in the Lower Southern Aranda area, and was eventually linked with the Ilôara saltlake on the Western Aranda-Unmatjera border; other Waŋkaŋuru traditions, which went in an easterly direction, linked up with those possessed by tribes living along the Cooper and the Diamantina—the Waŋkamala, Waŋkatjaka and Dieri; Waŋkaŋuru traditions that crossed the southern border linked up with Arabana sites; and so on. Ŋĭljirka, a Waŋkaŋuru dingo centre situated in the heart of the Simpson Desert, was linked by a myth with Ḻŭkuljăla Ṇḍĭrtja (Mt Gillen), another dingo site lying in the very centre of the Aranda-speaking country. With the security given by this knowledge, the Waŋkaŋuru could enjoy the ample food supplies yielded in normal and good seasons by their sandhill and clay-flat habitat, which responded vigorously to any showers that fell on it; for every drop of rain falling on this country soaked into the local soil instead of being carried out of it by means of creeks and rivers, as happened so readily in areas favoured with a higher rainfall. In good seasons various kinds of grass seeds and acacia seeds could be gathered in profusion in the Simpson Desert, while carpet snakes and sandhill marsupials provided the meat element in a diet which was, according to Aboriginal standards, both varied and very rich. Intertribal social links, provided by mythical stories, thus made possible the efficient exploitation of all natural food resources provided by the local geographical environment.

Some of these Central Australian linking myths were almost certainly based on actual long-distance travels and on historical events. The Eastern and Lower Southern Aranda *urŭmbuḷa* myth which linked such Simpson Desert centres as Akăra and Pmăṛ' Ulbŭṛa with Amēwara Tnăṭaŋa (Port Augusta) was without doubt one of these. Not only was the 600-mile route described in the myth a practicable one—human beings could have followed it with ease during good seasons—but the *urŭmbuḷa* verses sung at Port Augusta were composed, not in Paŋkala but in Aranda, and the Simpson Desert *urŭmbuḷa* verses sung at Akăra and Pmăṛ' Ulbŭṛa celebrated a *tnăṭantja* pole standing in the sea at Port

Augusta. Similarly, the singing of Aranda honey-ant verses at every centre situated along the 400-mile mythical route taken by the original honey-ant ancestors from Ṯâṯaṯa (a Pintubi place close to Ílbiḷi) through the Kukatja, Western Aranda, Northern Aranda, and Unmatjera territories to the Iliaura centre of Uŋgwâḷalanăma, can surely be explained most readily by assuming an historical basis for the events described in the corresponding honey-ant myth, which related that this Pintubi host followed the lead of a returning messenger who had first come from Uŋgwâḷalanăma to Ṯâṯaṯa. Throughout Central Australian mythology the traditions fitted in excellently with the landscape, and could be fully appreciated only by persons familiar with the places described in them. It cannot be stressed too strongly that Central Australian mythology did not concern itself with the sky, but with the earth; and all the human beings living in this land were believed to be linked indivisibly, by means of 'totemic' ties, to the supernatural creators, who were still slumbering in their midst at sacred centres dotted throughout the eternal landscape. (See T. G. H. Strehlow 1964.)

The Great Ceremonial Centres

These great ceremonial centres were by no means confined to a few major springs and permanent waterholes: their multitudinous presence dominated the whole of Central Australia, irrespective of the normal rainfall or the normal economic resources of any region in average years. As I have explained in an earlier paper (1965:145), the survival of all the inland tribes had necessitated the creation of social structures, and of an economic order, designed to bring about the utilization of the whole country so that every region could support some part of the well-distributed population. Hence it should come as no surprise to students of the Central Australian tribes to find that some of the greatest sacred centres had been established at sites where full-scale ceremonial festivals could be held only in excellent seasons. Thus, the three great Lower Southern Aranda sites in the Simpson Desert, Akăra, Pmăr' Ulbŭra and Ilbôra, were accessible only after exceptionally heavy rains had fallen over thousands of square miles in this area, and filled the large local swamp and flood-flat depressions with water. These three places could not even be reached during long drought periods, the nearest permanent waters at such times being located several days' walking distance away from them. Most of the important Waŋkaŋuru centres, such as Aljătjarkăka, Părapăra and Păḷani, were similarly situated. The Pintubi honey-ant centre of Ṯâṯaṯa lay in almost hopelessly arid country. Wăpirka, the greatest native cat centre of the Jankuntjatjara, depended for its water supplies on a few minor rockholes in the vicinity, and even the Unôwa soak—a few miles away—could not be regarded as a permanent water. Yet Wåpirka possessed what was possibly the greatest ceremonial cycle among the Western Desert groups living in the south-western corner of the Northern Territory. Even the Western, Northern, Eastern and Upper Southern Aranda, who inhabited the best-watered parts of Central Australia, had located some of their greatest ceremonial centres at sites where the water supplies were only of a temporary nature. For instance, Ilbåḷintja and Ljåba, both of which vied for the honour of possessing elaborate ceremonial cycles that required from four to six months for their full performance, drew their supplies from soaks that fell so low during dry seasons that the whole country around them had to be completely evacuated towards the end of long droughts. The same remark applies to the Upper Southern Aranda centres of Imǎṇḍa and Intêera, whose totemic acts formed the bulk of the ceremonies performed at the Alice Springs iŋkŭra ('Engwura') festival witnessed by Spencer and Gillen in 1896.

However, in spite of their lack of reliable water supplies in extended drought periods, all these great totemic centres were eminently suitable in good seasons as sites where long and elaborate ceremonial cycles could be staged in full by large assemblies of people. As I have pointed out (1965:122), the rainfall in Central Australia is not really low, but highly irregular. Even in the most devastating drought seasons isolated cloud bursts can produce rich food supplies in a few widely scattered areas; and in good seasons the country around all of the main totemic centres here mentioned yields food in abundance for many months. The country around Ilbåḷintja, Ljåba, Akǎra and Wåpirka, for instance, when soaked by several inches of rain, will yield in profusion a great variety of edible grass seeds, yams and native fruits. Kangaroos and emus and other animals will come flocking into these regions in droves, lured by the excellence of the bush feed. Hence the human population that came in quest of this abundance of food in pre-European days was able to range with impunity over hundreds of square miles of country, where scores of small swamps, claypans, rockholes and soaks provided temporary waters for some months for many hundreds of people.

The wide distribution of these ceremonial centres hence helped in good seasons to ease the strain on the food resources of the normal residence areas located around the permanent waters, giving the animals and plants in the vicinity of the latter a chance to recover after good rains from the normal depredations of hunters and food gatherers. The strength of the motivating religious forces which impelled, and compelled, these periodic migrations by large groups of people for the purpose of staging these great ceremonial festivals must not be underestimated. I shall leave its full discussion to the end of this contribution. However, it cannot be stressed too strongly from the very outset that all these migrations were of an orderly and compulsory kind. In the pre-European days, the Ilbãḷintja folk *had* to return as a united group to the Ilbãḷintja soak, the Lower Southern Aranda *had* to move out from their safe locations at Utjêra (Dalhousie Springs) and on the lower Finke River waterholes deep into the Simpson Desert; and the Jankuntjatjara *had* to return from the Musgrave Range waters to Wãpirka and the neighbouring ceremonial sites. These religiously motivated migrations were the main reasons for those long 'walkabouts', often lasting for months, that Aborigines used to indulge in during the first fifty years or so of European settlement in Central Australia. Before the aliens came, all the males who had been born or 'reincarnated' in a local group area had to return to their own main totemic centre on such ceremonial occasions. Even the Simpson Desert became totally uninhabited only after several decades of European settlement around its fringes had brought about the tragic depopulation of those Waŋkaŋuru and Lower Southern Aranda groups whose main totemic centres had been located in it from time immemorial.

Totemism and Social Organization

The religious necessity of visiting all major sacred centres in the local group area also had the effect of maintaining at strength the total numbers of each local group. This is a particularly important social aspect of the 'walkabout' institution. Since even local group areas situated in less well-watered parts of the country possessed important totemic centres whose ceremonial cycles had to be staged in good seasons at the sites where they were believed to have been first instituted by the totemic ancestors, the members of these local groups lived, by deliberate choice, for as long a time as the seasons permitted, in country whose poverty of resources outsiders might have scoffed at openly. Hence their children also tended to have their conception sites or birthplaces located in the group areas of the parents. This can be seen clearly in the Central Australian genealogies that I have collected, since these give also the conception sites of all persons figuring in them. Thus, in the Aranda-speaking area, the Akǎra and Pmǎr' Ulbǔra local group areas once could boast of having populations probably as large as some of those well-watered Western Aranda local group areas that were situated on the upper Finke River. While it is clear that the sizes of these local group areas varied according to the normal food resources located in them, all of them had, according to my genealogies, been able to keep the numbers of their group populations up to full strength within living memory.

This function of a geographically based form of totemism was of vital importance in those Central Australian tribal areas where the local group areas were associated also with a land-based kin-group class system. This was true everywhere in the Aranda-speaking area. I have described elsewhere (1965:136-9) the Aranda land-based kin-group class system in detail under the heading of the 'Aranda Njinaŋa Section (Local Group) Area'. This account also gives a map of the Western Aranda *njiŋaŋa sections*. Since Aranda marriages were exogamous, it was of the utmost practical importance that all populations in their *njiŋaŋa section* areas should be kept as far as possible at full strength. Only in this way could it remain feasible for marriages to be arranged on a kind of reciprocal exchange basis between members of different local groups. The Aranda genealogies show that marriage arrangements had become normalized to a very high degree within certain definable geographical limits. The Western Aranda genealogies reveal, for instance, that while the majority of marriages were contracted between persons who were members of the various Western Aranda *njiŋaŋa sections*, a considerable amount of intermarriage used to occur also with certain Matuntara local groups. On the other hand, marriages with Eastern Aranda spouses were virtually unknown, and no marriages at all had occurred in living memory with Lower Southern Aranda people. Yet the Western Aranda occupied the upper reaches of the Finke River, and the Lower Southern Aranda its lower reaches and flood-outs.

It may be added in passing that it is impossible to demonstrate in detail how the Aranda marriage system functioned except by means of detailed maps showing the locations of the normally intermarrying *njiŋaŋa sections*. Ample material for future research of this kind exists in my Central Australian genealogies and in the vast amount of mapping information that I have gathered in the interior since 1932.

The following is a brief recapitulation—stripped of all the details given in my 1965 paper—of the main features of the Aranda *njiŋaŋa sectional* organization:

(a) The men in each *njiŋaŋa section* area belonged almost exclusively to two kin-group classes which stood in a father-son (Aranda *njiŋaŋa*) relationship to each other.[2]

(b) The boundaries of each *njiŋaŋa section* area were demarcated by episodes in the sacred myths, and were therefore not subject to revision. This provision prevented the raising of boundary disputes by neighbouring groups: their geographical borders had been fixed by their own supernatural beings.

(c) All Aranda kin-group classes were based on these geographically delimited *njiŋaŋa section* areas; and each kind of father-son unit was repeated many times in the Aranda-speaking area:

Thus, in the Western Aranda dialectal territory there was a Purula-Kamara *njiṇaŋa section* area at Ntằrea, another at Krằntji, and a third at Emặlkŋa. Each of these Purula-Kamara areas was a self-contained unit, completely separated from the other two. In other words, the three Western Aranda Purula-Kamara groups were just as distinct from one another as they were from the Palṭara-Kṇuarea group of Lṭằlaḷṭúma or the Ŋala-Mbitjana group of Pằr' Erŭltja (1965:139).

(d) Each totemic clan area normally contained one major totemic centre (known as *pmằra kǔtaṭa*), whose totem gave a general appellation to all the males of that *njiṇaŋa section* area, thereby forming them into what may be called a *totemic clan*.

The numerical strength of the population in each *njiṇaŋa section* area in the pre-European era can only be estimated today. But there can be little doubt that it varied from about fifty to one hundred individuals. Since all of these could find their requirements of food and water within their own *njiṇaŋa section* area in normal seasons, the people constituting each Aranda local group always referred to themselves (and were referred to by members of other local groups) by the appellation of their major totemic centre (*pmằra kǔtaṭa*). Thus the Western Aranda fell into Lṭằlaḷṭúmarĭnja, Emặlkŋarĭnja, Irbmằŋkararĭnja, and so on. (These three names mean 'the men of—or the people of—Lṭằlaḷṭúma, Emặlkŋa, Irbmằŋkara'.) Each of these Aranda local groups thus formed an independent political and religious unit, under the guidance of leaders who belonged to one or the other of the father-son kin-group classes proper to their own local group. The word 'Aranda' was never used as a common tribal name in the pre-European days.

As other writers—such as the Berndts and Meggitt—have stated for the Western Desert tribes and for the Walbiri, the local organization of the people living west of the Aranda-speaking area was of a much looser and more fluid nature. This was undoubtedly due to the more arid nature of the environment in which these people lived. The Kukatja (C. Strehlow's 'Western Loritja'), however, had a land-based class system and a totemic clan organization virtually identical with that of the Aranda.

Meggitt (1965:147) has summarized the Walbiri local organization in these terms:

> Walbiri local organization differed, however, in several important respects from the over-simplified stereotype of Australian local organization created by Radcliffe-Brown. . . . In particular, there were no small, patrilineal, and patrilocal hordes (which Radcliffe-Brown asserted were the fundamental units of Australian Aboriginal social systems). The tribe comprised four local communities, each of which

constituted a major political and economic entity and occupied a finite but very large 'country' that spread over as much as 15,000 square miles. Within the community's territory hunted and foraged groups whose size and composition varied throughout the year. Sometimes, as in the dry season, the food-gathering unit might be no greater than the nuclear family; at other times it could include the whole community or even, when the ceremonial season was advanced, parts of several communities. Within a community, which numbered anything from 200 to 400 members, all kinship categories were represented, as were all eight subsections and both patri- and matri-moieties.

A. A. Yengoyan, who tried to map out the local group areas of people who came from the Petermann and Rawlinson ranges, had only limited success in reconstructing these areas. He came to believe that 'the resident group was always small in size, ranging from 20 to 70 people'. His main conclusions were as follows (1967:1):

> The resident group was loosely organized and flexible as regards membership. Yet in each case a patrilineal core of kinsmen was recognized. It was this core which possessed and transmitted a detailed knowledge of the traditional area of exploitation for each group. Although knowledge of geographical particulars was patrilineally transmitted, a broader knowledge of certain key water sources and areas of permanent foods was always known to different resident groups. Thus, in cases of extreme economic hardship, various groups would expand or contract to certain key waters where they would 'ride-out' the drought.
> Local group exogamy was the most important characteristic of resident groups. After initiation, males would serially link up with various resident groups and in turn would acquaint themselves with different areas. After marriage, a male might continue to reside in his wife's resident group, but at some time in the near future would eventually return to his own patrilineal core group.

This loose structure of the local group among the Western Desert people has also been commented on in my earlier paper (1965:130-1), where it has been pointed out that the Matuntara, Andekerinja, Jankuntjatjara, Pitjantjara, Pintubi and other Central Australian tribes living to the south and the west of the Aranda-speaking area, originally had no subsection systems: they completely lacked the main structural element of the Aranda local group organization—its *land-based* kin-group class system. According to Yengoyan (1967), the introduction into these tribes of subsection systems superficially resembling the Aranda-type class system in recent decades has not been able to do anything to rehabilitate the local groups.

The Waŋkaŋuru—like the Dieri, Arabana, and many other tribes in central-southern Australia—recognized only the two exogamous moiety divisions (*Mătari* and *Kăraru*), and counted descent matrilineally. Depending as they did for their very existence on a limited number of 'permanent' freshwater lakes in the Simpson Desert in normal seasons, and on the hospitality of their neighbours during long droughts, they would have found it virtually impossible to form themselves into strong and well-defined local groups. The one very detailed Waŋkaŋuru genealogy that I was able to obtain in 1967 merely indicated that Mick McLean Érinjĕli's paternal forebears and older relatives classified themselves as belonging to Pŭḷawĭni, their main permanent freshwater lake, and that this Pŭḷawĭni group was exogamous, their spouses coming either from more distant Waŋkaŋuru groups or from the areas of neighbouring tribes, in this case largely from the Lower Southern Aranda area.

Up to this point, I have limited myself here mainly to a discussion of some structural features (and linking arrangements) of the Central Australian tribes, and in particular—where applicable—of their main meaningful units, the local groups. In all cases, geography and climate were among the main factors that determined both the nature of the smaller structural units (local groups) and the long-range economic and political relationships that existed between the larger, geographically joined units such as tribal subgroups and whole tribes. The indigenous Central Australian population did not constitute a formless mass of nomadic humanity, drifting over the countryside purely in response to seasonal conditions, leaderless and lacking in purpose like herds of grazing or predatory animals. They were divided into socio-linguistic units called tribes, living in properly demarcated geographical areas; and these tribes, in their turn, were subdivided into smaller structural units. The latter found their most highly organized expression in the Aranda area, where geography and climate were particularly favourable. Here these so-called *njĭnaŋa* units lived in geographically defined kin-group areas; and each of these units had its own independent system of authority, but was linked with other *njĭnaŋa* units by a regularized interchange of marriage partners and by the links produced by a land-based form of religion.

We come now to a detailed consideration of the social functions which had been evolved in these clearly structured and geographically delimited Central Australian communities. They can be broadly divided into two main categories, religious and administrative—the latter term including all means of social control among members living within a defined geographical area.

Totemism: Religious Functions. Initiation and Iŋkŭra Festivals

The religious functions of the Aranda local groups have been discussed in several of my earlier writings. One of the latter was *Aranda Traditions* (1947:139-71), where they were set down in considerable detail in so far as they affected the Western, Northern, and Upper Southern Aranda groups, under the general heading of 'Tjuruṇa-Ownership by a Njiṇaŋ Section'. (For recent comments, see T. G. H. Strehlow 1964.) As has been mentioned in the present paper, each Aranda local group had the duty of staging, at irregular intervals, the complete ceremonial cycle associated with its own major totemic centre (*pmằṛa kŭtaṭa*). This could be put on only during an excellent season, and its staging could be carried out only in the presence of visitors from other local Aranda groups, and from any non-Aranda local groups whose major totemic centres were linked by myths with the *pmằṛa kŭtaṭa* of their hosts. The complete performance of any given cycle was thus always a rare event; for the members of the host-group had to attend the performances of the full cycles of their major visitor-groups in subsequent good years. Thus it is doubtful whether, even in the pre-European days, the full Ljằba honey-ant cycle would have been put on more frequently than once in fifteen or even twenty years; for the members of the Ljằba totemic clan (or, as it could also be termed, the Baṇaṭa-Panaŋka local group of Ljằba) had to attend subsequently, as visitors, the honey-ant cycles of Rŏuḷbmaŭḷbma (Western Aranda), Pŏpanji (Kukatja), and Kŏrbuḷa (Unmatjera), all of which places were major honey-ant centres (*pmằṛa kŭtaṭa*) linked by myths with Ljằba.

It has been made clear in my earlier accounts that each Aranda local group was believed to perform an indispensable economic service not only for itself but for the population around its borders as well. Thus, the Eastern Aranda Purula-Kamara local group of Ujĭtja was believed to have the responsibility of creating rain for the whole of the surrounding countryside by the performance of the Ujĭtja rain ceremonies. Other Aranda rain totemic clans—such as the Purula-Kamara local groups of Kằporĭlja (Western Aranda), Inŭŋamằḷa (Eastern Aranda), Mbŏrawằṭṇa (Upper Southern Aranda), and Erĕa (Lower Southern Aranda) —were credited with performing identical services for the populations in their local areas. In the same way, the members of kangaroo, euro, emu, carpet snake, grass seed, and other totemic clans were regarded as having the power of bringing about the increase of their totemic plants or animals not only within their local group areas, but throughout the adjoining regions as well. Consequently, the economic well-being, in fact the very existence, of the whole Aboriginal population of the Aranda-speaking area, was believed to depend on the continued existence of *all* the local groups found in it. Similarly, the religious acts performed by the totemic clan members of all the inland tribes at their respective totemic centres were regarded as being indispensable for the continuation of all human, animal and plant life in Central Australia.

This attitude was expressed clearly in a remark made by my Northern Aranda informant Mákarĭnja at the Njŏnta Festival in 1933. Nettled by the whispers of the Ilbâḷintja bandicoot clansmen, who claimed that he did not know how to perform the euro increase acts of Kâpuṯ' Urbŭḷa in their correct fulness, he remarked:

'The Ilbâḷintja men are always talking and boasting about their bandicoot (gŭra) ceremonies. But their ceremonies are utterly useless. Euros are to be found everywhere, and it is we who create them. The bandicoots have vanished long ago. Even we old men can remember eating bandicoot meat only when we were still mere boys. Where they have gone to since, I do not know.' (T. G. H. Strehlow 1970: 304-5.)

Rain, game animals and food plants were, however, not the only objects of totemic rites in Central Australia. Many local groups had as their main centres places which were associated with the deeds and travels of supernatural beings of the culture-heroic type. The lặkabặra hawks, who were credited with having introduced the rite of circumcision, the tjĭlpa (native cat) men, to whom the rite of subincision was attributed, and the bat men (who first sang the songs once used by Upper Southern and Eastern Aranda warriors who were about to set out as blood avengers), were all held in honour by powerful local groups who preserved their songs and their commemorative acts. The Lower Southern Aranda centres of Akặra and Pmặṛ' Ulbŭṛa celebrated in their great cycles ancestral heroes and heroines who had always appeared in human shape only: in all their actions they had revealed themselves as ordinary men and women, both on their travels and while resting: they had been personages impelled by powerful human emotions, in particular, by love, jealousy and frustrated passion. It was surely no accident that Akặra and Pmặṛ' Ulbŭṛa once boasted of possessing the longest and most elaborate sets of love charms that existed in Central Australia.

Though our knowledge of the religious acts of the non-Aranda groups of the Centre is still pitifully defective, it is clear that in the other Central Australian tribes, too, local groups or units associated in some way with definite geographic areas were responsible for performing either the increase rites which ensured the magic propagation of animals and plants or the commemorative ceremonies which celebrated the supernatural personages figuring in their mythologies. The Waŋkaŋuru, for instance, did not only have sacred traditions concerned with rain, carpet snake, acacia seed and similar 'useful' totems: fascinating 'semi-historical' traditions also inspired some of the finest items in their treasury of myth, song and dramatic action. Among these are the wanderings of the Seven Sisters (Ůljulakårikůmaṇa) from Ma͞uwuråni northward through the heart of the Simpson Desert, and the vivid account of the tortures of thirst inflicted between Kåntiwåṭa on the Kallakoopah and Påŋalůṇa in the Simpson Desert upon his hapless crane followers by their treacherous leader (whose song verses had the power to increase the heat of the sun to a dangerously high degree).

Among the Western Desert tribes living in Central Australia, the non-economic ŋåluŋka (known as 'boy corroboree' in 'pidgin' English) acts and songs actually outranked all others in point of sacredness and importance. These were the songs sung on the Western Desert initiation grounds, and the acts that could be staged only on these initiation grounds. Thus the songs and the acts in which the ŋindaka or giant goanna ancestor of Utjȇra, Mŭŋapiṭi, and Årinbåra figured were reserved purely for use on the circumcision grounds of the Lower Southern Aranda, the Andekerinja, and the Matuntara, through whose territories this personage had travelled.

The importance of the circumcision ritual among the Western Desert tribes may be assessed from the fact that totemic traditions relating to wandering supernatural personages who were honoured by Aranda and Kukatja groups in acts that could be witnessed on ordinary ceremonial grounds were frequently changed into ŋåluŋka traditions after they had crossed over some distance into the Jankuntjatjara or Pitjantjara areas. Thus the kangaroo acts linking the Kukatja kangaroo centre of Åjaii began by being ordinary commemorative acts, celebrating the southward travels of these kangaroos.[3] Upon entering the Petermann Ranges country, these kangaroo (wa͞ueri) acts had still remained commemorative (låka) ceremonies while depicting events that had taken place at Pȇijulaṭåra, Piͧtulu, Ṇŭlṭuṇa and Åwijůla. After their departure from Åwijůla, however, these kangaroo ancestors could be depicted only in Pitjantjara ŋåluŋka acts—that is, in sacred acts which, in the old days, could be revealed only on circumcision grounds.[4]

These remarks have been made in some detail in order to underline the difference between the main 'Western Desert' type of ceremonial gathering and the Aranda iŋkůra ceremonial festival. The latter was concerned with the staging of the great Aranda ceremonial cycles by the totemic clansmen before the members of their own local group and visitors from other local groups allied by myths with their own. The major 'Western Desert' type gatherings, on the other hand, were arranged for circumcision purposes—circumcision being visualized as the main act of initiating the male novices into the spiritual world of eternity.⁵ Hence all Western Desert verses that were sung on the circumcision grounds were regarded—unlike the corresponding Aranda verses—as being too sacred to be sung on any other occasions. How strong Western Desert feeling was on this point may be gauged from the reactions of the men at Ajûṛa, near the Amoonguna Reserve, when I played over to them, for identification purposes, the initiation verses collected by Spencer and Gillen in 1901 in the Lower Southern Aranda area. One of them was a ŋåluŋka circumcision verse from the Andekerinja region. Lockey Tjĭtuma, an elderly Andekerinja man present, was furious at its having been sung at all to Spencer and Gillen for a recording: women and children were certain to have heard it, and the original singer should have been killed for his crime. Toby Breaden, an Upper Southern Aranda man who had lived many years with Andekerinja men, said that he hated hearing this verse: the singer should have 'shut up' after singing it only a few times. The Western and Northern Aranda men, on the other hand, merely laughed at it, and thought it sounded 'funny' by comparison with their own circumcision verses.

From this consideration of the main religious and ritual objectives of the Central Australian gatherings it is clear that these meetings could have functioned effectively only under the guidance of strong-willed leaders—of men, learned in the sacred traditions, who commanded the respect of all men present on a ceremonial ground or on a circumcision ground.

Geographically Based Totemism and the Problem of Authority

This remark brings us to the problem of defining the agencies of authority and social control in Aboriginal Central Australia. In recent years there has been a tendency among some anthropological writers to dismiss the importance of leadership in this region. Meggitt, for instance, writes off present-day Walbiri leadership in these terms (1962:247-8):

> Whatever the source of the stimulus to action, its significance was at once apparent to the community members, who had early learned to recognize it. Similarly, they generally knew without prompting what roles to adopt in the subsequent activities. Most of these expectations were (and are) defined in genealogical terms. Consequently, the people did not have to make *ad hoc* plans for action; the norms of the religious and kinship systems constituted an enduring master-plan, which met most contingencies and to which there were few approved alternatives.
>
> Thus, although the actual communication of news of an emergency

posed a real problem for the Walbiri (one partly solved by sending out messengers), the organization of effective responses did not. Once a person was aware of the situation, he knew what to do about it. There was, therefore, little need for secular leaders in the community. Some men, better acquainted than others with certain rules, might be asked to expound them, but such requests chiefly concerned religious dogma and ritual behaviour. And it is only in this field that we observe an approximation to institutionalized leadership.

There were particular men, for instance, who were expected to co-ordinate the activities of Gadjari participants, and their status as 'Big Sunday bosses' was specifically defined and more or less permanent. Once a man was recognized as a Gadjari organizer (and there was no explicit procedure of election), he remained a leader of all such ceremonies in his community until he died or became senile. But unless he was an unusually forceful man, his authority did not extend into secular affairs, even in his own community.

Meggitt sums up the impressions he gained at Hooker Creek and Yuendumu between 1953 and 1955 as follows (*ibid.*: 250-1):

In short, the community had no recognized political leaders, no formal hierarchy of government. People's behaviour in joint activities was initiated and guided largely by their own knowledge and acceptance of established norms. European contact has not greatly changed this pattern, although there is an increasing (but still informal) delegation of authority by Europeans to men who have acquired new skills and who can speak some English. These men tend to stand between the Europeans and the camp people, transmitting instructions to the latter, voicing their complaints, and explaining to the Europeans the problems faced by the camp.

This absence of effective secular leadership, it should be noted, was by no means confined to the Walbiri area in the 1950s. It could be observed almost everywhere on the Central Australian Aboriginal stations in the post-World War II period. During the many decades of European settlement after 1870 Aboriginal leadership had been deliberately undermined by police officers, station owners and missionaries at all places where permanent contact had been established with the indigenous population. Up to 1950, however, this process of gradual erosion had been limited by serious deficiencies in the financial resources required to curb and repress Aboriginal culture effectively: neither the government[6] nor the missionary bodies had any considerable sums of money available for expanding their staffs. But with the official adoption of the so-called Assimilation Policy by the Commonwealth government in 1951, the nation's resources were, as it turned out, largely used to engage very considerable staffs of Welfare officers so that a paternalistic system of control could be instituted over all Aboriginal populations under direct Administration control. The newly established Northern Territory Aboriginal schools, too, encouraged the children to break with the Aboriginal past and to resist the authority of their elders. In the Walbiri area, however, there were additional reasons for a particularly severe breakdown in the authority of their elders. The best-watered part of the Walbiri country—the Lander River area—had already been the scene of severe police raids in 1928—the date of the last two punitive expeditions that were sent out against Aboriginal tribesmen in Central Australia. The police admitted that thirty-two people had been shot in the Cockatoo Creek-Lander River area in these two raids, but local station owners who had been members of these expeditions gave me a very much higher unofficial figure in 1932: according to their calculations at least a hundred Aboriginal men and women had been shot. As a result, the Lander River Walbiri group was largely scattered, and many refugees fled into the neighbouring Unmatjera area for protection. Very few of them ever returned to their own country. By 1932, both the Ŋalia, through whose territory I was taken for hundreds of miles by local guides, and the Yalpari (Meggitt's term for the Lander River community) whom I had met on the cattle stations, had become communities with the attitudes of near-refugee populations.[7] Walbiri leadership found it difficult to survive this wholesale uprooting process which began in 1928, and ended only with the establishment of the four Walbiri settlements by the Northern Territory Administration during the period 1946-56. Of these settlements, three (Phillip Creek, Hooker Creek, and Warrabri) were located outside the Walbiri area; the Yuendumu settlement, while situated inside Walbiri country, was no real substitute for Pĭkilji, a place rich with religious associations, which was dropped as a settlement site because of fear of court action by the station owner of Mt Doreen.

Authority in the Western Desert Area

In 1932 I still met on my travels through Walbiri country some elderly men who were quite clearly men of great authority in the Walbiri and Ŋalia communities. One of these, old Wĭririkăra, who was the guardian of the sacred cave at Kătna, was encouraged by Don Campbell, the owner of Mt Peake, to stay near his station premises as a sort of an insurance against any depredations by wandering Walbiri tribesmen, whom Campbell—like other station owners at that time—feared greatly as violent, cattle-killing nomads. Wĭririkăra was a man of importance not only at Kătna, but also at Ănka (Mt Leichhardt). Unfortunately, my hundreds of miles of camel travel in 1932 prevented me from accepting his offer to take me to Ȧnka, at the end of winter that year; and he had died before I had another opportunity of visiting this area. An even more honoured Walbiri man of authority was old Tŭma, the guardian and 'grand old man' of Pĭkilji. I met Tŭma first at Wŏṭulba, in the Ŋalia country 50 miles north-east of Mt Liebig, in July 1932[8] while I was being accompanied by his son Mĕrinȧṇa, who had wandered back to Mt Liebig after serving a term in the Alice Springs gaol for cattle-killing. Mĕrinȧṇa was told by his father to take me freely through the Ŋalia country. Tŭma's authority among the Ŋalia was never in doubt —he was both a ceremonial leader and a man who could authorize 'tribal punishments' with impunity. Pȧlpuwȧṇa, a Ŋalia man from Ėripilŏŋa, who had come under Tŭma's jurisdiction, had a spear pushed through his leg for some offence by way of punishment. Unfortunately he contracted a severe infection as a result, and lost not only his toes but even the main bone in one foot.[9] Men of lesser importance were in charge of the other groups I met in the Ŋalia area. One of the elders of the Ėripilŏŋa group, for instance, readily brought his folk back with me to Mt Liebig, where a temporary camp had been set up for that year's Adelaide University research expedition. None of the Ėripilŏŋa men would have come, had not this elder told them to do so; and the latter in turn had received Mĕrinȧṇa's assurance that Tŭma had authorized my request. While I did not bother—unfortunately—to keep any records of Tŭma's activities in the later 1930s, I well remember that his authority was great among the Ŋalia, not only in ritual matters but in the secular sphere too: he was the main pillar of 'tribal law' in this area till his death some time after 1941.

Among the Pintubi who lived in the country stretching from the Pŭṭati spring westward to the Kintore Range, old Kŏmutu, who was regarded as the guardian of the great centre of Ȉlbiḷi[10] in the Ehrenberg Ranges, held a similar position of authority in both the ritual and the secular spheres. Kŏmutu's prestige protected him from the vengeance that would have overtaken any other Pintubi man, after he had been forced by a band of Matuntara blood avengers (who had come to Mt Liebig from the Wȧṭarka area) to reveal to them the name of the place to which one of the younger Pintubi men had gone on a walkabout. Kŏmutu's forced betrayal enabled these Matuntara avengers to find and kill their intended victim; but none of the dead man's relatives raised their hands against Kŏmutu.

Without attempting to define the exact nature of leadership among the loosely organized Western Desert people—the Walbiri, the Pintubi, the Jankuntjatjara, the Matuntara, and the Andekerinja—I wish to point out that all of them of necessity organized their circumcision festivals and communal ritual activities through 'councils' of men who were personally associated in the eyes of their fellows with the totemic site chosen. This personal association was determined by reincarnation from the site's supernatural beings, by birth, or by the 'inheritance' of similar qualifications from male relatives. These small 'councils' were, in turn, dominated normally by older men,[11] who wielded considerable power over the ritual activities carried out by the whole gathering at the chosen site. All visitors from other places accepted this authority at that particular site for the duration of their stay. But at other times, too, the authority of ritual leaders carried over, to a greater or lesser extent, into the secular lives of the people who had personal ties with the areas surrounding the totemic sites of which these leaders were the main guardians. Outside his particular area, of course, a local leader could establish no secure claims for any pretensions to public power. But an aged and highly respected man, who was the recognized guardian of one of the major totemic sites—such as Ắnka among the Walbiri, Pĭkilji among the Ṇalia, or Ĭlbiḷi among the Pintubi—possessed the necessary religious reputation to win wide acceptance for his decisions in secular matters: his personal prestige could carry him far beyond the normal precincts of the religious power sphere. Whether this happened or not naturally depended on his personal qualities. This is, however, true generally of all human communities. A great leader, everywhere, is born, not merely created by rules.

The Pitjantjara, too, could be divided into totemic groups linked together by common ceremonial interest. The membership of the groups responsible for staging normal ceremonial acts (as distinct from the *ŋǎluŋka* rites) seems to have been similar to that found among the Aranda and the Kukatja. Thus the kangaroo acts linking Ắjaii and Ắwijǔla (mentioned earlier) were performed on the Jay Creek Reserve in 1950 by the following five men:

Ĭmaljǎŋu (aged about forty years), from Pĭtulu;
Ŋǔlitjǎra (aged about thirty years), from Mǔrkanti;
Nĭkutjĭlpi (aged about fifty), from Ǔtanta, south of Pĭtulu;
Ĕrinbǎṇa (aged about fifty-five or sixty), from Mǎḷupĭṭi; and
Njǔrkuri (aged about thirty), from Pēijulaṭǎra.

Ĭmaljǎŋu and Ŋǔlitjara, both of whom were regarded as reincarnations of ancestral kangaroos that had been 'left behind' (at Pĭtulu and Mǔrkanti respectively), were considered to be the two most important ceremonial performers. Ĭmaljǎŋu was regarded as the leader of the whole group of five men: for his father's brother had been Ǔḷṭuôtaṭǎra— who had been reincarnated as the waūeri (kangaroo) shown in one of the most spectacular linking acts; and Ŭḷṭuôtaṭắra had once been a part-owner of this act with two other men—Ĭmaljắŋu's father Ĭmalakŭnu, and Wåŋkarawônj' (who had been reincarnated as the kåŋala [euro] shown in this and one of the later acts). The normal leader of this group of men in secular matters, however, was Nĭkutjĭlpi, a person of great drive, whose ruthlessness had made him a feared man among those Pitjantjara folk who had drifted northward to Tempe Downs, Jay Creek and Alice Springs in the 1930s. Nine years before the Ắjaii-Ắwijŭla kangaroo acts were staged at Jay Creek, Nĭkutjĭlpi had successfully organized a death party composed of Pitjantjara men who were staying at Alice Springs, and led them to Simpson's Gap, 12 miles west of Alice Springs, where they speared to death an inoffensive Aranda man who was looking for camels. This cruel act was done as a 'reprisal' for the imaginary sorcery deaths of about a dozen Pitjantjara people at Alice Springs a short time before: in reality, these Pitjantjara people had died as the result of an epidemic introduced by European visitors.

The Kukatja, whose territory stretched from the western border of the Western Aranda territory westward as far as the westernmost outcrops of the MacDonnells, a little beyond Amŭṇurkŋa (Mt Liebig) and Pŭṭaṭi spring, had a local group system closely similar to that of the Aranda; and the description of the Aranda *njĭŋaŋa sections* in the following pages is applicable also to the Kukatja local groups. Ritual authority in the Kukatja local groups was vested in the ceremonial chief (*ắtanắri*) and his assistant elders (*tĭna* or *tjĭlpi*)—the Kukatja terms *ắtanắri* and *tĭna* (or *tjĭlpi*) corresponding to the Aranda *iŋkắṭa* and *kŋắribắṭa* respectively.[12]

Authority in the Aranda-speaking Area

In the Aranda-speaking area leadership rested on a much more solid and reliable base—the *njĭŋaŋa section* area. The Aranda local groups were located in *njĭŋaŋa section* areas, delimited by well-defined geographical boundaries. As has been stated earlier, the members of each local group were distinguished from those of other local groups by bearing the appellation of the most important totemic centre located in their *njĭŋaŋa section* area. The ceremonial chief of this totemic centre was not merely a kind of religious guardian of its rites, myths and songs: he was a person of very real secular authority as well in his own *njĭŋaŋa section* area. This secular authority derived inevitably from some of the religious functions exercised by him. It cannot be stressed too strongly that the ceremonial chief of a totemic centre was regarded, both inside his own area and by members of outside local groups, as the person responsible for ensuring, with the collaboration of the other fully initiated elders of his totemic clan, the effective performance of those ceremonial acts on which the economic well-being both of his own fellow clansmen and of outsiders was believed to depend. For the ceremonial acts were believed to be capable of producing their practical effects only if they were performed in their entirety, and without any deviations from the exact patterns that had been instituted by the supernatural beings at the beginning of time. Only the exact knowledge of the sacred ritual possessed by the ceremonial chief and his assisting group of elders (who had also been fully trained in the mysteries of the spiritual world) could bring about good rains and promote the increase of plants and animals upon which human life depended. In short, the ceremonial chief was not viewed by his Aboriginal community as performing merely the religious functions rendered in European communities by priests and ministers of religion: each ceremonial chief held, in a sense, also the status of a head of a vital food-producing organization. Even in present-day Central Australia one of the commonest Aboriginal criticisms made of the new order introduced by Europeans is that the whole country has been economically ruined by the wholesale destruction of all the indigenous forms of ritual activities. Ever since Central Australia's first major drought of 1927-29 the Aboriginal population has attributed the ensuing lengthy successions of poor and dry years to the disappearance of the older generations of ritually wise and traditionally educated elders who alone knew fully how to create rain and how to promote the increase of plants and animals. Derision has been heaped on their few and ill-trained successors, whose ritually faulty performances have been held responsible for their ineffectiveness in rendering the same communal services. During the grim eight-year drought which ended in 1966, many sophisticated Aboriginal agnostics and some Christianized younger leaders privately joined together in the same chorus of abuse: 'The old men always said that the rains would fail to come, that the animals and trees would die, and that men and women would fall ill, if the sacred songs were no longer sung and if the sacred acts were no longer performed. And what they said has come true. We young folk who know nothing about the old traditions are helpless to save the country; and the white people are just as useless.'

Because the religious functions exercised by the ceremonial chief in collaboration with his 'council' of elders were believed to be of overriding economic importance as well, any breaches of the ceremonial ritual and any refusal by any of the younger members of a local group to submit themselves to the directions of their elders in ceremonial matters were regarded as constituting sacrilege; and sacrilege was punishable by death everywhere in Central Australia. This power to inflict capital punishment for ritual offences was exercised frequently enough to ensure a deep fear of the guardians of the sacred places, the ceremonial chiefs, and the local group elders before the arrival of the first European settlers in Central Australia. It was a well-founded fear which ensured a great measure of respect for the 'advice' of these persons in all secular matters. (No younger men ever dared to shout at the older men—or, for that matter, at those older women who were the repositories of the women's secret lore.) Moreover, this fear did not disappear suddenly with the arrival of the European settlers in the 1870s; for 'tribal executions' in Central Australia continued everywhere into the first two decades of the present century, and, in the more outlying districts, into the 1940s as well.

Capital Punishment in the Aranda-speaking Area: Historical Examples

Since the next section of my paper is concerned only with the problem of Aboriginal authority and its relationship to geographically based totemism, I have deliberately refrained from discussing in it details of law and order in the secular sphere. The best account of law and order in Aboriginal Australia is to be found in R. M. Berndt's chapter with the same title in *Aboriginal Man in Australia* (Berndt and Berndt, eds, 1965); and readers of my paper are advised to consult this chapter. But since all effective authority ultimately rests on force, and since the power of inflicting capital punishment represents the ultimate use of force, some historical examples of the use of this power will show clearly one of the foundations of authority in Central Australia. Most of my examples are drawn from the history of the large Aranda-speaking area—by far the most populous territory of the pre-European days; but similar killings were carried out also among the other Central Australian tribes. The use of sorcery ('black magic') was always available for the punishment of offenders, and the fear of its use by the old men of authority was everywhere a powerful deterrent to possible wrongdoers. But the fear of this was strongly reinforced by the terror produced in the Aboriginal communities by the occasional killings of actual offenders.

A few selected instances of executions meted out in the Aranda-speaking area in the old days will now follow, in order to make clear to the reader the ultimate power over life and death possessed by the ceremonial chief (*iŋkáṭa*), supported by what has been termed, in anthropological treatises, his 'council' of elders (*kṋáribáṭa*), in cases of sacrilege.

At the full performance of the eagle cycle of Akắr' Intjôta at Urálawŭraka, east of Charlotte Waters, in the 1850s or 1860s,[13] men were gathered together from most eagle totemic centres situated in the Lower Southern Aranda area. The eagle commemorative ceremonies—known as *wắriĕra* acts—were performed at the foot of a large pole—'as thick as a tree'—set up on the ceremonial ground (kĕrinbĭnya). This pole stood on the kĕrinbĭnya for the duration of the festival—a matter of some weeks. Since there was only one waterhole available for all the festival guests, the women and children were permitted to camp near it. They could, however, come to their camping ground only at night; and then they were able to catch a glimpse of the pole some distance away, lit up by the glow of the fires around which their men folk were singing the eagle ceremonial verses. Each morning the women and children had to leave while it was still dark, and spend the rest of the day gathering food some miles away till well after sunset. The signal for their departure in the mornings was given out by a young man who climbed up on the pole in order to rattle the sea-shells suspended near its top, while the ceremonial chief below intoned one of the special wăriĕra verses. All went well at this festival till an unfortunate accident[14] happened one morning. This accident was deemed to constitute a grave act of sacrilege against the grim eagle ancestors. There were cries of alarm from the watching men and shouts of murderous anger from the ceremonial chief and his elders. The young men involved in the accident—there were either two or three of them—were immediately seized. Their necks were twisted around till the vertebrae had been dislocated, and they were probably choked to death as well. Holes were dug at the foot of the eagle totem pole, as a token that it was this symbol itself which had executed the offenders against its sacred dignity. After that the shocked spectators and all other male visitors rushed away from the desecrated ground, taking their wailing women and children with them without further delay. No one dared to lift his voice against the authority exercised by the ceremonial chief or his elders. For an objector to do so would have meant that he would be risking his own execution as well; for the men wielding authority on a ceremonial ground at such times were believed to be acting with the full power of the offended supernatural beings. However, the shock that ran through the assembled festival gathering which had witnessed the murderous grimness of religious power exercised so ruthlessly was so severe that no eagle wăriĕra festivals were ever held again either at Urălawŭraka or at Akặr' Intjọ̆ta. Men belonging to the eagle totem in this area had to be content with performing merely those eagle acts that belonged to them personally. Had no European settlers come into the Centre, it might have been possible for the local group leaders to revive the wăriĕra festivals after a lapse of many decades. But after 1870 the building of the Overland Telegraph Line and the setting up of the Charlotte Waters Telegraph Station effected revolutionary changes in the Lower Southern Aranda way of life; and the 'murderous eagle pole' was never again set up.

While tragedies such as that which happened at Urâlawŭraka did not happen frequently—otherwise most of the Aranda sacred cycles would in the course of time have slipped into oblivion—all men invited to the Aranda ceremonial festivals in the old days were keenly aware that they were camping on holy ground, where their ritual actions were being watched by the human reincarnations of supernatural beings; and they knew that these human reincarnations had the power of life and death over all people resident for the time being *at that particular totemic centre*. No man who did not belong to the local totemic clan, or who had not been invited by the leaders of the local totemic clan, had any right to be present; and the careful grading of all acts in the totemic cycle ensured that the ceremonial chief, in consultation with his assisting elders, determined what men were to constitute the audience for each act. There were acts that could be witnessed by all men present; and there were others that were reserved for the sights of a few elders only. Chanting, *rāiaŋkĭntja* calls, and the whistling or booming of bullroarers, gave warning to all persons within listening distance that there were men gathered in assembly on a sacred ground who were performing sacred acts that no unauthorized or uninvited persons would be allowed to witness. Any attempt at 'gate crashing' or 'spying' would have been punished by death.[15] It was also a capital offence for unauthorized persons to approach the storage places of the sacred *tjurunga*. Only the ceremonial chief and the local group elders had the right to do so. Other local males could go to such sites only if sent there on special errands by the ceremonial chief and his elders. Women and children were excluded at all times. Within living memory, a thirsty Eastern Aranda woman, when walking to the Ujĭtja spring to fill her kangaroo-skin waterbag, cut a corner in the mile-long mountain gully on her way, and passed within sight of the trees on which the Ujĭtja rain *tjurunga* were stored. Her tracks were discovered soon afterward, and she was killed by a spear thrust through the side of her chest.

The thirsty Southern Aranda woman, who ventured in to the sacred waterhole of Intêera (Spencer's 'Undiara'), and saw 'the ceremonial stone', must have been very lucky to have escaped death after discovery, if Spencer and Gillen were given a true version of the incident (1927: vol. I, p. 168). She was punished by being made 'for the time being common property to all the men'. Perhaps she was young and attractive, and knew it.

It should be observed that the powers of the Aranda ceremonial chief (*iŋkâṭa*) were limited in two all-important ways. First, he could put into execution only norms and directions accepted as having been instituted by the supernatural beings of the particular totemic centre of which he was the accepted religious head; and consequently his actions had to have the approval, or at least the consent, of the other fully trained elders (kŋăribăṭa) of his totemic clan. Second, the Aranda ceremonial chief possessed these powers only within his own local group area: outside the geographical limits set by its totemic landscape he enjoyed no special rights or privileges, except for the private prestige that he might have won for himself either by outstanding personal qualities or from his knowledge of the traditions of other local groups while acting as an assistant (kŭṭuŋŭla) to their ceremonial chiefs.

While in theory all Aranda men—because of reincarnation and *tjŭruŋa*-inheritance—had equal chances of reaching the position of supreme authority in their own local group, personal qualities naturally determined their relative degree of importance when they had attained the necessary age. The third part of *Aranda Traditions* makes this clear in detail. The account there given of the training received by my Northern Aranda informant Gŭra, the ceremonial chief of the *gŭra* bandicoot totemic centre of Ilbăḷintja, will bear repetition here (1947:125):

> The old men took me apart from the other young men of my own age at an early date. They showed me many gŭra ceremonies which they withheld from the other members of the bandicoot clan because they were still too young. I remember their teachings well. I often had my veins opened to supply blood for the ceremonies. I dutifully paid large meat-offerings for the instruction that I had received. Some of the ceremonies were too secret to be shown even to ordinary men of the bandicoot clan: only the oldest men of the clan and the born chief were allowed to witness them. None of the gŭra men of the present generation have seen them. My elders kept on repeating these ceremonies time and again in my presence: they were afraid that I might forget them. No other man of my own age was allowed to see them. Had I forgotten them, no one else would now remember them. Our old men have been dead for many years past, and our ceremonies have not been performed at Ilbăḷintja for a long time. They told me that after their death I should pass these ceremonies on only to proved men of their own age, when I felt that I was getting old and weak, and that my memory was beginning to fail me. I was to pledge these men to the same secrecy.

The same volume also makes it clear that the kin-group class of the aspirant for the highest position of authority was vitally important. My Northern Aranda informant Mǎkarǐnja, a Paḷṭara man, was readily accepted—in the absence of other men belonging to these particular totems—as the ceremonial chief of the Paḷṭara-Kŋuarea euro totemic centre of Kǎpuṭ' Urbŭḷa (his father's father's conception site) and of the Paḷṭara-Kŋuarea native cat centre of Kěrenběnŋa (his father's conception site). But many of the Northern Aranda men at the Njŏnta Festival in 1933 privately voiced strong reservations about his claims to be regarded also as the ceremonial chief of the Baṇaṭa-Panaŋka honey-ant centre of Ljâba, even though Mâkarĭnja had been inducted into full knowledge of the sacred traditions and acts of Ljâba, which was his personal conception site.

In spite of the modern doubts cast upon the authority wielded by the Aranda ceremonial chiefs outside the religious sphere, I cannot repeat too strongly at this point, from my personal knowledge of this matter, that men like Gŭra and Mâkarĭnja, and their counterparts in other local groups, were not merely venerated, but also feared. So was Lôatjĭra, the grand old man of Hermannsburg in my father's days, who had as a young man taken part in avenging expeditions. He had not only been an important *ŋâŋkara* (medicine man), but had possessed full knowledge of the dreaded death charms as well. All of my older Aranda informants gave me unasked the names of deceased ceremonial chiefs and elders whose decisions no one had dared to query in their lifetime. There were good grounds for this respect in the pre-European days. Among the Aranda, initiation into the sacred mysteries was a long drawn-out and highly painful process. Circumcision and subincision were the inescapable entrance requirements for gaining knowledge of the spiritual world. Then came head-biting and, in most Aranda-speaking areas outside the Hale River territory, evulsion of the finger nails. All of these excruciating operations were carried out on special grounds, to the singing of sacred verses, and with the ritual authorization of the supernatural beings of the appropriate totemic centre. Thus the ground-paintings of the honey-ant centre of Ljâba and the possum centre of Emặlkŋa used to be spotted with the blood from the ripped-off finger nails of all young men who had caught their first glimpses of them. Recalcitrant young men could be made to perform ceremonial acts celebrating minor totemic ancestors in a way calculated to make such performances highly painful. For instance, in the Southern and Eastern Aranda areas, arrogant young men used to be decorated for minor totemic acts in the blazing heat of midsummer, and then led to perform their acts in a sitting or kneeling position on hard or stony soil which burnt and lacerated their buttocks or their knees. These acts had to be performed for as long as the chorus of old men saw fit to chant the ceremonial verses proper to them. The singers naturally sat in the shade and took pleasure in prolonging the agony of the young men as long as they wished. In addition, most (perhaps all) Aranda subgroup areas included at least one totemic site associated with an act (or acts) in which fires were lit and live coals scattered over the persons of the actors.[16] The latter were not allowed to dodge the sparks or to brush off any live coals that had landed on them.

The resulting burns sometimes festered, and took several days to heal.

Again, when the sacred *tjurunga* were taken out of their caves or down from their storehouse tree platforms, the young men detailed for this task had to exercise extreme care: any unfortunate culprit who dropped and broke a stone *tjurunga* was later on speared to death at the behest of the elders entrusted with the care of the sacred objects. Thus a Western Aranda youth, who was the son of an Ellery Creek man called Kŭṭakŭṭa, was speared to death some months after he had dropped a stone *tjurunga* belonging to Lŭrkŋalŭrkŋa, a euro totem elder of Indáta, while bringing it down from a high mountain cave (T. G. H. Strehlow 1970: 339-40). An Unmatjera ṛắgia (native plum) stone *tjurunga* lost a chip from one edge when it slipped from the hands of a man called Ndắbuta who was carrying it to a Hanson River local group. The unfortunate bearer—he was the elder brother of my Unmatjera informant Tommy Kǻltjirbŭka, who eventually gave me the chipped *tjurunga* in 1932—was later killed at Ljĭlapŭntja, and no one was permitted to smoothen the damaged edge of the *tjurunga*. In this case the *tjurunga* was regarded as the actual changed body of an ṛắgia ancestor; and the chipped edge hence represented an injury done to this personage. Another damaged Unmatjera ṛắgia *tjurunga* in my possession came from Ulắlaŋa, where it had been broken on its storehouse tree platform when a blazing limb fell upon it during a bushfire several generations ago. Four men who had the duty of guarding the area around the storehouse site were subsequently killed for their failure to protect this object, which symbolized the most important ṛắgia ancestor of their local group. In this last case, however, the relatives of the executed men refused to accept the verdict of the elders, maintaining that the unfortunate guardians should not have been blamed for damage that had been caused by a bushfire. These relatives accordingly proceeded to avenge their dead kinsmen by killing some of the young men who had carried out the instructions of their elders. In this way a lengthy vendetta was started, and a number of men lost their lives because of a tragic accident.

Several of my older Aranda informants in the 1930s told me that, as long as they were still youths, they had always feared the worst whenever they had caught sight of a group of older men sitting somewhere outside the main camping area: they could not help dreading that perhaps their elders were hatching a further plot against the persons of the younger men. But even before their initiation, respect for the older men used to be inculcated into all Aranda boys and girls. While an extraordinary measure of latitude was normally shown by parents toward insolence on the part of their own children, offences against the ceremonial chief and his elders could well bring about severe punishment. An extreme instance was the drowning, before the turn of the century, of a Western

Aranda boy called Lŭpa, who had stolen some of the gifts of meat (gặra tjāuerĭlja) that the younger men of his group had donated to their elders in return for instruction in the sacred traditions. Lŭpa was flung into the boiling waters of the Ormiston River when it was in high flood. This case, however, also provided an instance of the rejection of the authority of the elders; for the matrilineal relatives of the drowned boy would not accept the decision of the older men. In other words, the uncles (i.e. mother's brothers) of Lŭpa—who came, of course, from a different local group, which was not subject to the authority of the Ormiston River 'council' of elders—refused to accept his drowning as a legal execution authorized by norms sanctioned by the supernatural beings. They accordingly speared to death soon afterwards both the dead boy's mother Nâpana (for having failed to prevent Lŭpa's thefts and for having neglected to rush him to safety upon learning of his thefts) and also the young men who had flung Lŭpa into the flooded river.

The power held by the ceremonial chiefs and elders over the members of their local groups in all religious matters provided for them an assured supply of food from men younger than themselves. In pre-European days the Aranda initiated males were not permitted to marry before the age of about twenty-five years. All unmarried young males had to sleep, as far as practicable, in special men's camps called *pmặra inkĭntja*; and they had to supply portions of hunted game animals to the older men who were keeping an eye on their activities, including any clandestine affairs with the opposite sex. Whenever any festival had been arranged, all young unmarried men, both from the appropriate totemic centre and from surrounding local group areas, were sent by their elders to the selected ceremonial ground. Upon arrival, they were classified as *ilĭara*; and their duties included hunting game animals for the assembled older men (so that the latter could devote their time and energies exclusively to the staging of the sacred acts), providing the personnel for the *wărkuntŭma* dances, and donating blood for the decoration of the ceremonial actors and objects. The elaborate ceremonial cycles of the great Aranda centres, some of which lasted for several months, could never have been staged without the active presence of scores of young men who were under the firm discipline of the appropriate local elders.[17] But even marriage did not end the obligations of the Aranda men toward their religious leaders. In order to advance to the status of a local group elder (*kŋăribăṭa*) it was necessary to acquire full knowledge of the sacred traditions of the major totemic centre (*pmặra kŭtaṭa*) of this local group. This could be obtained only from the local group elders, and these men—to use the normal Aranda idiom—had to be plied with gifts of meat before they released to any candidate for knowledge any important act or set of verses.

From these considerations it should be clear that the Aranda men of authority had full power over the younger men in all matters of ritual pertaining to their own group, and that they enjoyed a sufficiently high status to make their influence felt also in the personal affairs and the private disputes of the people in their particular *njiṇaŋa section* area. Most of the latter were, of course, linked to them by personal kinship ties as well. Men who held the power of life and death—in this case, for offences in all religious matters—could not be lightly disregarded in secular matters, or even in private quarrels that were nominally of no concern to any of the old men of authority. Violent-tempered and unruly males, whose arrogant actions could be held as constituting threats against the authority of their elders, or whose intimidatory behaviour habitually disturbed the peace of the local community, could, if the need arose, be charged with having committed sacrilege, and then executed on a hunt by young men authorized to do so by the offended elders. Insolent boys could be (and were) killed by the older men themselves. Lŭpa's drowning—a case in point—has already been quoted. In 1938 an uncircumcised lad called Billy—he had not yet been given an Aboriginal name—who had been insulting circumcised men at the Waite River Station on the border of the Iliaura territory, was killed by a man called George Ṛâljapŭŋa, at a camp on the opposite bank of the wide Sandover River one evening when E. Dixon, Billy's employer, was absent for a weekend in Alice Springs. Neither Dixon nor any of the other European station owners of the district was told what had happened; and Dixon believed that the boy had merely walked out on his job. About two months later, however, the story reached the ears of a full-blood police tracker at Barrow Creek. As the responsible Commonwealth Patrol Officer I went out, in company with Constable Clive Graham of Barrow Creek, to investigate the story. When reaching Utopia Station I began my questioning. I had anticipated days of evasive answers; but I was unexpectedly successful. Speaking in Aranda, I said to the first man I wanted to interview: 'A boy was killed somewhere here a short while ago, and I want you to take me to his grave.' The man I had addressed did not know me. Hearing me speaking to him in Aranda, he believed that I had already been told all the facts. He was so taken aback that he replied apologetically: 'I couldn't help it: the old men told me to kill him.' It was Ṛâljapŭŋa himself whom I had stumbled upon, and he willingly took me to the grave. By midnight on the same day Graham and I had located all the witnesses as well. Ṛâljapŭŋa was later on freed by a European Alice Springs jury.

Capital Punishment Outside the Aranda-speaking Area

The death penalty was meted out on a charge of sacrilege not only in the Aranda-speaking area but in all Central Australian tribal territories in the pre-European days.

The earliest recorded execution in the Kukatja area was that of the unfortunate guide, called Racehorse in Winnecke's *Journal* (1897:41-2), who had been tricked—by Europeans of high and honourable standing in the Adelaide community—into revealing the location of the Kạrkiljarkı̆lja sacred cave, in which both the Aranda possum totem *tjurunga* of Emạ̈lkŋa and the *kŭntaŋka*[18] of various Kukatja centres used to be kept: Kạrkiljarkı̆lja was a hill situated on the border of the Western Aranda-Kukatja border, about ten miles east of the present Haast's Bluff (Ănjali). The despicable theft of about fifty stone and wooden *tjurunga* from this cave by Dr E. C. Stirling (Director of the South Australian Museum) and Surveyor C. Winnecke, on 23 June 1894, despite the protestations of the frantic and helpless Racehorse,[19] was later on avenged by the latter's execution at the hands of the enraged men belonging to the local groups affected by this robbery. Spencer, who was also a member of this Horn Expedition (though he was fortunately not present at this robbery), later on announced Racehorse's execution in the following rather whitewashing terms (1927: Vol. I, p. 101, n. 4):

> It is regrettable that the true nature of the objects thus hidden away in a cave was not known at that time. We learned, later on, that the loss of these Churinga was very severely felt and mourned over by the natives, who remained in camp for two weeks, smearing their bodies over with pipeclay, the emblem of mourning. The act of treachery on the part of the native who showed the cave to the white men finally cost him his life.

Executions of the younger males, especially of those who were considered to be disrespectful to the authority of their own elders, on charges of sacrilege were, as in the Aranda-speaking area, also a feature of the accepted penal systems of all other tribes in the Centre. Instances of executions of young men who had been accused of revealing details of secret men's rites or traditions to unauthorized persons occurred among the Pitjantjara at Areyonga, and among the Iliaura, as late as the 1950s.

A 'tribal' execution, which had important administrative repercussions in the Northern Territory, took place in a Pitjantjara community which had moved from its tribal home into a recently taken-up station area. In 1934 a young Pitjantjara man, called Kai-Umen[20] in the Alice Springs police records, who allegedly came from a place called Kǎlaiamŭrba, north of Pı̆ltadi (in the Petermann Ranges), went to Ătila (Mt Conner) for a holiday, and joined a group of Pitjantjara men at Ăneri soak. He was secretly accused of betraying 'tribal secrets' to women, and the local Pitjantjara elders ruled that he should be killed. A number of young Pitjantjara men, who had been detailed to execute him, took him away one day from Åneri on the pretext of going out on a wallaby hunt. Kai-Umen was shot by a man called Nåmbala with a rifle which the latter had borrowed for the hunt from a European dingo scalper called Bob Hughes, who had also been camping at Åneri. After Kai-Umen had fallen down, the other men attacked his body with their weapons, in token of their common responsibility as avengers. The young executioners were later arrested by Constable W. McKinnon. Nåmbala and Ŋåntji—who had been found guilty as the leaders of the killing party—were each sentenced to ten years' imprisonment by Judge T. A. Wells on 21 February 1935, during the first Supreme Court session ever to be held in Alice Springs. The unusual severity of the sentence—'tribal killers' were normally acquitted by the Northern Territory courts till the 1950s—was without doubt due to the grave concern felt by members of the European jury that a rifle borrowed from a European dogger had been used to shoot the victim. Had the latter been speared in the normal way, no alarm would have been aroused.

Instances of other Central Australian 'tribal murders', or—as they should be labelled more correctly—'tribal executions', should be available in the records of the police stations at Port Augusta, Alice Springs and Darwin.

Protection for Authority of Elders

Marital disputes, arguments about spouses and personal quarrels of every kind between individuals were no concern of the Central Australian Aboriginal leaders anywhere: all private disputes had to be settled by the persons involved, sometimes with the assistance of willing kinsfolk. The community saw to it, however, that the penalties exacted were not excessive. For instance, to inflict bodily injuries on a rival was permissible; to kill him, was not. In the Aranda-speaking area, however, the exceptions to this generalization were those two marital offences that were believed to undermine the established order of society. The first was the breach of the absolute prohibition as regards marriage between a man and his real or classificatory mother-in-law. This was an offence punishable by death.[21] The other was the seduction of the wife of an elderly ceremonial chief by a rival who was a young man, especially if the latter was still unmarried. An instance of this occurred in the Owen Springs area about half a century ago. Normally, the two men affected would have fought such a dispute out with each other. But in this case the age of the older man and the prowess of the young offender would undoubtedly have settled the outcome in favour of the latter. The young man was accordingly ordered to take up his stance unarmed somewhere beyond the camping area, and the old man took up several boomerangs to hurl at him. The young man was at liberty to dodge this weapon. The boomerang, if thrown by an experienced man, was, however, a very difficult weapon to dodge. In this case, the young man's evasive actions failed against the old man's cunning: he was struck on the head, and the sharp edge of the boomerang entered his brain. With his brain seeping out, he was taken to Hermannsburg for attention by my father; but he died a day or two later.

Asylum

The geographical limitations to the power of the local group leaders made it possible for Aboriginal offenders in the pre-European days to seek asylum in communities not subject to their own elders. If the offence committed was deemed sufficient to merit death in its own community, the distance of the place where asylum was sought was sometimes very great. Thus a Pitjantjara man called Tjĭnakŭja, whose home was at Ĭlipĭṭi (allegedly a place in the Petermann Ranges not far from Mălupĭṭi), after committing a murder, fled from his own people into the Haast's Bluff area perhaps 300 miles away. Here he was later given a wife, Ŋuañita, who was a widow.

Asylum did not mean that the local group would protect an offender against the vengeance of his own people: it merely refused to take any punitive action against him, and generally agreed later on to let him take a local wife. Men who had committed minor offences sometimes fled only a short distance from their normal places of residence, in the hope that the men sent to punish them might act a little less severely in a different local group or tribal subgroup area. Thus Nămatjĭra, the father of the well-known Aranda artist Albert Namatjira, when eloping from Hermannsburg in 1901 with Ljŭkuṭa, against the wishes of the parents on both sides, fled with her to Owen Springs, only 40 miles away. Some Hermannsburg men followed the pair soon afterward, and Nămatjĭra had to submit to having a spear thrust through his upper leg as a punishment for having married a girl from a 'wrong' kin-group class. He was then able to return to Hermannsburg, where his son Albert was born on 28 July 1902. Nămatjĭra was, in addition, excluded from full instruction by his elders into the sacred traditions of his own conception site, the flying-ant totemic centre of Intălṷa, situated in a Paḷṭara-Kŋṷarea *njĭŋaŋa section* area; and the most important *tjurunga* slab of Intălṷa was later given into the care of a Kamara (later reclassified as Mbitjana) man called Arăŋa Ljĭnaŋa,[22] and not handed over either to Nămatjĭra or to his son Albert.

Punishment of Ceremonial Chiefs and Elders for Sacrilege

In the Central Australian tribes, the men who held supreme authority in all ritual matters were not a law unto themselves, nor were they persons inviolable at all times: the concept of *mana* was not found in Australia. Even the Aranda ceremonial chiefs, great though their religious powers were, did not stand beyond the reach of lawful punishment if they were considered to have committed sacrilege themselves. This was by no means impossible; for every breach of the correct local form of ritual behaviour constituted a deviation on the part of a human being from some mode of action instituted by a supernatural personage; and all deviations hence constituted acts of sacrilege. For instance, Atnĭtjĭlbŭntuka, the ceremonial chief of the Eastern Aranda rain centre of Erḗinta, while attending a ceremonial festival at Ujĭtja, another Eastern Aranda rain centre, was deemed to be acting sacrilegiously when he conducted himself in an arrogant and overbearing manner toward the Ujĭtja ceremonial chief and his elders during the performance of the rain ritual. The festival gathering grew impatient with him; and finally Wŭḷakǎla, a visitor from the rain centre of Kŋḗiakǎlkara, pointed the bone at him during the festival. Atnĭtjĭlbŭntuka fell ill and died, and was buried in the small gully called Itĭrkatneiwǎnuŋka, close to the Ujĭtja storehouse site. This happened some time last century, but well within living memory.

Atnĭtjĭlbŭntuka's death was not avenged by the Erḗinta local group, because it was felt that his death had been thoroughly justified by his behaviour towards the Ujĭtja totemic ancestors whose ceremonies he had sacrilegiously sought to direct, thus usurping the rights of the local authorities who were the reincarnations of these totemic ancestors. A different situation arose when the members of the Eastern Aranda Inŭŋamǎḷa rain totemic clan invited the Akǎṭa rain totemic clan to join them in their rain increase ceremonies. The Akǎṭa men brought along for their hosts a generous gift in the form of some ten of their own prized rain *tjurunga* stones. Aranda custom and ceremonial etiquette demanded that the Inŭŋamǎḷa men should present a counter-gift of at least equal value to their invited guests. However, the Inŭŋamǎḷa ceremonial chief at that time was a mean man called Antjṷǎntjṷarěnaka; and he persuaded his fellow elders to offer only three Inŭŋamǎḷa rain *tjurunga* to the visitors —an action which my informants, who were descendants of these Inŭŋamǎḷa clansmen, agreed was mean, dishonest and highly insulting. The visitors muttered complaints about their having been cheated; and a fight broke out, in which Antjṷǎntjṷarěnaka killed the Akǎṭa ceremonial chief with a spear. The visitors left immediately, and a lengthy blood feud began between the two groups. Eventually an Akǎṭa man called Ilȧntja surprised Antjuȧntjuarėnaka near Kȯḷba, and with a stone knife inflicted on him deep cuts from which he bled to death. To avenge Antjuȧntjuarėnaka for their Inuŋamȧḷa friends, the Ujítja men then organized a party and killed Ilȧntja. With the two principal figures eliminated, the vendetta was regarded as having been closed. This episode took place some time before the end of last century.

But sacrilege could be committed by a ceremonial chief even at his own local group's major totemic centre, if he departed from the correct ritual in any way. In such a case, the men who had the right to kill the ceremonial chief, and, in case of equal guilt, other members of the council of elders, could, of course, not come from the local group area; for that would have amounted to an act of sedition against supernaturally established authority. But each major totemic centre (*pmằṛa kŭtaṭa*) was linked by myths with major totemic centres located in other local group areas, and some of these centres were situated in different tribal areas. It was from these outside areas that punishment had to be meted out. The grimmest case illustrating this point in Aranda history is the massacre of Irbmȧŋkara, which took place somewhere about 1875. Irbmȧŋkara, a very important Aranda site located on the Finke River at the border of the Western and Upper Southern Aranda areas, was associated with the duck and mulga-seed totems; but its name featured in many other myths as well. Consequently a number of other totemic centres, situated in the Northern, Western and Upper Southern Aranda areas, were linked with Irbmȧŋkara by myths; and common myths also bound up Irbmȧŋkara with ceremonial centres in the Matuntara area. Because of its miles of lagoons that were fed by springs in the river bed, and its wealth of wild fowl, ducks and game animals, Irbmȧŋkara was often used as a convenient centre for full-scale festivals, and its ceremonial chief in the 1870s, Ltjȧbakŭka, was a well-known figure of authority far beyond the limits of his own group area. Somewhere about 1875, however, Ltjȧbakŭka and his elders were falsely accused by a man called Kȧlejĭka, after the latter's return from a visit to Irbmȧŋkara, of having committed a grave act of sacrilege. Since the nature of the act of sacrilege that was said to have been committed had been handed on after the massacre merely in whispers among the older men, my informants were not completely certain of Kȧlejĭka's allegations; but they believed that Ltjȧbakŭka and his elders had been accused of having given uninitiated boys blood drawn from the veins of initiated men to drink, in mockery of a particularly sacred initiatory rite. The Western and Northern Aranda men refused to believe this scandalous story, but the Matuntara men and some of the Southern Aranda men gave credence to it. To punish Ltjȧbakŭka and his men meant the wiping out of the whole camp of people normally resident at Irbmȧŋkara, so that no witnesses should be left alive who could have revealed the names of the attackers. A large party of avengers drawn from the Matuntara area along the Palmer River, and from some Southern Aranda local groups, was accordingly assembled and led to Irbmäŋkara by Tjĭnawăriti, who was described to me as having been a Matuntara 'ceremonial chief' (iŋkằṭa) from the Palmer River whose prowess as a warrior had given him a great reputation among the Southern Aranda as well. Tjĭnawăriti had the backing of another Matuntara man of importance called Kăpalŭru, allegedly the 'ceremonial chief' of Ắkaua, an important native cat site on the Palmer River; and Kăpalŭru had detailed a considerable number of young men from Ắkaua to join Tjĭnawăriti's party. Tjĭnawăriti and his men fell upon Irbmäŋkara one evening, after all the local folk, as they believed, had returned to their camps from their day's quests for food. Men, women and children were massacred indiscriminately, and the party turned back in the belief that they had not left behind any witnesses. However, their confidence was undermined when they came upon two more Aranda hunters soon after leaving Irbmäŋkara. They succeeded in killing one of them; but the other hunter, a man called Nămeia, managed to escape. In addition, a woman called Lặparĭntja and her infant son Kắltjirbŭka had survived the slaughter at Irbmäŋkara. Lặparĭntja, who had hurled herself over her child to protect him with her body, had merely been injured; and she successfully shammed death when she was being prodded by the spears of the attackers while these were making their final check of the slain before leaving Irbmäŋkara. After their departure Lặparĭntja made her way to safety by crawling into the banks of reeds and rushes along the Irbmäŋkara lagoons; and she took her son with her.

With Nămeia—who had Matuntara family connections with the Ắkaua region—and Lặparĭntja to identify the main attackers, it was possible for friendly Western Aranda groups to take revenge for the massacre of Irbmäŋkara. A small band of experienced warriors, led by Nămeia, went deep into the areas whence the killers had come. This party had to live off their enemies' lands and lie low, sometimes for weeks, between each kill; for they had to pick off their victims in singles or twos and threes whenever suitable occasions arose. But by patience and superb bushcraft they achieved their errand; and finally they managed to kill Tjĭnawăriti as well. When they returned into the Western Aranda area after an absence of about three years (perhaps in 1878), they found that their own world had been changed by the coming of Europeans; for the first structures erected at Hermannsburg greeted their eyes. (Hermannsburg was founded in 1877.)

Conflicts with European settlers and police officers put an end to any attempts at concerted reprisals upon the Aranda party by their Matuntara victims. Tjĭnawăriti's death, however, rankled in the memories of his Matuntara friends and relatives. It was avenged, in 1890, by the slaying of Nămeia at the newly established police camp of Boggy Waterhole (Alĭṯera) by a band of Matuntara avengers.

It must be stressed that the Western Aranda counter-raid into the Southern Aranda and Matuntara territories was organized only because the men in Western Aranda local groups involved in this counter-raid firmly believed in the innocence of Ltjâbakŭka and his elders. For there was general agreement among all parties concerned that Tjĭnawăriti and his band would have acted in accordance with 'tribal law' in punishing the Irbmăŋkara men, had the charge of sacrilege been true; for men from all totemic centres linked by myths had the *obligation* to guard the 'sanctity' of the various centres linked in this manner.

In all cases described up to this point the legal principles involved would have presented no difficulties to the minds of the Central Australian tribesmen affected by similar situations within their own geographical areas. However, in the most unusual—perhaps unique—case with which I want to close this discussion of legal rights and wrongs involving religious authority in the Aboriginal communities of the Centre, the persons involved in the tragedy could arrive at no solution deemed just or acceptable by the whole local community; and the innocent survivors finally sought safety by seeking asylum in a different Aranda local group area. Somewhere about the middle of last century a serious personal dispute arose between two respected Southern Aranda elders, Urāĭukurāĭa, a man belonging to the iltjĕljera (gecko) totem of Itĭrkawăra (Chambers Pillar) and his father-in-law, Iŋkămarĕḷaka, a tjŏnba (giant goanna) man from Ilkănŋiltĭḷa (Morris Gap). Urāĭukurāĭa had earlier married Iŋkămarĕḷaka's eldest daughter, Kămbarkŋăṇaka, and their son Tjĭta was still a boy aged about eight or ten years. They also had a daughter, Kăṇaka, who was a few years younger than her brother Tjĭta. Urāĭukurāĭa now wanted Iŋkămarĕḷaka to give him Kămbarkŋăṇaka's younger sister, Iwŭparătiṇăka, as his second wife. When Iŋkămarĕḷaka kept on delaying his answer, Urāĭukurāĭa grew incensed. Finally there was an open quarrel between the two men; and Urāĭukurāĭa, in a violent fit of anger, struck his father-in-law down and killed him. The whole community was aghast at this crime. In Aranda society the father-in-law was a figure of complete respect to his son-in-law. In many cases, it was the father-in-law who had carried out the circumcision operation on his future son-in-law, and thus engendered in the latter a sense of real fear based on great pain. In Aranda terminology, the man who had actually circumcised a youth was virtually compelled to give to him some years later his daughter by way of compensation. On no account was any man permitted by Aranda society to revile his father-in-law, still less to strike him;

and upon the death of the father-in-law, the son-in-law was forced to cut the longest and deepest possible mourning scars into his body to show his sorrow for the man who had given him his greatest treasure—his daughter as a wife.²³ For the son-in-law to kill his father-in-law was a crime where the community was forced to intervene in order to ensure the stability of its basic social structure. Normally, the relatives of a murdered man had to avenge his death; but there were no precedents entitling men to kill their own affinal kin. Again, it was impossible for any young men to be ordered to kill an important local group elder on a charge that did not involve sacrilege. However, Uraīukuraīa could not be allowed to live either; and men who were of his age and standing were unwilling to risk their own lives against his known prowess with weapons. Eventually some of the old men from his father-in-law's local group decided to dispose of him by treachery. Under the pretext of revealing a new sacred act to him, several of the older men of Tŭṇa invited Uraīukuraīa to go with them to Mǎlaṇa, a waterhole 3 miles upstream from Tŭṇa on the Finke River. He was told that he was to be decorated as the main performer in this act, and the chanting began. All went smoothly, till Uraīukuraīa's eyes had been covered with down. Then one of the men whipped out a sharp stone knife that he had kept hidden up to this stage, probably in his hair. Uraīukuraīa, who had naturally remained suspicious throughout the decorations, started up on his feet, but was quickly tripped and overpowered. His throat was cut with the stone knife; and, immediately after his death, his body was sliced up like the carcass of a butchered animal. The pieces were then hung on bushes surrounding the space where the decorating had taken place. The person of a decorated ceremonial actor was normally sacrosanct, for he impersonated a supernatural being; and the killing of the decorated Uraīukuraīa accordingly constituted not merely a treacherous murder but a blatant act of sacrilege. The men who had killed Uraīukuraīa were in their turn attacked when they returned to Tŭṇa, and their leader narrowly escaped being drowned in the Tŭṇa waterhole. Only their own age in the end saved them from death. After her father and her husband had both been murdered, Kǎmbarkṇǎṇaka, fearing for her own life, fled from Tŭṇa and took her two children, Tjǐta and Kǎṇaka, with her into the Western Aranda area. Here she married a Western Aranda man, her son from this second marriage being Ḻṭǎlaḻṭŭmarĭnja, the later ceremonial chief of Ḻṭǎlaḻṭŭma. The two children from her first marriage, Tjǐta and Kǎṇaka, also married Western Aranda spouses. Tjǐta, though he lived for the rest of his life in the Western Aranda area, either with the Ellery Creek *njĭṇaṇa section* or at Hermannsburg, was always regarded as an *ankĭeḻṭa* (guest) only, whilst his son Tjǎlkabŏṭa (known in his old age as Old Blind Moses) was readily accepted as a member of the Hermannsburg (Nṭȧṛea) local group, since he had been born on the mission station.

SUMMARY: GEOGRAPHICAL AND RELIGIOUS FOUNDATIONS OF ABORIGINAL AUTHORITY

From the above examples the foundations of Aboriginal authority in Central Australia may be summarized briefly as resting on religion and on geography. In other words, Aboriginal authority was regarded as being both validated and limited by the geographical environment as expressed in the totemic landscape. For Central Australia this is the answer to the problem posed by L. R. Hiatt (1955:147):

> The available data may be summarized by saying that observers in the middle of the last century denied that Aborigines had governmental institutions but did not indicate satisfactorily how affairs were conducted despite the lack. Observers later in the century asserted that Aborigines had governmental institutions but did not explain in any detail how these functioned. Observers in the first half of the present century described Aboriginal government as gerontocratic, but the evidence they themselves supplied indicates that the old men had little authority outside the sphere of ritual. Finally, in recent years Meggitt and I found no governmental institutions in two different areas and have described how, nevertheless, the people organized and controlled their activities.

This confusion among anthropological observers has been caused, without doubt, by the fact that most of them approached the problem of authority from insights gained in European, or at least in non-Australian, communities, where the centralization of authority in urbanized situations, the rights of certain individuals to govern by hereditary succession to rule, the continuous authoritarian influence exerted by a special class of aristocratic or at least leading families, and the compacting and consolidation of a multitude of people speaking one dialect or one language into a 'tribe' or nation ruled over by a small central body of men, have all come to be regarded as essential elements of those firm power structures that are normally classified as 'governmental institutions'. These easily definable elements are all lacking to a striking degree in the authoritative structures of the Central Australian local and tribal groups. No independent community that could be defined as a tribe, or even as a subgroup of a tribe, possessed a central political organization of a type familiar to European observers. There was no ceremonial chief or even a council of elders with the power to make religious or legal decisions for, say, the *whole* Western Aranda subgroup or the *whole* Northern Aranda subgroup, let alone for the *whole* of the Aranda-speaking area: the very considerable powers of the Aranda ceremonial chiefs and of the Aranda elders could be exercised only within the limits of their own two-class *njiṉaŋa section* areas. All marriage arrangements and all large-scale religious activities hence depended on the manipulation of the permanent social and religious links that existed with other *njiṉaŋa section* areas, which, however, had their own authorities. Thus, the Western Aranda area alone was divided into ten 'politically independent' *njiṉaŋa section* areas. (See map in T. G. H. Strehlow 1965:137.) Again, since all major totemic sites (*pmạra kŭtaṭa*) in these *njiṉaŋa section* areas were deemed to rank equally in importance, and since these major sites were linked *according to the nature of their totems* with the totemic sites of other subgroups and even of other tribes, not one of them was fitted in any sense to act as a sort of central 'capital' site for a whole tribal subgroup or a whole tribe. Thus, in the Northern Aranda area, the honey-ant *pmạra kŭtaṭa* of Ljâba was linked by myths with other honey-ant *pmạra kŭtaṭa*, such as Rôuḷbmaŭḷbma and Lŭkaria (Western Aranda), Pôpanji (Kukatja), Ṭặṭaṭa (Pintubi), Kôrbuḷa and Arặmbēa (Unmatjera); but it had no links with the other great Northern Aranda *pmạra kŭtaṭa* that were associated with non-honey-ant ancestral beings. (See T. G. H. Strehlow 1964.)

Spencer and Gillen's statement that the Imặṇḍa *iŋkŭra* festival witnessed by them in 1896 was 'the most important and lengthy of the Engwuras' (presumably in the Aranda-speaking area) is a completely mistaken claim: the frog and bat totemic centre of Imặṇḍa had links only with a few other *pmạra kŭtaṭa* in the Central and Eastern Aranda areas; and there were in existence at that time many better-known centres in the Aranda-speaking area than Imặṇḍa: Ljâba, Ḷṭặlaḷṭŭma, Akặra and Ilbậḷintja were only a few of the latter. Considered purely as a major totemic centre linked by myths with other local group totemic centres, the utnŭruŋĭta (green caterpillar) *pmạra kŭtaṭa* of Ṇṭŭrka (Emily Gap)—which was linked with such important utnŭruŋĭta (or tnŭruŋặtja) *pmạra kŭtaṭa* as Uḷậṭerka (Western Aranda), Ŭlba (Southern Aranda), Lĭrumbŭra (Hale River Aranda), Wặraṭặra (North-eastern Aranda) and many others of equal importance—would have been considered by its totemic clansmen as constituting a far greater ceremonial site than Imặṇḍa; and the totemic clansmen of the Alice Springs-Emily Gap utnŭruŋĭta group greatly resented the southern invasion by the Imặṇḍa men in 1896. Visitors from other Aranda local groups privately agreed that this *iŋkŭra* festival, specially arranged at a site convenient to the European visitors, far from being the greatest of the traditional Aranda ceremonial celebrations, constituted in reality a grave act of sacrilege. In 1933 many of my own Northern Aranda informants who had taken part in the 1896 festival as *iliara*, lamented the passing both of the original utnŭruŋita group of Alice Springs and the Southern Aranda group resident in the Imǎṇda area in these terms (1947: 109-10):

> The old men said that the men of Imǎṇda were committing sacrilege by putting down the tjĭlpa earth-mound[24] in the ancient territory belonging to the tnŭruŋǎtja clan. But they would not listen: they were greedy for the white men's gifts. They have vanished almost completely. Only one or two men may be left. There are no more children. Their *tjurunga* alone remain, and there is no one to claim them. The old men were right: it was sacrilege for mere boys of later generations to offend the great tnŭruŋǎtja ancestors by laying down a tjĭlpa earth-mound in territory that had belonged to the tnŭruŋǎtja ever from the very beginning.

In Central Australia, then, the structure of Aboriginal authority was such that no central authoritative body could come into being over any tribal subgroup, still less over any tribe; nor could any single geographical centre of authority ever have been established.[25] All territorial units, too, were inalienably linked with the population living in them: the lack of a centralized system of authority meant that no wars of conquest were possible in Central Australia. Here, then, was a land where men and women in a sense lived in those ideal communities envisaged by Karl Marx (and by William Morris in *News from Nowhere*)[26] where there were no social classes or castes, and where men could not be tyrannized by well-organized central governments. There were no families holding any hereditary rights of government over the rest of the population, and there was no special caste of priests. Since the land rights of all tribal units and, where they existed in the Aranda form, even those of the local *njĭṇaṇa section* areas were believed to have been laid down for all time by the supernatural beings, no organized wars of aggression or territorial conquest were possible in Central Australia: the natural combative instincts of aggressive males could find outlets only in killing expeditions for the punishment of sacrilege and in blood feuds organized to avenge grievous personal wrongs.

Generally, the manner in which men's motives are channelled into approved social actions is largely influenced by ideas and ideals beyond the effective control of cold and bloodless scientific considerations: this is one lesson that can be learned, even by materialistically conditioned, sociologically oriented experts, from certain European and Asian historical events in this century which have resulted from the deliberate application of systematized political ideologies. It might reasonably be assumed that long before the rise of all ideologies, men had experienced longings for a state of brotherhood with other men, for peace with foreigners living in differently structured communities, and for a security of assurance in the permanence of the great achievements of the human spirit. They had based their hopes for these things on beliefs that claimed to point to a valid bridge between Time and Eternity; and to these beliefs the name of 'religion' should surely be given, no matter in what form they may have been stated. I have no intention of defining what 'religion' is—that is a task for others; but one of the most important characteristics of religious thinking is, in my opinion, the attempt made to prove that human life, despite all disappointments and disasters, is meaningful in terms of eternity. Hence all religions seek to instruct the faithful how they should conduct themselves in order to live in harmony with the purposive universe into which they have been born. In brief, a living religion is something practical, something that is concerned with every-day life. It is probably because of its failure to convince men and women of its relevance to everyday living and of its applicability to the scientific, moral and community problems of the twentieth century, that the Christian religion has lost so much ground everywhere within the last fifty years. At the time of the Reformation fanatical discussions about dogmas could cause bloody massacres and disastrous religious wars; today the occasional verbal tiffs between professional churchmen on denominational matters are deemed to merit at most a few occasional columns of reportage in the better-class newspapers. There are many practising Christians who have begun to feel that the hour or two spent at church each Sunday is a sufficiently generous amount of time in which to devote their attention to a religion whose professional leaders, while zealous and eloquent in answering all those questions that no one any longer asks, studiously avoid committing themselves to authoritative replies about matters that do worry modern man—such as racial antagonisms, the problems of politically and economically underprivileged communities, birth control, chemical and bacterial warfare, the use of atom bombs against the populations of large cities, and so on. Many cynics feel that the Christian Churches everywhere are so obsessed with, and embarrassed by, their substantial material possessions that they no longer dare to speak out effectively on any matters of real public anxiety or national concern. On the other hand, a living religion cannot dodge the vital issues of the day: the attempt to whittle down the community-wide ideals and purposes of religion to the status of household commodities issued for private consumption by individuals only, must eventually bring about its death: man can realize his full powers only as a member of an organized society.

In Aboriginal Central Australia the situation was entirely different. Here religion was regarded as all-important because it was completely practical in all its intentions. I do not wish to develop this theme here: readers interested in the characteristic aspects of Aboriginal Australian religion are advised to turn to the two important discussions of it, which are to be found in articles by W. E. H. Stanner (1965) and Mircea Eliade (1968). In my own view, the great and specifically Australian contribution to religious thought has been the unquestioning Aboriginal conviction that there was no division between Time and Eternity. Since *every* person carried within himself, through reincarnation, an immortal spark of life derived from the original supernatural personages, men and the totemic ancestors were believed to be interlinked inseparably.[27] The perpetual well-being of the universe, and the whole welfare of the material world, hence depended on the continued singing of the original creative words and the continued repetition of the original creative acts of the original supernatural beings by their human reincarnations from generation to generation.[28] These things, however, had to be done at the original geographical sites if they were to be fully effective. The totemic acts and their songs, it should be noted, related not merely to animals and plants, but also to heavenly bodies such as the sun, the moon, the Pleiades and some of the stars, and also to such natural phenomena as sun-heat, frosts, winds and rain. The universe that was being perpetuated in this way continued to embrace, with relentless logic, not only those things that gave life and joy to mankind but also those other things which caused hurt and pain. Centipedes and scorpions, mosquitoes, flies and fleas, bull-ants and processional caterpillars, and the whole tribe of venomous snakes were mentioned, even if only in some rarely sung verses, in creative songs attached to certain of the totemic centres. So were whirlwinds, dust-storms and droughts. Moreover, there were a few centres set apart for the preservation of sorcery charms and avengers' songs, and there were sites, too, for the commemoration of Death's entry into the unquiet world of men and the totemic ancestors. All men, and not merely a special class of professional priests, shared in this task of perpetually renewing the universe; and in carrying out the rites enjoined by religion, all men acquired a sense of having a purposeful role to play both in life and in eternity: all the labours of humanity were necessary to keep nature functioning harmoniously. It was because of this conviction that the old religious leaders kept on urging younger men never to cease carrying out the traditional rites at the original sacred sites. In the Central Australian communities the 'profane crowd' of passive worshippers was unknown. Probably as a result of this, there were no parts of the population that corresponded even vaguely either to the slave elements found in the ancient civilizations or to the underprivileged sections which constitute disturbing components of certain modern industrialized communities. Aboriginal religion fostered a deep respect for the individual, and for all human values.

Because of its practical functions, and because all men in these localized permanent Aboriginal communities belonged to totemic clans, there was no sharp division between religious and secular authority. This is a division which seems so obvious to us, who have grown up in countries where the secular authorities are not only distinct from the religious leaders, but are often even at variance with them. But we should not forget that this distinction would have appeared completely irrational to communities where the religious organization was so all-embracing. In European-type communities the Church no longer has any legal machinery at its disposal for ordering and directing the daily lives of the citizens: the rights and wrongs of the latter are a matter for determination by secular courts. In these courts the state concerns itself mainly with criminal actions that endanger the welfare of society or the very base of authority, while the private citizen has to seek redress through civil actions in matters that concern him personally. The division found in the judicial systems of the Central Australian tribes between sacrilegious acts on the one hand and offences against private persons or ordinary marital misdemeanours on the other was of a rather different nature. The reason given for this division was that the totemic ancestors themselves had instituted sickness and death as punishments for sacrilege, and that secular offences (that is, acts that would approximate to our 'civil' offences) had been left to human beings for punishment or to settlement according to long-established 'tribal' precedents (which dictated how severe a punishment could be inflicted on an offender by a wronged individual with the tacit approval or connivance of the community). However, since all social actions and all marriage arrangements had, in the first place, been instituted by the ancestral beings, religious[29] attitudes here too influenced the behaviour of all parties involved in these disputes; for appeals to mythological precedents were often made, even on occasions at which they would have been considered as being quite irrelevant by ourselves.

These summarizing remarks point to the vital tie which bound up the social, political and religious institutions of the Aboriginal Central Australians with the economic facts of their geographical environment and the details of their totemic landscape. In a land where the supernatural beings revered and honoured by their human reincarnations were living, not in the sky, but at clearly marked sites in the mountains, the springs, the sandhills and the plains, religious acts had an immediate personal intimacy rarely, if ever, equalled in other religious systems. The human reincarnations turned into living symbols during the impersonations of the supernatural beings at the sacred sites. The visible totemic landscape was considered to be an integral part of the reality of eternity. There was no need of hereditary ruling families: the major totemic sites continuously sent out sparks of the life, from which future elders and ceremonial chiefs could become reincarnated: each major sacred site was the geographic fountain of authority for the territory surrounding it.

We have already seen that in Central Australia the whole economic resources of the country were utilized to the full. Man believed that he was living in harmony with Nature, not as its destroyer or conqueror. That unfortunate role was played by the later European immigrants into this country; and their blind destruction of the indigenous plants and animals has already had disastrous results in many parts of the Centre. But until that time even the most desolate portions of the most arid lands in the Centre were lit up by myths and songs with the light of the eternal landscape; and so their geographical features acquired, in the eyes of all folk born near them, those emotional aspects that made them revered as the handiwork of supernatural beings. A European standing on the low rise of Akạ̈r' Intjōṭa in the Simpson Desert would have seen only the vastness of desolation in the treeless plain, the red tops of the long dune ridges, and the mean and broken rubbly hills, in the circular-horizoned landscape around him. A Lower Southern Aranda man's vision would have been filled with different and far more magnificent sights. In his mind's eye he would have caught sight of the great Amêwara Tnạ̈ṭaŋa totem pole brought from Port Augusta, towering against the western horizon, the flames of its plumed crest-top shooting skyward at night toward the desert-bright stars. Close at hand he would have seen the broad trunk of a great casuarina tree rising up and touching the sky above him with its branches, forming a firm bridge between the sky and the earth. He would have seen the native cat travellers from Port Augusta winding their trail across the vast plain of Akạ̈ra on their way to the Eastern MacDonnells and beyond. And finally he would have seen the two eagle brothers, whose nest had been placed on top of the nearby casuarina tree, rushing forward into their last fight with the Ṭạ̈ŋka avengers 10 miles away at Uṭy̆ra, after the latter had cut their tree down and destroyed the bridge between the earth and the sky.

It is little wonder that Kŋêitnǎma, whose father and father's father had both come from Akạ̈r' Intjōṭa, after spending some weeks in 1955 in the mountainous country close to Alice Springs, said to me with deep feeling: 'If only I could get away from these ranges that shut out everything from my eyes to that beautiful open plain where there is scarcely a tree to block my view. Here I am shut in everywhere—there everything is open to the eyes. And it is my own country, and that of my fathers.'

It takes little imagination to visualize the catastrophic effects upon all Aboriginal institutions of the severing of the Central Australian tribal groups from their geographical environment after European settlement had begun. The breakdown of Aboriginal authority started as soon as the aged guardians of the great totemic centres were forcibly evicted from their local group areas. Mission and governmental establishments, often unwittingly, helped the process of social disintegration by raising to authority at the new settlements men who were not entitled to this honour by the correct geographical considerations. Thus, during the early history of Hermannsburg, men who were in Aboriginal eyes only the ceremonial chiefs of Ḷṭâlaḷṭŭma, and of the Ellery Creek local group, were looked on by the missionaries as the pillars of the Hermannsburg congregation, because they had embraced Christianity. On the other hand, Lôatjĭra, the venerated ceremonial chief of Nṭărea, who should have been the most important man of authority at Hermannsburg, exiled himself most of his life from his local group because he remained, till a couple of years before his death (on 4 October 1924), a strong champion of the old order. The European missionaries were thus forced to assume the mantle of supreme authority themselves; but some of Hermannsburg's present troubles with members of the younger Aranda generation could without doubt have been avoided if the old system of leadership had not been destroyed so thoroughly. At most other Aboriginal settlements in the Centre similar troubles either have already made their appearance or will almost certainly do so in the not too distant future.

For the Aboriginal Central Australians the totemic landscape formed a firm basis for religion, for the social order, and for established authority itself. To understand these things thoroughly the European anthropologist, too, must become familiar with the geography of Central Australia, and study all Aboriginal institutions of the tribes of the interior against the backdrop of their geographical setting.

Notes

1. The names of the larger clay freshwater lakes (known as *kwâtja amặla* and *ekrâra* in Lower Southern Aranda, and as *jĭkara* in Wăŋkaŋŭru) were: Pŭḷawĭni (north of the Kallakoopah), Mărabăti, Mŭrkarăṇa, Kăḷjikăṇa, Jătalkṇa, Pălkuru, Pălarĭŋuṇa, Pĭrbaṇa, Pĭlakāīja, Kăḷalŭmba, Părapăra, Wălbarka, Pŭrupŭṭu, Păḷani, Mădluṇa (north of Poeppel's Corner) and Păŋalŭṇa. In the northern part of the Simpson Desert lay Wăḷara, an overflow lagoon or swamp flat marking the end of one of the northern rivers, probably the Plenty.

2. The Aranda had an eight kin-group class system in the Western, Northern and Central subgroups, and in the Unmatjera area, and a four kin-group class system in the Eastern, Upper Southern and Lower Southern areas. However, after the turn of the

century the eight-class system gradually spread into the latter as well, particularly after the depopulation caused by the 1919 influenza epidemic. The Imăṇḍa group began substituting Ŋala and Mbitjana classes for their original Purula and Kamara classes after the 1896 festival held in honour of Spencer and Gillen. This represented a deliberate adoption of the Northern and Western Aranda system; for Ŋala and Mbitjana classes are to be found only in an eight-class system.

3. Two of these later on became mates and were thereupon called 'a kangaroo and a euro pair'—the latter being an original kangaroo which had changed its fur to that of a euro en route.

4. A similar change occurred in the acts depicting the wanderings of the mălu (kangaroo), the kăṇalạ (euro), and the tjŭrki (owlet nightjar) from Ărkowăla, near Granite Downs, past Ărapa towards the Musgrave Ranges. Up to Kărbakŭṭara (near Wăpirka) their ceremonies were of the *wămulu* (commemorative) type, and were known as *bĕria*; but at their next western point of call (Ŭḷalba) they had turned their acts into *ṇăluŋka* acts. Spreading their initiatory acts from this point onward, they had then continued as far as Erăntjirănŋa, a mountain in the eastern Musgrave Ranges.

5. Among the Aranda circumcision was only an operation preparing youths for entry into the company of the initiated men. The actual initiation of the circumcised youths into the mysteries of the spiritual world took place at a later stage when the sacred *tjurunga* were being revealed to them, and it reached its full height during the staging of the great ceremonial cycles with their carefully graded series of secret acts.

6. The Commonwealth government's total expenditure on Aborigines in the Northern Territory was £6,921 during 1936/37. In 1950/51 it rose to £175,094 and in 1956/57 to £495,510.

7. This uprooting of the Walbiri after 1928 undoubtedly had a deep effect on the social organization of the Walbiri, as I have explained in detail in my review of *Desert People*, in *Nation*, 12 January 1963.

8. Tŭma was staying there at the time with four other men and four women; there was also a child in this group. Most of the Ŋalia were still pursuing a nomadic way of life in 1932. During the winter of that year they were scattered throughout their extensive semi-desert lands, living on sandhill yams which were growing in profusion within reach of scores of small rockholes and limestone soaks. The Ŋalia groups I met on my travels in that year were all rather small in size. A group met at Jĭlbartji soak consisted of seven men, six women and about half a dozen children. Two elderly women, who were accompanied by a number of young children, were met at the Jămabănta soak: they were on their way south, hoping to rejoin another small group. The largest group I came upon was engaged in gathering yams around a large quartzite hill ridge, whose main water was called Ĕripilŏŋa. It consisted of seventeen persons—ten males and seven females: this sex count included all the children as well.

9. This foot bone was extracted by Professor H. Whitridge Davies, on 28 January 1934, and only the ankle stump was left behind. Professor Davies at the time was working on a research project at Ăjantji, south of Mt Liebig, assisted by a Sydney University medical party.

10. Kŏmutu's personal totemic site (by conception or birth) was, however, the wăru (rock wallaby) centre of Ṭŭŋiṇa, near Wăluŋuru, on the edge of the Kintore Range.

11. The serious decline of all authority in the present-day communities living on the Central Australian stations and settlements tends to encourage bitter disputes among the remaining elderly men who still possess some measure of prestige in religious matters. These disputes inevitably lower their status still further in the eyes of those younger men who are willing to listen to their advice. Thus the continual bickering between Măka and Tjĭtuma, two Jankuntjatjara elders, both of whom derived their status from their

knowledge of the Wåpirka traditions, caused grave discontent among their assistants during the staging of the final Wåpirka acts at a site on the Goyder River in 1965, and eventually brought about the break-up of the gathering. I was assured by the younger men present that their two leaders could never work together amicably. Every ceremonial occasion would end with a walk-out by one or the other of these two old men.

12. It is to be regretted that C. P. Mountford's recent book, *Winbaraku* (1968), contains a great amount of misinformation about the Kukatja area, and that the Kukatja myth of Wĭnbarku itself ('Wĭnbarku' is the correct Kukatja form of Mountford's 'Winbaraku') has been incorrectly given. I collected both the Wĭnbarku myth and song in the Kukatja language from the Kukatja owners in 1936 (together with a number of other Kukatja myths and songs); and I have witnessed the sacred acts of many of the important Kukatja ceremonial centres. My information was gathered from authorities like Wåpiti, the åtanåri of the yam and native cat centre of Mêrini, Ŭkili, the åtanåri of the kangaroo centre of Ãjaii, Ṯŭṉala, the åtanåri of the emu centre of Ŭrṯurṯåti, and their elderly assistants (the best informed of whom were Mŭlda, Ilbĭljaŭrka, Erãka, Wĭnuinṉa, Ṯånatji, Tŭṯaṉa, Ṯåpani, and two other men who also bore the name of Ṯŭṉala).

13. This so-called *warièra* festival took place while my informant Kṉêitnåma's father was still a boy, some time before the construction of the Overland Telegraph Line.

14. Because of tabus against the free discussion of serious acts of sacrilege, my informants had never been given by their fathers the exact details of what had actually happened at Urålawŭraka. The young man who had to give the signal—and who had probably been assisted by one or two of his friends to climb the eagle pole—had either slipped and fallen off, or had broken the string from which one of the sea-shell clusters had been suspended and dashed the shells to the ground below. Again, my informants had not been told exactly whether two or three young men had been killed for this accident; but Kṉêitnåma, who as a young man had still seen the bleached skulls and skeletons lying at Urålawŭraka (where they had been exposed by the action of wind and weather), thought that there had been three skulls.

15. Actual instances of such punishments have been given to me by several informants. H. Basedow (1925:282; see also the picture of the *Etominja*, plate XXXVII) similarly refers to the power of the Aranda ceremonial chief to execute unauthorized persons:

> Once constructed, this drawing, which is known as '*Etominja*', is zealously guarded by one of the old men. If, peradventure, an unauthorized person happens upon the sanctified place, he is killed and buried immediately beneath the spot occupied by the design; thereupon the ground is smoothed again and the Etominja re-constructed. Nobody in camp ever hears what became of the person, and should any relative track him in the direction of the area known to be tabooed, he is horror-stricken and runs away.

The ceremonial verses quoted by Basedow confirm that his *Etominja* is the etåmintja ground-painting associated with the låtjia yam totem of Iwŭpaṯåka (Jay Creek).

16. The actors impersonating the Northern Aranda hawk ancestor of Kĕrenbĕnṉa and the Upper Southern Aranda sandhill wallaby (kwåḷba) ancestor respectively squatted between burning fires and swished live coals over themselves and over the young *wårkuntŭma* dancers that were racing around them. The Eastern Aranda pŭṯia ratkangaroo sire of Bêjapŭṉa advanced at blazing fires with two crouching *pŭṯia* novices moving on their knees in front of him: sometimes he pushed these youths almost into the circle of the wind-blown blaze while beating the fire with long branches till sparks and small live coals flew into their faces and on to their bodies.

17. Similarly the preparation of the elaborate and constantly changing ground-paintings of such Unmatjera honey-ant centres as Alkŭpitja or Kôrbuḷa, and the daily decoration of scores of painted shields during festivals held at the north-eastern Aranda euro totemic sites ranging from Ḹâlkararŭra to Mbŏkuṇaḷṭáta, demanded such large quantities of blood that these could have been obtained only from the veins of scores of young and vigorous men.

18. The Kukatja word *kûntaŋka*, which is the exact equivalent of the Aranda *tjŭruṇa*, was given by both Stirling (in the form Kundŭnga) and Winnecke (in the form Koondunga) as the name of the Ḳárkiljarkĭlja cave, which both of these men had clearly found impossible to pronounce.

19. In Winnecke's words: 'Accompanied by Dr. Stirling, Taylor, and the two blacks I started in search of the corrobboree stones. Racehorse now seemed loath to proceed in the direction of the hills where these treasures were hidden, and endeavoured to persuade me not to go. But all his excuses and objections were futile, and fortunately the information I secured from him last night rendered his further assistance of little importance.'

20. His correct Pitjantjara name could not be ascertained after his killing. He had in any case left his group and come as a young boy into the Matuntara area, where he had worked almost continuously for the white station man, W. Liddle. In 1969 I was told that Kai-Umen's real name had been Kāíjuwåna.

21. Spencer and Gillen give an instance of the killing of an Iliaura man who had 'married within the forbidden degrees of relationship' by an Aranda avenging party (1927: Vol. II, pp. 444-5), and of the attempted killing of a Lower Southern Aranda man at Charlotte Waters (*ibid.*: 446). The latter escaped only because he was a formidable fighter who killed two of the men who had attempted to punish him. However, it was almost certainly the influence of the European settlers in this area which saved his life in the long run.

22. Arảṇa Ljĭnaṇa's mother's father had been Iltĭṇterȧka, the ceremonial chief of Intâḷua.

23. If these scars had not been cut deeply enough, it was permissible for the relatives of the dead man to punish the son-in-law by cutting them still deeper. Spencer and Gillen (1927: Vol. II, p. 507) give an actual instance of a visitor who was publicly taunted because 'he had not properly cut himself and mourned when his father-in-law, a local man, had died'. The visitor in the end 'inflicted a slight wound on himself with his stone knife, and then they all became reconciled'.

24. Even this tjĭlpa earth-mound may have been an innovation: the ancestral tjĭlpa horde from Arêtowảṭṇa by-passed Imȧṇda by 2 miles.

25. This lack of any centralized system of authority extended into the spiritual sphere as well. Each set of the multitudinous earth-born totemic ancestors exercised their power only in relatively small geographically delimited areas; and such sky dwellers as the Western Aranda or Kukatja Great Fathers exerted no influence whatever on the earth or its weather or its plants or its animals or its human inhabitants. The only myth to the contrary is that concocted for Sir Baldwin Spencer's consumption by the Alice Springs police tracker Charlie Cooper. It is ironic that Spencer, who had jeered at C. Strehlow's Western Aranda myth of 'Altjira' (C. Strehlow, 1907-20: Part I, pp. 1-2), was taken in by Charlie Cooper so completely that he wrote the whole of Chapter XIII in *The Arunta* on this subject. Yet C. Strehlow's Western Aranda myth is correct as it stands, except perhaps for the two sentences in which he referred to the completely otiose Western Aranda Sky Being as being the benevolent Supreme Being of the Aranda. Spencer, however, claimed that his 'great original *Inkata Alchera Numbakulla*' (1927: Vol. I, p. 356) 'gave rise to all the original Kurunas [=spirits, souls], Churingas, and

Knanjas [=totems]'. Unfortunately, the very name given to Spencer's Supreme Being shows that his informant had syncretized Aboriginal beliefs with the new doctrines of the Hermannsburg missionaries: for 'Iŋkâṭa Altjỉra Ŋâmbakâla' was merely the Hermannsburg translation of a common title given to the Christian God: it means 'Lord God Eternal'.

26. In Chapter XI of *News from Nowhere* the idyllic state of the English people after all governmental authority has been abolished and Parliament House itself turned into a 'dung-market' is described as follows:

> The old man answered.... 'Now, dear guest, let me tell you that our present parliament would be hard to house in one place, because the whole people is our parliament....
> 'It is true that we have to make some arrangements about our affairs, concerning which you can ask presently; and it is also true that everybody does not always agree with the details of these arrangements; but, further, it is true that a man no more needs an elaborate system of government, with its army, navy, and police, to force him to give way to the will of the majority of his *equals*, than he wants a similar machinery to make him understand that his head and a stone wall cannot occupy the same space at the same moment.'

Morris's Utopian England was not far removed spiritually from that Walbiri tribal area in which Meggitt has claimed to have found a similarly leaderless community.

27. When my Pintubi guide Lỉlitjukŭrba pointed to the water in the Ỉlbiḷi soak in 1932, he told me: 'That water is no good—it stinks. There is a dead man in there.' What he alluded to was that the human reincarnation of the totemic ancestor of Ỉlbiḷi had been speared to death a few weeks previously; and his advice was that we should not drink from the soak so soon after the death of the reincarnated person. We accordingly filled up our canteens at a rockhole about ten miles away. (This incident has been quoted by H. K. Fry 1933.)

28. Eliade's comments (1968:261) on the lack of European-type interest of history among the Aboriginal Australians are pertinent in this connection:

> In fact, the distinctive characteristic of Australians and other primitive peoples is not their lack of history but their specific interpretation of human historicity. They too live in history and are shaped by historical events; but they do not have a historical awareness comparable, say, to that of Westerners; and, because they do not need it, they also lack a historiographical consciousness. The aborigines do not record historical events in an irreversible chronological order. The changes and innovations, which imperceptibly but continuously transformed their existence, were telescoped into the mythical era; that is, they became part of the tribal sacred history. Like most archaic peoples, the Australians do not have any use for *real* chronology. Their sacred history is meaningful, not because it narrates the events in a chronological order, but because it reveals the beginnings of the world, the appearance of the Ancestors, and their dramatic and exemplary deeds.

29. Stanner's apt conclusions on the relationship between Aboriginal society and religion may make the general Aboriginal Australian attitudes clearer for the reader (1965:237):

> Students with the patience to look beyond the symbol to the symbolized will find that the end of Aboriginal religion was in Confucian terms 'to unite hearts and establish order'. Understood in that way, a 'totemic' system shows itself as a link between cosmogony, cosmology, and ontology; between Aboriginal intuitions of the beginnings of things, the resulting relevances for men's individual and social being, and a continuously meaningful life. The associating of a totem with a collection of people was that which transformed them from just a collection into a group with a sign of unity.

When everything significant in the world was thus parcelled out among enduring groups, the society became made up of perennial corporations of a religious character. Each group was corporate *in* all that its totems signified and symbolized. Aboriginal totemic groups were thus sacred corporations in perpetuity. The yearly round of rites let the Aborigines renew both the sources and the bonds of life constituted in that way. The religion was not the mirage of the society, and the society was not the consequence of the religion. Each pervaded the other within a larger process.

REFERENCES

BASEDOW, H. 1925 *The Australian Aboriginal*. Preece, Adelaide.

BERNDT, R. M. 1965 Law and Order in Aboriginal Australia. In *Aboriginal Man in Australia* (R. M. and C. H. Berndt, eds). Angus and Robertson, Sydney.

ELIADE, M. 1968 Australian Religions, Part V: Death, Eschatology, and some Conclusions, *History of Religions*, University of Chicago.

FRY, H. K. 1933 Body and Soul, *Oceania*, Vol. III, No. 3.

HIATT, L. R. 1965 *Kinship and Conflict*. Australian National University, Canberra.

MEGGITT, M. J. 1962 *Desert People*. Angus and Robertson, Sydney.

——— 1965 Marriage among the Walbiri of Central Australia: a Statistical Examination. In *Aboriginal Man in Australia* (R. M. and C. H. Berndt, eds). Angus and Robertson, Sydney.

SPENCER, B. and F. J. GILLEN 1927 *The Arunta* (2 vols). Macmillan, London.

STANNER, W. E. H. 1965 Religion, Totemism and Symbolism. In *Aboriginal Man in Australia* (R. M. and C. H. Berndt, eds). Angus and Robertson, Sydney.

STREHLOW, C. 1907-20 *Die Aranda- und Loritja-Stämme in Zentral-Australien*. Joseph Baer, Frankfurt.

STREHLOW, T. G. H. 1947 *Aranda Traditions*. Melbourne University Press, Melbourne.

——— 1964 Personal Monototemism in a Polytotemic Community. In *Festschrift für Ad. E. Jensen*. Klaus Renner Verlag, Munich.

——— 1965 Culture, Social Structure, and Environment. In *Aboriginal Man in Australia* (R. M. and C. H. Berndt, eds). Angus and Robertson, Sydney.

——— 1970 *Songs of Central Australia*. Angus and Robertson, Sydney.

WINNECKE, C. 1897 *Journal of the Horn Scientific Exploring Expedition, 1894*. Bristow, Government Printer, Adelaide.

YENGOYAN, A. A. 1967 Field Report No. 2, 1 November 1966–1 March 1967. Australian Institute of Aboriginal Studies, Canberra. (Cyclostyled.)

NANCY D. MUNN

*The Transformation of Subjects into Objects
in Walbiri and Pitjantjatjara Myth*

In his classic study of gift exchange, Marcel Mauss (1954) was concerned with social relationships in which people are bound together through the agency of things, and in which, therefore, the things are imbued with notions of person. The binding force of obligation between persons is thus expressed through notions about the nature of the objects as 'forming a part of human persons' (p. 54). Mauss's work implies that such objects are symbols of the social relationships they define because they condense within themselves the structure of these relationships. They are, in effect, icons or expressive symbols of them.

In this paper I explore certain transformations in the myths of Walbiri and Pitjantjatjara Aborigines of the central and western deserts[1] which involve the creation of a binding relation between persons and things. By 'transformations' I mean on the one hand various recurrent operations through which an ancestor—a sentient being—takes on or produces a material form, an object, consubstantial with himself, and on the other hand the products of these operations, the resultant objects. I do not deal here with transformations of one sentient being into another, but rather with shifts between a subject and an object, a mode of transformation that is far more common in Walbiri and Pitjantjatjara thought. Indeed, subject-object transformations form a pervasive substratum in these, as in many Australian Aboriginal mythologies, since the major features of the country are systematically regarded as the products of ancestral transformation.[2]

The purpose of this paper is to push our attempts to understand transformation beyond the artificial boundaries of 'mythology' into the domain of socialization or, more generally, the problem of the relationship between the individual and the collectivity as mediated by the object world.[3] My primary aim is to suggest a possible framework of enquiry and the sorts of inferences it may yield, rather than to develop a detailed analysis or comparison of transformations in each society.

The Structure of Walbiri and Pitjantjatjara Transformations

Three types of transformation are prominent in Walbiri and Pitjantjatjara myth: (1) metamorphosis (the body of the ancestor is changed into some material object); (2) imprinting (the ancestor leaves the impression of his body or of some tool he uses), and (3) externalization (the ancestor takes some object out of his body). Of the three, externalization is more specialized; the first two are most common, and need not be sharply distinguished from each other. In general, any object created in any way by an ancestor is thought to contain something of himself within it, and the various creative modes all imply a consubstantial relationship between the ancestor and his objectifications.

Metamorphosis is verbally expressed in Walbiri and Pitjantjatjara by a morpheme meaning 'become, change or develop into' which is suffixed to the term for the resultant object. For instance, 'to become a waterhole' is *ngaba-djari* in Walbiri, *gabi-ri* in Pitjantjatjara. (The latter also has a special term *burga-ri* which I discuss later.) Externalization may be indicated by expressions such as *urgu* ('pull out') or *udi-ma* ('make visible or outside') in Pitjantjatjara, and *wilbi-ma* ('take out') in Walbiri.[4]

In both languages there are terms meaning 'mark' which are widely used in the context of ancestral acts. These terms refer in general to any sort of identifying marking, or determinate pattern including imprints. Thus any sort of visible form resulting from the presence of an ancestor can be regarded as his 'mark' (Walbiri, *jiri*, also *guruwari*; Pitjantjatjara, *walga*). Pitjantjatjara say, for example, that the ancestor *walgadjunu*, 'put his mark'. This generally carries the specific implication of an imprint, as well as the more general sense of any visible, identifying form being left by the ancestor.

The Walbiri terms *jiri* and *guruwari* are somewhat more complex.[5] *Jiri* means 'name' and 'song' as well as 'visible mark'. *Guruwari* has two primary senses: (1) ancestral totemic designs (which the Pitjantjatjara class under *walga*); (2) the invisible fertility powers or essence of the ancestor which, like his visible marks, he leaves in the country. *Guruwari* may, however, be used to refer to *any* visible phenomena, for example, footprints or hills, left by an ancestor. For instance, Walbiri may say that when he walks along he 'puts' (*jirani*) his *guruwari* (i.e. footprints).

In both Walbiri and Pitjantjatjara thought there are certain associations (more pronounced amongst the Walbiri) between 'putting marks', that is, transformation in general, and 'naming' a place. The Walbiri term *jiri*, as I have indicated, can cover both senses. Pitjantjatjara also sometimes refer to ancestral transformations by the expression *ini* (name) *djunu*: 'he put his name (mark)'. The initial naming of ancestral sites is attributed to the ancestors, just as is their physical creation. Indeed, the one tends to imply the other. The names of sites are also thought of as the ancestors' proper names. The object world is both verbally and visually constituted: ancestral naming and transformation create a determinate, fixed phenomenal reality grounded in the specificity of form and verbal sign (proper names).

The Aborigines relate the ancestor to his transformations either by reference to the process of transformation itself (e.g. A becomes B) or to the state of identification which results (A and B are 'the same thing').[6] The identification expresses the permanence of the incorporation of the ancestor or subject in the object; the processual statements express the primary grounding of these permanent properties in a dynamic relation between subject and object, sentient being and external object world.

Ancestors may be wholly human or, more typically, partly human and partly non-human. Although for convenience I refer to them in general as male, they may be male or female. In this region, however, male ancestors are emphasized. The number of distinctive ancestors is indefinite, and the objects they create constitute, in effect, the total, non-sentient environment as epitomized by the country itself. Transformations which are not directly a part of the topography (such as string crosses or oval boards) are variously linked to the country in Aboriginal thought.[7] The country is the fundamental object system external to the conscious subject within which, as we shall see, consciousness and identity are anchored.

There are certain distinctive features of transformations on which our interpretation must hinge. In each instance the operation shifts the mode of being of a mortal, transient person into a permanent form such as a hill or rockhole, or an artificially renewable one such as a string cross or 'churinga'. The mobile person either travels on or dies (goes into the country). If he carries an object along the track with him then he may leave it behind when he 'goes in'. The general assumption, irrespective of particular incidents, is that ultimately only the transformations remain visible and available to human observation. An ancestor may leave an indefinite variety of such records of himself: he is not uniquely embodied by a single transformation.

There is thus a disappearance linked with a new appearance; a transient 'will', temporally located, from which emanate atemporal, static embodiments. The ancestors continually move from place to place, or they travel around one place until they go in forever. A kind of perpetual motion is remedied by images of permanence, yet at the same time this motion and the dynamic subjectivity it presupposes are, as it were, incorporated into permanent objects: transformations contain the ancestral being and his 'strength' at the same time that they are disengaged from him.

For traditional Walbiri and Pitjantjatjara, as for many other Aboriginal societies, time is split into two broad temporal ages, that of ancestral times (*djugurba*), and that of the ongoing present and recent past (Walbiri, *jidjaru*; Pitjantjatjara, *mulaba*). There are also two corresponding categories of human or humanized subjects: ancestral persons (*djugurba*) and contemporary human beings (Walbiri, *jaba*; Pitjantjatjara, *aṇangu*). Since transformations were created in *djugurba* times but remain visible forever (or may be perpetually remade), they condense within them the two forms of temporality, and are thus freed from specific historical location. As we shall see, both human beings and ancestors can be freed from their 'historicity' or 'mortality' by integration within these objects; their mutual identification with the latter in turn reintegrates the two categories of subject (the ancestral and human).

We may say, then, that a transformation is constituted by a kind of 'double movement': on the one hand a process of separation from the originating subject; on the other hand, a binding of the object to him in permanent, atemporal identification. I shall refer to this characteristic as the 'bi-directional' structure of the transformation, since it involves a tension within the object between subject-object engagement and disengagement. This 'tension' is critical to the overall significance of transformations as symbols of social mediation.

If we consider further the nature of ancestral creativity we find that it may be conceived as ranging from conscious to more or less unconscious objectification (or at least to a situation in which consciousness of the objectifying act is irrelevant). The most fundamental assumption is that the object emerges as the automatic result of an ancestor's presence and activities; for instance, where he sits down a waterhole appears. In this case, there is no consciousness directed toward the objectifying process.

At the other extreme, the ancestor may be thought of as consciously constructing an object as when, for instance, in Walbiri myth, the two kangaroos made their 'tails' (their penes and ceremonial poles) by pulling them out of their bodies (or, in another version, out of a hill). Here the subject consciously creates his transformation. In general, it is inherent in the psycho-physical nature of ancestors to freely objectify aspects of themselves,[8] either as conscious productive acts or as automatic effects of their bodily presence or actions.

There is, however, a more explicit set of notions concerning the psychology of creation which is well developed in Walbiri thought, although not, it would appear, in that of the Pitjantjatjara with whom I worked. In both societies the term for ancestors and ancestral period also means 'dream'. Only the Walbiri, however, appear to develop the significance of this fact in detail. In their view, the ancestor first dreams his objectifications while sleeping in camp. In effect, he visualizes his travels—the country, the songs and everything he makes—inside his head before they are externalized. Objectifications are conceived as external projections of an interior vision: they come from the inner self of the ancestor into the outer world.

Since these objects all refer back to the ancestor himself (they are regarded as his 'marks' or 'names', his essential figurations), it is as if he were visualizing himself in his dreams through the imagery of the objective world. The dream images are in this sense incipient acts of self-consciousness which are completed by their externalization. As I have pointed out elsewhere (1964:92):

> The concept of the ancestral dream focuses an idea which appears to be at the base of Walbiri thinking in this matter: the ancestors created their own names, their identifying marks, from their inner beings, so these marks are an intrinsic part of them sharing in their own nature.

If we begin with the ancestral subject, then movement is initially from subject to object; for the Walbiri at least, the movement is really from the interior of the subject to an external, sense termination—that is, from 'inside' to 'outside'.[9] Objectification is conceived as a process linking the interior subjectivity of the person with the external world. But if in the ancestral situation the subject is prior to these objects (he is the original creator of objects), for the living individual the object is prior, and the initial direction of movement must be, as we shall see, from object to subject, from outside to inside.

In sum, ancestral transformation involves a free, untrammelled creativity and 'self-objectification' inherent in the nature of the subject. This kind of originating power—the power to create one's own identity without limitation—is thought of as split off from contemporary human beings and localized in the ancestral world. Human beings must initially 'submit' to the existence of this world. The significance of this 'submission' will become apparent in the subsequent discussion.[10]

Land Claims and Local Ancestral Ties

As we have seen, the object transformations of an ancestor are permanently bound to him by ties of substance. Human beings also have certain unbreakable bonds with particular parts of the country, and these bonds serve to fix their social identities relative to the ancestors. Before examining transformations themselves more closely, some brief background on the nature of these bonds is necessary.

Pitjantjatjara.[11] Among the Pitjantjatjara, small groups of agnates usually constitute the landowners for specific localities or countries (*ngura*) in the Petermanns region. Such groups also have a residential focus since, in the pre-European period, the men of the group ideally based themselves after marriage in their father's home country (even though at any given time they might actually have been living or hunting elsewhere).

The rights of landowners (exercised primarily by men) refer to the sacred resources of the area, that is, to control of ancestral transformations (sacra), and associated songs and ceremonials. No part of the country—whether it is the design-marked sacred boards and stones lodged in crevices and caves, or any of the ordinary stones which might also be ancestral transformations—should be 'touched' (removed or molested) without their approval. A single country (*ngura gudju*) generally includes in its close-lying cluster of sites the bodily remnants of more than one ancestor, but only one is ordinarily dominant or representative. The ancestral transformations thus constitute a homeland to a particular group of men and women, ritual rights over it being inherited ideally from the father.

The importance of these sacred countries is not economic in the sense that the sites do not define the limits of the region over which those in residence may forage for food.[12] Rather, the home country must be seen as a symbol of stability, a spatial and temporal anchorage conceptualized in terms of specific place-names and the originating ancestors bound within it.

In addition to homeland ties and claims, an individual has close associations with his (or her) birthplace and its ancestors. He may sometimes identify himself with the ancestor of his birthplace as well as his homeland (if these two differ) by referring to him as 'I'. Birthplace ties are also expressed in the beliefs concerning birth-marks (called *djuguridja*, 'of or pertaining to the ancestors'). Pointing to various body markings such as moles, warts or skin discolorations, Pitjantjatjara would say that they were marks left by the ancestors at their birthplace. For example, one woman explained that a marking upon a particular ancestral rock at her birthplace was also on her body. The rock was the transformed body of the ancestor lying down and the marking was originally his hair. Similarly, another man claimed that a small skin marking on his body was the scar on a carpet-snake ancestor speared in a fight at his birthplace. The result of this fight was the emergence of specific topographical features (and no doubt the scar was recorded in them although my informant did not state this explicitly).

Through his identification with a particular locality at birth an individual may be imprinted with ancestral markings which on the one hand are aspects of the ancestor's own body, and on the other, parts of the countryside. In this way a person's own body may be identified with the ancestor's body through the mediation of the object world of ancestral transformations.

For the human subject the country is an experiential 'given', a pre-ordained structure which as 'homeland' or 'birthplace' (or both at once) provides a stabilization of 'self' in object form. This inverts the relationship which Aborigines conceptualize between ancestral subjects and objects: relative to the ancestor the world is a novel stabilization of self which he can create freely and extemporaneously out of his being. In doing so he automatically limits the possibilities of free creation, since he is forming the determinate, post-*djugurba* order of reality. In effect, his transformations betoken his recession from the overt life-scene; as he discloses his identity through his 'marks', he displaces or transforms his own mode of existence. The living Aboriginal, on the other hand, is confronted with a *fait accompli*, a fixed topographical structure within which he must operate.

Walbiri. Among the Walbiri, rights over land are also lodged in patrilineal groups, but the adult men of these groups do not constitute the core of a residential unit, localized at the sites. Walbiri communities in the immediate pre-European era could include men united by various kinship ties and representing all subsections. The sites of ancestors associated with particular patrilineal groups were to be found within the general region surrounding the residential focus of the community where men of these groups based themselves. One can find within the same area sites belonging to patrilineal groups of different father-son subsection couples.[13]

As in the Pitjantjatjara case, the rights men exercise over these sites are of a ritual nature and involve the maintenance of ceremonial paraphernalia connected with the associated ancestors who made the place. Sacred boards are also stored at some of these locales and are regarded as amongst the 'marks' left by the ancestors of a place.

As I have pointed out elsewhere (Munn 1964:88, 89), Walbiri men may justify claims to site ownership by reference to the fact that an ancestor has left his marks there, thus establishing a claim to the place. For example, in one instance, the rights of a particular patrilineal group to certain sites were explained by pointing out that the ancestors of the present owners had travelled there, singing as they went. To sing one's way from place to place implies that marks and names are being 'put' at each place—that is, that the site is being claimed. Thus group claims are based ultimately upon ancestral claims made through the marks of personal identification with which the ancestor imprints a place.

In addition to ancestral affiliations determined by patrilineal descent, an individual identifies himself with the ancestors of the site where he or she is believed to have been conceived. A person is thought to have the ancestral powers (*guruwari*) of that ancestor inside him, and these powers are also thought to have entered his or her mother at that place. In this sense, it is through the object world, the country with its stores of ancestral power, that the human subject is brought into being. Conversely, as we have seen, the ancestral subject brings the object world (and its inherent potency and fertility) into being out of himself.

In the imaginations of both Walbiri and Pitjantjatjara, the country consists of a network of places joined by various ancestral routes, as well as by routes over which Aborigines travel in hunting and gathering. The spatial order is parcelled out into discrete sites consisting of defined topographical features, and having identifying names; the sites are owned by different patrilineal groups and in this sense geographical space is socially segmented. This world of forms (a visually defined, named and socially segmented order) laid down by ancestral beings, mediates the relationship between the untrammelled creativity of ancestors and the dependent receptivity of living human beings who care for the ancestral products.

THE CONTENT OF TRANSFORMATIONS

I shall now look in more detail at some specific features of transformations in the ideology and myths of the two societies. My aim is not to provide a close comparison of the two, but to bring out different points about transformations available in my data for the two societies.

Pitjantjatjara. In addition to specific expressions of metamorphosis (for example, that the ancestor became a rocky hill or stone, *buliringu*) Pitjantjatjara also have a general transformative notion conveyed by the term *burga-ri*, which means that an ancestor was changed from a mobile being to a permanent feature of the country.[14] Informants emphasize that this term is not to be precisely equated with the usual terms for dying, *ilu-* or *wiya-ri* (became nothing), for the ancestor did not 'become nothing'; rather, he went into the waterhole and 'became the country'.

In general, imprinting of a place implies the bodily metamorphosis of an ancestor as well. For example, where an ancestor sat down, a waterhole, his imprint, results. Informants commonly give as a meaning for the spiral-concentric circle in designs the phrase *djugurba nyinantja* (the ancestor who was sitting; where the ancestor sat down). The circle can also be explained as 'buttocks' (*maṇa*) and more generally as 'body' (*bundu*). The camp is the place where the ancestor sat down; it *is* the ancestor, his body.

Notions of the body and body parts are constantly assimilated to notions of topographical forms. For example, in explaining to me the use of terms for the design-marked stones and boards kept at the sacred sites, one man pointed to the wood of a fire to illustrate the wooden objects (*gulbidja*), and to stones on the ground to illustrate the stone objects (*djalgarara*).[15] The ancestors, he explained, *burgaringu*; they became respectively wood (*bunuringu*) and stones (*buliringu*); both types of objects are *bundu*, the ancestor's body.

The media of the sacred stones and boards or 'churinga' (i.e. the stone and wood) ties them in very closely with the country itself in Pitjantjatjara thinking. Moreover, as I have pointed out, they are stored in the crevices and caves at sacred sites. In one instance they were themselves referred to as 'camps' (*ngura*) or 'country'.

In addition, they are closely identified with the progeny (*guranidja*)[16] left by ancestors at the sacred places. *Guranidja* are said to be 'like *gulbidja*' but they are also people. For example, one man drew a picture of the *guranidja* of a corkwood ancestor as a number of ovoid forms placed within a large slightly rectangular shape representing a rockhole at a particular site. He identified the circles as being *guranidja*, *wadi djuḍa* (many men) as well as the nectar of the corkwood flower, and remarked that *guranidja* are like *gulbidja*. The *guranidja* concept thus condenses within it the notion of persons on the one hand (and also procreative power) and object form on the other.

In the important myth of the two kangaroos and the owl who travelled across the country together, the kangaroos are said to have pulled *guranidja* or 'many men' out of their chests, leaving some of them behind at each place to which they travelled. In one instance these were depicted by the concentric circles for 'camps' or rockholes. In this and the previous case the fundamental transformational principle is reiterated with an intervening term: the ancestral emanations are progeny, but the progeny are also merged with the forms of the object world.

Just as the notions of ancestral progeny are objectified, so also living individuals or the particular remembered dead may be 'thought of' in the guise of ancestral transformations, or as being the *djugurba* (i.e. ancestors) at a particular place. For example, one young man drew a site connected with certain grub ancestors in which he represented the grubs as oval sacred stones incised with grub designs lying by a waterhole at the site. Pointing to these stones he said: 'My father, my old man (*djilbi*) is lying down.' He was referring to his own father, an old man who was still living; the drawing represented a major site of his ancestral (patrilineal) homeland.[17] The ancestral subject and the living subject, the young man's father, were both assimilated into his conception of the stones.

There is thus a constant assimilation of subject to object, whether the ancestral side of the time barrier is referred to, or the human, present day side. The country is redolent with the transient beings who have occupied it. Subjective identifications with the object world are symbolically expressed by the absorption of notions of 'persons' into the meanings of objects. While the Aborigines conceive of a split between the ancestral and human modes of subjectivity and 'will', the two are, as it were, *reintegrated* within the object itself.[18]

This reintegration is expressed in other ways. Pitjantjatjara sometimes say of a dead person that he or she *burgaringu*, the rationale being that having 'sat down' at a particular place the individual left something of himself there. Commenting on the *gulbidja* boards and their designs, one old man said that the ancestors *burgaringu* and so after them did the men of the past: 'Many dead men afterward became country at that place, ancestors'. Referring to the dead as *guranidja*, he remarked further that the first *guranidja* died and so after them successive generations until finally only the last (i.e. current) generations remain. On this view all the generations of dead are successively transformed into country; as the mode of being involving conscious will and awareness is eclipsed, the subject takes on the determinate, unchanging structure of the object world.

At death the living relinquish their claims to a country, and it is their patrilineal descendants who must care for it and guard the ancestral relics. Yet they are also bound within the country, and in this sense they maintain a perpetual claim upon it, a claim which is itself epitomized in the originating ancestor's permanent ties to the country through transformation. But the notion of ancestral transformation can actually be seen as expressing both aspects of this complex relationship because of what I have called its bi-directional structure. I would suggest that the transformation asserts the inalienable rights of ancestral landowners (they are contained within the country) at the same time that it expresses the transmission of control from the ancestors to the heirs (the object world or country is disengaged from the ancestor's mortal person, and the latter disappears).

In this view, the ancestral acts of transformation express in mythic form the devolution of rights over the country which occurs at death. The type of inheritance they epitomize is one through which the deceased and the heirs are perpetually bound together within a vital social relationship. We shall find later that in some Walbiri myths the idea of transformation as a process of inheritance is quite explicitly suggested.

Because of the nature of this 'inheritance', alienation of any part of the country from the rightful heirs is a violation of the essence of the moral order. It is a *desecration*, not merely a theft. This point emerges more clearly if we glance briefly at Pitjantjatjara notions about the grounds of 'lawful' behaviour.

Contemporary Pitjantjatjara use the English term 'law' in expressions such as *wadigu law* (the law of man) to refer to their traditional modes of life: all customary and socially sanctioned (thus 'lawful') behaviour patterns. The same concept may be phrased as *mirigu law*, the law of the dead; *tjamugu law*, the law of [our] grandfathers. The equivalent native term for 'law' is *djugurba* (i.e. the term for ancestors and ancestral times). The country and the sacred boards and stones are viewed as the very foundations of this law. As one man said: 'The law is the *gulbidja*.' In the words of another: '[They are] the law of the dead; the ancestor became country.'

Violation of the country is a violation of the very essence of the 'law of the dead'. Put in Durkheimian terms it involves a desecration of the symbols which contain the socio-moral heritage, for the moral imperatives of the dead are bound within the country through their transformation.

Thus when the ancestors created the country they laid down a world of determinate forms not only in the senses suggested earlier (see above), but also in that they created the constraining moral imperatives, the 'lawful' behaviour patterns or mores, of the traditional society. The human individual is therefore born into a world that is wholly formed: visually defined, named, socially segmented and morally constraining.

Walbiri. Like the Pitjantjatjara, Walbiri think of the 'law', the 'straight way' (*djugaruru*), as having been laid down by the ancestors. Their views of metamorphosis and imprint are also similar, and like the former, they think of the ancestral camp as becoming some particular geographical feature, usually a hill or waterhole. This notion may be combined with that of the metamorphosis of particular parts of an ancestor's body: for example, the breasts of certain ancestral women (their camps) changed into hills. Various activities of an ancestor yield topographical forms: for instance, a possum ancestor dragging his tail behind him as he travels makes a creek (his tail print; also the metamorphosed form of his tail). In general, *guruwari*, country (*walja*) and body (*balga*) are bound up together in Walbiri thought.

Transformation and Inter-generational Transmission

I shall consider here some distinctive incidents of transformation pertaining to certain ceremonial artifacts. In one Walbiri account of some kangaroo, possum and other ancestors who travelled through Walbiri country to a site far to the south,[19] the kangaroo was said to have danced on the fire. As he did so, he took out of his stomach a string cross which he showed to many people. He and all these people then disappeared within the country, and human beings (*jaba jidjaru*, people of today, real people) came and picked up the string cross.

Speaking of string crosses belonging to another kangaroo ancestor, one Walbiri man stated that the kangaroo carried crosses with him along the track and when he finally went in said: 'Body [*balga*, also meaning here, a large important object] I carry, left behind [*jambidja*]. You now become "boss".' This man, who belonged to the Walbiri lodge which controls the important 'Two Kangaroo' ancestors, was referring directly to the patrilineal transmission of rights over ceremonial objects.

In the first incident the cross is 'born' from the kangaroo who then dies: the combination of elements of birth and death is very apparent in this transformation. In both instances the whole triadic relationship, *ancestral subject-object-human subject*, is contained within the accounts of the myths; the recession of the ancestor's will and authority as a living being is locked into the human assumption of authority ('You now become boss').

At the same time, ancestral authority is not rescinded, since its moral force is embedded in the transformation. For example, one man remarked that if too many strangers (he was referring here to non-Aborigines) should see the string crosses of his patri-lodge,[20] 'I might lose my country'. The string cross would, in his view, 'strike' (*bagani*) the Walbiri people because of this sacrilege. Major ceremonial objects are sometimes said to be able to strike or kill persons committing sacrilege, the main premise being that it is *djugurba*, the ancestors, who administer the punishment *via* the object. In this respect, the object is explicitly thought of as being imbued with the moral force or will of the ancestor. It is a *djudju wiri* (powerful sacra).

The notion that the ancestor pulled something out of his body which was left behind also occurs in my data in connection with the two Walingari men who pulled out of their bodies the leafy *widi* poles (their penes) used in boys' initiation ceremonies. One man explained that they had then 'lost' (*wadjiwadji manu*) them when they 'went in'. Men also make this reference to 'losing' in connection with patrilineal inheritance. For example, one man, speaking of the ancestral sites in his lodge, said that they first belonged to his father's father (*waringi*) and then to his father (*girana*): 'My father lost them, the living then hold them.'[21] According to another man, a father might say to his son when the latter was first seeing totemic 'increase' ceremonies: 'I might die, you must hold this *djugurba* for me.'

Thus the kangaroo transformations recounted above suggest the beginning of an inter-generational chain of transmission requiring the original separation of the object from the ancestral holder. If we imagine the cross (or any ancestral transformation) being inherited along a chain from father to son, then each man plays successive roles of *heir* and *donor*. As *heir* he is recipient of rights over objects which have been controlled by previous generations, most immediately by his father's generation, and is therefore in a passive position. In effect, he is subordinated to the determinate socio-moral order represented by the authority of the senior generation, and the ancestral inheritance of which these men are the *donors*. As *donor*, or potential donor, he moves into the position of authority, becoming in this respect ancestor-like, a transmitter (or potential transmitter) of objects which are now permeated with his own will and authority, as well as those of previous generations.

The object itself integrates the two roles, functioning as the pivot of the subordinating-receptive experience (inculcated most obviously in the important male circumcision ceremonies) and the superordinating one which is developed in masculine adulthood. The latter involves full participation in the ancestral cult, including identification with the ancestor in dances dramatizing his activities.[22]

The process through which sacra and ritual rights over the country are transmitted between the generations begins for a boy at circumcision when sacra are revealed to him for the first time. Since it is at this ceremony that he is separated from his family of orientation and publicly acquires affines (or potential affines), he now first enters the intergenerational chain as a potential father.

This is not the place to discuss the initiation ceremonies, but a brief comment on the revelation of sacra to the novice may be relevant. The string crosses may serve as an example, since these objects are prominent amongst the sacra first revealed to a boy at this time. Meggitt (1962: 302) describes the highly dramatic scene where the boy is first brought into contact with a string cross which has been passed in the air above the heads of a line of dancers: 'As it hovers above the foremost dancer, the boy is told to open his eyes. At that moment two brothers snatch him up and press his chest against the design on the cross to enable the lodge patrispirit to enter him. The savage, guttural chanting rises to a crescendo . . .'

This sort of situation, in which the boy, generally in a dazed condition, is brought into bodily contact with the sacra, reverses the physical, bodily relation between an ancestor and his transformations. Whereas the ancestor's powers and being are transferred to the object, here the powers of the object are imprinted in the novice; whereas the ancestral situation involves an autonomous creation, here the boy is wholly submissive, subordinated to his seniors.

Walbiri think of initiation as a kind of dying (cf. Meggitt 1962:294). The novice is then 'reborn' into a world where he may begin to participate in ceremonials involving the re-creation and control of ancestral transformations. Similarly, as we have seen, ancestral transformation has associations with notions of death and birth, loss or relinquishment and benefaction. In both initiation and transformation there is a passage out of the temporal locus of experience into an identification with atemporal objectifications, but from polarized positions in the temporal scheme, as well as polarized statuses in the social order. The ancestor releases his creative power and authority within his objectifications, while the boy, through initiatory passage, enters into the early phases of masculine adulthood and potential authority by means of identification with these objects.

It is interesting to find the theme of inter-generational transmission directly connected with the concept of transformation in a myth belonging to Walbiri women rather than to men and associated with women's ceremonies.[23] In the account, two old women go down to a fire and, burning to death on it, are transformed into charcoal. As they burn they sing: 'Take up the fire, take up the charcoal.' According to my informants this means that the fire speaks and says that the younger women should take up the bodies of the old women and paint designs with them on their own bodies. Thus the sacra (the charcoal) transmitted between the generations is the objectified, immortalized 'body' of the dead. The myth is most explicit in emphasizing that the transformation is a gift from the older to the younger women; indeed, it appears as an active relinquishment of self.

Transformation and Birth

There are a variety of associations between transformation and fecundity in Walbiri myth, but I shall discuss only one sort of connection here: that between ancestral progeny and certain sacred, oval boards.

Boards called in general *julguruguru* or by other more specialized names are commonly equated with ancestral progeny. The latter are usually thought of as metamorphoses of the boards. For example, the *Jaribiri* snake ancestor carried design-marked boards on his head, as men wear ceremonial headdresses today; as he travelled along from place to place he danced wearing the boards. But men think of these objects as being both the ribs of the snake (i.e. part of his body) and also his progeny. One man suggested that they were 'wood first' (*wadijawi*) and 'then became people' (*jabadjaridjalgu*). There is then a series, *subject → object → subject*; the boards objectify both the parent (father snake) and the child. Here again two sorts of subject (parent-child, ancestor-people) are integrated within the object, the latter functioning as the ground of their mutuality and yet the emblem of their separation. The snake dancing with the boards is ceremonializing both his own objectification and that of the subsequent generations, his progeny.

Another myth illustrates a similar series with certain special features. Some of the basic elements, abstracted from one man's account, are as follows (transformations relevant to the argument are italicized):

> At the request of his sons, a father snake *emits from his body oval design-marked boards* called *julguruguru*. These *boards change into women* who with their digging sticks dance along from place to place creating waterholes with the impress of their digging sticks into which their many progeny go. They are followed by two men [the sons?] who pick up the *faeces emitted by these women which are also sacred boards* of various kinds (including *julguruguru*). The men make headdresses of these boards and dance with them, but every night when they go into the women's camp to sleep with them they leave these headdresses outside the camp so that the women will not see them. These events constitute the core of the narrative and recur at each site along the track.

Here we have different sorts of transformations in a series: *subject* (*snake*) externalizes *objects* (*boards*) which become *subjects* (*women*) who externalize *objects* (*boards that are also body parts, faeces*).[24] This pattern of thinking parallels the one suggested in the Jaribiri snake example, but extends it in form:

| Jaribiri snake | ribs | = | boards | = | children | |
| Father snake | emits objects from holes in body | = | boards | = | women emit faeces | = boards |

In these examples the transformational process is closely associated with the reproductive one. The women are the children of the father snake who are emitted from his body in the form of boards, while the boards emitted by the women would also appear to be *their* progeny in object form. The transformations in this and the Jaribiri myth well illustrate the underlying assumption that a subject 'contains' an objectifying potential within it and, conversely, the object 'contains' a subjective aspect or potential.

An important feature of the myth about the women is that the boards the women emit are left behind them and are then picked up by the men. The situation is reminiscent of the incident in the kangaroo myth:

| kangaroo takes out of stomach | string cross | leaves cross behind; 'goes in' | human beings (men) take up |
| women emit | oval boards | leave boards behind; travel on | men take up and dance with them |

The women 'lose' the boards to the men who take them up and dance with them, rigorously keeping them from the women (as of course men do today). The narrator of this myth, identifying with the ancestral men (whom he referred to as members of his own subsection), actually illustrated himself dancing with the boards. Thus it is living men who inherit the boards of the ancestral women, and have the right to dance with them.

If we take the boards as being progeny of the women and as also containing the women's substance within them, then what the men take over is the objectified form of the 'women-children'—that is, they take control of the immortal, objective aspect epitomized in the sacred boards. It is the men of the patrilineage who celebrate and transmit this permanent objectification in ceremonial.[25] The corporeal, sentient aspect, on the other hand, is associated with the heterosexual intercourse of the camp.

Although I cannot adequately develop the point here, it may be suggested that the women's loss of their boards in the myth is parallel to their loss of the novice to the male corporation at initiation; in addition, the compulsive separation of the boards and the women in this account can best be understood through considering the dynamic of male initiation ceremonies. In Walbiri initiation, adult identity is developed by two articulated and opposed processes: that of separating the boy from the women on the one hand, and of revealing to him certain ancestral objects on the other. These objectifications come to incorporate the novice's new masculine identity at the same time that the old one of childhood is displaced.

Although the process is accompanied by overt instructions to the boy that he should never reveal these sacra to women, the compulsion for maintaining these separations would appear to be built into the patterning of the process itself: just as the boy's identity must be disengaged from its childhood identification with his mother (and by extension with other women), so the new foci of identification (the ancestral objects) must contain a boundary-maintaining 'tabu' which keeps them apart from women. Thus the positive 'moral binding' inherent in the process of identification with these ancestral transformations contains negative controls on sex relationships and roles.

Summary and Conclusion

The most obvious feature of Walbiri and Pitjantjatjara transformations is that they form a bridge between a sentient being or subject, and the non-sentient object world. I have suggested that they have a bi-directional structure: on the one hand, they permanently incorporate the substance of a subject; on the other hand, they are detached from him as 'external objects', permanently present or artificially renewable outside him. Transcending individual subjectivity, they are also permanently bound to it as its objectifications.

In Aboriginal thought the object world was first created freely by the ancestors out of themselves. Since each generation must come to experience these forms as self-objectifications, it is not simply the ancestral transformations, the objects themselves, which are perpetuated over time, but also the underlying pattern of transformation—its bi-directional structure—which through a continuous process of subject-object identification is reiterated in each generation. There is, however, a fundamental difference in the relationship to the object which distinguishes ancestral and human objectification: the human being participates in objectifications already created by the ancestors, and bound to them. For human subjects, objects which come to embody 'intimations of themselves' already contain 'intimations of others'—who are superordinate to them and precede them in time.

In these societies, land or 'country', and certain objects that refer back to the country, are the focus of descent group inheritance. I have suggested that this property itself, as ancestral transformation, is an icon of a particular kind of inter-generational transmission: the transformation's bi-directional structure suggests the holder's relinquishment of a claim to the country at the same time that his permanent claim to it (expressed as identity of substance) is maintained. The country is like a *lingua franca* which 'translates' all the generations into a common currency.

If we ask in what this 'currency' consists, the most obvious answer, of course, is the Durkheimian one: it is the collective socio-moral order with its grounding in seniority and the past which has been objectified as the determinate, compelling forms of the external environment. But it is possible to deepen this interpretation. For it would seem that what is being inherited *via* ancestral transformations is not simply the moral order and authority structure itself, but also the *a priori* grounds upon which the possibilities of this order are built.

On this view, it is a fundamental *mode of orientation* to objects in which experience of self is firmly anchored in objective forms incorporating moral constraints, that is being transmitted down the generations. These fixed attitudes about the relationship of human subjectivity to the external order are pre-requisite to the transmission of the Aboriginal 'law'; without them, the moral patterns of Aboriginal culture cannot be adequately communicated or maintained. Put in another way, it is not merely a particular kind of object and meaning content which is being transmitted, but also a particular form or mode of experiencing the world in which symbols of collectivity are constantly recharged with intimations of self. Without the assurance of this mode of experience, the moral content cannot be effectively learned, or its 'force' internalized.

How then shall we interpret the psychological grounds of this orientational mode? An older Anthropology regarded orientations of this type as indicative of a 'confusion of categories' or a failure to distinguish the subjective from the objective, the self from the object world.[26] On the contrary, it should be apparent from the present analysis that this orientation is grounded in the awareness of subject-object distinctions. Indeed, it seems obvious enough that it is merely a recasting in institutionalized form of certain general psychological processes of individual development: on the one hand, the separation of the self from external reality which is a necessary part of the maturation and socialization process; on the other hand, the symbolic reincorporation of the self into the external world which occurs through the infusion of this world with ego's subjective life experience. As a result of this projective process, the material world comes to provide the individual with images or 'fragments' of himself. In the normal personality these 'images' are recognized as being outside the person and separate from him, and yet are experienced as inextricably bound up with him. Furthermore, one may expect in traditional societies, where the life span is usually locked into a limited geographical space, and where new artifacts do not constantly swell the existing repertory, that the symbolic potential of the material environment will be intensified.

The Aboriginal world view institutionalizes these individual experiences of separation and incorporation, fixing the symbolic foci and standardizing the experiences in particular beliefs which bind the individuals to common imaginative centres. The material world as 'collective symbol' stands over and apart from the self because it is a socialized phenomenon stabilizing within it the authority and precedence of 'other selves'. In identifying with it, therefore, ego's symbolic reintegration with the external world involves a co-ordinate integration with these 'alters'. As long as an individual can anchor his own identity in ancestral transformations, this anchorage binds him to the authority of previous generations, and hence to the wider group. Basic psychological processes are thus utilized in a system of social control, and the perpetual reinforcement of these processes *within the specified sociological frame* becomes requisite to the maintenance of the controls themselves.

I would suggest that basic differences between this type of traditional world view and that of 'modern' industrial society derive from the institutionalization in the former of the individual's symbolic orientation to a relatively closed environmental space, and from the functioning of this self-related orientation as a key structure in social control. As the sociologist Thomas Luckmann has observed (1967:102) in a trenchant study of religion in industrial society, the world view or 'sacred cosmos of industrial societies' is not constituted by a coherent system but by an 'assortment of religious representations' or 'themes'. The individual selects some themes from this pool and 'builds them into a somewhat precarious private system of "ultimate" significance'. Rather than a singular, socially centred or institutionalized symbolic universe, there is an indefinite number of individually centred, overlapping and labile symbolic universes which are no longer formed in 'approximation of an "official" model'.

An aspect of Walbiri and Pitjantjatjara world view which is critical to its regulatory functions is the split inherent in the Aboriginal concept of time. The temporal split can be seen as a model for the disposition of autonomy or 'will' and submission in the Aboriginal concept of self. The ancestral order is treated as the locus of autonomous free creativity set off from the Aborigines, hidden away as it were within the determinate forms of existence (literally, 'inside' the country). Since it is conceived of as being split off from the individual and outside him, bound to the ancestral past, this autonomy has to be reintegrated into the individual through identification with the external world—that is, through submission to the ancestral 'givens' of existence. Its attainment can never be separated from receptive submission to a given order of things. In this sense, subjective integration is forced into the external social field.

Each person regards himself as having been born with some ancestral components inside him through identifications occurring at conception or birth, and so he is immediately bound, as if by *fiat*, to an external authority structure. But the most important stress upon this external locus of autonomy occurs at male initiation[27] where the new identity of the novice is fashioned through submission to external authority combined with identifications with newly revealed sacra.

The most central acts of creative autonomy and potency occur within male cult where the individual constructs or renews ancestral objects and may play the role of his own ancestors in dramatic performance. Through these operations, in which he becomes 'ancestor-like', he can contribute in certain ceremonies to the reconstitution, or life maintenance, of the people, flora and fauna of the countryside—that is, to the maintenance of the country itself. In this respect the subject-object 'movement' reverses to its original ancestral direction: the living person becomes the originating source of the external world. Put in Walbiri terms, the objectifying movement is from 'inside' the subject to 'outside' him (cf. above). But the forms to which the individual gives visible shape (either through construction or performance) are forms in which, as we have seen, subjectivity has already been externalized, and which belong to the creative locus 'outside' the individual actor and 'inside' the country. These forms consist, therefore, of already constituted links between ego and alter, between the subject and the external object world, rather than novel objectifications of self.

Thus closure is effected: forms that emerge from within individual will—that are produced by the human actor as extensions of himself—are perceived as having their primary locus within the previously formed object world outside him. In this way the ritual actions fix creative autonomy to determinacy in a closed system of permanent symbolism.

NOTES

1. Field research amongst the Walbiri, supported by a Fulbright grant and sponsored by the Australian National University, was carried out at Yuendumu Government Settlement, 1956-57. My work with the Pitjantjatjara (also 'Pitjandjara' in the literature) was supported by the Australian Institute of Aboriginal Studies and carried out at Areyonga Government Settlement, 1964-65.* The people at Areyonga are primarily northern Pitjantja-speaking peoples who traditionally inhabited the Petermann Range region of the Western Desert; my data refer to this dialect group only.

2. The detailed mythological interpretation of the countryside is well illustrated in the photographs and Aboriginal commentaries provided by C. P. Mountford (1965) for a major site in the desert region.

3. I am grateful to Dr Terence Turner for helpful suggestions regarding the development of the subject-object theme, and for the label 'bi-directional' which I use to describe the structure of the transformations.

4. In this paper I use the following orthography: the b-d-g series transcribes native plosives, dentals and glottals rather than the p-t-k series; the palatal, y, is rendered in the common Australian transcription j.

5. These terms are more fully discussed in Munn 1964.

6. Identifications or equations may be expressed by terms meaning 'same' (Walbiri, *djindadjugu*; Pitjantja, *balurudu*), or simply by saying, for example, 'waterhole, body' meaning 'the waterhole *is* the body'.

7. They may, for example, have designs representing features of the countryside on them, and/or they may be thought of as lodged at sacred sites, etc.

8. Cf. Gould 1968:113. Referring to Western Desert (Ngatatjara) beliefs he says: 'It is an essential characteristic of totemic beings that these transformations [into stone, ridges, rockholes, etc.]' are made 'by themselves (*yungara*)'.

9. See Munn (in press) for a discussion of the importance of 'inside' and 'outside' in Walbiri thought.

10. In what follows I shall be concerned primarily with the question of masculine identity, since it is men who are most intensely socialized in these societies through the agency of symbolic objects, and it is from men that, given the secrecy of male cult, information regarding ceremonial objects must be acquired. The basic structure of the world, however, and its socio-moral implications are part of the common culture, as is the basic imagery of transformation.

11. Parts of this section and of the later section on the 'content of Pitjantjatjara transformations', are adapted from my (unpublished) research report to the Australian Institute of Aboriginal Studies (Munn 1965). The report also contains more detail on the social organization and on variations in the nature of the landowning units which I do

not take up here. On landowning, ritual and residential groupings in the Western Desert, see Berndt (1959).

12. On the distinction between ritual and economic relationships of people to land in some parts of Australia see Hiatt (1962) and Stanner (1965).

13. Northern Pitjantjatjara do not use the section or subsection system (see Munn 1965). In Walbiri society the principle of patriliny also receives more structural elaboration and emphasis than amongst the Pitjantjatjara, since the Walbiri recognize father-son patri-couples of subsections categorizing the patrilineal groups, as well as patrimoieties. Particular places and ancestors are classified according to the subsection couple of the actual owners, and men of this couple and the relevant patrimoiety as a whole regard themselves as classificatory owners.

14. According to the southern Pitjantjatjara vocabulary lists from the mission at Ernabella the term *burga* means 'cool'. My informants suggested various explanations: e.g. that the ancestor went inside the water (i.e. he changed into the waterhole and thus the locality); another suggestion was that the term implied 'having become tired he sits down'. In general, *burga-ri* is always used with reference to ancestors or the ancestral dead, and conveys the notion of transformation into natural features.

15. *Gulbidja* may also be used as a cover term for both stone and wooden objects. *Djalgarara* (possibly an Aranda loan term?) is less common.

16. The term *gurunba*, which refers to the life source within human beings, may also be used.

17. Gould (1968:114) says that his Ngatatjara guides to a sacred site in the Western Desert, approaching a rock at the site, addressed it as 'my father'. Here the kin term no doubt has a primary reference to the ancestor himself, but one can see how memories of specific individuals (e.g. 'my *own* father') who have been associated in the individual's mind with the sites, can become objectified and lodged in the ancestral objects; certainly, the ritualized use of the kin term (and the modifying possessive) for the ancestor in this context reinforces the sort of specification in the individual's private experience that is illustrated by my informant's conception of the grub 'churinga' as his own father.

18. The practice of pressing sacra against the individual's body provides an example of how these identifications can be expressed and reinforced in ritual action. Mountford (1962:398) remarks, for example, that Pitjantjatjara men press sacred boards against them to obtain some of their ancestral potency. Here the potency of the object passes into the subject, and conversely, the individual is identified with the object. In this sense the person's identity becomes symbolically lodged in the object, just as the ancestral potency becomes lodged in the subject. See also the Walbiri use of string crosses at initiation on which I comment in this paper.

19. This myth was associated with ceremonies which had recently (as of 1957) come into Walbiri country from the Pintubi to the south. The site referred to in the myth was apparently in the country of Western Desert peoples south of the Pintubi. The Pitjantjatjara also use string crosses and identify them with the country, as do the Walbiri.

20. String crosses are not restricted to particular ancestors; all ancestors may be represented in this way.

21. The term *maḍa* means 'to hold' or 'care for'. It does not imply permanent possession.

22. A man constructs and decorates the ancestral objects of groups of the opposite patrimoiety, and dances decorated with designs and carrying (or wearing on his head) the sacra of his own patrilineal group.

23. The ceremonies referred to are the well-known *Jawalju* ceremonies which women may perform for various purposes including love magic, but also in association with men's initiation ceremonies. (As far as I know, there is no initiation for women in the specific

area in which I have worked.) The particular designs referred to belonged to women of one section of the Yuendumu community. Women's designs are not transmitted through lineal descent groups, and the inter-generational transmission referred to in the myth is not connected with a lineal principle of inheritance.

24. The waterholes the women make with their digging sticks are also, of course, transformations. However, I am not concerned here with an interpretation of the myth as a whole, only with some suggestions regarding the board transformations. It may be noted that the *julguruguru* boards, which figure prominently in the myth, have wide ramifications in Walbiri thought, and are generally associated with women and procreation.

25. Men also say that they are taking care of the ritual and sacra for the female members of the descent group, even though the latter may not participate directly.

26. This view has recently been reconsidered and criticized by Mary Douglas (1966:80 *et seq.*), but a cogent discussion and refutation is to be found in A. I. Hallowell (1955:75 *et seq.*). According to Hallowell, 'self awareness is a major component of the personality structure of man' (p. 110). By 'self-awareness' Hallowell means the ability of the adult individual 'to identify himself and refer to himself in contradistinction to other selves and things, to represent himself to himself . . .' (p. 82). This awareness, Hallowell suggests, is developed concomitantly with the separation of the self from the external world which occurs in maturation; it is on this psychological basis that man builds up symbolisms that express the relationship between his own nature and that of the outside world.

27. I have commented only on Walbiri initiation here, but, of course, both societies have circumcision ceremonies for males. For one brief description of *southern* Pitjantjatjara initiation, see Tindale (1935).

* I am also indebted to the American Philosophical Society for a travel grant aiding this research.

References

Berndt, R. M. 1959 The Concept of the Tribe in the Western Desert, *Oceania*, Vol. 30:81-107.
Douglas, M. 1966 *Purity and Danger*. Routledge and Kegan Paul, London.
Gould, R. 1968 Living Archaeology: The Ngatatjara of Western Australia, *Southwestern Journal of Anthropology*, Vol. 24:101-22.
Hallowell, A. I. 1955 *Culture and Experience*. University of Pennsylvania Press, Philadelphia.
Hiatt, L. 1962 Local Organization among the Australian Aborigines, *Oceania*, Vol. 32: 267-86.
Luckmann, T. 1967 *The Invisible Religion*. Macmillan, New York.
Mauss, M. 1954 *The Gift* (I. Cunnison, trans.). Cohen and West, London.
Meggitt, M. 1962 *Desert People*. Angus and Robertson, Sydney.
Mountford, C. 1962 Sacred Objects of the Pitjandjara Tribe, Western Central Australia, *Records of the South Australian Museum*, Vol. 14, No. 2.
―――― 1965 *Ayers Rock, Its People, Their Beliefs and Their Art*. Angus and Robertson, Sydney.
Munn, N. 1964 Totemic Designs and Group Continuity in Walbiri Cosmology. In *Aborigines Now* (M. Reay, ed.). Angus and Robertson, Sydney.
―――― 1965 A Report on Field Research at Areyonga. (Mimeo.) Australian Institute of Aboriginal Studies.

Munn, N. The Spatial Presentation of Cosmic Order in Walbiri Iconography. In press (Wenner-Gren Symposium).

Stanner, W. 1965 Aboriginal Territorial Organization: Estate, Range, Domain and Regime, *Oceania*, Vol. 36:1-26.

Tindale, N. 1935 Initiation among the Pitjandjara Natives of the Mann and Tomkinson Ranges in South Australia, *Oceania*, Vol. 6:199-224.

MARIE REAY

A Decision as Narrative

Aboriginal communities in Australia adjust to the intrusion of an investigator by incorporating him or her into their kinship system and any other systems they have of classifying themselves and each other. This paper tries to explain why the women of Borroloola put me into one subsection rather than any other, suggests a particular narrative method for studying the making and the implementing of decisions, and presents evidence that Aboriginal women use the narrative of myth as a model for social action. I offer it here for the light that events in a non-traditional system may bring to the possibilities inherent in the traditional system.

I

Borroloola lacked all the qualities Herbert Read attributed to a good adventure story: 'speed, suspense, visibility, with the incidental details standing out significantly'. There were arrivals and departures, but my notes of what else occurred read more like jottings for a landscape with figures than a dynamic account of on-going events. When the sullen, tittering women accepted the fact that I was there to stay, they told me I belonged now to Nangalama subsection.[1] Why Nangalama? I asked, but the only explanation they would give me was that anyone could tell by looking at me that I was Nangalama. My physical imperfections, which they enumerated ruthlessly, were typical of Nangalama women and they told me, looking me straight in the eye, that women of this subsection always tended to be 'a little bit silly'.

My allocation to a subsection signalled my acceptance as one of the still figures in the landscape. This was evidently a consensual decision taken by the women themselves, or by some of them, without reference to the men. Since I could not find out, from a reconstruction of how they had reached this decision, what had led them to make it, I have looked at the activities they performed regularly in the absence of men to find an explanation. Their hunting expeditions were no good for this purpose because the men could, and occasionally did, come along.

I was studying the women's secret ceremonies, which included the mythologically based *yawalyu* songs and dances and also provided a context for the singing of *ilbindji* love songs and the performance of love magic.[2] Women who had lovers, women who wanted to obtain certain men as their lovers, and women who wanted other women to accept them as lovers co-operated with one another in holding an intensive series of *yawalyu*. A mission based on the other side of the river had forbidden the women to hold their secret ceremonies, and they compromised by obeying this edict on the days of the week when the missionary crossed the river. They were well aware that a few sly mission converts would report their indulgence in these sports of Satan, but this did not deter them from the task of arranging repetitive *yawalyu*. How did the women arrange this task of holding a secret ceremony? How was the wish of one or two women transformed into a collective decision, a plan of action?

At least the arrangement of a task moved the figures across the landscape. A study of these movements *could* turn out to be a 'tremendous trifle', like the postponement for the obvious cure for Chesterton's complete ignorance and profound curiosity about what he would find in his pocket. On the other hand, there was a chance that it might turn out to be the perfect simple case, a demonstration of something always reiterated but rarely practised in Aboriginal studies, that Anthropology is concerned with the minutiae of social life, that the humdrum, the mundane, the trivial, is worth serious study. Confronted with Australian Aboriginal society, giants of the discipline like Durkheim, Radcliffe-Brown and Lévi-Strauss have tried in their several ways to draw sufficient conclusions from insufficient premisses. The complexities of marriage arrangements and religion have dominated the anthropological depiction of Aboriginal society. Edmund Wilson's comment on Proust's greatest novel, that it is a symphonic structure rather than a narrative in the ordinary sense, is precisely applicable to the monumental work on Aboriginal religion, Stanner's elegant analysis of myth and ritual. But Aboriginal religion is a large and dramatic topic for study. There were no large and dramatic topics available for study at Borroloola unless I hoped to draw sufficient conclusions from insufficient premisses. We know that involvement in change is an ordinary, predictable condition of society so long as it is autonomous, which the still landscape of Borroloola was certainly not. We can only begin to understand it when we see it as the base for a ranging ethnic segment of the wider society of the Gulf-Barkly Tablelands region. Important Aboriginal choices were taken care of by the terrible triad of official authoritarianism, mission interference and employer demands. The purposive element had been largely lifted from their activities. The presence of the ration depot boss, with his ultimate threat that they could be deprived of the means of life on displaying forbidden behaviours, and of the missionary with his shaming habit of publicly denouncing backsliders, was the lid on the pot of their sluggishly simmering discontent. The pot boiled over in a boomerang fight in 1962 during the temporary absence of the boss of the ration depot, but ordinarily only a wisp of steam escaped from under the lid as an individual saw some private advantage in reporting other people's defections to the authorities. It was a sick segment of the wider society. It illustrates an analogy that can easily be drawn between certain characteristics of contemporary Aboriginal society and a mob of uninformed individuals wandering aimlessly about the restricted environment of a psychiatric ward.

II

My Borroloola material grew up as a poor relation of my New Guinea material—a little bit thin, showing symptoms of fact deficiency. I am therefore suggesting a thin model to deal with the durations of decision-making: a trifle, perhaps, but not a 'tremendous trifle' if it steers clear of specifying temporal vectors in section, or the orchestration of retrospect and expectation in overlapping durations, or any other complexities that could easily overload it. The narration of a sequence of events or series of actions is a literary matter, and I am suggesting a literary model—a particular kind of story I shall call a 'dramaticule'. A dramaticule is a miniature or insignificant drama. I define 'dramaticule', in the sense of a tool for analysis, as 'a trivial series of actions or course of events connected by a purpose which finds achievement or denial in the final event of the series'. I see it as a particular kind of short story, rather than as a dramatic form, because the three parts into which it divides are not in any sense the acts of a drama. There is the introduction of the characters; next, what they did and said, and what was done and said to them; and finally the outcome. Now let us look at these women who were bucking the missionary's edict and using an unsuspecting anthropologist to help them carry out their evil purposes in the moral theatre of their paltry world.

There were five main characters. I am using fictitious names.

One of these characters was the present narrator of this dramaticule. I shall introduce myself by citing in condensed form a story related by Dr Catherine Berndt (1950:31-2):

> Mabel, a Nangala woman, slept one night at Pigeon Hole, on Victoria River Downs, when the two Mungamunga came and showed her a

ceremony. She considered herself under an obligation to put these rituals into practice. Her daughter, Blanchie, married to a man at Wave Hill, has the duty of 'mustering up' the Wave Hill women to perform the ceremony and see that it is done correctly.

The Mabel of Dr Berndt's story was a Nangala woman, my 'Nangalama', to use the female form of the name. For some reason the women of Borroloola had put me in this subsection. Let us look at Dr Berndt's story as a dramaticule. There are four main characters—Mabel, the two Mungamunga girls, and Mabel's daughter Blanchie. The story mentions Blanchie's husband, but only to account for her association with Wave Hill, not as an additional character in the story. There is also a chorus of women, who are mustered by Blanchie to perform the ceremony. Following Aboriginal versions of what occurred, Dr Berndt does not draw attention to the analytic opposition we ourselves can make between the two 'natural' (i.e. actual and observable) characters, the woman and her daughter, and the two 'supernatural' characters, the Mungamunga girls. Her account does, however, give prominence to the 'mother'-'daughter' opposition, from which it is possible to hypothesize that the mother has a creative or activating role in being chosen by the Mungamunga to reveal this ceremony to earthly women, whilst the daughter has an executive role in getting the ceremony performed and in seeing that it loses nothing in the performance.[3]

The plot of the story is a simple line of communication, the ceremony being conveyed from the Mungamunga to Mabel, from Mabel to Blanchie, and from Blanchie to the chorus of Wave Hill women. The outcome or denouement is the satisfactory performance of the ceremony.

At Borroloola I was the only Nangalama woman who attended all performances of the various *yawalyu* over the relevant period. One result of my becoming Nangalama was that I acquired immediately a mob of 'daughters'. Any woman who could find any excuse for calling a Nangalama 'Mother' called me 'Mummy', no matter what other relationships could be posited. The conclusion was inescapable that the women of Borroloola wanted mothers, and it was very tempting to look for a universalistic psychoanalytic explanation of their putting me in the subsection where I could be mother to most. But this may well be just the idiom they use for expressing something else, as Walbiri symbolization of their natural world in terms identical with Freud's suggests.[4] 'Mother' is not simply the womb-site and the mate of 'father': she gives more than birth to her daughters, as Dr Berndt's story of the *djarada* ceremony attests. Mabel gave Blanchie the responsibility for organizing the ceremony. At Borroloola it was important for this 'mother' to be Nangalama because she could benefit her 'daughters' in ways a non-Nangalama 'mother' could not. But I am anticipating the outcome of the dramaticule. Another relevant feature of the anthropologist as a character in this trivial drama is that I had been making explicit inquiries about women's ceremonies and a girl who was something of an expert on the myths of the Mungamunga was relating them to me whenever I could persuade her to do so by satisfying her addiction to Aspros.

This girl, whom I shall call Clytie, gave beautifully full accounts of the Mungamunga on eleven Aspros each morning. (More than that, I found, made her as silly as a rabbit and her stories unintelligible.) Clytie had a small, slight figure for a woman of the Salt Water tribes whose women had always struck observers as burly and formidable in stature.[5] She was unusually quick in her movements, darting about like a gadfly in the presence of goannas. The other women used to say, when she roused them from their swags with gay invitations to hunting and fishing, that she was 'little bit Mungamunga' herself. The two distinguishing characteristics of the Mungamunga were traits they carried over into everyday life from their prodigious sexual life, namely teasing and devouring. Clytie's physical movements and her manner of initiating encounters with others were as teasing as the Mungamunga were supposed to be. Her devouring quality was harder to document, apart from her performance on the Aspros, but she was a particularly expressive performer in the women's ceremonies, preening her breasts as she danced and portraying in the rhythmic trembling, the shaking, the twisting and always graceful jerking of her lower body all the sex manuals have to say about the orgasm: there was always a stage in Clytie's dance when the attribution of this quality of devouring to the sexual proclivities of the Mungamunga made absolute sense to the observer. Clytie's motives in participating in *yawalyu* and helping in the arrangement of these ceremonies were, so far as I could discover, rooted in her enjoyment of the dance and the opportunity it gave her to display her unusual talents, which most of the other women appreciated and envied. Clytie had an aged husband, to whose camp she went sometimes, and (from the other women's accounts) she had two lovers, one male and one female. According to her sister, who enters the dramaticule now as a third character, Clytie had no worries like the rest of the women. I think she was probably wrong about that, but certainly a magpie's song sounded no less carefree than Clytie's arpeggio of giggles.

Clytie's sister, Big Taylor, was grossly fat and had a habit of shaking with gargantuan laughter. She was currently infatuated with Roy, a stockman rather younger and more vigorous than her weedy husband and at present unattached. She treated her husband abominably, as I am sure she would not have done if he had been a match for her in brute strength. She spent a lot of time washing her clothes, singing them to sparkle in Roy's eyes and make her irresistibly attractive to him. She had ambitions to elope with Roy when he was due to return to the Tablelands but Roy, being a male, was slow to realize that he was wasting his time in staying unmated. Whenever Big Taylor encountered the other characters in this dramaticule she related audacious dreams of Roy crawling into her tent at night and pestered us for news of his daily movements in the hope that she might learn that he was passing closer and closer to her camp. She saw the *yawalyu* as a means of securing Roy's attentions. The Mungamunga girls of mythology were sisters, as she and Clytie, the girl who was 'little bit Mungamunga' herself, were. The Mungamunga were mainsprings of the *yawalyu* and, whilst Clytie was a prominent practitioner of the dance, Big Taylor was one of the leading singers. Her dancing was slovenly, and she did not seem to know the ritual very well. She tired early and sat beside the fire to sing. But she was eager that the men back in the main camp where Roy was could hear her and learn of her desire, though she could not specify the object of it. Sometimes she would stand up and bellow the words of the song (which often she did not understand) from the depths of her massive lungs.

The fourth character was a widow I shall call Beulah, a burly Salt Water woman of about my own age, who was as surly as Big Taylor was jolly and as sluggish and awkward as Clytie was graceful and quick. Beulah brought herself to my attention by trailing me wherever I went, occasionally exclaiming her admiration for my hat or my shoes or my hand-watch. Beulah called to see me on her way home to the single women's camp and I could not always be away somewhere else. On these occasions she would place her chair so that she faced me directly and was as close as I would tolerate and gaze fixedly at various parts of me. Like Big Taylor and Clytie, she was one of the women who called me 'Mummy'. Embarrassingly, Beulah described with relish certain acts she said she would like to perform on particular parts of my anatomy. I reproved her for having such wishes in respect of someone she was always calling 'Mother'. 'But *my* Mummy's Nangalama', she said, laughing slyly. 'You're the Old Woman, and I'm a Mungamunga.' She repeated the story I had already heard from several women about the Mungamunga's activities both before they left the sea and also between their teasing visits to earthly men. The Mungamunga were the daughters of the Old Woman of the Kunapipi myths: sometimes they debauched with earthly men they met on their travels, and sometimes they debauched incestuously with each other and their mother. Beulah told me the *yawalyu* would make me desire her as she desired me. The ceremonies were punctuated with her suggestions that it was time for Nangalama to strip off and give a performance, and she stole a dirty Kleenex tissue and a bandage I had used in order to sing magical songs over them in the intervals between the dancing.

The final character was Clementine, the oldest of the five of us. Clementine had occasional fits of chattering and clucking irrationally, allegedly through failing to recover completely from boomerang and axe wounds inflicted on her cranium in youth. During these fits of irrationality she would wander gibbering along public tracks; people said, though I did not witness this, that she would lift her skirts in a public place and execute an orgiastic dance. Though not a virtuoso like Clytie, she was a spirited and energetic dancer and displayed a certain style. Despite her age, she was a mainstay of the 'playabout corroborees' and the secular camp ceremonies held at Borroloola. She had a magnificent singing voice. Her relationship with her husband was more companionable than that between most spouses, and she quarrelled with him as with an equal, unlike Clytie, whose 'fatherly' husband would either ignore her or give her a clout when she offended him, and Big Taylor, whose relatively minute mate suffered miserably at the hands of the flabby Amazon. Clementine had occasionally developed light romantic attachments, which did not appear to trouble her unduly, to younger men but she was reticent about her sex life and gave us no hint that she might be languishing for a particular lover. She confessed to having pleasant dreams after the women's ceremonies, but did not specify their content. The enjoyment she showed when participating in them appeared to be the same as that she derived from proficient performances in open camp ceremonies. In addition, she seemed to like the company of the other women and, since she herself addressed me as 'father's sister' rather than 'mother', saw it as her duty to protect me from the obvious attentions of Beulah.

Like Dr Berndt's story already quoted, this dramaticule progressed as a communication process. What was communicated was an intention to hold a *yawalyu*. The triviality of the miniature drama derives from the absence of opposition to this intention. Two of the characters, Clytie and Clementine, wished the ceremonies to be held frequently to provide them with an opportunity to spend an evening in a congenial manner. Two of the other characters, Big Taylor and Beulah, wished to use the *yawalyu* as a potent means in their campaigns to secure the sexual services and affections of particular persons. The fifth character, the anthropologist, wished to record the ceremonies in notes and on tape, but was inhibited from initiating any suggestion that the ceremonies might be held by the wish to interfere as little as possible in the life she was studying. Of the four other characters, Big Taylor, Beulah and

Clementine all initiated the idea at various times, and at other times Clytie would visit one of them, not to make the suggestion directly but to provide the opportunity for one of the other women to do so. Clytie, the Mungamunga girl, was the principal agent of communicating the intention. I thought that this was because she was unusually energetic and did not mind walking about the scattered camps in the hot sun, but her sister, Big Taylor, largely assumed this role during Clytie's absence and, since it is easier to keep a particularly lazy and vocal buffalo in one's sights than a teasing gadfly, I was able to discover precisely what was being communicated. Clytie's procedure had been to visit us in turn in our scattered camps and then proceed to the single women's camp and notify both the occupants and the other women camped nearby. Big Taylor, however, shrank from walking over a mile in the hot sun and, after visiting myself and Clementine, who did not live far from her, would shout in the direction of the main camp the message she wanted the single women to pass on. The message was that 'that Nangalama', the term they used for me, wanted all the women to assemble that evening in the usual place for a women's corroboree. It sounded as if the *yawalyu* were a command performance to satisfy the anthropologist. Clementine also used this device. At last I knew that the missionary was not wilfully lying when he accused me of stirring up the sports of Satan and disbelieved my denials that I had ever persuaded the Aborigines to revive old ceremonies. His informants, the mission converts, were in the main camp where the message was being received as 'That Nangalama wants all the women to assemble'.

III

That is why I had to be Nangalama. Most of the most potent *yawalyu* ceremonies, like some elements in the open camp ceremonies, were dreamed by Nangalama women. Sometimes the Mungamunga sisters appeared to the dreamer and showed her the ceremony, as in Dr Berndt's account. In a dream a Nangalama woman related to me at Brunette Races, she herself became the Old Woman of Kunapipi and, hypnotized by the great snake, drew him into her belly, her own body movements following as in trance his agitations within her. Awakening, she remembered her cries of pain and pleasure as particular words forming a song. When a Nangalama woman dreams a ceremony it is, in a sense, the 'property' of Nangalama subsection. It should not be performed unless a Nangalama woman decrees that it shall be, and there should be at least one Nangalama participating or at least present. Nangalama the creator, or Nangalama who belongs to the subsection of the creator, delegates the organization of the ceremony to women of Nulyerima subsection and any other 'daughters' she may have. This is a service the Mungamunga do for their mother, the Old Woman. There was a shortage of Nangalama women at Borroloola: those who were not absent on the Tablelands were converted or contemplating conversion to the austere Christianity of the missionary.[6] But there were women at Borroloola who desired strongly to hold the forbidden ceremonies, and they used the unsuspecting anthropologist to escape censure for doing so. So long as I was Nangalama and could be identified with the Old Woman, their decisions to hold forbidden ceremonies had to be attributed to me in order to conform with the model from mythology. They cast themselves as messengers or executives to convey and implement my policies.

After months of *yawalyu* Big Taylor and Beulah were no closer to securing their intended lovers than they had been when I arrived, despite the vaunted potency of the songs and dances and their incidental tricks. Beulah was becoming diverted from her interest in the anthropologist by the threat of being left alone in the single women's camp at the end of the season when elopements were in the air. Big Taylor had bragged so much about her ability to ensnare Roy that it had become a matter of honour for her to do so, and she was getting desperate. As my Nulyerima 'daughter' she mustered up not only the women but the men as well, invited ostensibly by me to a recital of songs on the tape recorder in my camp. Clementine's husband, who thought he knew that her singing was for him, expressed delight and congratulated me on 'my' ingenuity in using a tape recorder to let the men enjoy the women's songs without having to steal a peep at the forbidden ceremonies. The fiction was maintained to the end that these were my own decisions that I have narrated, for in that sick segment of Gulf-Barkly Tablelands society the only thing the women could use as a model for social reality was the structure of myth, something certain and their very own.

Notes

1. Concerning the subsection system at Borroloola in the Northern Territory see M. Reay (1962:90-115).
2. For a general discussion of women's secret life see C. Berndt (1965: Chapter 9).
3. In fact I found in Dr Berndt's account (1950) an apt illustration of an hypothesis already developed from the Borroloola material.
4. This is an inference from Dr Nancy Munn's account (1964:83-100).
5. I know of no scientific grounds for this impression, which I myself shared.
6. Indeed, since this subsection has never been reported to have a monopoly of *yawalyu*, it is possible that the shortage of Nangalama women may even have determined which ceremonies the Borroloola women concentrated on performing during that period.

REFERENCES

BERNDT, C. H. 1950 *Women's Changing Ceremonies in Northern Australia.* L'Homme, Hermann et Cie, Paris.

―――― 1965 Women and the 'Secret Life'. In *Aboriginal Man in Australia* (R. M. and C. H. Berndt, eds). Angus and Robertson, Sydney.

MUNN, N. 1964 Totemic Designs and Group Continuity in Walbiri Cosmology. In *Aborigines Now* (M. Reay, ed.). Angus and Robertson, Sydney.

REAY, M. 1962 Subsections at Borroloola, *Oceania*, Vol. XXXIII, No. 2.

―――― (ed.) 1964 *Aborigines Now*. Angus and Robertson, Sydney.

KENNETH MADDOCK

Myths of the Acquisition of Fire in Northern and Eastern Australia

In his *Mythologiques*, Lévi-Strauss brings out how South American mythology coheres to form an aetiology of some of the cultural features by which men are distinguished from animals, though part of the force of his demonstration is lost in the detail and ingenuity of the accompanying argument that myths are structures composed of forms and sensible qualities. *Le Cru et le Cuit* and *Du Miel aux Cendres* aim at establishing that their 353 myths are permutations upon one another, and that structural analysis is uniquely fitted to reveal meaning. Although Lévi-Strauss holds the myths to be representations of passage from nature to culture, he subsumes, under the latter term, 'neolithic' as well as 'palaeolithic' achievements. Thus the mastery of fire and practice of cooking must have long preceded such arts of civilization as cultivation, domestication, weaving and pottery-making. It does not appear, however, that Lévi-Strauss wants to maintain that there are structural differences between the mythical accounts of neolithic and palaeolithic achievements. On the evidence of *Le Cru et le Cuit* and *Du Miel aux Cendres*, tales explanatory of fire and cooking are central to the investigation. Fire transforms raw into cooked, a process which is both a cultural homologue of the natural transformation of raw (or fresh) into rotten, and a culinary symbol of passage from nature to culture.

Fire may be taken as a cultural acquisition that is eminently comparable. It is not merely that 'the acquisition of power over fire stands out as a quite exceptional achievement, without a prototype', as Freud thought (1930:50), but fire is universally possessed and is essential for the universal practice of cooking. In this paper, I shall examine fire myths recorded in northern and eastern Australia.[1] Despite the diversity of their surface detail, the myths incorporate only a few themes. The events narrated are expressed in conceptual codes recurring in widely separated places. An interesting feature which, at this stage of investigation, is found only in Arnhem Land, is that different myths

FIRE MYTHS

can be ordered as segments of a super-myth on the acquisition of fire. America probably constitutes a privileged ground for inquiry into mythical representations of passage from nature to culture, for the Indians were scattered on both sides of the 'neolithic' threshold, but the myths of the 'palaeolithic' Australians lend themselves to the same type of structural and semantic analysis.

I

I shall take as myth of reference a Dalabon myth collected during fieldwork on the Beswick Reserve in the far north of the Northern Territory (see map).[2] I give the myth virtually as recorded, for the manner in which the events narrated are repeated and elaborated is not without interest.

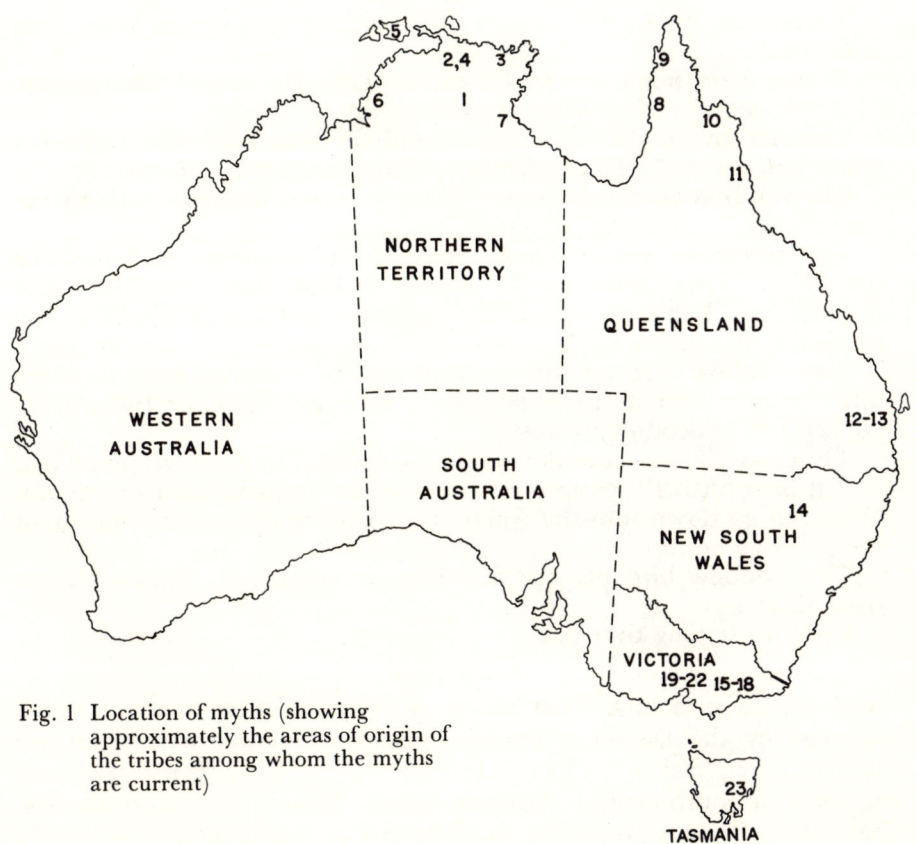

Fig. 1 Location of myths (showing approximately the areas of origin of the tribes among whom the myths are current)

M₁   The crocodile possessed firesticks. The rainbow bird would ask for fire, but was knocked back every time. The rainbow bird was without fire: he had no light, slept without a camp fire, ate his food (fish, goanna lizards, mussels) raw.

The rainbow bird could not get fire because the crocodile was 'boss' for fire and would knock him back.

'You can't take fire!'

'What am I to do for men? Are they to eat raw?'

'They can eat raw. I won't give you firesticks!'

The crocodile had fire. No man made it. The crocodile had had fire from a long time ago. Then the rainbow bird put fire everywhere. Every tree has fire inside now. It was the rainbow bird who put the fire inside.

The rainbow bird spoke. '*Wirid, wirid, wirid!*' He climbed into a tree, a dry place, a dry tree. Down he came, like a jet plane, to snatch the firesticks, but the crocodile had them clutched to his breast. Again and again the rainbow bird tried.

'You eat raw', the crocodile told him, 'I'm not giving you fire.'

'I want fire. You are too mean. If I had had fire I would have given it to you.'

'*Wirid, wirid, wirid, wirid!*' Down he came. He missed. He flew up.

'*Wirid, wirid, wirid!*' They argued again.

'I'm not giving you fire. You are only a little man. Me, I'm a big man. You eat raw!' That is the way we had been going to eat.

The rainbow bird was angry. 'Why do you knock me back all the time?'

The crocodile turned about. Snatch! The rainbow bird had the firesticks! '*Wirid, wirid, wirid!*' Away he flew. The crocodile could do nothing. He has no wings. The rainbow bird was above. 'You can go down into the water', he called, 'I'm going to give fire to men!'

The rainbow bird put fire everywhere—in every country, in every kind of tree (except the pandanus). He made light, he burned, he cooked fish, crocodile, tortoise.

The crocodile had gone down into the water. The two had spread out.

'I'll be a bird. I'll go into dry places', the rainbow bird called out, 'You can go down into the water. If you go in dry places you might die. I'll stay on top.'

The rainbow bird put the firesticks in his behind. They stick out from there now.

That was a long time ago.

The crocodile is of a fresh water variety, harmless to men, called *nalagmumu* by the Dalabon. Its diet is said to include items that are *nura* ('stinking', 'rotten'). The rainbow bird is called *wiridwirid* in several languages of south-central Arnhem Land. This is an approximation to its call. In Djauan *wirid* is the word for tail, so that *wiridwirid* is literally 'tail-tail'. The reference is to the pair of long feathers protruding from the bird's tail, and which, as the myth relates, were once firesticks.

It is common for Aboriginal myths to represent their protagonists as animals endowed with human capacities and wanting in obvious features of the kinds of animal that they are supposed to be. Crocodiles that do not live in the water are not crocodiles at all, we would say, and rainbow birds that eat fish, mussels and reptiles and do not live in trees are not rainbow birds. The protagonists, then, are hazily defined, but become unambiguous in form, habit and habitat at the myth's end. If differentiation of the human and animal worlds is a concern shared by my myth of reference with most Australian myths, what marks it off is the momentous transaction that it records. Fire, formerly the exclusive possession of the crocodile, was freed for men, making it possible for them to eat cooked where they had been constrained to eat raw. This momentous transaction is bound up with marvellous transformations: 'crocodile' into crocodile, 'rainbow bird' into rainbow bird, 'trees' (hitherto implied to be incombustible) into trees. The path is cleared for cultural acquisition by men, and simultaneously a part of the non-human world acquires its natural contours. It is precisely this double significance that makes the Dalabon myth more than a mere just-so story.

In his paper on 'The Structural Study of Myth', Lévi-Strauss (1963:229) suggests that myths are logical tools for overcoming contradictions. My myth of reference evokes two 'contradictions'. One is of the myth's own making. The myth purports to explain a feature of the real world: the possession of fire by men generally, and by men alone. It does this by positing an initial situation which is in some sense the opposite of the real situation. In reality fire is readily and generally available to all members of one species, the human, and humans alone cook their food. Fire is shared and is symbolic of sociality. Yet according to the myth, fire is possessed successively by two species, both animal, who cook their food by it, while men eat raw. Fire is denied to him who wants it, and is a thing competed for. Together with the contrast between the real situation and the imagined situation is a double, but inversed, progression: from a natural to a cultural condition for men (by the events narrated in the myth they will acquire fire and eat cooked); from a cultural to a natural condition for the animals (they lose or renounce fire and will eat raw or rotten or both). The other 'contradiction' expressed in the myth arises out of the general world view of the Aborigines. There is among them what can only be described as a profound resistance to crediting themselves with their own cultural achievements. All that they will claim credit for is fidelity to tradition or, as they put it, for 'following up the Dreaming', the cultural features of human societies having been established entirely by the acts of mythical beings who, demiurges or animals-to-be, are alone conceived of as active and creative, men being passive beneficiaries of unmotivated generosity. As men deny the creativity which is truly theirs, they can explain their ability to make fire only by falsely attributing responsibility for the technique to beings who are not human.

The Aboriginal conception of men as passive is perhaps linked to the ecological relations sustained by hunters and gatherers with nature: they gather the fruits of nature, but do not cultivate them. In South America, although demiurges and animals-to-be play a vital role in aetiological myths (see Lévi-Strauss 1964; 1966), men are not conceived as of merely passive: often they transact actively with non-human characters. The South American view of men as active in cultural acquisition might be thought to be linked with the partial mastery of natural forces that the Indians established with their techniques for producing food. Thus in myths of the Gé-speaking tribes (Lévi-Strauss 1964: 78-81), fire originates with jaguars, but the events by which men come to possess fire and jaguars to lose it include human acts of appropriation. The Aborigines, then, in contrast to the Indians, achieve an 'inverted world consciousness' by denying human responsibility for human creations, even withholding from men the promethean-type roles attributed to them in some South American myths. The events by which these creations come to be possessed by men are also often the events by which they cease to be possessed by animals. Hence the creation of culture and the establishment of nature are viewed as coterminous. If the world view implied by the myths were to be expressed in a Lévi-Straussian formula, it would be something like:

Humans : Animals : : Cultural Consumers : Cultural Producers

or:

Humanity : Animality : : Tradition : Innovation

The point is that to create or innovate culturally is to be more or less than human. Consistently with their world view, the Dalabon do not suppose that once the rainbow bird had distributed fire to all trees men made fire. Instead, the cycle of Gunabibi myths and songs celebrating the Nagorgo heroes relates that they taught men how to operate firesticks.

Given that Aborigines commonly attribute a culturally creative role to animals, the question arises why it should be crocodile and rainbow bird, instead of some other pair, in the Dalabon myth (cf. the analysis of moiety totemism by Radcliffe-Brown 1951). Recalling the 'oppositeness' which is built in to the myth, the selection of crocodile and rainbow bird is intelligible by the fact that their contrasting qualities particularly fit them to form a pair of opponents. The myth portrays them occupying the same element, the earth, but in reality the earth is not their regular habitat. The crocodile's is water, the rainbow bird's is the air. The one shuns men, who hunt it as food; the other is conspicuous for its brilliant plumage, its swooping and darting flight and apparent lack of fear of men. Rainbow birds are not hunted, ostensibly because of their prototype's aid to men. The events related in the myth account for the pair becoming vertically separated, one going down, the other up. But they both come to earth for breeding. Female crocodiles bury their eggs in low-lying sandy ground. Male and female rainbow birds nest in holes in sandy soil in more elevated places. Before becoming vertically separated, the protagonists share an interest in cooking, but then one is deprived of fire and the other renounces what he has captured, once again vacating human ground, for in reality only men cook food. Crocodiles are active by night (in the dark) as well as day (in the light), rainbow birds only by day. Crocodiles eat fish chiefly, and rainbow birds insects, but both eat raw (crocodiles eat fresh and rotten indiscriminately). In the myth these contrasting physical characters find their counterpart in the contrasting moral characters of the pair: the crocodile refuses to share, preferring to keep for himself alone what is of value and, in consequence, loses once and for all what he has unsociably tried to keep; the rainbow bird expresses willingness to share, strives to aid men, and finally renounces in their favour the valued thing that he has captured.

Thus the myth contains several conceptual codes in terms of which the narrative is organized: a vertical register of low, middle and high; a corresponding elemental register of water, earth and air; a culinary register of raw and cooked, with rotten implied; a moral register of selfishly interested and generously disinterested conduct; and registers consisting in the contrasts dry/wet and light/dark. In the course of the myth a differentiation is achieved amongst its protagonists which may be tabulated thus:

Fireless	Rainbow bird	High	Air	Raw	Disinterested	Dry
Fire-possessing	Men	Middle	Earth	Cooked		
Fireless	Crocodile	Low	Water	Raw	Interested	Wet

Now this differentiation is consistent with the observed compatibilities and incompatibilities of fire. Water, the natural abode of crocodiles, is an element incompatible with fire. Flames spring from earth into the air, which is the abode of rainbow birds. Fire transforms raw into cooked, which is how men eat their meat. Men's conduct incorporates both interestedness, attributed in the myth to the crocodile, and disinterestedness, attributed to the rainbow bird, without either state of mind expanding to exclude the other. The trees in which rainbow birds perch provide, if dry, materials for making firesticks and sustaining fires.

My myth of reference is current among several tribes in southern Arnhem Land. I collected a version quite like the Dalabon from a Djauan tribesman, the Djauan being western neighbours of the Dalabon. Robinson (1966:97-9) recorded a similar tale from the Ngalagan, who are south of the Dalabon. At Oenpelli, to the north of the Beswick Reserve, Mountford (1956:216) recorded a crocodile and plover myth, which begins and develops differently, but whose ending recalls the crocodile and rainbow bird myth. A summary is given below.

M_2 The crocodile and plover possessed the only firesticks in the world. Because of the plover's laziness, most of the work was done by the crocodile. One morning before going out hunting, the crocodile asked the plover to light the fire ready for his return so that the game could be cooked. The crocodile returned carrying a large kangaroo only to find the fire unlit and the plover asleep. The crocodile abused his companion, snatched the firesticks and ran to the river to extinguish them. But the plover was too quick. He snatched the firesticks back and ran into the hills. Since then crocodiles have lived in and about water, plovers in the hills. But for the plover men would have had to eat raw.

Again the myth opens by positing a fantastic situation, and then narrates events leading toward the real situation, that is, the exclusive possession of fire by men. Unlike the Dalabon, who invoke the Nagorgo heroes in order to explain how men came actually to make fire, the Oenpelli myth merely explains the rupture of relations among the fire-possessing animals. Although both myths recount the capture of fire from the crocodile by a bird, the rainbow bird of M_1, which is habitually in trees and the air, is replaced in M_2 by a hill bird of a variety that spends much time on the ground. The vertical and elemental registers are retained, but the plover's habits being what they are, the representative of the upper terms is closer than in M_1 to the representative of the lower terms. The moral register is used differently. Instead of a mean crocodile and a generous bird, M_2 begins with a crocodile whose moral character recalls M_1's bird, and a bird who recalls M_1's crocodile. A reversal of moral roles occurs at the end of the tale. If both myths represent the capture of fire by a bird from a crocodile, in one the seizure is at the expense of a crocodile who wishes to keep fire for himself alone, and in the other at the expense of a crocodile who shares until failure in reciprocity drives him to wish to extinguish fire. The pattern of correlations and contrasts between the two myths may be brought out schematically.

M_1	M_2
	Men are without fire and eat raw; an animal or animals possess fire and eat cooked.
Crocodile and rainbow bird live apart, the former refusing to share fire with the latter, who is constrained to eat raw;	Crocodile and plover live together sharing fire, the bird neglecting his share in work about the camp, the crocodile doing more than his share;
The bird requests fire repeatedly, but his requests are refused and he is told to eat raw;	The crocodile requests the bird to make fire, so that they may eat cooked, but the bird ignores his request;
After several attempts the bird captures fire from the crocodile;	The crocodile seizes the fire in order to extinguish it, but the bird recaptures the fire;
The protagonists separate: the crocodile into water, the bird into the trees;	The protagonists separate; the crocodile into water, the bird into the hills;
	If the crocodiles had had their way men would have eaten raw to this day, but the birds saved fire for men.

These contrasts in narrative, which lead to like conclusions and develop within the same conceptual codes, are all the more interesting because the myths are from nearby places. It is as if the Aborigines were holding the codes and conclusions constant while varying the events narrated.

M_1 and M_2 raise a problem which neither states: How did the possessors of fire come to possess fire? In my experience, the Aboriginal narrators do not try to resolve the problems implied by their myths. (Cf. M_1: 'The crocodile had fire. No man made it. The crocodile had had fire from a long time ago.') Yet if the fire myths collected from different places in Arnhem Land are examined it looks as though they fall into place as segments of a super-myth on the origins of fire and the vicissitudes it underwent until it became a human possession. This long and involuted story is not known by any one group, but each group knows a fragment of the whole, a fragment which is self-sufficient except for the unresolved problem which it implies. If the region were better known ethnographically, then the super-myth might be extended and its segments seen to join more perfectly than they do at present. The sequence consists in each myth's raising a problem which is in some sense solved in another myth of the series.

The unstated problem of M_1 and M_2 is: How did the crocodile, or crocodile and plover, acquire fire? A 'Murngin' myth published by Warner (1958:519-20) explains how the crocodile acquired fire.

M_3 The crocodile took a firestick with which to make fire, for there was then none in the world. But every time he tried he broke the drill. Soon his hands were cut and bleeding and broken firesticks lay about. Then the frilled lizard arrived. He sat down and continued work on a basket that he had started. The crocodile asked him to try making fire. The frilled lizard, who had firesticks of his own in the basket, told the crocodile that he had been gripping the drill incorrectly, and then made fire. 'Waku (sister's son) of mine', said the crocodile, 'it is a good thing you are my relative and it is a good thing that you made fire for us, for all people.' The crocodile took grass, lit it, and built a huge fire.

The theme of capture of fire is replaced here by that of generation of fire. Positing the non-existence of fire, but not ignorance of the means of producing fire, M_3 solves the problem of M_1 and M_2, for it relates how the crocodile came to have fire, but only at the price of a problem of its own, which is neither stated nor solved: How did the crocodile and frilled lizard know about fire and firemaking? Before taking up myths logically prior to M_3, we may consider the conceptual framework within which it is organized.

As in the first two myths, the protagonists form a pair. The behaviour of one is marked by inability to fulfil a wish (he wants to make fire, but breaks the drills), and the behaviour of the other by a complementary ability (he generates fire without difficulty). This contrast finds its counterpart in M_1 and M_2, for in both there is a crocodile whose wish to keep or to extinguish fire is frustrated, and a bird whose wish to capture fire is satisfied. The vertical and elemental registers recur, but as compared with M_2 the distance between the representatives of upper and lower positions is reduced (in M_2 there is a reduction compared with M_1), for the crocodile is now paired with an arboreal lizard. The progressive narrowing of the gap is achieved by the upper position's representative coming down, the lower's representative remaining the same, and is correlated with the successive modification in the moral quality of the relation between the pair.

M_1	No co-operation	Crocodile paired with an aerial bird
M_2	Partial co-operation	Crocodile paired with an aerial and terrestrial bird
M_3	Full co-operation	Crocodile paired with an arboreal lizard

The culinary register is absent.

M_2 is a better sequel to M_3 than M_1 would be, for the initial helpfulness of the crocodile in M_2 is consistent with the co-operativeness of his relation in M_3. M_1 could be seen as an alternative ending to M_2, for it opens with the crocodile acting unhelpfully, which is how he acts in M_2 after the bird's failure in reciprocity provokes a rupture in their relation. A long myth collected at Oenpelli from the now extinct Kakadu by Spencer (1914:305-8) explains the crocodile's knowledge of fire and firemaking. I do not know of any myth explaining the frilled lizard's knowledge.

M_4 Two men went hunting with their mothers. While the men caught ducks and plovers on the plain, the women collected lily roots and seeds from water pools. The women possessed fire, but sought to keep it secret from the men, who were ignorant of firemaking. The women cooked their food while the men were away, and on seeing them returning hid the live ashes in their vulvas. The men asked where the fire was. The women denied that there was fire, a row broke out, but the women gave the men cooked lily cake, and after they had eaten cake and meat, they all slept. Then the men went hunting and the women cooked.

The weather was very hot. The uneaten remains of the birds went bad. The men brought a fresh supply and again saw the fire burning in the distance. A spur-winged plover flew to warn the women, who hid the fire as before. The men arrived, they argued, the women denied the fire. 'The men said, We saw a big fire; if you have no fire, which way do you cook your food? has the sun cooked it? If the sun cooks your lilies, why does it not cook our ducks and stop them from going bad. There was no reply to this.' They slept.

In the morning the men left the women, found that they could make fire by rubbing sticks, and then decided to turn themselves into crocodiles, of which there were none. They made crocodile heads, pierced their lungs so that they could breathe underwater, practised swimming, and then hid the heads and returned to camp. Again they saw fire, again the plover gave warning. The women wanted to know what the men had been doing, 'but the men said nothing at all.'

Late in the afternoon the women set nets for fish. In the morning when they went to take in the nets, the men arrived first, turned themselves into crocodiles and dived into the water. They hung onto the nets so that the women could not pull them in. When the women felt for what made the nets heavy, the crocodiles dragged them under. The men brought the women up on the bank; 'Get up, go. Why did you tell us lies about the fire? But there was no reply from the women; they were completely dead.'

The men 'threw away their sticks and spears, in fact everything that they had', changed themselves completely into crocodiles and 'dived into the water in which they have lived ever since.'

The vertical and elemental registers are retained. Women, who originally collect roots and seeds from water pools, are left on the bank; men, who originally hunt ducks and plovers on the plain, enter the water. Crocodiles-to-be are opposed to birds, particularly to plovers, for they prey on plovers which they are constrained to eat raw because the women withhold fire. A plover co-operates with the women in their attempt to keep fire from the men by warning the women of the men's approach. Thus a plover who fails to help a crocodile in cooking kangaroo (M_2), is replaced by a plover whose kind is eaten raw by crocodiles-to-be and who tries to help women to keep fire from them. The culinary register is enriched with the explicit introduction of the rotten (birds putrefying in the heat). As for the moral register: in M_4, as in M_1 and M_2, refusal to share fire leads to the loss of fire by those who refuse to share. But now it is women, not crocodiles, who refuse to share, and it is men who will become crocodiles, not birds, who wish to share. Instead of fire being exclusively claimed (M_1) or seized with the intention of extinction (M_2), it is denied that fire exists. Instead of fire being captured (M_{1-2}) fire is extinguished, or so one may presume from the immersion and drowning of the women in whose vulvas it was hidden, and firesticks thrown away. In keeping with these variations in plot, it is vegetable foods, unmentioned in the other myths, which are cooked, meat being eaten raw or thrown away after becoming rotten. The moral code is impoverished in comparison with M_{1-3}, for there seems to be nothing of disinterested generosity. Perhaps this absence is compensated for by the extending of the culinary code in the inhuman direction of rottenness.

Throughout M_4 there is a marked emphasis on low positions. The women collect in the pools, the men hunt ducks (water birds), the men practise swimming, the women set nets for fish, the women are drowned and the men become crocodiles (water reptiles). The emphasis is explicable on the view that the myths are concerned with the observed incompatibility of fire and water, the observed compatibility of fire and air. Whereas M_{1-3} portray fire saved or generated by the intervention of a bird or arboreal lizard, M_4 portrays fire lost by the (unwitting?) act of the crocodiles in drowning the women in whose bodies the fire is concealed. It appears from the first four myths that if fire is to be distributed widely or saved from extinction or generated, it will be in spite of the crocodile, that wittingly or unwittingly the crocodile is the enemy of fire.

The unstated problem of M_4 is: How did the women come to possess fire? A Melville Island myth reported by Mountford (1958:25-6, 29-30, 35) relates the accidental discovery of fire, the wish to extinguish fire and the distribution of fire. These motifs suggest comparisons with the myths already discussed.

M_5 Food was eaten raw. The wedge-tailed eagle and the fork-tailed kite were rubbing two sticks together when they noticed a speck of light where the heat caused by the friction between the two sticks had ignited the powdered wood dust. The eagle placed the smouldering dust in the pith of a dead pandanus palm and blew. The speck burst into flame. The two were afraid and ran to Purukupali (son of the old blind woman who created Melville Island) to ask him to destroy fire. But Purukupali, realizing that men (real men did not then exist) would get light and warmth from fire and would be able to cook their food by it, called his sister, Wuriupranala, and gave her a bark torch, telling her always to keep it alight. Tjapara (whose parents the aborigines do not know) was given a smaller torch. Purukupali ultimately descended into the sea at a place which became a dangerous whirlpool. In the same sequence of events Tjapara rose into the sky to become the moon. Wuriupranala became the sun.

Instead of a withholder (M_1) or would-be extinguisher (M_2) or actual extinguisher (M_4) of fire entering the water, in M_5 it is a saviour of fire who does so, but as a dangerous whirlpool, not as a crocodile. The crocodile in M_1 is of the harmless fresh water variety; it is to be regretted that Mountford, Warner and Spencer do not identify their crocodiles, which may be of the dangerous salt water kind. Birds figure again, but now as the chance discoverers and would-be extinguishers of fire, not as distributors (M_1) or saviours from extinction (M_2) or accomplices in exclusive retention (M_4). This exchange of roles between 'higher' and 'lower' is correlated with a change in postulate: it is no longer a case of fire existing or fire not existing but known about; it is a case of the accidental discovery of what had been unknown until then. It may be remarked that the 'higher' creature's role in M_4 contains an element of ambiguity, for the plover, by aiding the women to keep fire for themselves, was thereby helping to keep fire from the men. The birds in M_4 and M_5 therefore play ambivalent roles.

M_5 is the primary segment in the super-myth, and as it postulates the chance discovery of fire no logically prior myth need be sought. Indeed, there could not be one. The super-myth unfolds in the order:

M_5
M_4
M_3
M_2 (with M_1 as an alternative)
The Nagorgo episode

That fire myths from various Arnhem Land tribes fit together as segments of a longer, more 'explanatory' narrative raises a problem. Perhaps the Aborigines knew one another's myths, and addressed themselves to resolving the problems posed by the myths when taken separately. Perhaps there was once a series of fire myths associated with a cycle of fire rituals, of which each tribe knew only a portion, just as today there are cycles of myth and rite extending over wide areas and of which no group possesses more than a fraction, though each knows that the cycle continues beyond its own territory. In the absence of direct evidence to support either conjecture, the puzzle remains that Aboriginal groups do not merely reproduce one another, as they often do in social and local organization, but that they also take up where others leave off, as if problems were receiving cumulative solutions.

II

So far I have considered only southern, central and northern Arnhem Land myths. Fire myths to the west and east include elements familiar from M_{1-5}, and use the same conceptual codes. A fragment of the long Kunmanggur myth recorded by Stanner (1961:246) from the Murinbata of the Port Keats region repeats the motif of attempted extinction of fire in water. As in M_2 the attempt is by a creature associated with water, for Kunmanggur is now a water-dwelling serpent dangerous to men, and the rescue is by a bird. Like M_2's crocodile, Kunmanggur is portrayed as a formerly benevolent figure. The fragment includes a making of fire by friction, recalling the episodes of M_{3-5}; furthermore, the creature responsible for this achievement is the kestrel which, like the eagle and kite of M_5, is a diurnal bird of prey. But the kestrel's firemaking is deliberate, as in M_{3-4}, not accidental as with the *two* birds in M_5.

M_6 Kunmanggur took all the fire and entered the water, meaning to take the fire for ever. The fire was on his head. When only his fiery head-dress could still be seen, the butcher bird snatched the fire. Then the kestrel made fire with firesticks, the first time they had been used, and set alight the grass on all sides, giving this country its characteristic fire-scorched appearance.

In another article (1960a:252) Stanner notes the Murinbata belief that fire and water were once possessed by the two patrilineal moieties: 'Each possessed a vital resource—fire or water—without which the other could not live.' I take this as corroboration that the Arnhem Land Aborigines see fire and water as antithetical.

A brief myth recorded by Spencer and Gillen (1904:628-9) from the Mara and Anyula south of the Roper mouth, links the Arnhem Land with the Cape York myths.

M_7 Kakan, an old hawk, discovered how to make fire by twirling one stick upon another. In a dispute with a white hawk the country was set on fire. A pine tree, by which every day a number of men, women and children used to climb into the sky and come down again, was burnt, so that the people stayed in the sky. Starlight comes from the crystals implanted in their heads, elbows, knees and other joints.

The old hawk is evidently the chickenhawk, known as *gargan* over much of Arnhem Land. In the Jabuduruwa cult at Roper Mission and the Lòrgon at Croker Island, the chickenhawk is celebrated in rituals in which fires are lit. Although it is not clear whether the primary aim of the myth is to explain fire or the stars, several of its features are found in Arnhem Land fire myths. Discovery of fire by a bird of prey, discovery of the method of generating fire by friction, and the lighting of a fire which sweeps destructively across the country, recall M_{5-6}, M_{4-6} and M_6 respectively. The vertical register is retained in the motif of people from the earth trapped in the sky, with the upper position (the stars) being higher than in the preceding myths. The elemental register is weakened by the absence of water, there is no culinary register, and it does not seem that a moral register could be constructed from the incidents recorded.

Four Cape York myths are available for comparison. The Mungkan myth reported by McConnel (1957:62-5) is strongly reminiscent of the Arnhem Land myths.

M_8 Men had no fire. They piled up wood and said, 'Let's burn grass to catch kangaroo for meat!' Tu:mauwa twice made firesticks ineffectually, then correctly. Fire came. He dropped the spark into the grass, which caught alight.
   Tu:mbeya, a small bird, said, 'The fire is mine as well as yours. Give it to me!' 'I will not give you fire!' replied Tu:mauwa.

Tu:mbeya's meat was raw. It stank. He again asked for fire, and again his request was refused. Then Tu:mauwa slept, and while he did so, Tu:mbeya lit a bark torch from the fire and ran up river, setting the grass alight. 'Let's chase him!' cried the crow, 'He's stolen our fire, and by and by everything will be on fire!'

Tu:mauwa heaped up wood, erected a forked stick in the hole at the fork of which he had placed fire, stood close against the firewood, and sank down, coming out in the river. He is now a place that the Aborigines avoid in their canoes because the water 'boils' and the currents swirl.

Generation of fire after ineffectual attempts, a bird's rejected request for fire, raw meat which putrefies, capture of fire from him who will not share, pursuit of the thief, and transformation of the being from whom fire is stolen into a 'thing' in the water, respectively recall M_3, M_1, M_4, $M_{1-2, 6}$, $M_{2, 6}$, and $M_{1-2, 6}$.

Roth (1903:11-12) reports three fire myths from Cape York.

M_9 According to the Pennefather River Aborigines, Old Mother Wallaby, who lived in the neighbourhood of the ant-hills, was the first to make fire, of which she had plenty. One day the fire went out, with the result that the bat could not see what he was doing, and accordingly he tried the various kinds of timber until he discovered the right one (to make fire by friction?).

M_{10} According to the Kokowara of Princess Charlotte Bay, because of the cold weather the little wagtail could not keep himself warm. He begged the owl for fire, but was refused. Waiting until nightfall, he stole the firesticks from off the owl's hut during the owl's absence, lit his fire, flew to Rocky Island (where he then lived and which, in those days, had plenty of grass, timber and food), burnt off all the verdure and then returned the sticks. The owl, finding a large part of his hunting grounds destroyed, set out to fight the wagtail, but the latter made a crocodile with whose aid he was successful (in resisting the owl?). Even now, wagtails and crocodiles are often seen in company.

M_{11} According to the Cape Grafton Aborigines, a small red-backed wren (*Malarus* sp.) went into the sky to get fire, there being none on earth. Not wanting to share with his friends on earth, the wren hid the fire under his tail and reported that his quest had been fruitless, but suggested that his 'friend' (unidentified) should try to extract fire from wood. The friend's attempts at making fire by twirling were unsuccessful, his hands became very sore and he gave up. Then the friend, on turning round suddenly, burst out laughing, and when asked by the wren why he laughed, answered that there was fire on the wren's tail, indicating the red marking. The wren admitted that he had fire and showed his friend from what wood it could be extracted.

Although the myths published by Roth largely repeat codes and motifs found in myths already examined, they contain several points worth commenting upon. The large marsupial in M_9 plays a role in marked contrast to that of the large marsupials of $M_{2,\ 8}$. Instead of being an object to which fire is applied, she is presented as the first possessor of fire. The contrast between light and dark, referred to in earlier myths, is important in M_{9-10}, with their stress on bat and owl, both nocturnal creatures, on the bat's inability to see after fire went out, and on the wagtail's action by night. M_{10} is the southernmost myth in which the crocodile occurs, and he is shown not as the enemy of fire, but as a supporter of the bird who steals fire. Reversal in the crocodile's role in a theft of fire myth is associated with another reversal: it seems to be 'lower' who steals from 'higher'—wagtail from owl.

Taking the Cape York myths as a group, and comparing them with the Arnhem Land myths as a group, a notable feature is the weakening in the elemental register, water being referred to or evoked in only two out of four tales in the former group, as against six out of seven in the latter. Associated with this weakening is a disappearance of the motif of deliberate attempts at extinction of fire. Conflict between birds over fire (M_{10}), fetching or taking fire from the sky, trickery and laughter (M_{11}) are new motifs.

The myths from northern Australia, and particularly those from Arnhem Land, are more thoroughgoing in their contrasts than the fire myths from the Gé-speaking tribes in central Brazil discussed by Lévi-Strauss (1964:74-86). In the Gé myths fire is possessed originally by a jaguar, who befriends a seeker of birds abandoned in a tree or on a cliff face, takes him to his camp and provides him with roasted meat and a bow and arrows. The jaguar's human wife evinces dislike of the young man, who kills her without incurring the jaguar's ill will and returns to his own people, whom he leads in an expedition to rob the jaguar of fire. Between jaguars and men, Lévi-Strauss argues, the relation is of null reciprocity, for in mythical times men ate raw and jaguars cooked, whereas now men eat cooked and jaguars raw; moreover, jaguars eat men, but men do not eat jaguars (1964:91). Like the northern Australian myths, the Indian myths begin by positing a situation in some sense opposite to the real situation. The events narrated in the myth lead from one situation to the other. Unlike the Australians, however, the Indians attribute something of a promethean role to men, for they organize to steal from the jaguar who had befriended one of their number. The jaguar's morality thus contrasts with human morality.

In South America the contrasts fire/fireless and raw/cooked are not bound up with vertical and elemental registers in the systematic manner found in northern Australia. The Australian myths are at once more dialectical and more specialized than the Indian. More dialectical because of their play on compatibilities and incompatibilities: jaguars occupy an element compatible with fire, but water 'things', be they reptiles or whirlpools, are in an element in which fire cannot exist. More specialized because they relate how fire was obtained by men, or how the path was cleared for men's acquisition of fire, but, unlike the jaguar myths, not concerned with other cultural techniques. The Gé-speaking Indians put their fire myths in a setting of cultural elaboration (several techniques are acquired); the Aborigines prefer a setting of natural elaboration (various creatures acquire their present-day forms, habits and habitats). This difference is correlated with another: the jaguar is shown interacting with humans, to his eventual undoing, for he is married to a human, befriends a human, and is robbed by humans, aided by animals; in the Aboriginal myths it is largely animals or animals-to-be or beings who become places in the water who interact.

III

I propose now to examine fire myths from further south in Australia, following the eastern side of the continent to eastern Victoria and Tasmania. It will be seen that, although the northern conceptual codes recur, the mythical protagonists begin to be differently arranged within them and transformation occurs in the vertical positions of takers and losers of fire relative to each other. The southern myths contrast in motif with those from Arnhem Land in a manner foreshadowed in Cape York. Howitt (1904:432) gives a myth from an unnamed tribe near Maryborough:

M_{12} Birral, the culture hero who placed the blacks on the primitive earth, was asked by them how they should get warmth in the day and fire at night. He told them that if they went in a certain direction they would find the sun and, by knocking a piece off it, would get fire. Going far in this direction, they discovered that the sun issued from a hole in the morning and entered another in the evening. Rushing after the sun they knocked a piece off.

M_{12} differs from M_5, according to which the discovery of fire antedates the sun, though in both myths the sun antedates the use of fire by humans.

It seems from Howitt's account that fire was secured while the sun was at the level of the earth. If in that early period the sun rose into the sky by day, M_{12} would resemble M_{11}, according to which the wren brought fire from the sky. Howitt does not record whether the sun resisted the taking of fire. Myths collected from the Kabikabi and Waka Waka in south-east Queensland by Mathew (1910:186) and from the Euahlayi in north-east New South Wales by Parker (1953:39-42) reintroduce the motif of conflict for the possession of fire.

M_{13} The death adder was in sole possession of fire, which he kept inside himself. All the birds tried to get some, but in vain, until the small hawk's ridiculous antics provoked the adder into loss of gravity and laughter. Then fire escaped, becoming common property.

M_{14} The blue crane and the kangaroo rat discovered fire when rat rubbed sticks together. They resolved to keep the art to themselves, but the difference in appearance between the fish they cooked and the fish that was sun-dried in the old manner excited attention. Crane and rat insisted that their fish was sun-dried too, but were spied upon by the night owl and parrot, who discovered the secret. It was determined to take possession of the firestick, which the crane and rat kept in a bag. A corroboree was held. The dancing of the brolgas caused the crane and rat to relax their vigilance. They laughed. The rat dropped the bag, which was snatched by the hawk who took out the firestick and set the grass alight, outdistancing the crane in her pursuit.

In these myths a lower creature(s) keeps fire *within*, inside the body (M_{13}) or a bag (M_{14}: the crane and rat had also hidden firesticks in the open-mouthed seeds of the needlebush scrub). These modes of concealment recall the concealment in vulvas of M_4. In M_{14}, as in M_4, suspicion is aroused by the differences between cooked and uncooked food and birds play a 'spy' role, but the spying is on behalf of the fireless, not of the withholders of fire. Laughter by the possessors of fire brings about their undoing, whereas in M_{11}, in which laughter also occurs, it is from a figure who wants, but is denied, fire. The change in the identity of those who laugh correlates with a change in the identity of the trickster(s). In M_{11} the trick is perpetrated by the possessor of fire at the expense of his friend who wants fire; in M_{13-14} the characters who want fire trick the jealous possessors. As in all but one of the more northern myths containing the motif of the taking of fire from a character who will not share ($M_{1-2, 6, 8,}$; the exception is M_{10}), 'higher' takes from 'lower'. But the two new myths are distinguished in several ways. The elemental register is weakened in M_{13} by the absence of water (death adders live in dry places). Water is found in M_{14} (cranes spend much of their time wading in search of fish; the myth refers to fish), but the stress is reduced by the pairing of the crane with a land animal as joint possessor of fire. Moreover, in M_{14} the distance in the vertical register between takers and losers of fire is narrowed, for although those who co-operate to capture fire are all birds (owl, parrot, brolgas, hawk), one of those they take fire from is also a bird (crane). M_{14}'s arrangement of characters recalls M_{10}, in which a wagtail and a crocodile are set against an owl. In M_{10}, however, the pair, one member of which is a bird, is opposed to a jealous possessor of fire; in M_{14} the pair, one member of which is a bird, consists of the jealous possessors.

M_{10}, in which the wagtail takes from the owl, is possibly an example of 'lower' taking from 'higher', and thus an exception to the rule prevailing so far that if fire is captured the loser is lower than the taker. (M_{11-12} do not seem to be exceptions, for in the form in which they are recorded they do not recount conflict over the possession of fire.) Even so, any vertical disparity between wagtails and owls must be minute. Myths from eastern Victoria published by Smyth (1878) and Frazer (1930) indubitably permute the vertical relation between takers and losers. Two Gippsland myths (Smyth 1878:472, 478-9) relate the vicissitudes of fire. Like most of the earlier myths they presuppose the prior existence of fire.

M_{15} Bowkan, conceived of as a cloud-dwelling spirit, was angry with the blacks. He took their fire, but the fire-tail finch stole it back without Bowkan's knowledge, and restored it to the blacks. That is why this finch is red-tailed.

M_{16} Bowkan was angry with the gins (Aboriginal women) because they would not give him any of the fish they were catching. He took their fire and outdistanced them. A crow picked up a black snake and threw it at Bowkan, who was so frightened that he dropped the fire and the women recovered it.

In both myths fire is taken by a higher being, by a cloud-dwelling spirit from folk on the ground (what eventually becomes of them is not recorded by Smyth). He is unable to keep what he has gained, losing it to a creature 'lower' than himself, either finch or crow. Curr (1887:548) records a fragment from the Brabralung tribe of Gippsland (M_{17}), according to which the ancestors of the Aborigines obtained fire from the fire-tailed finch. No other details are given. The fragment may be from a myth resembling M_{15}. Smyth (1878:458) gives another Gippsland myth (M_{18}), according to which a man, who is now a little bird with a red mark over the tail, stole a firestick from two women who guarded fire very strictly and kept it for themselves. The bird 'feigned amity and affection, and accompanied the women on their journeys', until one day he hid a firestick behind his back and, on an excuse, left the women and gave fire to the Aborigines. What happened to the women after the theft is not recorded. The motif of the two women, jealously keeping fire, not only recalls M_4, but anticipates myths recorded from the vicinity of Melbourne in greater detail than M_{18}. In these myths, which Frazer (1930:19) suggests may be called 'the Melbourne legend', one, two or a group of women searching for ants' eggs have fire at the end of their sticks. A male character captures the fire, but loses it in favour of men or gives it to men. The version summarized below is taken from Smyth (1878:459):

M_{19} The only one who could make fire was a woman, now the Pleiades or Seven Stars, and she would not share. She kept the fire in the end of her yamstick. The crow formed a plan. He made snakes, put them under an ant hill, and invited her to dig for ants' eggs, of which she was fond. When she turned up the snakes he advised her to kill them with her yamstick, the fire fell out and the crow ran off with it.

The crow was nearly as selfish as the woman had been. The Maker of Men (a sky spirit), became angry, gathered the blacks and had them speak harshly to the crow. Frightened, the crow threw fire to burn them, but they picked it up and went off.

The Maker of Men is the culture hero whose name is variously rendered as Bunjil, Pund-jel and Pund-jil. He figures in all versions of the Melbourne legend, either directly or as the father of Tarrang, who plays in one myth the thief role assigned in the others to the crow. I know three variants on M_{19}. Their points of difference may be indicated briefly. M_{20} (Smyth 1878:459), as Frazer (1930:16) notes, 'involves certain repetitions'. While cutting a tree to get ants' eggs two women were attacked by snakes and, in fighting them, one woman broke her stick. Fire came forth, and was stolen by the crow, who flew off with it, but was frightened into dropping it by two men who later became stars. There was a great fire, which frightened the Aborigines, but Bunjil descended from the sky to tell them that they should not lose the fire. Eventually fire was lost. Snakes became numerous. A woman of the same name as the Pleiades woman of M_{19} was sent by Pal-yang, who had brought women from the water. She fought the snakes. One day she broke her stick in striking a snake. Fire came out and was stolen by the crow, who hid it on a mountain. The two men who had become stars descended to tell the Aborigines of this. They flew up again, but one of them returned, bringing the fire, and taught the Aborigines the use of firesticks. M_{20} is the only version of the Melbourne legend in which the sticks are not yamsticks, in which it is not actually stated that the women became the Pleiades and in which the thief does not play tricks. Furthermore, M_{20}, alone among the myths from eastern Victoria, seems to account for the original appearance of fire; the other myths presuppose fire's existence. M_{21} (Howitt 1904:430) relates that the crow stole by a trick the fire kept by a group of women at the end of yamsticks used for digging ants' eggs. The trick is not described. At Bunjil's command the musk-crow released the whirlwind from his bag, sweeping the women into the sky as the Pleiades. M_{22} (Frazer 1930:18, cited from *The Scottish Geographical Magazine*) attributes the theft to Bunjil's son, who plays on a woman the trick performed by the crow in M_{19}. He gives the fire to the Aborigines. Bunjil's son, whose ultimate fate is not recorded, acts a role which combines something of the crow in M_{19-21} and the two men who become stars in M_{20}.

The Melbourne group of myths contains several interesting features. Trickery is a recurring motif, linking them with $M_{11, 13-14}$. The motifs in M_{20} of female possessors of fire and of extinction of fire constitute links with $M_{4, 9}$, and in particular with M_9, which also refers to ant-hills, though not to ants' eggs. Water is absent, except for the reference in M_{20} to the woman sent by Pal-yang, who had brought women from the water. High positions in the vertical register are strongly stressed, though questions of vertical relation are complicated by repetition in the taking and losing of fire. In all of the eastern Victorian myths recorded in sufficient detail ($M_{15-16, 19-22}$), characters active in taking or losing fire belong to the element of air, as stars, birds or sky spirits. They no longer include creatures bound to the elements of water and earth. When such characters occur they seem to be present merely as victims (the Aborigines of M_{15-16}) or as means to the ends of aerial creatures (for example, snakes in $M_{16, 19, 22}$). Contrary to the northern pattern of 'higher' takes from 'lower' (as a bird from a crocodile), 'lower' takes from 'higher' (as a bird from stars or sky spirits). At least two of the eastern Victorian myths relate a taking by 'higher' from 'lower', as in M_{15-16} in which a sky spirit steals fire from Aborigines, but I find it significant that he loses by the intervention of a 'lower' creature, crow or finch, what he has taken. In the south, then, if fire is lost to a higher position in the vertical register, the loss is only temporary. One of the northern myths contains the motif of a temporary loss of fire: in M_2 the crocodile takes fire formerly shared with the plover, but the plover quickly recovers it. I would interpret M_2's temporary inversion of the northern 'higher' takes from 'lower', and M_{15-16}'s temporary inversion of the southern 'lower' takes from 'higher', as devices to confirm the general pattern of the two areas. The point is that any taker of fire who is in the wrong vertical position relative to his antagonist quickly loses what he has anomalously captured. M_{20} is of particular interest here. According to the first part of the myth, the two men who frighten the crow into dropping fire become stars. In the second part of the myth, they return from the sky to tell the Aborigines where the crow has hidden fire. In some accounts, one of the men then dies on a mountain, though in other accounts this is denied, and he is said to have become the planet Mars. The other man took Aborigines to a mountain to teach them the use of firesticks, and then flew up—where to is unexplained. Now Smyth's presentation of what I have summarized as M_{19} brings in two men, one of whom has the same name—Trrar—as one of the men in M_{20}, and who, as in M_{20}, are opposed to the crow, though not instrumental in taking fire from him. They finish as stones at the foot of a mountain. It is not clear, therefore, taking M_{19-20} together, how the two men are to be placed relative to the crow in the vertical register, for although as stars they would be higher, as stones at the foot of a mountain they would be lower, and their ultimate position in the myth in which they became, for a while, stars, is unstated for one man and disputed for the other.

The last myth that I wish to consider in this paper is the only known Tasmanian account of fire (Smyth 1878:461-2, cited from *Proceedings of the Royal Society of Tasmania*).

M_{23} Two men who are now the stars Castor and Pollux were seen by the aborigines standing at the top of a hill. They threw fire which fell among the aborigines, who ran away frightened, but then returned to make a fire with wood.

The possession of fire by the two men who are now stars is unexplained. M_{23} recalls features of the Melbourne legend: possession of fire by beings (female in $M_{19, 21-22}$; male in M_{23}) who become stars; association of a pair of men with a mountain or hill ($M_{19-20, 23}$); a pair of men who become stars (permanently in M_{23}; at least temporarily in M_{20}); Aborigines initially frightened by fire ($M_{20, 23}$). In view of the long separation of Tasmania from the mainland, it seems reasonable to interpret these shared features as indicative of the ancient fire mythology of an indefinite area of south-east Australia. At the same time, it must be noticed that the Tasmanian myth shows impoverishment, relative to those from the mainland, in that it does not relate the conflicts over the possession of fire that seem to be the commonest motif of the myths collected in the various areas of northern and eastern Australia.

IV

Although the analysis of the fire myths from northern and eastern Australia could be deepened, and the study extended to include the rest of the continent, what has been attempted here is sufficient to bring out a number of structural and semantic features that might otherwise have remained hidden. As these have been indicated in the course of the paper, they will only be summarily stated here.

(i) The myths characteristically posit situations which, from the point of view of everyday experience, are fantastic. The events narrated lead in the direction of the real situation. The incidents described are momentous for everyday life and include marvellous metamorphoses by which the world acquires part of its form.

(ii) The incidents described in the myths can be classed as expressions of a small number of motifs, some of which are limited in distribution even in the part of Australia studied. For example, the motif of accidental extinction of fire is found in Arnhem Land, Cape York and eastern Victoria, but that of the deliberately attempted extinction of fire is found only in Arnhem Land. The motif of laughter incapacitating the possessors of fire is found only in what may be termed the central group of myths (comprising M_{12-14}), whereas that of the obtaining of fire by trickery is found not only in the central, but also in the southern group (M_{15-23}). Trickery occurs in the northern group (M_{1-11}), but in marked contrast to the central and southern myths the trick is played either by the possessor of fire (as in M_{11}) or by the witting or unwitting enemies of fire (as in M_4). Withholding of fire, concealment of fire, capture of fire, rejected requests for fire and pursuits are motifs occurring in all groups.

(iii) In the northern group, several myths (M_{1-5}) can be understood as segments of a super-myth giving a complete account of fire from its chance discovery to its acquisition by Aborigines. It does not seem that myths belonging to the other groups could be joined to form super-myths, even though most of them give incomplete accounts of fire.

(iv) The events narrated in the myths are organized within frameworks of conceptual codes, the eliciting of which provides objective criteria for comparison. The codes include vertical, elemental and moral registers, and registers consisting in such contrasts as raw/cooked, dry/wet and light/dark. Among these, the vertical and elemental seem the most useful for analytic purposes. By eliciting them it becomes possible to grasp some of the presuppositions of Aboriginal thought. I shall conclude the paper by indicating why I think this possible.

It has been seen that a theme of many of the myths is the taking of fire from its non-human possessor by a being also represented as non-human. Humans acquire fire after, and in some sense because of, this transaction. The primeval takers and losers are objectified as spirits or natural phenomena or species. In all but one of the northern myths incorporating this theme, the loser is identified with water, as either a water reptile or a place in the water. The takers are birds, and hence identified with air and higher in the vertical register. The exception is M_{10}, in which taker and loser are both birds. In the southern myths, with the possible exception of M_{20}, the positions of taker and loser relative to each other are inversed, birds taking from stars or cloud-dwelling spirits. Takers and losers are thus both identified with the air. From a southern point of view all the northern myths except M_{10} would seem to be inverted, to be upside-down. From a northern point of view, the southern myths, except possibly M_{20}, would give the same impression. In the central group, the relevant myths (M_{13-14}) are conceptually intermediary between north and south.

Turning now to beliefs in the fate of spirits of the dead, it seems that there is a correlation between the vertical position of mythical takers and human possessors of fire relative to mythical losers, and that of possessors of life in the flesh relative to losers. According to the Dalabon, the authors of M_1, the spirits of the dead enter totemic waters. Elsewhere in Arnhem Land and Cape York (see, for example, Berndt and Berndt 1964:414-17; Mountford 1958:61; Roth 1903:17-19; Warner 1958: 445-7), they dwell in totemic sites, including waters, or haunt the bush or their burial place or late home, or travel across the sea to an island of the dead. That is to say, losers of life in the flesh are either on the same level or lower than possessors of life in the flesh. They occupy the same element (earth) or a lower element (water). Losers of life in the flesh therefore have something in common with mythical losers of fire who occupy a lower position and element than the mythical takers and the human possessors of fire. A comment made by Stanner (1960b:120) on the Murinbata Rainbow Serpent myth is of interest: 'The myth of The Rainbow Serpent tells—among other things—how the very condition of humanness, the possession of fire, was at the expense of the death of the father's father of one moiety of men and the mother's father of the other.' Here the possession of fire is mythically linked with questions of life and death.

In the north, the correlation is weakened by the fact that losers of life in the flesh are not always lower than possessors. Sometimes they are on the same level. With the exception of M_{10}, mythical losers of fire are always lower than mythical takers or human possessors. In the south, the correlation is stronger. The prevailing belief is that the spirits of the dead go to the sky, a belief found also to the north and west of the area of my southern group of myths (see, for example, Berndt and Berndt 1964:412-13; Dawson 1881:51; Howitt 1904:434-40; Parker

1905:90-1; Thomas 1906:204). Losers of life in the flesh are therefore higher than possessors, just as, with the possible exception of M_{20}, mythical losers of fire are higher than mythical takers and human possessors. Subject to the qualifications and exceptions noted, it looks as though certain presuppositions of Aboriginal thought can be formulated from a combined study of fire myths and beliefs in the fate of spirits of the dead. The formula is:

Losers of life in the flesh : Possessors of life in the flesh : :
Losers of fire : Takers and possessors of fire

The formula, which is more thoroughly applicable to the southern group of myths than to the northern, is unaffected by the inversion occurring between south and north in the position of takers and possessors of fire relative to losers. That a similar inversion should occur in the position of possessors of life in the flesh relative to losers, may be taken as indicating that the correlations expressed in the formula are not merely accidental.

Addendum

Since writing this paper, I have read A. Massola's *Bunjil's Cave* (Melbourne: Lansdowne, 1968). Massola (pp. 111, 142-3) records two beliefs relevant to my argument. The Wotjobaluk of north-west Victoria held Castor and Pollux to be two hunters who pursued and killed a kangaroo at the beginning of the 'great heat' (summer). The Beehive is the smoke of the fire by which the hunters cooked the kangaroo. The Wotjobaluk belief evidently belongs to the same family as the Tasmanian myth. Further, if the two are considered in relation to each other, they look like segments of a super-myth, the Wotjobaluk being earlier in the sequence than the Tasmanian. The Kulin of central Victoria believed that spirits of the dead sometimes return to earth to visit their burial place. While on earth spirits could sustain themselves by killing game with magical spears, but could not light a fire, even though they were interested in fire. Spirits often warmed themselves at camp fires left by the living (left, that is, by possessors of life in the flesh). That the Kulin should impute to the spirits of the dead inability to light fires is logical, given the relation presupposed between loss of life in the flesh and loss of fire.

Notes

1. The present paper is a revised version of a paper prepared for Symposium No. 42, Wenner-Gren Foundation for Anthropological Research, Burg Wartenstein, 1968. I hope in later papers to examine fire myths collected in other parts of Australia. In the meantime, I have thought it preferable to study a limited zone more intensively than the entire continent less intensively.

2. I conducted fieldwork on the Beswick Reserve and neighbouring places in several periods between 1964 and 1968 under the auspices of the Australian Institute of Aboriginal Studies and the University of Sydney.

References

Berndt, R. M. and C. H. 1964 *The World of the First Australians*. Ure Smith, Sydney.
Curr, E. M. 1887 *The Australian Race* (Vol. 3). Government Printer, Melbourne.
Dawson, J. 1881 *Australian Aborigines*. Robertson, Melbourne.
Frazer, J. G. 1930 *Myths of the Origin of Fire*. Macmillan, London.
Freud, S. 1930 *Civilization and its Discontents*. Hogarth Press, London.
Howitt, A. W. 1904 *The Native Tribes of South-East Australia*. Macmillan, London.
Lévi-Strauss, C. 1963 *Structural Anthropology*. Basic Books, New York.
―― 1964 *Mythologiques: Le Cru et le Cuit*. Plon, Paris.
―― 1966 *Mythologiques: Du Miel aux Cendres*. Plon, Paris.
McConnel, U. 1957 *The Myths of the Mungkan*. Melbourne University Press, Melbourne.
Mathew, J. 1910 *Two Representative Tribes of Queensland*. Nutt, London.
Mountford, C. P. 1956 *Records of the American-Australian Scientific Expedition to Arnhem Land* (Vol. 1). Melbourne University Press, Melbourne.
―― 1958 *The Tiwi: Their Art, Myth and Ceremony*. Phoenix House, London.
Parker, K. L. 1905 *The Euahlayi Tribe*. Constable, London.
―― 1953 *Australian Legendary Tales*. Angus and Robertson, Sydney.
Radcliffe-Brown, A. R. 1951 The comparative method in social anthropology, *Journal of the Royal Anthropological Institute*, Vol. 81:15-22.
Robinson, R. 1966 *Aboriginal Myths and Legends*. Sun Books, Melbourne.
Roth, W. E. 1903 Superstition, magic and medicine, *North Queensland Ethnography*, Bulletin 5. Government Printer, Brisbane.
Smyth, R. B. 1878 *The Aborigines of Victoria* (Vol. 1). Government Printer, Melbourne.
Spencer, B. 1914 *Native Tribes of the Northern Territory of Australia*. Macmillan, London.
Spencer, B. and F. J. Gillen 1904 *The Northern Tribes of Central Australia*. Macmillan, London.
Stanner, W. E. H. 1960*a* On aboriginal religion: II. Sacramentalism, rite and myth, *Oceania*, Vol. 30, No. 4:245-78.
―― 1960*b* On aboriginal religion: III. Symbolism in the higher rites, *Oceania*, Vol. 31, No. 2:100-20.
―― 1961 On aboriginal religion: IV. The design-plan of a riteless myth, *Oceania*, Vol. 31, No. 4:233-58.
Thomas, N. W. 1906 *Natives of Australia*. Constable, London.
Warner, W. L. 1958 *A Black Civilization* (2nd ed.). Harper, New York.

NICOLAS PETERSON

Buluwandi
A Central Australian Ceremony
for the Resolution of Conflict[1]

In 1901 Spencer and Gillen witnessed a 'Fire Ceremony' held by the Warramunga. They described it in detail but commented (1904:392) that they '... could find no satisfactory explanation of what it meant' except that '... its object was to finally settle up old quarrels and to make the men friendly disposed towards one another'. Several versions of this ceremony are still held in Central Australia by the Walbiri, western neighbours of the Warramunga. They offer the same explanation for holding the ceremonies today as the Warramunga gave to Spencer and Gillen in 1901. It is likely that the problem for Spencer and Gillen stemmed from the fact that only a limited range of people are able to give vent to their aggression in these ceremonies. Since they did not establish exactly who could do this, they were unable to begin to answer why. This paper describes which categories of kin are able to display anger and argues that it results from conflict between patrikin and matrikin over rights to bestowal. Though the Walbiri have an Aranda type kinship system which is usually described in terms of D (daughter) exchange, it is a model of ZD (sister's daughter) exchange that provides the most economical explanation.

In the context of a totemic religion the term 'Fire Ceremony' is perhaps misleading, since the ceremonies are not associated with fire 'totems'. The term is descriptive, referring to self-inflicted burns and the use of flaming torches, which suggested 'fiends escaped from Hades' to Gillen (1968:255). Fire features in many Aboriginal ceremonies and is often associated with burning people, but in none is its use more spectacular or so public. For this reason Spencer and Gillen's term is retained.

THE WALBIRI FIRE CEREMONIES

The Walbiri perform three versions of the Fire ceremonies at Yuendumu Government Settlement today. Two have names similar to (probably the same as) those mentioned by Spencer and Gillen as being celebrated by the Warramunga; they are the *Djariwanba* (Spencer and Gillen's *Thaduwan*, 1904:376) and the *Ngadjagula* (Spencer and Gillen's *Nathagura*, 1904:375-92). The third version, *Buluwandi*, is associated with the northern Walbiri and regularly performed at Hooker Creek Settlement. Unlike *Djariwanba* and *Ngadjagula* it is only of recent[2] standing in its present form at Yuendumu. *Djariwanba* belongs to the djuburula, djagamara, djambidjimba and djangala subsections,[3] which together form one patrimoiety. The mythology associates it in particular with the travels of *Yaripiri*, a snake, of the djuburula and djagamara subsections, who went from Winbago (Blanche Tower) to an unknown destination north of Hooker Creek. Both *Ngadjagula* and *Buluwandi* belong to the opposite patrimoiety (djabaldjari, djungarai, djabanungga and djabangari). The mythology of the former relates to the travels of a rat kangaroo, *mala*, from Mowerung, south of Yuendumu, to Walaya near Hooker Creek. *Buluwandi*'s most important associations are with a bird and a snake resident at Inabaga on the Lander River flood-out.

Though the song cycles and mythology connected with each ceremony vary considerably, and even from performance to performance of the same ceremony, the manner of celebration and pattern of interaction is always the same. Each of the ceremonies has the following features:

1. All adult participants until the final night are married.
2. A period of several weeks preparatory singing of the song cycle at a site close to and in view of the general camp.
3. The participation of women once the ceremony is under way.
4. Basically similar ground plans.
5. The use of tall saplings bound round with dry leaves to make long torches called *wanbanbirri* (Spencer and Gillen's *wanmanmirri* 1904:380).
6. The throwing of small pieces of bark, *wandabi*, by men of the worker patrimoiety at the women and children.
7. The decoration of the men of the owner patrimoiety with cotton high hats (*gudari*) and their individual dancing before the assembled community.
8. A central fire at which the decorated dancers 'burn' themselves (*buramiga*), tended by relatives of the opposite patrimoiety who smother (*ngalkinba*) the sparks.
9. A climax to the ceremony in which the torches are set alight and the dancers attacked with them.
10. The same structural relationship between the subsections of the two patrimoieties in each version of the ceremony.
11. The same explicit function, to settle up quarrels.

The patrimoieties form the basic division in all important Walbiri ceremonies. One patrimoiety owns each ceremony and is termed *kira* or owners and the other patrimoiety is termed *kulungulu* or workers. The owners perform the ritual whilst the workers prepare the ritual paraphernalia, help paint the owners and stage-manage the ceremony. Though the Walbiri speak of ritual organization mainly in terms of subsection affiliation, the reasons why some people are connected with one ceremony and not another are based on kin and community ties. These ties are considered in the analysis of the pattern of interaction, but until then I will use the subsection categories, as the Walbiri do when discussing ritual in general terms.

TABLE 1

SUBSECTION GROUPING IN RITUAL

The pairs on the right 'look after' those on the left

Kira = Owners   *Kulungulu* = Workers

Djabaldjari ⎫   Djambidjimba ⎫
             ⎬ F/S   ⎬ WMB/ZDH
Djungarai   ⎭   Djuburula   ⎭
                 ←MBS/FZS→
Djabanungga ⎫   Djangala   ⎫
             ⎬ F/S   ⎬ WMB/ZDH
Djabangari   ⎭   Djagamara   ⎭

In ceremonies where behaviour is governed by the patrimoiety division, the owners are grouped in father-son subsection pairs, while the workers are grouped in the *malilangu* or WMB/ZDH relationship; that is, of men who are *djuraldja* to each other and may marry into each other's matrilines. In the smaller ceremonies shortage of people may obscure this pattern of co-operation, but in the large intercommunity Fire ceremonies in which at least sixty men and women are involved, they are strongly evident.

The Buluwandi

Buluwandi, a stork (pelican?), lived at Inabaga and made visits to the surrounding sacred sites. During his travels he observed ancestral men holding a Fire ceremony and descended to participate in parts of it. At a number of stages he transformed himself into various other forms, a snake *Banangula*, an owl, a cockatoo and a *Gurrgurrba* bird. At the end of the ceremony he returned to Inabaga.

Though the basic features and sequence of events remain the same in each performance, there are variations in other respects. These seem to be the result of *Buluwandi* belonging primarily to the djabaldjari and djungarai subsection pair, so that if men of the other father-son subsection pair in the patrimoiety wish to emphasize their role they introduce song cycles, emblems and mythology that are directly associated with their subsections. This means that there may be a pole-emblem for the *Banangula* snake as well as for *Buluwandi* proper, and there may also be emblems related to *Djamangula*, the blanket lizard, when men from further north are heavily involved. The ceremony I describe here had only one rather poorly decorated pole. It was performed in August 1967 at the settlement. I saw the final days of a second *Buluwandi* the following year, also at Yuendumu. The latter ceremony had much more elaborately decorated poles and a separate minor sequence of events was performed for the *Djamangula* away from the main ground on the penultimate day. I describe the first ceremony, however, since it has been filmed.[4]

The Ceremony

From informants' accounts of the beginning of the ceremony, men of all subsections gathered at the edge of the camp on most evenings and sang parts of the song cycle as the sun set. Sometimes they continued for an hour or two after dark. This was the pattern for about four weeks until men from Hooker Creek and neighbouring cattle stations arrived. The most important group expected were to have come from Willowra cattle station, but as they were slow in arriving, the ceremony proceeded without them. Some time after the second week, the women started to participate.

The worker patrimoiety, the men and women of the djagamara, djangala, djambidjimba and djuburula subsections, cleared a ground approximately 100 feet wide and 250 feet long and oriented north-south. Thirty feet in from the southern end a 12-foot pole stood surmounted by feathers, and painted with a snake design in red. In the late afternoon the worker men would gather at the ground, followed casually by the members of the owner patrimoiety, the djabaldjari, djungarai, djabanungga and djabangari subsection men and women collectively referred to as *Dia Dia*. The owner males would sit in a semi-circle facing north with their backs to the pole. Those of the djungarai and djabaldjari subsections sat to the west, with worker men of the djambidjimba and djuburula subsections standing behind them also facing north. To the east sat the owners of the djabanungga and djabangari subsections, with the worker men of the djangala and djagamara subsections standing behind them. Behind the pole, the women and children sat in a straight line facing north. The women of the nabaldjari, nungarai, nambidjimba and naburula subsections sat on the west, that is, behind the men of the same subsections, and the women of the remaining subsections to the east. As the men sang, the women danced toward the pole in a hopping shuffle, forearms raised vertically, palms opposed, calling out on a single high note as they moved forward. The worker and owner men

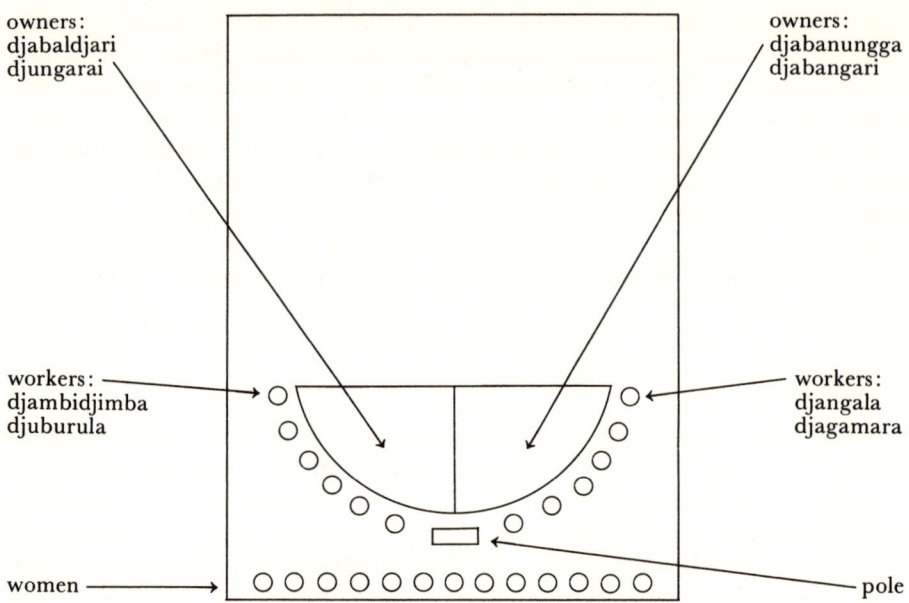

Fig. 1 Ground plan until the penultimate day

sang together and from time to time some of the workers would run round behind the seated owners and then dance out in front facing them. The men of the djagamara and djangala subsections ran round in a clockwise direction and the men of the djuburula and djambidjimba subsections in an anti-clockwise direction. The dance, described by Spencer and Gillen as grotesque (1904:376), involved leaping up and down holding boomerangs in a threatening manner as if about to throw them at the owners. Slightly to the north of where the worker men danced, a small triangular stone with a hole in the apex was suspended from a thin stick and kept rotating by a young worker man. On it was painted in red a design of a snake that lived at Inabaga.

This was the pattern of the ceremony each evening until the day before the climax and completion. In the early morning of the penultimate day some of the worker men repainted the pole standing on the ground. Others decorated two large and one small digging stick and three shields, and made a large number of small clapping sticks for the owners. At 3.30 p.m. the workers commenced to paint themselves with designs similar to those used by women in their *Jawalju* ceremonies; the designs, in red, were outlined in white or black. The owner men and a small number of owner women painted themselves up, 200 yards away from the ground to the south-west. When they were ready, some worker men danced across to them, surrounded them and danced back on either side of the long file that moved toward the ground; the women brought up the rear. As the procession approached the ground the owners went down on their knees and circled around the tall pole, with a group of fifteen women of the nungarai and nabaldjari subsections dancing beside them. They then wheeled around and sat in their normal position facing north. The suspended stone was replaced with the two painted digging sticks planted upright before the men, and the small stick before the women. The pattern of the ceremony remained the same as the previous evenings, except that the worker men, instead of using boomerangs when they danced in front of the owners, now took up the digging sticks and danced with these, standing them upright in the ground each time they stopped dancing at the end of a verse. Just before sunset the owner men, led by the djabaldjari and djungarai subsections, proceeded in single file, on their knees, to circle round the two digging sticks, rising to their feet one by one as they passed them and returning to where they had been sitting before. The leader carried one of the painted shields.

After a break at sunset, dancing continued as on other evenings. The small digging stick that had been in front of the women during the afternoon was now beside the two the men had been using. A hole (*raku*) was dug in front of the owners for them to urinate in, for from the commencement of the singing at 8 p.m. till dawn the next morning they were not allowed to leave the ground. The same was done for the owner women. The worker men sometimes performed the taunting dance in front of the owners holding one of the painted shields (*guridji*, a term also used for WM). At 10.30 p.m. one of the two other, and as yet unseen painted shields was brought out and briefly revealed 40 feet away from the men; the women were not meant to look. Later in the night it was revealed again much closer to the owners. Before midnight the workers constructed a large leafy hut, *minjirmurru*, at the northern end of the ground, and a smaller one at the southern end of the ground immediately behind the women. Sometime[5] after this the owner men and women moved to stand in a semi-circle around a fire built in front of their respective huts, facing the entrances. The worker men and women stood behind the owners, shielding them whilst they singed their pubic hair. After this all returned to where they had been before and continued singing till dawn. As the first light of dawn flushed the sky the owner men, led by the djungarai and djabaldjari subsections, proceeded in single file on their knees toward the men's hut, the leader holding one of the painted shields. As each man reached the half-way point he got to his feet and stooping low proceeded into the hut. The owner women then moved into their hut. Within the men's hut the owners sang in shifts all day, those not singing taking the opportunity to sleep.

The triangular stone and the painted shield were displayed inside.

In the middle of the morning the worker men went off to make the *wanbanbirri* torches and to cut a number of small pieces of bark, 9 inches square or so-called *wandabi*, or *wadamirri*. The worker women went off separately and cut green branches and bark squares too. By 3.30 p.m. the worker men had completed their tasks and a group of six of them came out of the bush near the ground where they had been working. Dancing in their hopping style, and making whooping noises, they approached the hut where the women were. As they drew near they hurled the bark squares in the direction of the women and children, who laughed and screamed. No one was hit.

The owner men and women in their separate huts then started to paint up. In the men's hut, which was not big enough for all of the twenty-six owners, only the djungarai and djabaldjari men were inside painting up, the men of the djabanungga and djabangari subsections sitting outside to the north where they could not be seen by the women. The blood used by the owner men in their decoration was donated by young worker men, but the work of decoration was carried out by men of both patrimoieties. The worker men made high hats, twig-bundles (*maribi*), and wrapped the small *mana-baganu* bullroarers, referred to as *ngindi* (tail or penis) in pieces of cloth to hang about the neck, for each performer. As the sun set, the twenty-four torch poles were placed in the ground in two parallel lines between the men's and the women's huts, to form an avenue 20 feet wide. Owner men who had not taken an active part in the ceremony until this stage sat in a freshly made clearing (*mina*) at the southern end of the ground on the eastern side. Two small fires were started outside the men's hut at either corner, and a single large fire not far from the pole at the southern end of the ground. At sunset the owner women, chests painted in a white curvilinear design, emerged on their knees in two groups, nungarai-nabaldjari and nabanungga-nabangari, then moved to stand near the pole where they remained motionless for the rest of the evening. The worker men danced around the clearing and then in a large circle on the ground near the fire; then stopped. One moved to the entrance of the men's hut, several others to stand by the large central fire. A throng of spectators, men, women and children, gathered to watch.

After a formalized cry from inside the hut the first owner emerged wearing his high hat and decorated in a red and white cotton design. He knelt before the western fire. A shadowy figure of a worker man holding a fighting stick lurked in the background. Then, holding his hands behind his back, the dancer stood up and stepped out with elaborate caution, for the central fire. A small core of djambidjimba and djuburula men stood by the fire whilst all the members of the

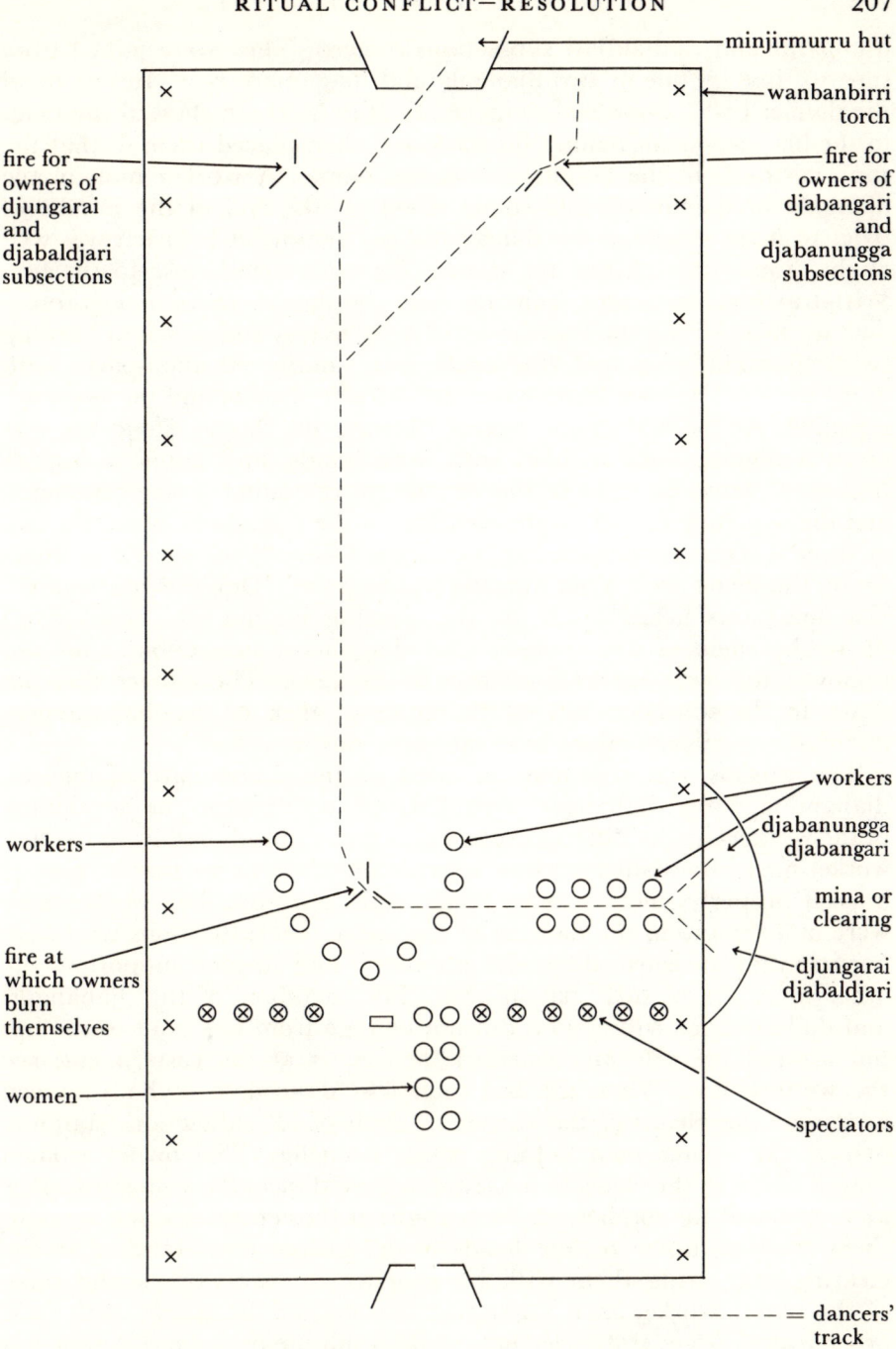

Fig. 2 Ground plan on the final night

djungarai and djabaldjari subsections danced. They were joined from time to time by one or two djangala and djagamara men. In one hand the dancer had a bundle of twigs. At the fire he knelt, showed the twigs to the fire, put them behind his back and then placed them so that the top two-thirds of the bundle was in the flames. A worker man of the djangala or djagamara subsection stood on the end of the bundle of twigs to make sure that the dancer did not remove it before it was well alight. Some men chided the dancer for not getting close to the fire. Withdrawing the bundle from the fire, the dancer shook it vigorously over his head so that he was showered with sparks and pieces of burning twig; djambidjimba and djuburula men smothered the sparks with green leaves. The twig bundle was put back in the fire and the sequence repeated. At the end of the second burning the dancer stood up, was given a digging stick to hold with both hands, and made to hop or high-step[6] across in front of the women participating in the ceremony, and the watching crowd, to the clearing on the east. As he went, the two or three workers accompanying him abused him: 'You are not as smart as you think you are', 'Your dancing was no good', 'Don't be big headed'. The spectators heard it all. At the clearing his hat was knocked off by worker men of the djangala and djagamara subsections who also removed the *mana-baganu* from around his neck. The dancer then sat down in the southern half of the clearing; men of the djabanungga and djabangari subsections later sat in the northern half.

The process was repeated for each of the djabaldjari, djungarai, djabanungga and djabangari men. Changes occurred in the positioning of the workers as the different subsection men danced, and as individual worker men who wished to abuse a particular man, or see that he burned himself properly, moved to be in the right position. The worker men were more polite to the dancers of the latter two subsections who were participating to learn about the ceremony and to give support to the other members of their patrimoiety. The members of the djabangari and djabanungga subsections did not emerge from the front of the hut but around the side and warmed themselves at the eastern and not the western fire. When the last man had danced, everybody moved nearer to the clearing, the worker women of all subsections standing behind the owner men holding green branches. The owner women moved closer to the clearing too. After a brief dance, the younger worker men uprooted the torches, set them alight at the central fire and brought them crashing down on the heads of the people now standing in the clearing, showering them with burning leaves; the women and some of the senior worker men attempted to smother the sparks with their green leaves. A general mêlée ensued for a minute or so until the torches had burnt out. This marked the end of the ceremony. Four nungarai women removed the central pole and all went home. The following day an exchange of possessions took place between the owners and the workers at the ground.

The Pattern of Interaction in the Buluwandi

From the viewpoint of any owner man in any of the Fire ceremonies the primary attack comes from the subsection of the MB and DH (*ngamini*)—real and classificatory in all cases mentioned unless otherwise specified. Primary support comes from the subsection which includes the MBS (*bangu* or *wangili*) and MF and DS (*djamidi*). From the workers' point of view they are attacking their WFs, real ZSs and classificatory ZSs who are also potential WFs (they are actual WFs in over 50 per cent of the marriages [Meggitt 1962:199]). It is from among these potential WFs that a man's circumcisor is most generally chosen (*ibid.*: 299-300).

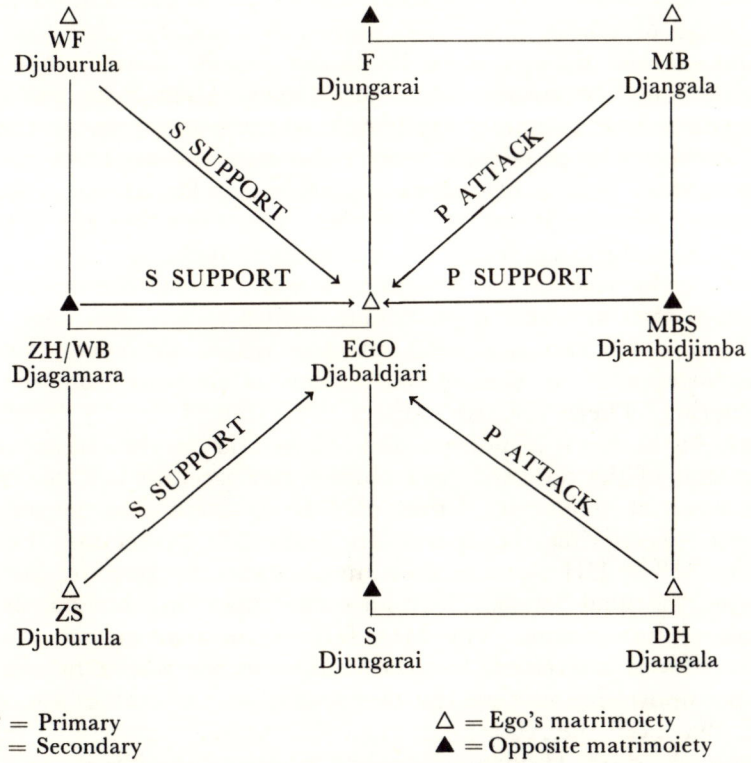

P = Primary △ = Ego's matrimoiety
S = Secondary ▲ = Opposite matrimoiety

Fig. 3 Ceremonial interaction between workers and owners

Though the men of the other subsections have a theoretical obligation either to attack or to support, they have in practice the opportunity to choose as far as their classificatory relatives are concerned. The men of an owner ego's WB and ZH (*ngumbana*) and FMB and ZSS (*jabala*) subsection are primarily concerned with burning their 'WFs' (that is, ego's F and S) and must support their real WB or ZH. The men of ego's own WF and ZS (*wandiri* and *nguniari*) subsection whose primary task is the support of their MBS (ego's F and S) must support their DH. The distinction between who should attack and who should support is based on the matrimoiety division. A man calls the opposite matrimoiety *magunda-wanu*, the origin of shame, or *gulu-wanggu*, without anger. This refers to the fact that it includes a man's actual and classificatory mother-in-law, and the relatives who have given him a wife, which in some circumstances they could take away (*ibid.*: 192). By contrast, a man's own matrimoiety is *magunda-wanggu*, lacking shame and by implication *gulu-wanu*, with anger.

In the actual performance of the ceremony the role of the workers as protectors is more clearly seen *vis-à-vis* particular individuals than that of the attackers. The male protectors stand on each side of the fire and smother the sparks as the dancer 'burns' himself—that is, they are protecting the owners from themselves. They may also barrack for the dancer. It is mainly the female workers and a few of the senior male workers who physically protect the male owners from the attack of the others. This is of particular interest as far as the women are concerned, because it means that they are protecting the men their brothers are attacking: that is, their sons and husbands.

Though the role of the attackers is less obvious, there is room for individual men to seek out particular owners to 'punish'. This may be verbal, in which case it is most effective whilst the owner is hopping (or high-stepping) in front of the women on the way from the fire to the clearing. There are two opportunities for physically burning the owners. At the fire it is indirect; the MB or DH has the chance to stand on the end of the dancer's twig bundle and see that it is really alight along much of its length. If they do this, it means that the other men who are smothering the sparks are indirectly protecting the owner from his MB or DH. A more substantial chance for burning the owners is during the final attack. After an owner man has danced, he sits in his half of the clearing. The MD, DH or, for that matter, any other worker who is interested, has the chance to see where he sits down. This is important, because the decoration on the face of the dancers means that even the Aborigines may have to look twice to be sure who is who in the dark. Having established where a man has seated himself, they stand a good chance of being able to burn him, particularly if the signal for the actual burning is given discreetly to surprise the owners, as it often is. However, younger owner men who are nervous of the burning they are about to receive may sometimes move surreptitiously about the clearing, though this is not good form. One young man spoken to moved twice and avoided severe burning though two MB were after him. Generally people do not move about because they think '. . . no one will worry about me, I can just sit and join in and sing'. (Barrett 1964.) Thus, in terms of the interaction of the owner and worker patrimoiety males, the primary attack is between generations but within matrimoieties, and primary support within generations but between matrimoieties.

The two common ceremonies at Yuendumu are *Djariwanba* and *Ngadjagula*, which are owned by opposite patrimoieties (now *Buluwandi* seems to be replacing *Ngadjagula*, but as they belong to the one patrimoiety the change is largely in fashion since the formal structure is the same), so that the owners in the *Djariwanba* become the workers in the *Ngadjagula* or *Buluwandi* and vice versa. Since the ceremonies are generally performed alternately, the cumulative effect of the primary burning action is attack on junior members of matrilines by the senior members, 'down' the matriline, and by the circumcised against their circumcisors, that is 'up' or 'against' the direction of the circumcision relationship and the giving of daughters in marriage. Primary support is exchanged between MBS/FZS and MF/DS; the former are traditionally expected to be ritual friends, and the latter are also close (Meggitt 1962:145).

THE PATTERN OF CO-OPERATION: ZD EXCHANGE AS AN EXPLANATORY MODEL

The ceremony cannot be for the settling of all or any quarrels since the pattern of interaction and co-operation is severely limited. Certain people, such as males of the patrimoiety, never have a chance to attack each other. It is therefore legitimate to think that the ceremony is concerned with primarily allowing for aggression that arises out of a fairly specific sphere of social relations. It is clear from Meggitt's material that the sphere of social relations which gives rise to many quarrels is rights to and over women (e.g. see case of Romeo, *ibid.*:173-84; and under 'Disputes' in index). In his discussion of marriage arrangements he emphasizes the role of the matrikin (*ibid.*:197-8) and the importance of the circumcision relationship (*ibid.*:281-310); both are involved in the Fire ceremony. Though he explicitly denies (*ibid.*:198) that actual niece exchange occurs among the Walbiri, it does provide an economic explanation of the pattern in the ceremonies.

In terms of the ZD exchange model, the co-operation of the MB and ZH of an owner ego is comprehensible, for these relatives stand in the relationship of potential WMB/ZDH—that is, of men potentially exchanging nieces. They, like the other worker pair, are *djuraldja* to each other—that is, belong to intermarrying matrilines (*ibid.*:196-7). A true MB, particularly as he becomes older, would have ample motivation to burn men of ego's patriline if his wishes had not been considered in the bestowal of his ZD, and she had been given to a man other than the one he planned. He cannot direct his antagonism at his ZH (ego's father), because he is of the opposite matrimoiety and has his Z. The ZS, however, over whom a MB has a recognized authority relationship (*kiwayila*), is the obvious alternative because he belongs to the patriline that has failed to recognize his rights and is of the MB's own matrimoiety. Though ZHs are not meant to burn their 'WBs', they inevitably do in the final mêlée because their ZSs are standing together with them in the clearing, and the sparks are bound to fall on both. This gives a ZH a good excuse if he does want to burn an owner ego whose sister he has been led, by ego's MB, to expect as wife but who has been given to somebody else, because he can claim he was after a ZS.

In the final attack it is noticeable that the torches are mainly wielded by the younger men, often a number of unmarried men who have only been watching until the last night. Those who are potential DH to an ego have the motivation to burn their 'WF' if there has been a delay or failure to give a daughter promised. 'DH' are in a potential niece exchange relationship with ego's WB who may have promised his ZH's D to one man but have been thwarted by her father giving her to another 'DH'.

Primary support comes from MBS, the only close male relative in the opposite patri- and matrimoiety who is rarely involved directly in ego's own matrimonial arrangements (*ibid.*:163) and also a man with whom traditional ritual friendships are commonly established. The MBS has a niece exchange relationship with the men of ego's WF's subsection which includes 'ZS' who are often WF (*ibid.*:199), but the nieces that they are exchanging are not the sisters and daughters of ego. So although the WF, who probably circumcised ego, is in the same matrimoiety and could therefore legitimately attack him, there is no reason for this under a ZD-bestowal system and there is every reason why he should co-operate with his *djuraldja*, ego's MBS. The MBS subsection also includes the MF, *djamadi*. In terms of the formal structure rather than the actual interaction, these people are important. Ego's 'MF' will include his WMMB, who is a full member of his wife's matriline and therefore *djuraldja* to ego. It is these men that perform the taunting dance in front of the owners with the painted shield bearing the *Buluwandi* design. The name for the shield is *guridji*, a term also used for WM. Under a system of ZD bestowal the 'MF' who is WMMB would have bestowed the WM and if still alive would have rights in the bestowal of her daughters, ego's wife.[7]

The ceremony also allows the fathers of girls the owners are likely to be having affairs with (classificatory MBD; *ibid.*: 163) to attack the lovers physically. Since these would be 'ZS', this is important because in normal daily life there is a prohibition on MBs hitting ZSs. This prohibition is not reciprocal.

Conclusion

Though I have offered no direct evidence here that the Walbiri do bestow nieces,[8] or at least try to do so, the model does provide an explanation of the behaviour in the Fire ceremonies and the limited range of interaction they allow.

Contrary to what Meggitt says (*ibid.*: 198), ZD exchange is at least a possibility in an Aranda-type system, and as Hiatt (1967) and Shapiro (n.d.) have recently pointed out, was probably widespread in Australia. A model of daughter exchange would not explain why the matrilineal divisions were important, why the matrilines and circumcision relationship were involved, nor why the workers were formally grouped in the *malilangu* WMB/ZDH relationship when they could be in F/S pairs just as the owners were. But the ZD model alone is not adequate to explain the conflict, for unless the bestowal were opposed in some way, there would be none. Indeed, the discussion of the pattern of interaction and co-operation has assumed that the niece bestowers have been giving vent to anger arising from a failure of their rights to be acknowledged. That is, that the owners, since these are the people the workers are attacking, have been D-bestowing and ignoring the rights of the matrikin.

To spell out this implicit aspect of the explanatory model, it can be said that the conflict which the Fire ceremonies attempt to resolve results from an opposition of interest between patrikin and matrikin in the bestowal of the former's Ds who are the latter's ZDs. That is, that an individual will, when he is the father of a girl being bestowed, conceptualize his rights in terms of D-bestowal; but when he is the MB, in terms of ZD bestowal. The alternation of these positions is reflected in the alternation of the Fire ceremonies in which the owners in one become the workers in the other. The objection may be raised that I have not shown that the ceremony is concerned specifically with conflicts over women, merely that the model has an explanatory function.

I would agree, but point out that authors from Malinowski (1963:125) to Meggitt (1962), Hiatt (1965), Hart and Pilling (1960) and Goodale (1962) discuss the politicking associated with women and indicate that many if not the majority of fights and quarrels in Aboriginal society are over them.

NOTES

1. I collected the material for this paper during two brief visits to Yuendumu Government Settlement when I was anthropological advisor to the Australian Institute of Aboriginal Studies' Film Unit. Though we filmed *Buluwandi* it was secondary to our main project, the filming of a 'Lodge' ceremony. I relied heavily on Dr Meggitt's book on the Walbiri. Dr Hiatt has made many valued comments on the paper, though he is not of course responsible for its contents.

2. This does not mean that the ceremony itself is recent but only the current style of performance.

3. Though the evidence indicates that the section and subsection system are less than a century old amongst the Walbiri (Meggitt 1962:168), this is not an indication that the ceremonies are new. The Walbiri already possessed double unilineal descent groups, merged and alternate generation levels and preferred marriage with a type of cross-cousin. They are, as Meggitt has said, a useful shorthand, much used in the discussion of ritual.

4. The film is held by the Australian Institute of Aboriginal Studies in Canberra.

5. At this stage I was tired and glad to be told I would not miss much if I turned in. The main event to take place before dawn, I was told, would be the building of the huts. It was only on the second occasion that I learnt that late at night they singed their pubic hair and that this always happens. In the past there was group copulation with a promiscuous girl immediately prior to the singeing of the pubic hair; there is some indication that this may have taken place in this ceremony. I was not well enough known to the people to establish this for certain.

6. The men of the djungarai and djabaldjari subsections hop; those of the djabanungga and djabangari high-step.

7. Shapiro, in this volume, suggests that WM-bestowal may have been a common practice in Australia. This observation would support it as a possibility. However, I feel that when it does occur it is just one ploy by a matriline to protect its jural rights from the girl's patrikin.

8. Both Hiatt (personal communication) and myself have unpublished data that suggest ZD-bestowal was an ideal arrangement.

REFERENCES

BARRETT, M. J. 1964 A tape recording made at Yuendumu. Australian Institute of Aboriginal Studies Tape Archive, No. A57.
GILLEN, F. 1968 Gillen's Diary. Libraries Board of South Australia.
GOODALE, J. 1962 Marriage Contracts Among the Tiwi, *Ethnology*, Vol. 1.

HART, C. W. M. and A. PILLING 1960 *The Tiwi of North Australia*. Holt, Reinhart and Winston, New York.

HIATT, L. 1965 *Kinship and Conflict*. Australian National University, Canberra.

—— 1967 Authority and Reciprocity in Aboriginal Marriage Arrangements, *Mankind*, Vol. 6:468-75.

MALINOWSKI, B. 1963 *The Family among the Australian Aborigines*. Schöcken Books, New York.

MEGGITT, M. J. 1962 *Desert People*. Angus and Robertson, Sydney.

SHAPIRO, W. n.d. Some Aspects of Marriage on Elcho Island. Unpublished paper presented at the Australian National University, 1966.

SPENCER, B. and F. GILLEN 1904 *The Northern Tribes of Central Australia*. Macmillan, London.

RONALD M. BERNDT

Traditional Morality as Expressed Through the Medium of an Australian Aboriginal Religion[1]

THE PROBLEM

Aboriginal man has been variously conceptualized as being either moral or immoral, or a-moral. On one hand, in the abundant literature on these people it is often assumed, sometimes without empirical validation, that their ethical systems are highly developed and based on religion; that they are articulated in everyday action, ensuring fairly rigid adherence to what are regarded as correct or good ways of behaving and acting in relation to others; and that these are reinforced by religious sanctions. On the other hand, the converse view has been put forward: that morality is dependent on self-interest; that Aboriginal religion is not necessarily concerned with the interaction of man with man, but only of man with deity or with what these supernatural beings can provide for man when induced (through ritual or otherwise) to do so. Neither of these two extremes fits the actual situation.

In traditional Aboriginal Australia the boundaries between the sacred and the mundane are blurred. These are (or were) repetitive societies that place a tremendous emphasis on traditional precedent—specifically on what is believed to have transpired in the beginning, in the 'original' form of social living established by the major creative beings. Reference to this particular dimension, not limited by time, and often translated by the words 'Eternal Dreaming', underlines the Aborigines' traditional reliance on a body of knowledge and belief that is relevant not only to the past but also to the present and the future. Within this scheme is provision for change and individual interpretation, but change in terms of variation on a recognized theme and interpretation within a relatively closed system. The mythical beings are believed to have been responsible not only for creating the natural species, which included man, and much of the physiographic features of the country associated with them. Importantly also, in this context, they are believed to have established an Aboriginal way of life, its social institutions and its patterns of activity: in other words, they established a moral order, comprising a series of 'oughts' and 'ought nots', indicating what people should and should not do. But such injunctures are not necessarily explicitly articulated; they are usually recognized implicitly. There are certain exceptions, and the way the ethical system functions in any one Aboriginal society is in terms of both the 'good' and the 'bad' example. However, it is not expressed as simply as this.

Aboriginal religion was, and is, intimately associated with social living, especially in relation to the natural environment and its economic resources. The 'deities' were not only the creators but the stimulators of continuity: their power, released through human rituals, ensures the maintenance of the *status quo*. In one sense, they are independent of man. In another, they are bound to man by ties of familiarity and great intimacy. The gods are immortal: they are creatures of the Dreaming, of the eternal. They moved across the country, leaving possessions which are now enshrined as specific sites, meeting others of their own kind, creating, instituting—and finally being metamorphosed as stone, or in some other form, or disappearing into the territory of an adjacent group, going into the sky, into the ground or water. But in doing so, they left behind them tangible evidence of their presence on the earth and what they left was imbued with their spiritual charisma. The gods are also shape-changing. In many cases, they could be called totemic. They are closely identified with some of the natural species or elements, or are manifested through particular creatures or elements. In this sense, their spirits live on in the mundane world. If, for example, a specific spirit character is also a shape-changing goanna man, then *all* goanna today are a reflection of that spirit, all contain its essential Dreaming essence. The spirit character concerned is perpetuated in its continued presence on this earth, through them. This orientation is communicable to man. It emphasizes the essential unity of man with nature, where man is viewed as being for general purposes part of nature, not opposed to it; as having a close and personal interrelationship with his natural and physical surroundings.

Many Australian Aboriginal deities, not all (and the exceptions do not invalidate the rule), are *ancestral*, credited with having created the progenitors of contemporary man. (See R. M. Berndt 1952; Berndt and Berndt 1964:188.) Beliefs about such a direct linkage with the major mythical beings imply, also, the belief that man is not fundamentally dissimilar to them—that both share a common life force which is sacred. This is brought out most tellingly in dramatized ritual performances when postulants assume the guise of such beings and re-enact the mythic incidents. It is because of this quality, shared by man and his deities, that man is in a position to activate ritual and bring it to bear on essentially mundane situations. The assumption here is that ritual is a symbolic means of solving problems of everyday significance, whether these are directed toward initiation, the resolution of life crises, the maintenance of environmental fertility and/or the reaffirmation of socio-cultural identity, over and above wider and more abstract and not immediately recognized implications.

The connection between contemporary man and the spirit beings, then, is putatively ancestral. But in addition, much more directly, is the general belief that these mythic characters are manifested through and in man. (See Berndt and Berndt 1964:189 *et seq.*; R. M. Berndt n.d. *i.*) Through birth and/or conception, a person comes to possess the same spiritual quality as that of a particular spirit being, *in personal terms*. For instance, a woman eats some substance associated with a specific site: she vomits when normally she should not: she is thus made aware that a spirit has entered her, that she has conceived. The child she eventually bears has a direct affiliation with that particular spirit. The norm (where this is relevant) that a woman should give birth to, or conceive, children within the local group territory of her husband, ensures a patrilineal linkage from father to son through the generations. Variations on the theme serve to emphasize the general point. For example, a man (whose wife may not, up to that point, have realized she was pregnant) may injure or kill or disturb a local spirit at a particular site, one that is manifested in animal or some other form. As a result, the child born to his wife becomes a manifestation of it; or, the site-spirit 'turns into' the child, and evidence of the transaction is believed to be discernible on the child's body or in its character. If it had been in animal shape and he had killed it by spearing, the actual wound-mark may be identified on the child.

Between Aboriginal man and the non-empirical inhabitants of his world was a relationship not only of mutual interdependence but also of mutual identification. They are, however, conceptually divisible in specific mytho-ritual contexts. In myth, for instance, the characters are often portrayed as having an existence independent of man. This is deceptive, if only in that what they do (or some aspects of what they do) reflects or is reflected in traditional Aboriginal life. In ritual, the relationship between human and spirit beings is straightforward, whether this be expressed in social or in personal terms. In all cases, such characters are directly concerned with the affairs of man, and exhortation and supplication are not necessary to ensure their attention. They do not stand apart from man. But, through ritual performance, their sacred power is believed to be released and focused broadly for the benefit of man. In individual terms they are also deeply concerned in relationships between persons—usually, but not always, in a symbolic sense, and not explicitly in the pronouncement of moral precepts.

The contention I explore here is that, in mytho-ritual contexts, incidents are noted which can be evaluated as being either good or bad. The mythic characters themselves provide a pattern or blue-print for human behaviour, including interpersonal behaviour. Specific social actions do not necessarily bring condemnation and approbation, punishment and reward, in the myths themselves. It is sufficient that these human beings have before them a body of mythic information in which they believe, oriented in terms of a way of life that can be identified as being basically similar to their own, traditionally.

Supernatural punishment can (is believed to) follow if there is violation of the sacred code. Mostly, however, such threats are oblique and not framed in relation to specific spirit characters. Usually, if there is no intervention by a human agent who is acting in his capacity as a protector of the sacred heritage, the violator must be prepared to await the consequences—it is assumed that he is bound to suffer in some way. (See Berndt and Berndt 1964:285.) But because ritual and myth bear so centrally on social relations, including relations between the sexes, 'what these media have to say about the arrangement of social units, the rules governing behaviour between persons, the breaking of such rules or the means by which they are enforced, or the types of behaviour which are enjoined or deplored' (*ibid.*:249) is always important.

Morality and religion are not conceived of as being separate spheres of experience. However, it is also true to say that only acts against the spirit characters themselves in their varying manifestations and within the ritual context (or in emblem form), can be regarded as being really sure to incur their displeasure. In the majority of situations it is *taken for granted* that the majority of people will follow the socio-cultural patterns laid down in the creative era. But 'following a pattern' would seem to differ from the kind of response involved when particular moral precepts or values are enunciated, and sponsored by a being who is incensed by any infringement. Examples of this last were very rare in Aboriginal Australia. As Stanner (1965:217-18) says, '. . . the authority of spirits and other potencies . . . was only vaguely a moral-ethical authority'. I would agree with him here. However, as Stanner also notes, mythic beings acted also in ways which are not ordinarily acceptable as far as human beings are concerned. They are seen not simply as moral or a-moral, but as (in some cases) beyond the 'law', or beyond the range of conformity set for ordinary men (see Berndt and Berndt 1964:249, 280). They were law-makers, but also law-breakers. Stanner (*ibid.*:218) speaks of 'two faces, one well drawn and the other less so'. The former concerns those acts by spirit beings which are contrary to what are regarded as 'right', but in the myths themselves are not explicitly condemned (although they may be by implication). In discussion that may follow the narration of myths, either in prose or in song form, someone may point out that 'this is what the spirits did, but we do otherwise!' Also, a myth itself may deal directly with the implications arising from wrong actions, in terms of their consequences. In the case of 'right' behaviour, as I have said, there is no need for underlining: this speaks for itself.

In Aboriginal religion there is certainly no 'intellectual detachment', no codification of principles and no 'challenge that would have forced morals and beliefs to find anatomies' (Stanner 1965:218). But to my mind these are not essential features of a religious ethical system; and they are obviously not considered essential in Aboriginal terms because, despite this lack, the ideological system of belief (manifested as it is through myth) seems to have been entirely adequate. It provides a stable setting against which actual behaviour can be measured, and it also indicates the limits of both 'rightness' and 'wrongness'—recognizing the frailty of human character. It is true that, viewed superficially 'this made the moral aspect of the religion rather amorphous' (Stanner *ibid.*:218). But this has two facets. The more important (i) is that relating to myth. To quote Stanner again (*ibid.*:218-19): 'Many myths reveal a mounting of incidents to a crisis or culmination that exhibits a cluster of meanings with a distinct moral quality.' This is certainly the case with a large number of Aboriginal myths—but not necessarily those of a sacred nature, or those which have, for instance, direct ritual implications. As far as these last are concerned, a particularly long cycle may be made up of a series of crises which in themselves have *ethical* (but not necessarily *moral*) overtones and undertones. A particular mythic crisis occurs when a statement is made evaluating an action on the part of the characters concerned, as being *im*moral or *a*-moral. It is, as it were, as if an immoral act must occur *in order to demonstrate what can be categorized as being moral*. For instance, a mythic being commits incest and may consequently be killed; no further reference is necessary to emphasize the moral injuncture concerned. There are two legs to this. The first is the one already noted—both direct and positive in its negativity. In the second, action of a sort traditionally viewed as immoral brings about a result which is for the common good. For instance, through an incestuous union, the human progenitors of the local Aboriginal people come into being; through treachery, a malignant spirit is killed; a mythic being is killed to enable his sacred emblems to be made available to man; and so on. These are 'immoral' acts, but their consequences are considered to be good. Other actions performed by mythic beings are *beyond* ethical question; they are presented without reference to their implications, whether these be good or bad. In such cases, they are non-moral: it is simply, as noted, that the mythic characters concerned are beyond the law to which ordinary man is subject. In ritual, as an example of this, there is a difference between what is regarded as moral or immoral in secular life and its meaning in sacred life. Ritual licence, for instance, may include sexual intercourse between ordinarily prohibited kin or affines; ritualized swearing between kin who normally treat one another with constraint; symbolic use of menstrual blood, which men usually regard with abhorrence; and so on. Such non-mundane acts enhance the sacredness of the occasion, over and above their symbolic intentions. In passing, Meggitt (1966:23) mentions that contemporary Wailbri men, as custodians of the myths, see the behaviour of Dreaming mythic women, for example, as being immoral by present-day standards and 'openly deplore such behaviour when recounting the myths'. Strehlow (1947:38), for the Aranda, speaks of the older versions of myths being toned down by narrators today. And this is of common occurrence.

The other facet (ii) is religious ritual. It is true that, as Stanner (1965: 219) says, in specific cases 'the myths ... may have served as the implicit moral "theory" of the rites'. This should be regarded in two senses, as Stanner implies. One is the sense of mythic re-enactment within the context of ritual, with varying recognition of symbolic allusion, perpetuating a traditional scheme which is regarded as being of direct benefit to man, over and above the *practical* implications of specific rituals—that is, what they are designed to accomplish. The Dreaming, with its expression through myth and ritual, among other things, is believed to be possessed of a moral rightness of its own. As Stanner has put it (*ibid.*:220), it 'was said to, and to all appearances did, weigh on the present with over-mastering authority'. In the second sense, is initiation through ritual in broad terms—not solely the initiation of youths or their involvement in physical operations (that is, in disciplinary terms), but revelatory rites which are correlated with increasing knowledge and participation by adults. Such progression could be regarded also as paralleling moral development. This is, of course, more obvious in regard to the initiation of young men, where in many cases specific injunctions are articulated—often with mythic connotations—stipulating what to do and what not to do in particular circumstances, both ritual and mundane.

The Dingari as a Moral System

In the present study my concern is with myth as the most likely source of moral statements. Their translation into action is, of course, another matter and it is one which will be considered only indirectly in this context.

In brief, my contention is that morality and religion are not really separable here—they belong together within the same sphere of experience; and, on the treatment of moral issues in Aboriginal mythology, that 'right' and 'wrong' actions are a part of ordinary living: that the results speak for themselves, and that these do not necessarily need to be spelt out as a series of moral admonitions or maxims (as is the case in the eastern Highlands of New Guinea: see R. M. Berndt 1962).

The material I am using comes from the north-western sector of the Western Desert of Australia. The 'tribes' are the Walmadjeri, Gugadja, Mandjildjara, Wonggadjunggu and Ngadi, representatives of which now live at Balgo Pallottine mission station on the northern fringe of the Desert. These people have come out of the Desert in recent years but retain close ties with their own territories. They have been subjected to fairly intensive alien contact, but may still be described as traditionally oriented. The mythology, and the land that is intimately associated with it, along with ritual, continue to be significant to them. (For a summarized statement, an overall view of Desert socio-cultural life from the perspective of Balgo, see R. M. Berndt n.d. *i*, where additional references are provided.)[2]

The *dingari*, a mytho-ritual complex or tradition which is secret-sacred, is by far the most important of its kind throughout this region. It is associated with many mythical characters. The primary ones are the Ganabuda, also known as the Gadjeri, the Old Woman or Mother: but there may be a group of Ganabuda or Gadjeri, and they may have male counterparts. The *dingari* ritual group, as they are collectively called, travel across the country, moving from one site to the next; they may be a group of men followed by women, or vice versa, accompanied by novices; and the presence of the Ganabuda or Gadjeri is usually implied if not expressly stated. The *dingari* initiate young men and perform rites, and meet various other characters in the course of their journey.

The Ganabuda *dingari* I shall consider here, in summary, has a particular Desert flavour. In one sense, it is reflective of this socio-cultural situation and therefore has unique characteristics (that is, unique to this region). In another sense, it is not bounded by Desert cultural limitations; in both structure and content it may be identified with eastern and north-eastern myths and rites which are also known under the general label of Gadjeri, and there are connections even further afield. The *dingari* of the Walmadjeri-Gugadja (to name but two of the dominant 'tribal' dialect-units concerned with our example) is made up of an accretion of myths that are not necessarily woven into an integrated pattern of mythic knowledge. Their neighbours to the east, the Wailbri (Walbiri), also have the Gadjeri (Gadjari). In their case, it is the myth of the two Mamandabari men 'whose exploits provide the rationale of the Gadjari rituals' (Meggitt 1966:4). The full myth (as set out by Meggitt *ibid.*:5-22, along with a description and analysis of the ritual) contains no reference to the Gadjeri Mother. However, in the Wave Hill-Birrundudu areas, north of the Wailbri, the Gadjeri (or Fertility Mother) and her two daughters (the Mangamanga) are much in evidence. (See C. H. Berndt 1950; my own material on this, from that area, is still unpublished.)

The Gadjeri has, additionally, many linkages with the Kunapipi cult (see R. M. Berndt 1951), which is widely distributed throughout Arnhem Land and in other parts of the Northern Territory. Closely associated with this is the myth of the Old Woman, Mutjingga, connected with the rite of Punj (among the Murinbata of Pt Keats, Northern Territory: see Stanner 1960:260-2). Stanner's interpretation rests on what he considers to be a 'persistent suggestion' of a mythic 'immemorial misdirection' in human affairs—a 'Wrongful turning of life', as he puts it, and through the killing of Mutjingga, 'men are committed to its consequences'. The content of the myth lends itself to other, different interpretations. I shall not, however, pursue that possibility here. Stanner (*ibid.*:265-6) makes a connection between 'suffering' and 'good', in order to underline the moral side of the mythology he discusses. (It will be noted that in my framework 'suffering' can be and is equated with evil, and regarded as immoral.) Stanner observes, too, that there is no concept of a 'Golden Age': Strehlow (1947:38-42), on the other hand, in an early work, mentions the concept of a 'Golden Age', but at the same time emphasizes the absence of moral and ethical values in Aranda myths.

Stanner comes closer to the core of the significance of myths (*ibid.*:266) when he writes that they 'are a sort of statement about whole reality, a declaration about the penalties of private will, and by implication a thesis on the spoiling of possible unity'; 'they deal less with origins as such than with the instituting of relevances—the beginnings of a moral system . . .'; 'the myths rationalize and justify *familiar* entities, forms and relations'. It is this view which is closer to the content and symbolism of the *dingari*. Mythology inspires and contemporary ritual sustains a way of life sanctified by the Dreaming, where good and bad are accepted conditions of living. There is no 'fall from grace', no mythic beings possessed of an innate goodness to be emulated by Aboriginal man, beings ready to punish the transgressor and reward the person who adheres to ideal norms. Mythic beings were both good and bad, and badness was a necessary corollary of goodness.

The *dingari* is linked with similar cults in other parts of Aboriginal Australia. As far as we can tell, it spread into the Kimberleys of Western

Australia and west to La Grange (Petri 1968:188-9), and also down into the Western Desert. However, as Meggitt notes (*ibid.*:23), the Wailbri 'have grafted elements of an imported Gadjari cult on to a typical indigenous hero myth and in doing so have dropped the Mother concept from the former'. The Walmadjeri-Gugadja have integrated the introduced Gadjeri with indigenous myth forms, while at the same time not adopting many essential features of the northern versions. They have retained the Gadjeri as Mother, but not so directly as in the north.

The following examples are presented in summary, omitting many references to actual sites which the mythic beings pass through or are associated with. Most versions actually include much detail. Additionally, the myth is generally presented as a series of songs which *in toto* make up a cycle, although each song may require further explanation. There are also numerous versions. Those presented here were collected during fieldwork at Balgo in 1958 and 1960 and belong to the Desert tradition.[3] They are arranged as a series of myth-sections (I to X), all related to the *dingari*; for convenience of reference each is divided into parts.

Myth-Section I

1. Ganabuda women with *dingari* men move across the country in the vicinity of Lake White, with a pre-circumcisional novice. They possess secret-sacred ritual boards (called *darugu*);[4] they erect some of them on a hill, and their power causes fire to issue from the apex of each board. The fire spreads across the country and forces the Ganabuda to seek protection in a pit, but some are burnt to death. Eventually, they continue on their way, with their long *darugu*.

2. They go into the ground at Wilgungara and come out at Djawuldjawul. A mythic lizard man, Gadadjilga ('spiky head'), emerges. Through the aid of love magic, he is able to have sexual intercourse with one of the Ganabuda: however, she is related to him as a *jumari*, an avoidance relationship. This is considered *wadji* (wrong), and punishable. He is eventually killed by the other Ganabuda. (A detailed rendering of this section of the myth up to this point is contained in R. M. Berndt n.d. *i.*) To kill Gadadjilga, the Ganabuda hit his testes with sharpened digging sticks and finally cut his penis, which was elongated, and which he had caused to travel underground and come among them. (This is quite a common theme in Desert mythology: see Berndt and Berndt 1964:208-9, on the Julana-Njirana myth. The *dingari* myth reiterates that Gadadjilga was the 'wrong' man for the girl he seduced: also, that he was an old man with grey hair—too old for any of the Ganabuda, among whom were, 'genealogically', potential spouses from his point of view.)

3. Leaving here, they go from site to site; they cut and make *darugu*, dance, meet another group of Ganabuda, and collect food. At Gunjin, they are frightened by a man named Mungamadju; some enter this place, but others continue on.

4. (At this juncture, emphasis is placed on the ritual activities of the women: the older women make *darugu*, while the young girls hunt and so are able to compensate those who show them the sacred objects. This situation is paralleled in contemporary ritual life as far as the men are concerned.) The young girls are the Mangamanga (or Mungamunga: see C. H. Berndt 1950:18; R. M. Berndt 1951:13).

5. In the myth, the Mangamanga travel ahead of the older women, who come behind carrying the heavy *darugu*. In one instance, they look back but cannot see these older women; they wait and then search for them, but without avail: they have disappeared.

6. They continue, however, and meet another group of Ganabuda; the routine sequence of events is repeated. Eventually, at Jandeia, they perform special dancing using a sacred *wedi* (*widi*) pole and finally 'go in' there, where they remain.

Myth-Section II

1. The Ganabuda travel across the country, hunting (near Lake White); they kill animals by throwing sacred *darugu* at them.

2. They are watched by a man named Djalaburu, who is astonished to find that they possess *darugu* and swing bullroarers while the men have no sacred objects. In his country (Wailbri-Woneiga), it is the other way about.

3. In the night, Djalaburu steals power (*maia*) from under the armpits of the women.

4. In the morning, the women find they have lost their power and cannot use the *darugu*.

5. The men change places with the women, taking over the *darugu*. In return, the women receive digging sticks and wooden dishes, and Djalaburu explains the situation to them, giving them a firestick. (A more detailed version of this section is contained in Berndt and Berndt 1964:224.)

Myth-Section III

1. An old man, Djangimanda, is with a large *dingari* group of young men. He tells them to go ahead and he will follow with the sacred *darugu*.

2. Instead he 'tricks them': he covers all the camp fires, except for a piece of lighted wood he takes for himself. He then collects some of the

darugu, tying them together with *ngaljibi* fibre, placing them on his head and shoulders and suspending them from his waistband; some he holds in his hands.

3. The power of the *darugu* enables him to fly away with these boards, leaving no opportunity for the others to follow him. He comes down at Gulei, on the Canning Stock Route, and enters the ground, where he remains.

4. The *dingari* go in the opposite direction (east), hunting and performing ritual as they travel from place to place.

5. (Details are given of each place where they camp.) At one, they frighten a man, Gurgul (night owl), who is making a boomerang. At another, they make waterholes by standing their *darugu* upright in the ground. At still another, they perform the *nanggaru* hole ritual. (See R. M. Berndt 1951: e.g. 17 *et seq.* concerning the significance of this in the Kunapipi.) Novices go inside this, and firesticks are thrown over it and them.

6. Eventually they come to Ruldu where, in anger at not finding Djangimanda, the *dingari* begin to quarrel among themselves over the *darugu*. One man, Guninga, puts his foot on a *darugu*, deliberately breaking it. The extreme seriousness of this action immediately results in a cessation of fighting: their differences of opinion are resolved and they become friends again.

7. They continue on their travels. Finally, at Jaran, they hold a big ritual. Next day they are so tired that they can hardly walk: and the country is hilly and they find it impossible to climb. In desperation, they all enter Bargunbargun rockhole, in Wailbri country.

Myth-Section IV

1. *Dingari* men begin their travels at Warawara, on the Canning Stock Route. They make *darugu* boards. A euro (kangaroo) is frightened by the feathers attached to a *darugu*. They perform ritual and make stone flake blades for spears.

2. They meet two old men who possess a large number of *darugu;* the *dingari* kill them with one of their own *darugu*, using it as a throwing stick; after hitting them it continues for some distance and finally falls, forming a mountain ridge.

3. The *dingari* follow it and meet Lon (the kingfisher man), who is a *dingari* leader. (Lon is important in Petri's versions: *ibid.*: 188-9.)

4. They continue travelling, coming back to their old home: they sing, make *darugu*, use *darugu* for grinding grass seeds, and finally mount their *darugu* and fly through the sky to Ngalgildjara soak. (A more detailed version of this section appears in R. M. Berndt, n.d. *i.*)

5. They then continue to Garalja soak, where they meet an old man, Djilgamada (echidna). While the *dingari* are out hunting, he steals some of their *darugu*.

6. They discover the theft and follow Djilgamada's tracks, but he dives down into Bulgalilji soak with all the boards, to hide from them. In the dark, they miss him and continue on to Jugu where they camp in a *ganala* (ritual trench: see R. M. Berndt 1951: e.g. 43, 58 *et seq.*, in relation to the Kunapipi).

7. Djilgamada follows the *dingari*, and during the night teases them by throwing stones and hitting them, but runs away at dawn.

8. They follow Djilgamada, but cannot find him. Tired, they rest in the evening, cooking and eating possum. Then they light one of their *darugu*, using it as a torch in order to follow the old man; but he has a similar torch. Eventually they camp at Lindabaru. Here, in the night Djilgamada comes stealthily up and knocks them over with a *darugu*. (He also makes a bush fire. He teases them 'all the way along': and this is why novices today are teased in the relevant rituals.)

9. The *dingari* dance at Bilbiga and paint the youths with arm-vein blood; they stand up their *darugu* in a row. As a result, there is a big creek here, made by their dancing feet.

10. They follow Djilgamada. At Burudu they circumcise novices.

11. They continue in their search for Djilgamada, and see his fire in the distance.

12. Another travelling group of Ganu lizard men come upon Djilgamada: they put stone flakes inside him and sticks all over his body 'because he stole all the *darugu*'.

13. In the morning, Djilgamada leaves the camp, still holding his *darugu*; he is sick, and drags them along the ground.

14. The *dingari* easily track and encircle him. Djilgamada, however, is cunning: he goes under the ground and comes up some distance away, in Wailbri country.

15. The others follow him again and throw spears and *darugu* at him: these stick into his body. But he is still relatively strong and continues on. Eventually he falls, at Wirilji-wirilji. They drag him along the ground and throw more spears at him. But he evades them and goes into a rockhole there, making it larger so that all of his attackers fall into it too and are unable to escape.

Myth-Section V

1. A *dingari* group comes from Ganingara (Kaningara), on the Canning Stock Route: they possess a large number of unincised *darugu* (which they incise later: see paragraph 8). They move across the country.

2. As they fly over Gudal riding on their *darugu*, they see an old man, also named Gudal, who is afraid of them.

3. They land at Djindidjindi, searching for water. Garangalgu (turkey man) brings it to them.

4. They are hungry and seek food, but without success. They pierce their arms for blood (to drink). They hear a noise; at first, they believe it is the sound of their own arm blood flowing, and they staunch this to listen. It is a man named Buradjidin, who is snoring in a cave at Jalbilbungu. At night they surround the cave and try to spear him, but he runs away. They follow, and kill him at Gwial. They had intended to eat him, but his flesh is too salty: they leave his body there.

5. They continue on their travels, swinging bullroarers, painting the bodies of novices, and so on, until they come to Ladada, named after Lightning, who made a creek here by striking the ground; the *dingari* are afraid of him.

6. Continuing, they throw their *darugu* like spears, following them to where they fall. Lightning strikes again and frightens them: they seek shelter in a cave. They can find no water. They swing their bullroarers, but one breaks into pieces—they weep over this calamity.

7. They continue, dancing along (as in contemporary ritual). At Djarudjaru one man, Galan, tries to chew wild tobacco leaves; others copy him, but all burn their mouths, and they are sick.

8. At Widjindi, the *dingari* exchange *darugu*, recounting the myths and the waterhole routes symbolized by the incised lines on the surface of these boards. They are instructing the younger men, who in turn should compensate them with meat and other food they have caught. No food, however, has been obtained.

9. They throw a large *darugu* into the sky, where it travels by itself; they follow it to Djilmanda, where it has fallen, making a soak.

10. They continue to Winbubula. An old woman named Badara (a Gadjeri) makes four holes for novices, in which they are ritually smoked: the holes become rockholes. (A similar ritual of smoking novices is carried out today.)

11. They burn *darugu*, using them as torches so they can travel at night. They stand *darugu* upright in the ground, and as a result they 'find water': the *darugu* make soaks.

12. While they are sleeping here, a woman named Wonadjura comes for water. In the morning, the *dingari* notice her tracks and those of other women. The women have seen the *darugu*. The young men go after them and kill them all, putting their bodies in trees at Gwibiljaru.

13. They continue on, making wells and soaks with their *darugu*, and performing ritual. Again they search for water, but find none—in this case, their *darugu* are of no avail. They do, however, find sand

dampened after rain, and cover themselves with it to obtain its moisture.

14. Eventually they come to Manggi. Here they make a *ganala* trench (symbolizing the Gadjeri womb). The Gadjeri Mother is here: men enter her belly. As she walks along, her footprints form rows of waterholes (at Rubudjungu). From time to time she permits the men to go out for hunting, but they always return to her. They perform ritual: they enter the *nanggaru*, and fire is thrown over them.

15. They come to Jugul and, mounting their *darugu*, fly to Gulgan where they perform ritual.

16. At Ilgalidja, they hunt with *darugu*. After killing a kangaroo rat, the *darugu* passes through it and falls to the ground, making a waterhole; ducks and pelicans appear on its water.

17. They continue travelling, hunting and performing ritual; they swing bullroarers and ride their *darugu* through the sky. (It is explained, in this part of the myth, that the *darugu* they use is/are really the Gadjeri.)

18. At Widjinbi, they meet an old man named Bindin (a small water bird); he is a *dingari* leader. With him, they fly to Imbirwanu and prepare for ritual and for the initiation of young men (that is, the showing of *darugu* to them).

19. Eventually they come to Wonggu, in Wailbri country. Here they meet a group of women, the mothers of the youths who have been initiated into the *dingari;* it is a long time since they have seen their sons. There is a ritual presentation, and Bindin finally 'hunts them away'. The men continue on their travels.

20. Finally, two young men become ill at Galiaga (in Wailbri-Woneiga country), and die. The others mourn their death and 'sing themselves' — they clasp one another, forming a heap, and die. All of their *darugu* turn to stone.

Myth-Section VI

1. The *dingari* men sit together on a hill segregated from the women (the Ganabuda), who assemble on low flat ground, at Wilgin (Lake White). The men are ritually within the Mother (Gadjeri). (In a commentary on this, it is said that previously it was the 'law' to keep the young men and women apart from one another; two old men looked after the women.)

2. One man goes hunting and spears a kangaroo. However, it is not immediately killed and drags the protruding spear shaft along the ground; the hunter follows and kills it, then returns to the other men.

3. One of the old men attached to the women collects some of this meat, which he takes to the women. When dividing this, they find a broken piece of the spear point which had killed the animal. Before this,

the women had no idea that men were living nearby. They talk among themselves and agree that there must be some young men among them.

4. The women make a large ground-seed cake and give this to the old men, asking them to pass it on to the other men. (This is the present-day *mididi* ritual feast.)

5. The men come down from the Mother and meet the young women for the first time. They have intercourse.

6. In anger, the old men make a bush fire, hoping to kill both the men and the women; the fire burns the men, but the women escape by diving into a lake. The old men leave this place, one of them going to Gulul.

7. The women emerge from the lake to find all of the young men dead. They follow the tracks of one of the old men and find him digging a hole, his testes hanging down. They have obtained *darugu* from their 'husbands'. First they pinch his testes. Then dancing round him, they spear him with *darugu*, killing him, and bury him in the hole he has dug. (The *bandiri* dancing used in this section of the ritual refers to that episode.)

8. The women continue travelling, walking at night rather than during the day because it is so hot. At Gunanganu, they meet Gaanga (the crow man); he has intercourse with two women who are his *jumari* (a tabued relative) and *gabali* ('mother's mother') respectively. They are young girls, and since his penis is abnormally large, he injures them. The other women kill him with their *darugu*.

9. Later, the two girls die at Gunagari.

10. Continuing, they meet another Gaanga, who is digging a hole. When he sees the Ganabuda, he disappears into it. They stand around him, calling to him to come out—but he remains there, turning into a snake.

11. They continue to Bangur, where they find another Gaanga who is making a hairbelt: they grab this and scatter its hanks of hair. Gaanga is angry, but his anger turns to fear when the women run after him; they beat him with their *darugu* until he dies.

12. They go on to Lirinmanu, where they enter the ground. (Comment made at this point: these women did not like men; they became embittered after all the young men were burnt.)

Myth-Section VII

(Several sections relate to the adventures of the Ganabuda women at Wilgin. Then the myth continues.)

1. Two Ganabuda leave Wilgin, crawling all the way along—they

are tired. They drag themselves from place to place. As they push their hair back from their faces, bush potatoes fall from it.

2. When they urinate or prod the ground with their digging sticks, springs gush forth; in the former case they are salty; in the latter, fresh.

3. They come to Darbaibanda, where they hear a *darbai* malignant man-eating spirit singing outside his cave. The Ganabuda are frightened and throw stones to keep him away.

4. Finally they enter Gabulula, a sandhill in the middle of this dry lake.

Myth-Section VIII

1. The Ganabuda are sorry because the young men have been burnt (see Myth-Section VI, 6).

2. They spread out across the country as they leave Wilgin, dancing from place to place, hunting with their *darugu*.

3. At Bundaldjining, they cut the hymens of two young girls. (This is equivalent to subincision: see Berndt and Berndt 1945:216-18.) These two girls 'turn into' stone (their spirits are left here, but they do not die).

4. They continue on, hunting. At Jamabundubundu, a man named Gadadjilga smells the women; he creeps up stealthily, planning to have intercourse with them. However, when they hear him they run away, because his penis is too large. He follows them.

5. At Djuwandu he comes upon the women sleeping; he has intercourse with two, who in consequence are seriously injured and die.

6. The women run away: he follows them. Eventually they all go into the ground at Djalwa-djalwa.

Myth-Section IX

1. The *dingari* move across the country. Among them is Dangidjara. At Jumari, he has intercourse with a tabued 'mother-in-law' (*jumari*), named Magindi. He goes out hunting and brings meat back to her. Eventually, Magindi bears a son.

2. Dangidjara continues on to Nundjil. There, while he sleeps, some ants bite his testes and penis, which detach themselves from him and run away.

3. He goes in search of his genitals, but they have set off in the opposite direction. He calls out for them to return, but they refuse to do so.

4. He travels from place to place looking for them and at last, at Lungulurul, he finds them.

5. He goes on to Mandangunda, where the Mangamanga (see above)

are living. They are searching for him: but he dives down into a hole and comes out at Djindara. He teases them, and runs away to Njiringgi. The Mangamanga follow him.

6. They find him at Gunawiri. Again he escapes. He puts his *darugu* in a tree there; they are now stone. Standing on one leg, he gathers up all the *dingari* men and, with them, enters a hole.

Myth-Section X

1. *Dingari* move across the country. Among them is Wirangula. Ants bite his testes. He hunts for euro, but is unable to find any. He puts spinifex grass around the holes in which the euro are hiding, and lights it to smoke them out. The smoke, however, temporarily blinds him.

2. He continues, and regains his sight at Madjud. He sees a kangaroo rat: having no weapon, he pulls off his pubic fringe and throws it at the creature, but misses.

3. At Naberi-naberi he meets a husband (Jilbril) and wife. He is jealous; he sneaks up to the man and breaks his neck with a firestick, and then has intercourse with the woman. He is cold and goes back for a firestick; while he is away, the woman escapes.

4. Wirangula goes on to Rilana soak, which he enters, and there he remains.

These ten sections are not sequentially arranged. I have preferred to present them in the order in which I recorded them. Also, as I have noted, they are considerably compressed and do not mention all the actual sites through which these mythic characters passed. Since, in this context, I am emphasizing moral values, I have not set out details relevant to hunting or to ritual, or to the creation of the landscape. The myths themselves are dense with meaning, especially regarding the relationship of these characters to the land, fertility and ritual symbolism. This applies particularly to the *darugu*: there are many different kinds; various parts of the *dingari* ritual are described; and the mythological associations of each site are noted. All that I have presented here are clusters of events which, at one level, speak for themselves: that is, as they are told, they provide us with a glimpse of aspects of behaviour which require no further explanation. They are highlights which can readily be identified and reveal the 'character' of the main mythic beings: but they do other things as well. (See later.)

The Overall Conception of the Dingari

I have called the *dingari* a moral system. First, let us think of it as a system, or perhaps more precisely as a design. The foregoing myth-sections are only excerpts from, portions of, the total patterning of the *dingari*. All Desert myths are territorially anchored and are therefore in the possession of those people who claim particular stretches of country. It is only through obtaining myth-sections from a number of representatives of these 'countries' that a broader picture can be ascertained. Mostly, the really great Desert myths are fragmented. Also, they are meandering in style, often almost elusive: in them is a compulsive and vitally necessary mobility, of characters wandering from site to site, disappearing, 'turning into' something else, and usually reappearing. Further, many of them are almost prosaic (although this is not true for the song versions), with their reiteration of routine happening and ritual act. However, their structure is consistent.

The mythic setting, the décor, is familiar to listeners: it is commonplace, and so are the great majority of the activities of the characters. Against this backdrop, contrasts are provided in the form of incidents which disturb the smooth-flowing course of events—and it is these which interest us particularly. The *dingari* complex is not a story *per se* and should not be evaluated as such; it is not meant to be a tale, even though some, including Aborigines themselves, may regard it in that way. The plot element is incidental to the overall conception, or intent. It is, rather, as I have already suggested, a statement about Desert living. At the level of reality, these people take their life very much for granted. At the level of reflection in myth, they are able to stand back from it and consider it as it is, or was. These are two interrelated levels of perception. Before considering the implications of this, we can look briefly at the content of the myth itself.

The *dingari* contains two orientations, each made up of a number of ingredients. Together, they form what can be called the ethical universe of these people, using the term ethical in a broad sense to cover the whole field of conduct—moral as well as immoral. Tentatively, we can conceptualize this in Figure 1.

Around a central core focusing on social relations are two concentric circles with arrows leading clockwise and anti-clockwise; a diagonal line divides them, forming two interdependent spheres which I have designated 'moral' and 'immoral'.[5] The outer circle includes a *sine qua non* of Desert life—relatively constant movement across limited stretches of territory in the quest for food. For the most part, this is an arduous business. While the seasons remain good, and people are able to move about and collaborate actively and 'normally', they can achieve reasonable satisfaction. But through drought and consistently bad hunting, illness or accident, the situation can change radically. It can bring hunger, thirst, exhaustion and finally tragedy, because these people live so close to the land and rely utterly on its natural

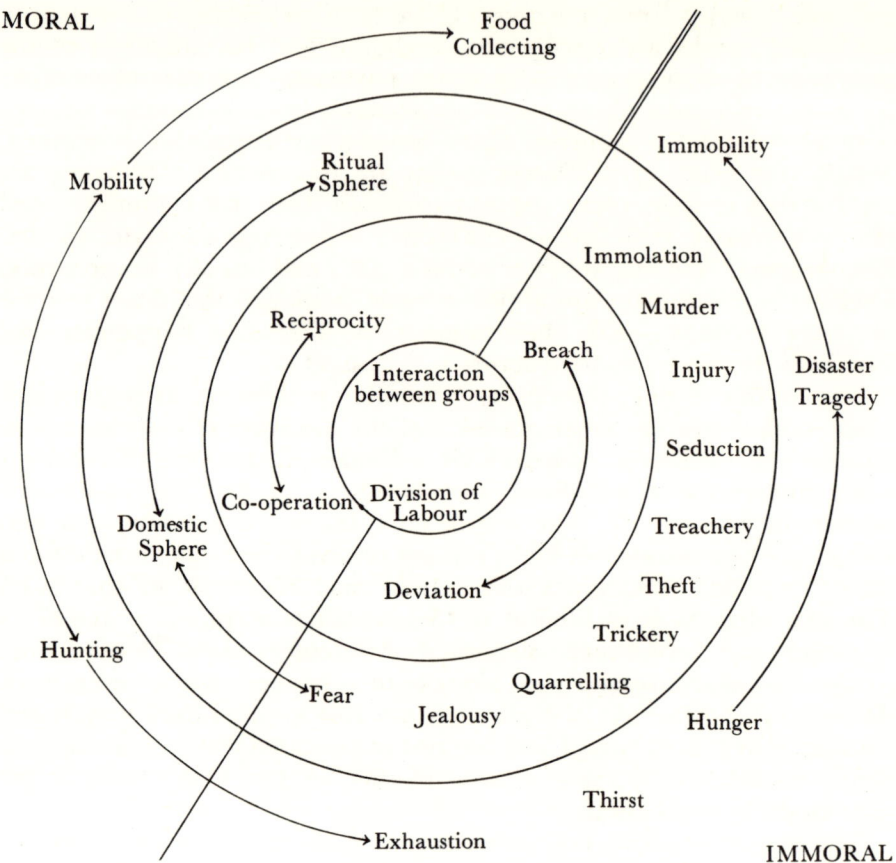

Fig. 1 Ethical universe of Desert people

resources: they are absolutely dependent for survival on nature, and on their own limited skills. Under these circumstances, the 'moral' can change to the 'immoral', *as part of the condition of living*.

Within the middle circle are the two primary spheres for the channelling of human social activity: the 'domestic' (directly relevant to family and other interpersonal relations), and the 'ritual'. Each sphere is characterized by co-operation and reciprocity—dependence on others in the course of social living. These are the spheres of 'moral' behaviour in the conventional meaning of the term: the area of good, proper, morally right behaviour, in which conformity with moral rules is expected to be at its maximum. However, social living involves breaches of the peace, behavioural deviation and so forth. Fear, jealousy, quarrelling, trickery, theft, treachery, seduction, injury, murder and immolation infiltrate the moral orientation. These immoral acts are highlighted in the *dingari*. They are, of course, subject to various forms of control, which are often indifferently applied; they are, however, 'wrong' in the same way as are drought, accident, and so on: they too can turn to tragedy and disaster; they, too, are 'immoral'. Because, in this situation, the social dimension in the broadest sense embraces the total environment, natural and 'supernatural' (or non-empirical), we can logically extend the use of the term 'moral' (or 'immoral') to this wider range of phenomena and events, not limiting it to purely inter-human affairs. What I am saying here is that the *dingari*, as a total ethical system, covers both the moral and the immoral *viewed as the natural condition of man*, as an accepted constant of Desert living. It is true that one is virtually outside his control and the other more or less within his control; but both involve common expectations—moral, and immoral.

I said before that in this context I was not attempting to deal with *dingari* symbolism. Of course, by identifying the elements that make up a 'moral' universe for man and his deities, I am touching very closely indeed on the *dingari*'s basic symbolism. To repeat, the *dingari* is a religious myth. Among other things, what it has to say, both directly and indirectly, is recognized as having especial significance and calling for especial concentration of effort and activity in the ritual sphere. It is concerned, specifically, with maintaining a sequence of events, including social actions and ideas, that have critical relevance to everyday life: and, more broadly, with sustaining the *complete* ethical universe created and established once and for all in the Eternal Dreaming by the mythical characters of the *dingari* and other important cycles—and this includes sustaining the immoral with the moral, as necessary conditions of life.

The two primary symbolic patterns, as recurring themes, concern: (i) relations between men and women; and (ii) secret-sacred and secular (or mundane) life. These are seen as two complementaries (to think in Lévi-Strauss's terms: see R. M. Berndt n.d. *ii*). The first includes the symbolism of women's original possession of the sacred *darugu* (e.g. Myth-Section II) and men's use of trickery to take over their power; and antagonism between the sexes (e.g. Myth-Sections VI, IX, 5). In the second, we have the Gadjeri Mother (e.g. Myth-Section V, 14): postulants and novices enter her womb for ritual (see R. M. Berndt 1951; 1952) but leave it for hunting. Wherever the *nanggaru* and *ganala* trenches or pit are mentioned, this implies the Gadjeri's womb; and the *darugu* are variously interpreted as being the body of the Mother or of phallic man himself. I am *not* saying that, at this level, these interdependent features are conceptualized as symbolizing the moral and the immoral—because this would be to fall into the quagmire of dead or moribund controversy on the issue of the sacred-profane dichotomy. But it is true that these are seen as contrasts: woman is the source of life, as expressed in the conception of the Gadjeri—as was the case in the beginning when she possessed the keys to the sacred, which are in fact the keys to life; and as she is now, as the ritual protector of man, symbolized as she is in the Gadjeri. But she is also a major source of dissension, and possible death. I do not want to over-emphasize this, because the Gadjeri, Ganabuda or Mangamanga (or Mungamunga) are often relegated to the background. One hears much more about the *dingari* and other spirit beings, especially in the Desert; after all, the Gadjeri has, as far as we can tell, come into the Desert and been integrated into and adapted to the local socio-cultural environment.

I have already commented on the relationship between the *dingari* myth and its expression through ritual. Table 1 demonstrates this.

TABLE 1

RELATIONSHIP BETWEEN DINGARI MYTH AND RITUAL

	dingari myth	*dingari* ritual
I, 1	novice travels with *dingari*	pilgrimage of novices to sacred sites
	use of *darugu*	*darugu* used in variety of ways
	fire spreads across country; Ganabuda seek protection in pit	ritual re-enactment; use of *nanggaru*. Novices sit in shallow trench (*nanggaru*) while firebrands are thrown over them*
I, 2	the Gadadjilga incident	re-enacted by postulants*
I, 3	Ganabuda make *darugu*	cult leaders make *darugu*
I, 4	Mangamanga appear	re-enacted in ritual*
	young girls 'pay' Ganabuda with meat for ritual knowledge	similar situation regarding men performing *dingari*, who expect such gifts from those they initiate
I, 6	women perform special dancing using *wedi* pole	complementary *dingari* ritual by women in main camp or separated from men*
III, 1-3	Djangimanda incident	re-enacted in ritual*
III, 5	*dingari* perform *nanggaru* rite	re-enacted*
IV, 6	*dingari* camp in *ganala*	*ganala* trench used in ritual*
IV, 5, 8, 12-15	Djilgamada sequence	re-enacted*

* Items distinctive to the *dingari*

	dingari myth	*dingari* ritual
IV, 8	Djilgamada knocks *dingari* with *darugu*	*dingari* novices teased in same way*
IV, 9	*dingari* anoint youth with arm blood	also done in ritual
IV, 10	*dingari* circumcise	also relevant to section of contemporary *dingari*
V, 4	drink blood to quench thirst	ritual drinking of blood
V, 5, 6	swing bullroarers	also feature of *dingari* ritual
V, 7	special form of *dingari* dancing	also performed in ritual*
V, 8	ritual exchange of *darugu*	also feature of this ritual as form of instruction
V, 10	Badara makes four holes for novices, and smokes them	ritual smoking of novices in depressions*
V, 12	killing of women	sanction used in relation to uninitiated who see or seek to see secret-sacred ritual and objects of initiated men
V, 14	*dingari* make a *ganala*	see above*
	appearance of Gadjeri Mother	ritual ground symbolizes the Mother: men enter and leave her*
	throwing of fire	see above*
V, 18	initiation of young men	see above
V, 19	meeting the mothers, and 'hunting them away'	women see novices as they come down from the secret-sacred ground: ritual presentation, and ritual 'hunting away', with wailing*
V, 20	death of *dingari*	ritual re-enactment*
VI, 1	sexual division	maintained in *dingari* ritual
VI, 4	women make ground-seed bread for young men	*mididi* ritual feast in *dingari*: prepared by specific women*
VI, 7	women dance around old man they kill	*bandiri* dancing by women as complementary to men's: held near secret-sacred ground*
VI, 8, 10, 11	Gaanga incident	re-enacted in ritual*
VII, 1-3	Ganabuda women crawl along from place to place	postulants crawl on ritual ground*
VIII, 3	Ganabuda cut hymens of two young girls	ritual hymen-cutting performed in secret, away from men: regarded as complementary adjunct of the *dingari*, and equivalent to subincision. Rarely carried out*

I have made no attempt to provide a framework of *dingari* ritual arranged sequentially, since my main emphasis is on myth. In ritual performance only sections of the myth are dramatized, and not the total myth. Those items marked with an asterisk are distinctive to the *dingari*. A structural analysis of these two dimensions, myth and ritual, would be rewarding: but here it is necessary simply to repeat that the basic ethical pattern I have been speaking of is upheld and reinforced by ritual action which has direct relevance to everyday life.

Ritual has to do with maintaining the state of affairs which, men affirm, has continued to exist since it was instituted by the major mythical beings. It is also the way through which contact can be made with these beings, to ensure that the power (*maia*) they possess is brought to bear on social living. This is relevant, primarily, in two ways: one is natural increase and fructification of the countryside, maintaining and sustaining the material things of life; the other is spiritual renewal or stimulation. Indeed, within the ritual sphere men particularly, and women also, are brought close to the essence of things. Human and spirit beings are not distinctly separate entities. In this view, man is the contemporary manifestation of these sacred characters. He does not have to urge the release of this power, this *maia*, by supplication or exhortation: it is transmitted to him through ritual performance, by his identification with those characters themselves. And he emerges from the ritual ground, symbolized by the Mother, as a new man.

At the same time, all myth-inspired ritual is an area of formal instruction. It involves teachers (the big men, men of experience and knowledge) and learners (the novices, young men, or those undergoing particular stages of the ritual, as onlookers, active participants and so forth). In this context, learning refers to the *total* ethical system, including the moral and the immoral.

There are, as we have seen, two dimensions of the immoral. The one that immediately concerns us here is the sphere of human social relations. Table 2 sets out the main *dingari* incidents which can be categorized as immoral in this sense, and how each situation is resolved, along with comments.

I have categorized what can be distinguished as basic crimes—that is, those considered to be immoral. In the first bracket (A), theft, no direct punishment is involved except in Myth-Section IV, 5-8, 10-15, where all the *dingari* suffer as a result. The three cases under this heading concern theft of sacred objects, along with trickery used to obtain them. In real-life situations, sacred objects are rarely stolen, and I have recorded no examples—except in the case of those removed by Europeans without the authority of the local custodians. If such objects had been stolen, the crime would have been regarded very seriously indeed—so much so that it could be conceived of as an irretrievable loss, likely to bring disaster to the group as a whole and not solely to the thief. To some extent, this situation is mirrored in the culminating results of Myth-Section V, 6, or more specifically of Myth-Section III, 6. What would happen is really open to conjecture.

In C, seduction, three incidents involve four women in incestuous unions; two other cases involve three women, and in their case incest is not relevant. In ordinary life there is strong condemnation of incestuous intercourse; and in the myth, death is the result in two cases, with death and/or injury of the females concerned. What the myth is saying is that only a man with abnormal genitalia (and, by implication, an abnormal sexual appetite) could contemplate entering into an incestuous relationship, and that if he does put his desire into action only tragedy can ensue. In the third case, even though the culprit escapes the avenging Mangamanga, he suffers the temporary loss of his penis and testes. In the other two cases, where the women do not stand in a sexually tabu relationship to their seducer, he escapes punishment: but it is shown that such promiscuous behaviour can bring disaster—injury and death for two women, and the murder of the other's husband.

In the cases of murder (D), and this is also relevant to C, the situations differ, and seem to be dependent on circumstances which in, for example, IV, 2, are not entirely clear. In V, 4, is the example of intended cannibalism. (Cases of cannibalism are mentioned in Desert myths and stories, but I have recorded no actual incidents—except one to the effect that east from Jabuna, two starving Europeans on camels shot two Aborigines for this purpose, cut up their flesh, cooked and ate some, and salted down the rest. This enabled them to return to Hall's Creek. It is said that this happened some years ago, when a man now living at Balgo met them on the way into Hall's Creek and was able to see what they were carrying.) In the example noted in V, 4, the breaking of the bullroarer could be interpreted as portending disaster as a direct result of this killing, as indeed was borne out in the concatenation of events leading to the immolation of all those involved. The violation of the sacred objects by women (who were killed in consequence) follows sequentially in building up the theme of disaster. In Myth-Section VI, although a mass killing occurs, and one old man is killed as a result, it is really the breaking of the religious law which could be said to bring about the succession of further immoral acts. The youths are in fact enticed down from the Mother by the food prepared by the women: they have not completed their *dingari* initiation

(to p. 243)

TABLE 2

DINGARI INCIDENTS SEEN IN MORAL–IMMORAL TERMS

Reference	Immoral Acts	Resolution	Comment
A. *Theft* II, 2-5	Djalaburu steals ritual power from Ganabuda women	men take over the ritual position of women	women are compensated for the theft, and the situation explained to them
III, 1-3	Djangimanda steals sacred boards	escapes without his followers finding him	is aided by power of *darugu*
IV, 5-8, 10-15	Djilgamada steals *darugu* and aggravates the situation by teasing the *dingari*	is followed by *dingari*; eventually aided by Ganu men, who weaken Djilgamada, leaving him to be dealt with by the *dingari*, who spear him	evades final punishment by disappearing into a rockhole and causing all the *dingari* to fall in too
B. *Quarrel* III, 6	*dingari* quarrel over *darugu*	Guninga deliberately breaks one	breaking the *darugu* resolves the quarrel. In real life, such an act would be tantamount to attempted destruction of spirit being and subject to supernatural sanctions. Note, however, that *darugu* are used for a variety of mundane purposes in the myth, including use as firewood or as a torch, as a spear in hunting, etc.

C. Seduction			
I, 2	Gadadjilga seduces a tabued relative	punished by death: abnormally long penis cut	specifically stated that Gadadjilga's action was wrong; but statement modified by saying he was too old for the women, implying he would probably have been acceptable if younger. Although the act is regarded as incestuous, no reference is made in the myth to the girl's death
VI, 8, 9	Gaanga seduces two women, one a tabued relative and the other a classificatory mother's mother	Gaanga is killed by the Ganabuda; the two girls die through injury from Gaanga's abnormally long penis	punishment of Gaanga and death of the girls because this was regarded as incestuous
VIII, 4-6	Gadadjilga (see I, 2) seduces two women	the two women die, injured by his abnormally long penis	Gadadjilga disappears with the Ganabuda; no punishment; no reference to incest
IX, 1-4	Dangidjara copulates with tabued mother-in-law, lives with her and has a son	implied punishment: loses his testes and penis, but these eventually return to him	the Mangamanga follow him; he teases them but finally escapes. This case was regarded as incestuous
C, D. Seduction and Murder			
X	Wirangula kills husband of woman he seduces	woman afterward escapes	no actual punishment implied; relationship between Wirangula and the female is not one of avoidance
D. Murder			
IV, 2	*dingari* kill two old men who possess a number of *darugu*	no reasons given	—
V, 4	*dingari* kill Buradjidin	in hunger; but flesh inedible	an attempted resolution – but unsuccessful

Reference	Immoral Acts	Resolution	Comment
D. *Murder* (cont.)			
V, 12	women supposedly see *darugu* and are killed	no further action involved	normally regarded as punishment for women who see secret-sacred emblems, etc., guarded by men
VI, 6, 7	old men kill by fire youths who have copulated with Ganabuda women	one old man escapes; the other is followed and killed	youths are punished for associating with females before their *dingari* initiation is completed. An old man is killed by women who are angry at being deprived of the young men and so came to hate all men
VI, 11	a third Gaanga is killed, beaten to death with *darugu*	—	explanation as above: the women have become embittered after losing the young men
E. *Other*			
V, 6	bullroarer broken	—	sorrow expressed; symbolic prediction of final disaster which befalls the *dingari*
V, 20	death of two young men; immolation of the rest	—	disaster and tragedy have dogged this particular *dingari* group. Hunger and thirst lead to the killing of Buradjidin; a bullroarer is broken; the women see the sacred *darugu* accidentally in their search for water. In one sense, the *dingari* are punished for this act. But it also underlines the influence of the environment on the moral life of man
VI, 10	a second Gaanga is attacked	escapes attentions of women	—

and are therefore too young to marry or to have sexual intercourse—
they must therefore be punished. Novices are warned at initiation to
beware of women, not to be promiscuous: ritual should, in the myth,
have strengthened them to withstand the overtures of the women,
who in turn are punished in their own way—by the lustful Gaanga,
and through becoming embittered against all men.

Conclusion

It is clear that in these mythic examples, in the majority of cases,
wrong action can lead to punishment, disaster and tragedy. In other
words, the mythical characters are subject to more or less the same
processes of social control as those relevant to contemporary human
beings; they are not to be regarded as being entirely beyond the law,
although they are endowed with power which makes them more than
human in particular circumstances. This is not the place to discuss
their superhuman qualities. What is striking, however, is their close
approximation to man. This cannot be said of all mythic characters
in Aboriginal Australia. But in the Western Desert the physical, social
and cultural environments of mythic man virtually coincide with those
relevant to traditional and present-day non-acculturated Aboriginal
man, and this is true too as far as their psychological make-up is concerned. Perhaps I should make this clearer. I have already said that
myth is more than a direct statement. It is palpably false to assume that
in myth we have a view of the world as it is, or as it was. I have already
demonstrated that the *dingari* reveals a concern with basic issues of
social living mostly couched, symbolically, in terms of relations between
the sexes and relations between the sacred and the non-sacred, between
materialism and spirituality. Further, there is underlined a preoccupation
with the vicissitudes of Desert living, an endeavour to cope with an
essentially unpredictable environment, *by making it ritually predictable.*

At the same time, myth is a reflection of reality, and in this context
the reflection is not over-distorted. It is as if Desert life were encapsulated
in the myth. What it contains is a guide for action. Shorn of their
magical and superhuman qualities, the mythic beings could well be
taken for human characters. It is possible to argue, on the basis of
Aboriginal epistemology, that they are no more or no less than human,
and the same can be said of man. Because myths of this kind, like their
ritual expressions, belong to the Dreaming, they are part of the sacred-
past-in-the-present. Moreover, a direct relationship exists between
Aboriginal man and the mythic characters who are manifested through
contemporary man by virtue of conception and cult 'totemism' (see
R. M. Berndt 1969, n.d. *i*, *ii*). An indestructible essence or life force

continues, it is believed, uninterruptedly from the beginning of time, and is present today in two ways—one, in the continued spiritual existence of the mythic beings at specific sites or elsewhere, and in their animal, bird, etc. guise through the natural species, for instance, or in certain natural phenomena; and, two, in man himself, each person being affiliated with a particular Dreaming spirit. 'Affiliation' is the wrong word here, because it is, rather, that each individual is a contemporary representation of the relevant spirit being. Man is identified through the myths, and identifies himself within them: indeed, his character as a person is derived from this source.

This means that the mythic spirits (like their human counterparts) have a direct concern in issues relevant to the welfare of man: and this means, too, in moral issues. The religious system of the *dingari* is also a system of morality, and this is one of its primary functions. This is not conceived of in terms of divine punishment for the wrongdoer, nor is there stipulation of sin where 'offences against ethical rules cause the displeasure of supernatural beings' (C. von Fürer-Haimendorf). Rather, the conception of sin is irrelevant in this context: supernatural sanctions may be imposed, aided by human agents, only where there are specific ritual infringements. The interest of the mythic beings is not, however, limited to this. What we have is a statement of the total life situation, in which these mythic characters demonstrate by their own actions that there is both good and bad within it; that they are part of the inevitable and irreversible framework of existence, and that wrongdoing will almost certainly precipitate its own disastrous results. That they themselves, as mythic beings, as supernatural creatures, were not exempt from these conditions and did in fact suffer as a result of wrong action, is amply borne out in the *dingari*. As Stanner has remarked (1965:218), '. . . myths contain much of the "human-all-too-human" character of man'; and from an Aboriginal point of view it is unreasonable to expect the personality of man and that of his spirits to diverge appreciably.

In this respect, then, we perceive a pattern laid down in the Dreaming, by spirit beings, for men to follow; a series of incidents in which they themselves are actors, as are men; a range of possibilities from which Aboriginal man may select, according to circumstances, in due (but not necessarily full) awareness of what that choice will involve. I would not say, however, that this is consciously carried out: people do not pause to reason out the implications of their actions, any more than did the spirit beings themselves. Nevertheless, the *dingari* system as a pattern of living is an accepted part of their ideology, an ideology embracing both that which is conceived of as being good and that which is conceived of as being bad—in the recognition that reality is a mixture of both, that there is no morality without immorality. In fact, it is not the good which is emphasized in the *dingari*, but the evil. The good is accepted—it is the norm or custom, if one wishes to use such words: it requires no specific highlighting and is taken for granted. On the other hand, evil does require particular attention to be paid to it. It is true that, as I have said, it is a necessary condition of social and physical living: this is not denied. But it is also true that it must be controlled. Wrong actions not only make those that are good more desirable; they sharpen realization of inherent dangers. As we have seen, the continuum of the moral-immoral does not concern only human social relations: it also has a much wider relevance in Aboriginal terms. Living so close to nature means inevitably that there are times of plenty and times of hunger: and these last may be times of tragedy and disaster. The spirits themselves were in many cases creative, they were possessed of superhuman powers, they wielded the water-producing *darugu*, they were responsible for the increase of the natural species, among other things—but they were also vulnerable. How much more so is man? And this is one lesson the myth purports to teach.

Notes

1. This paper was originally presented at the VIIIth International Congress of Anthropological and Ethnological Sciences held in Japan in September 1968, in a symposium on 'Religion and Morality' organized by Professor C. von Fürer-Haimendorf of the University of London.

2. Fieldwork in this region was carried out in 1958 and 1960 at the old Balgo Hills settlement, in 1962 at Hall's Creek, and in 1969 at the new Balgo (Ngarili) settlement and at Hall's Creek. During this last period, also, full song cycles of the *dingari* were obtained, but this material is not used in this contribution. Professor Helmut Petri of the University of Cologne has been studying the *dingari* complex from the perspective of La Grange mission station near Broome, where he has carried out fieldwork. See Petri, in Nevermann, Worms and Petri 1968, where further references are provided concerning his work. In this study I am not making cross-references to his work, and am referring only selectively to others. R. Tonkinson, too, has material on the *dingari* from the Jigalong area (see Tonkinson 1966), as has Dr R. A. Gould for the Warburton Range area (1966). I have also collected *dingari* data from the Warburtons in 1957, and at Birrundudu in 1944-45.

3. The bulk of this material is retained for detailed treatment.

4. The word *darugu* can be translated generally as meaning secret-sacred, set-apart, tabu, or dangerous and is used in a religious sense for any thing or any person within that context. In this paper it usually refers to sacred objects, particularly incised wooden boards of varying size—some as long as 12 feet, some as small as 1-2 inches. There are different categories of boards within this general heading, each with specific names.

5. I am not discussing in this context the Aboriginal equivalents of these words which are usually translated as 'good' or 'not good' (or bad). In one sense, I follow

Durkheim (1949:398) when he says, 'Everything which is a source of solidarity is moral, everything which forces man to take account of other men is moral, everything which forces him to regulate his conduct through something other than the striving of his ego is moral . . . [This] . . . consists in a state of dependence.' What Durkheim is saying is that morality is based on interpersonal and intergroup interaction in terms of reciprocity and co-operation, and it is this which is expressed in the diagram to this paper. To spell this out: co-operation and interaction are essential in the domestic and ritual spheres, and in all aspects relevant to maintaining the social order in terms of obtaining food and ensuring, by spiritual intervention, that its supply is continued. This is a *three-sided* discourse between man-man, man-god, man-natural environment (natural species), in which interaction between the three is considered paramount. Thus:

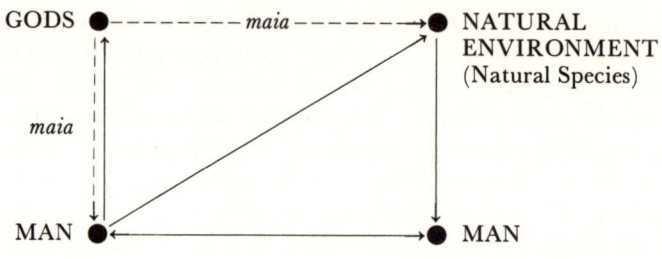

Fig. 2

Interaction is between gods and man, gods and environment (through species) via *maia* (power). The social world is expanded to include this three-dimensional world.

However, this could well be put in Radcliffe-Brown's terms (1952:166) when he says: 'The cosmos is ruled by law.' In other words, a pattern is involved. Or, again, 'For him [the Aboriginal] men and women ought to observe the rules of behaviour that were fixed for all time by the events of the World Dawn [that is, Dreaming], and similarly the rain ought to fall in its proper season, plants should grow and produce fruit or seed, and animals should bear young. *But there are irregularities in human society and in nature.*' (Italics mine.) The point I am making here is one that Radcliffe-Brown did not follow up. It is the 'breaking down' of the three-dimensional interaction that brings about an immoral state. To take this further: it is the rupture in social relations which is categorized as being immoral, and social relations are three-fold—existing between man and man; between man and his deities; between man and his environment and that which is within it and is directly relevant to his well-being.

The 'irregularities in human society and in nature' constitute part of the total system and are written into it as part of the condition of social living. A total ethical system, within the context of the Aboriginal society reviewed here, embraces what is regarded as both moral and immoral, and these are seen in *social* terms.

REFERENCES

BERNDT, C. H. 1950 *Women's Changing Ceremonies in Northern Australia*. L'Homme, No. 1, Hermann, Paris.
BERNDT, R. M. 1951 *Kunapipi*. Cheshire, Melbourne.
——— 1952 *Djanggawul*. Routledge and Kegan Paul, London.
——— 1962 *Excess and Restraint: Social Control among a New Guinea Mountain People*. University of Chicago Press, Chicago.

BERNDT, R. M. 1969 *The Sacred Site: the Western Arnhem Land Example*. Australian Aboriginal Studies No. 29, Australian Institute of Aboriginal Studies, Canberra.
—— n.d. *i* The Walmadjeri-Gugadja Constellation. In *Simple Societies* (M. G. Bicchieri, ed.). Holt, Rinehart and Winston. *Forthcoming*.
—— n.d. *ii* Two in One, More in Two. In the Claude Lévi-Strauss *Festschrift*, Mouton, Paris. *Forthcoming*.
BERNDT, R. M. and C. H. 1945 A preliminary report of fieldwork in the Ooldea region, Western South Australia, *Oceania Offprint*, Sydney. (Also see *Oceania*, Vol. XII, No. 4 to Vol. XV, No. 3.)
—— 1964 *The World of the First Australians*. Ure Smith, Sydney. (Second printing, 1965; paperback, 1968.)
—— (eds) 1965 *Aboriginal Man in Australia*. Angus and Robertson, Sydney.
DURKHEIM, E. 1949 *The Division of Labour*. The Free Press, Glencoe, Illinois.
MEGGITT, M. J. 1966 Gadjari among the Walbiri Aborigines of Central Australia, *The Oceania Monographs*, No. 14, Sydney.
PETRI, H. 1968 In *Die Religionen der Südsee und Australiens* (H. Nevermann, E. A. Worms and H. Petri, eds). Kohlhammer, Stuttgart.
RADCLIFFE-BROWN, A. R. 1952 *Structure and Function in Primitive Society*. Cohen and West, London.
STANNER, W. E. H. 1960 On Aboriginal Religion, *Oceania*, Vol. XXX, No. 4.
—— 1965 Religion, Totemism and Symbolism. In *Aboriginal Man in Australia* (R. M. and C. H. Berndt, eds). Chapter 8.
STREHLOW, T. G. H. 1947 *Aranda Traditions*. Melbourne University Press, Melbourne.
TONKINSON, R. 1966 Social Structure and Acculturation of Aborigines in the Western Desert. M.A. thesis in Anthropology, University of Western Australia.

HELMUT PETRI
GISELA PETRI-ODERMANN

Stability and Change: Present-day Historic Aspects Among Australian Aborigines[1]

The observations described here result from anthropological fieldwork, which was first carried out in 1954/55 and then systematically at intervals in 1960, 1963 and 1966. The purpose was, first, to record all those features of the Aboriginal traditional cultures still to be found among the social units of the northern regions of Australia's Western Desert. Second, it was to examine at regular intervals a specific form of culture contact—that is, those changes which were slowly taking place in present-day Aboriginal social and cultural life under the influence of the Australian-European civilization. We are dealing here with a kind of anthropological field research which gives equal weighting to both poles of the concepts 'stability' and 'change'. This has, in our personal opinion, proved its fruitfulness when the fieldwork has been limited in principle to narrow, and therefore easily encompassed, geographic as well as historic areas, and when it is repeated also with a certain regularity. Such studies, which could help us gain a deeper insight into the past and present cultural situation of so-called underdeveloped peoples are, unfortunately, not as common as they should be.

Introduction

Various publications have appeared, dealing with the deep-rooted traditionalism of these human groups, the overwhelming majority of whom find themselves today within the socio-economic field of interest of the wider Australian society, and whose small number, varying between 45,000 and 60,000 persons, represents an ethnic minority. (See Berndt and Berndt 1964:420 *et seq.*, 1965:377 *et seq.*; Meggitt, 1962; Petri 1956, 1967; Petri and Petri-Odermann 1964.) For this reason we may be spared the necessity of explicating the matter to its full extent. A short synopsis may suffice. The pre-European social order of the Australian tribes, which determined the constitution of the local groups, continues to exist today as a functioning system only in isolated instances; however, as an idea and a historic reminiscence it still continues to play a large role among the numerous Aboriginal units in the north of the Western Desert. The former local groups, as extended families with territorial ownership rights, which represented the units of economic and political life in a continental framework, gave way slowly to European principles of order. The Aborigines, whose former hunting grounds became areas of stock-breeding or other forms of Western economic planning, lost thereby the basis for gaining their livelihood by means of the former hunting and gathering economy. Most of the Aborigines were forced to migrate and find new possibilities of social and economic life. In the wide arid areas, the so-called outback, of central and northern Australia, a new type of local group, which in many cases can be dated back to the early nineteenth century, came slowly into being. Aborigines of different social, territorial, tribal and linguistic groupings joined to form new communities. They were bound to a particular area and became in time economically dependent on various Australian-European settlements. It is to this new type of local group that the cultural anthropologist must look, if he wishes to gain access to the Aborigines and all their former and present problems of existence. Even contacts with so-called 'bush natives' (that is to say, with those small social units made up of people who, either temporarily or continuously, are still leading a life of hunting and food gathering: Petri 1962:291 *et seq.*) are possible only through local groups of this new type. It is, then, these people, those in the new communities, who hold the keys to the traditional culture of their forefathers as well as to all levels of adjustment to the Western economic and social order. These local groups prove to be the focus of Australian Aboriginal cultures in the 'coloured-white' contact situation of today. They reflect a definite historic development characteristic of the present situation; they become the manifestation of the particular temporary incongruity between traditionalism and the processes of change which are taking place under the pressure of Australian-European civilization. R. M. Berndt considers these new local groups, which can be termed 'acculturated' in only a limited sense, to be units of 'mixed orientation', which tend toward the European cultural and social type on the one hand, but on the other adhere to their traditional system of values (R. M. Berndt 1959:105).

According to everything we were able to establish in the area of the Western Desert in which we worked during the years between 1954 and 1966, it was clear that there was an accent on the traditionalism of the Aborigines and on their conservative view of life. The majority of all the individuals of both sexes and of very differing ages with whom we came in contact during that time, persist in a rather clear-cut cultural introversion. Even those people who in their status and outward behaviour seem largely to have adjusted themselves to European ways of life, tend generally not to make a secret of their indifference and mistrust toward the European value systems and social order. The old forms of social and religious life and their cult performances continue to remain basically in their former contexts. Generally this is not altered even if the Aborigines come into a temporary or permanent occupational relationship with Australian employers (Petri 1962:297). In spite of the numerous challenges of a civilization which is foreign to them and which has only partially been revealed to their understanding, it is the 'Law' (as the whole complex of all traditional values is called), which provides their lives with a sense of balance and existential security. Considerations of this kind appeared constantly in conversations with people who claimed not only to be integrated into this still very much traditionally oriented Aboriginal society but also to wield influence on the destiny of their own community. Sex and age levels revealed scarcely any difference of opinion in this context.

The Survival of Aboriginal Tradition

During the years 1954-55, such rather uncompromising viewpoints and ways of behaviour were noticed only in individual cases. They were limited to a few persons who had drawn certain consequences for themselves personally out of their experiences with Australian society. The majority of the Aborigines of the new type of local groups at Anna Plains, Mandoorah, Wallal, Thangoo and Broome gave little thought, in spite of their 'traditional orientation', to the dangers posed by the Europeans to their way of living. The Aborigines had to deal with settlers who were interested in them primarily as labourers and who had, if any at all, only a curious layman's interest in their internal affairs (Petri 1962, 1963). In 1960 the situation was a changed one. In the meantime, the Government Aboriginal Depot at La Grange had been transformed (on 1 January 1955) into a Roman Catholic mission station. This was the beginning of the first serious European intervention into the spiritual life and traditional value systems of these Aborigines, which until then had been taken for granted. The mission's activity, reaching far beyond the original local radius, naturally questioned the Aborigines' traditional religiosity. For the first time in the course of their unwritten history, they saw themselves confronted with the necessity of reflecting on the values of their own world of belief and philosophy of life in a more or less changing world.

Unfortunately, we had no opportunity to study the early efforts of the La Grange mission in terms of its success or failure in this respect. When we chose La Grange in 1960 as a particularly well-suited base for fieldwork, the situation was approximately as follows. Almost all the members of the two new types of local group which were settled near the mission attended mass, at least on Sunday, at the local church. We shall not attempt to judge to what degree we are dealing here with an outwardly manifested adjustment to a new situation or with a newly awakened spiritual need. A constantly obtruding phenomenon was, at any rate, that, with the exception of Briemie Jack (a former leader of the Garadjeri local group of La Grange, who had given up the old 'Law' and considered himself to be fully Christianized), all others (among whom were also young boys of initiation age, some being altar boys in the mission's services of worship) continued to participate in the traditional and esoteric cults, which were performed in the usual way at secret bush places. The impression we received was that such 'syncretistic' behaviour was accepted by the Aborigines as being completely natural. At that time, beginnings of a kind of revivalistic movement could be seen, which might be considered as a reaction against the teachings of the mission, that were questioning for the first time the validity of the old Australian norms of value and reasoning. The spokesmen for this reconsideration of a given cultural heritage (having as its goal on the one hand a revival of traditional complexes which were falling into oblivion and, on the other hand, a more intensive care of the cults and ceremonial life) were, strangely enough, not the 'old men' acting as 'past masters' (Elkin), but young and middle-aged men, aware of their traditions. They had lived in contact situations and had attempted to incorporate their experiences intellectually, seeking adequate solutions for the problems facing them. (See Petri 1962:305; Petri and Petri-Odermann 1964:462.)

What we observed in 1960 and what had in no way stood out six years earlier in the same area, was more or less the outline of a 'culture consciousness'. This should be understood as an attempt to preserve those institutions and concepts of the past which were considered essential for the continuity of life in the present and future. This was observable in an intensive cultivation of their own, but also of alien traditional elements. The main motivators were middle-aged and elderly men. Younger initiated men who had been educated at a mission were also involved. In most cases small or large groups would, without any perceptible reason, set out for the tabued areas in the bush in order to sing through certain 'lines' of mythic historic character, reviving the wanderings and achievements of the 'Dreamtime' ancestors. The motivation was always: 'We have to keep the old Law going.' All this took place away from the mission and actually stood in opposition to mission policy at that time—which was to have as little as possible to do with the existing norms of Aboriginal social life, and to replace their traditional religion completely with the concepts of Christianity. In spite of this conflict of aims, there were scarcely any upsets between the mission management and the 'reformers' in the camps of both local groups settled near La Grange.

The only critical problem leading to actual conflict was the mission's resistance to the system of *rites de passage*. In the northern districts of the Western Desert, these consist of the old or elderly men 'grabbing' young boys at puberty and putting them through the long process of initiation. This begins with the ritual operation of circumcision, followed by a definite period of instruction in the isolation of the bush. It means that novices are introduced to their community's basic principles of social and spiritual life. In fact, this is the usual Australian pattern. This system of instruction is temporarily completed by a second ritual operation, subincision, which takes place between the ages of eighteen and twenty, and immediately after that the youths have the right to marry. It is well known that every Aboriginal man wishing to gain status in his society must undergo this kind of initiation. The numerous attempts made by the mission and secular bodies to alter this extend back as far as early settlement in this area, and seem to have brought little result. Even the so-called 'acculturated' and 'Christianized' Aborigines are today considered to be 'men', with the right to take part in the process of decision making, only when they have been circumcised and have attended the bush schools provided by the 'Law' experts. The second operation, subincision, is not a *sine qua non* condition of 'man-making'. There are many men, even elderly ones with a firm traditional orientation, who have not been subincised but have not, consequently, suffered any loss of prestige. This attitude toward subincision, over and above its being a painful operation, could be because it was taken over only secondarily—probably from the eastern regions of the Western Desert. Originally, and this is inferred from the 'Two Men' traditions within this geographical region, circumcision only was practised as a first step toward becoming a man and attaining maturity. To a certain extent, one can view this as being a symptom of the growing cultural awareness which has been increasingly observed during the past eight years. In this context, the question of the origin of subincision (that is, its mythical history) became a serious subject of discussion during the different kinds of 'meetings' which one of us attended. Widely divergent viewpoints, concepts, and attempted interpretations were put forward. Even in 1966 a solution to this controversial issue was not forthcoming. Such discussions, however, were of particular interest because they demonstrated that these Aborigines, contrary to still widely held ideas, are in no way bound to a fixed and unmodified pattern. These and similar findings, discussed elsewhere, permit us to recognize that Australian Aborigines are quite prepared to question their traditional values and moral code, to discuss these and, if necessary, to re-interpret them. (See Petri 1967:3 *et seq.*, 1963 and 1966.)

A measure undertaken by the La Grange mission in 1960, allegedly to prevent the boys being put through the initiatory process, was their removal to the Beagle Bay settlement, approximately 200 miles to the north. This was already a largely Europeanized and Christianized community made up of mixed-blood Aborigines. Whether this removal had really been planned to keep circumcisional candidates out of the hands of the custodians of the Law is not specifically clear. However, the fact remains that all members of both La Grange local groups were convinced that this was the reason, and they were consequently alarmed and annoyed. This was not expressed overtly, but smouldered beneath the surface. There was no open conflict between the Aborigines and the mission management. This was mainly for the following reasons. Around the end of 1960, a liberalized mission policy was set in motion at the instigation of His Lordship Bishop Jobst, the Catholic Bishop of Kimberley (Western Australia). All seemed to go smoothly at first, largely for the practical reason that the average Aboriginal accepted only as much of the Christian tradition and Christian ethos as fitted into his own thought categories and seemed to be at one with the concepts of his forefathers. The Catholic mission took a practical standpoint and did not continue to question the so-called old 'Law' as such. One immediate result was that a compromise was reached on the revitalization of initiation. The 'grabbing' of circumcision candidates was supposed to take place only after their elementary education in the state school attached to the mission. In practice, during the following years, a synchronization took place. Virtually free of coercion, the European-Christian and the Australian-traditional educational systems were co-ordinated. Between 1960 and 1966 several initiation ceremonies were held at La Grange, more or less under the patronage of the mission. These proceedings were communicated to us by letter. We were able to attend personally only two of these events which are so important for traditionally oriented Aboriginal life, in October 1963 and in August 1966.[2]

The Rise of a New Cult Perspective

Theoretically, such a liberalization of mission policy should have led to the emergence of a new syncretistic form of religion. As we were able to establish in 1963 and 1966, this actually happened—but in a different manner from what was theoretically expected. A few Aborigines belonging to La Grange local groups, as well as to those at Anna Plains and Broome, all of whom were in principle traditionally oriented, professed certain beliefs which attempted to bring Old Testament doctrines of the Protestant missionaries into accordance with the Aboriginal 'Law'. They had received their new orientation, combining traditional with Protestant beliefs, second-hand from people who had spent part of their lives within the Fitzroy River area. We were able to record the beginning of such a development at La Grange in 1963, and this has been discussed in detail elsewhere (Petri and Petri-Odermann 1964:461 *et seq.*). Particularly among the Udiallas (who were migrants from the central and eastern regions of the Western Desert, and who had formed their own new-type local group), nativistic anti-European feelings occasionally appeared. In this connection, the spokesmen expressed their discontent with existing conditions, taking every opportunity to emphasize that the country was theirs, that it belonged to the Aborigines; that the Europeans were intruders, since they had arrived later; and that there was no reason why they should comply with the wishes of the missionaries and 'station bosses'. Apart from this, there was a constant demand for the basic wage. It would be incorrect, nevertheless, to conclude—from these and other displays of displeasure—that the way was being paved for a social revolutionary awareness. A causative link between different ideas was not clearly established, and in all the discussions on these matters there was no apparent intention to change, in a broad sense, the existing *status quo*. If this was present, it escaped us. The cause of such 'anti-European' trends as manifested by this, then still relatively small, group of people can be interpreted, with some reservation, as follows. Around the middle of the 1950s the township of Talgarno was founded as a centre for missile experimentation, near the pastoral station of Anna Plains. This settlement, created *ad hoc* (whose very name had no reference to a local Aboriginal language, for instance Njangomada, but was taken from a non-identified language from Australia's south-east), was considered by Aborigines of the new Anna Plains local group to be a grievous infringement of their traditional order of things. Their *ngirbiri* (the tabued bush area in which the *gogur*, or sacred boards of *tjurunga* type, were stored, and where all cult activities were held) was confiscated and declared to be within a military restricted area. This event was significant since it forced the Aborigines at Anna Plains to make various changes in their traditional life pattern. It affected, also, neighbouring local groups at Mandoorah and Wallal in the south-west and at Nita Downs, Frazier Downs and La Grange in the north-east. It led to the first serious disharmonies in relations between European and Aboriginal groups, which until 1955 had been relatively free of crises. To be sure, the military project at Talgarno was disbanded after a few years, but the disturbance in the equilibrium of Aboriginal socio-cultural life remained unforgotten. Even in 1966, long after the dismantling of this experimental station, the same views were expressed whenever the name Talgarno was mentioned in conversations with conservative and traditionally oriented Aborigines.

A lasting impetus to this anti-European frame of mind and behaviour (which was quite diffuse in 1963, but more clearly formulated in 1966) came from a very different direction. The Udiallas, already mentioned as having come from various places in and around the Western Desert, maintain routine contact with groups focusing on the Jigalong Apostolic Mission, near Lake Disappointment. This interaction, which as such represents an interesting phenomenon of 'population dynamics' among these Desert people (and which has been studied by us) has at La Grange contributed significantly to this tension. Since about the end of World War II, differences between the Udialla on the one hand, and the Gularabulu ('the coastal people', that is, the local Garadjeri and Njangomada Aborigines) on the other hand, have become apparent. These tensions came into existence because of what seemed to be insurmountable differences between them on questions of cult ritual and mythic historic traditions: and they have continued to exist. This problem will be treated in more detail later, as it is important for understanding ethnic movements in this area.

The contacts between the Udiallas and the Jigalong peoples, who are bound together by a common linguistic background and a common cultural tradition, seem in a particular aspect to have been of some consequence for some years past. The propagandistic activities of Donald McLeod (a 'white' Australian and a Marxian social reformer, who for the last two decades—first near Port Hedland, then near Roebourne and also at Marble Bar—has founded mining co-operatives along socialistic lines, managed by full- and mixed-blood Aborigines) seem to be especially appreciated by those who have had minimal contact with Europeans. And these belonged principally to the Jigalong groups and their loosely associated Udiallas of the northern regions. It is clearly these people who have made the least compromise in respect of the traditional values of their forefathers. They have made themselves least accessible to the assimilation and integration plans of the Western Australian Native Welfare Department. Individual observations and informants' case histories illustrate these points quite plainly. McLeod's social progressivism seems particularly to have given wings to the fantasy of these Aborigines, since it is bound to the internationally standardized slogan of 'anti-colonialism' and sets as its objective the social and economic equalization of the 'exploiter' and the 'exploited'. Whether Donald McLeod was always successful in communicating such views to his followers is open to question. The recipients had other thought categories, and probably did not always understand him as he intended they should. But this remains to be seen. Up to now, the impression is that the majority of the Aborigines who did profess the axioms and principles known as 'Don McLeod's Law' have rather vague visions of a future egalitarian society without any colour-bar. Since even the Australian Aborigines are subject to the common human weakness of wishful thinking, they hope for a future which will permit them to lead a life with material advantages but without the obligation to work, and all this oriented within the framework of traditional values. It is possible to see this manifested in revivalistic and millenarian concepts, as in the Melanesian Cargo Cult idea. In the latter case, as in this part of Aboriginal Australia, critical issues have been raised in the process of interaction between the different worlds which have stimulated such contemplations—insofar as we can perceive, independently. Here as there, there is a tendency to push forward in a way, often inadequate in reality, toward a synthesis of both cultural and social systems, without recognizing overtly any kind of relationship between them. In such attempts a kind of tragedy is reflected in the very different expectations of salvation (*Heilserwartungen*): and this refers to people who previously came under such labels as 'primitive' or 'savage', irrespective of whether or not they have achieved political independence. Aside from a small Western-educated élite, people of Aboriginal descent were not in a position, socio-psychologically, to cope with these situations of conflict which were caused by their abrupt initial contacts with highly specialized and technologically oriented peoples.

The readiness of Udialla and Jigalong groups, who primarily concern us here, to accept the social reform programme of Donald McLeod cannot be explained simply by the direct relations which exist between them. His propagandists—we first had word of them at Anna Plains in 1954—occasionally travel through the whole of the north-west, soliciting for members among the new types of local groups. In doing so, they make use of specific means, as simple as they are effective. As an advance for the future wealth which will be placed at the disposal of the Aborigines, they give supplies of flour, tea and sugar. For Aborigines today, these are three necessary ingredients for the preparation of ceremonial meals, which follow all cult activities considered as important (Petri and Petri-Odermann 1964:463). One of the most active emissaries for the 'Don McLeod Law' is an elderly Njangomada named Dooley Bin-Bin, who has worked together with this almost charismatic social reformer for more than twenty years. He has continued to collaborate with him in spite of various difficulties. His trips have led him as far as Derby and to the lower Fitzroy River. In 1966 he belonged to the governing body of McLeod's mining co-operative near Marble Bar. By chance we had the opportunity at Port Hedland, in November 1963, not only to get to know this man, unusual in his own way, but also to hear him speak publicly. Being 'traditionally oriented', and convinced of the lasting validity of his people's old 'Law', he has endeavoured for years now to adapt this to a particular doctrine of Western origin. The results of this 'auto-acculturation' within a limited framework did not leave too encouraging an impression. Dooley Bin-Bin's eloquence, which could be shaken by nothing, was confined to monologues and recitals of studied programme mottoes and slogans, arranged one after another without logical sequence. A large part of these could easily have originated directly from his master's repertoire, providing little information on his own views. His stereotyped rhetoric was concentrated in a polemic against persons of different skin colouring and existing social institutions, and left the audience without comment. It was a rather disappointing display of prefabricated concepts, which could scarcely have stimulated a group of politically interested Europeans, let alone Aborigines. Yet it could be seen that this man (who, according to local Aboriginal opinion, took disagreement to be an insult) was in fact responsible for an important part of the formation of those anti-European attitudes and vague revivalistic-millenarian dreams which were current among some of these Desert Aborigines—at least from the perspective of La Grange and Port Hedland. In this connection, it can be said that among the coastal population, who can look back to an older and more intensive experience with Europeans, only isolated individuals were prepared to turn to these social revolutionary programmes and specifically to their Aboriginal spokesman, Dooley Bin-Bin (*ibid.*).

We regret that the findings, confirmed not only by ourselves, but also by officers of the Native Welfare Department, settlers, and missionaries, scarcely permit themselves to be brought into harmony with certain 'anti-colonialistic' trends of our times. If one, however, discusses with Dooley Bin-Bin questions relevant to mythic historic traditions of his people and the cult and ritual systems which vivify them, then he displays an intellectuality, free from Western doctrinairism, flexible and open to discussion, such as is often apparent among today's Aborigines (Petri 1966:331 *et seq.*, 1967:1 *et seq.*). The presence of this compartmentalization suggests a suspicion of mine, which has been expressed in other contexts (Petri 1962:307 *et seq.*), namely, that the readiness of Aborigines of this area to internalize what is conceived of as a body of Western ideas and concepts, is still in its very beginnings. Dooley Bin-Bin, who is ridiculed by most Europeans as a charlatan and feared by many of his 'coloured' colleagues because of the sanctions he threatens to enforce against those who disbelieve him, becomes an impressive case of the not so rare socio-cultural misfit. Whether he is ever to attain the status of a 'marginal personality' in the sense of socio-psychological adjustment, or maladjustment, is open to question. His advanced age may exclude this possibility.

In summary, then, we have considered various aspects under which it is possible to view the reasons for anti-European feelings among the Desert Aborigines specifically of the areas we have noted. These attitudes have been gaining more and more ground since 1963, and there is the possibility that they will be expressed more vocally as time goes on. It could be that there are other 'social revolutionary' backgrounds, as yet overlooked, which may come to light in future field research.

The Revelation of Jinimin

However, even the mythic religious systems of these Aborigines contain points of departure for this kind of critical phenomenon. As has already been mentioned elsewhere (Petri and Petri-Odermann 1964:463 *et seq.*), *Jinimin* (Jesus Christ), it is said, revealed himself personally (probably for the first time in July 1963) to the *marungu* ('human beings', i.e. a synonym for Aborigines) in Wonajagu or Woneiga territory (a tribal area in the east). He was manifested as being both black and white in skin colour. This two-sided aspect of his epiphany is probably coherent with his message of salvation, which he wanted to bring to the Wonajagu people. According to Wili-Guda (one of the Aborigines who resided at that time in La Grange, but had come from the east and belonged linguistically and tribally to the Walmadjeri or Djualin people), Jinimin had proclaimed that all land had from the beginning belonged to the Aborigines and that in the future there would be no differences between Aborigines and other Australians—all should share equally in that land. This reference to the ancient rights of Aborigines to their country (which was first articulated in this way in 1963), is still reiterated today (1966). It does not necessarily have its basis in the secularized socialistic ideology of McLeod; it is rooted partially in the syncretistic Jinimin belief.

Jinimin's future world without social and 'racial' differentiation can be realized, it is said, only if they (the Aborigines) have enough political power and achieve a sense of self-identification. Only under such conditions can they successfully counteract the designs of Europeans. One *pre*condition, however, is that the Aborigines must 'keep going' the old 'Law'. In other words, they must not depart from the path through life which had been prescribed by their forefathers and by the Dreamtime spirit beings. The Christian Redeemer, adapted to their own categories of thinking and values, assumes the role of protector and preserver of their traditional culture. A kind of syncretistic religiosity becomes recognizable: and this is familiar to us from the various millenarian movements (or *Heilserwartungsbewegungen*) which have appeared over the last hundred years or so in Oceania as elsewhere. However, in this context it has its own character, which is derived from the background of Aboriginal Australian traditionalism. In this connection, Wili-Guda reported that when Jinimin-Jesus revealed himself to an Aboriginal group in Wonajagu territory, they were singing *wanadjara* and *worgaia*. These are two traditional cult complexes which vivify the Dreamtime activity of female creators, and which in the course of the past two or three decades have spread (as a 'travelling business': that is, as migrating cult complexes) over a wide area of the Western Central Desert into the Northern Territory, where some Aborigines still live in organized social units. (Petri and Petri-Odermann 1964; Meggitt 1966; Micha 1965: spelt *workaia*.) Their celebration of these rituals is believed to contribute to a large degree to Aboriginal self-confidence and self-identification, providing them with courage and inner strength to cope with the future and the changing (and in their view, better) social order. The *worgaia* complex plays a particular role here, for it is regarded as 'God's Law'. Our first information on this dates from 1963 (Petri and Petri-Odermann 1964). Only in 1966, at La Grange, during an initiation ceremony of the *worgaia* type, did there appear to be such a relationship between the traditional religion and certain aims of a 'social revolutionary' character. And this was apparent in the ideas of a large group of people.

This exposition up to now enables us to reach some provisional conclusions. The nativistic manifestations, inimical to aliens, among certain Aboriginal groups of this area, have psychologically two basic foundations. In the west of the area under examination, the ill-feeling over the establishment of the missile base at Talgarno, and the propagandistic activity of the reformer McLeod, must take the main brunt of the responsibility in activating the kind of beliefs we have discussed. In the east, the Jinimin religion which is slowly pushing itself westward incorporates certain Christian concepts: it could have originated under the influence of missionary activity. It would, however, be incorrect to classify such an, as yet, modest expression as the beginnings of a *Heilserwartungsbewegung* within the definition of this term. The western and eastern variants indicate they are both secular *as well as* religious. In both cases—and indeed without a recognizable readiness for action, as of yet—the retention of the pre-European or traditional religious and cultural form is coupled with a utopian dream of an egalitarian society, in this world, patterned along Western lines.

A wealth of data which we were able to gather during our fieldwork in 1966, at Port Hedland and Lombadina, as well as at the La Grange and Broome mission stations, supports the above thesis—at least as a temporary assessment. We refer once more to Wili-Guda, who reported that the new Jinimin myth was accepted within his tribe, as well as by the Djualin or Walmadjeri at Myroodah Station on the lower Fitzroy. He spoke of a native doctor (or shaman) named Tommy Djilamanga who was employed as a stockboy on Myroodah. This man was the cult chief or prophet of the new teachings. That he had really played the role of a charismatic leader and prophet, during the re-appearance of the black and white Jesus, could be established only during the winter months of 1966. However, Tommy Djilamanga had become in the meanwhile the *gagural* (chief or leading expert) of one of the *worgaia* traditional cult complexes associated with the Jinimin belief. His name was on every lip, and he even enjoyed high prestige among Aborigines living in those localities already mentioned among people who knew little or nothing of what he represented. Despite all attempts, it was not possible for us to talk to him. We did meet his actual brother (from the same mother) in La Grange. According to the degree of veneration in which the Udiallas, particularly, held him, it was possible to gauge Djilamanga's own personal power and his charisma as a prophet of the old, as well as the new teachings of salvation. Djilamanga, moving around in the vast northern area between Port Hedland in the west and Fitzroy Crossing in the east during 1966, was a personality upon whom many of the Aborigines set great hope. From what we have said, it seems clear that we must discard the view that all Australian Aborigines have a uniform religious framework.

The Introduction of the Worgaia

Wili-Guda, together with Wiluridji, a Julbari-dja, was also the first who, in 1963, brought the basic elements of the *worgaia* tradition to La Grange. With this came the Jinimin myth, directly from Myroodah. Actually, that should have come by way of Broome, which was the old cult 'relay station' in present times, but there were other considerations against this which we are unable to go into now. The inauguration of the *worgaia* complex among the Udiallas at La Grange consisted, first, of the display of several cult objects of the Central Australian *tjurunga* type. These were small oblong boards incised with varying geometric designs, and no more than 2 inches long. No precise explanation was given concerning their meaning. Strangely enough, among them was a board supposedly from the sacra out of the east, termed a *djabanba* (which has the same name among the Walbiri: Meggitt 1966:8) and of south-western Australian origin. This had been given by one of us to the Udialla group at La Grange, for diplomatic reasons and as a gift, three years before. Probably it did not occur to Wili-Guda to mention this when he exhibited his *worgaia* relics from *Waringari* (the east): or else he placed it unselfconsciously within a new religious setting. Both possibilities are imaginable here.

The introduction of the *worgaia* to people at La Grange was, to our surprise, not yet completed by 1966. In the interim period between 1963 and 1966, the immediate contacts between La Grange local groups and those at Myroodah had become intensified. This took the form of reciprocal visits, with regular exchange of messengers, and even two circumcision ceremonies in which both groups participated. One of these was held at La Grange and the other at Myroodah. In this way the Udiallas became more and more acquainted with the basic elements of this eastern system of cults and tradition. In the latter part of 1966 it had come so far that the *worgaia* became the central focus of interest, and all other ritual forms were either neglected or incorporated into the new system. A particularly telling example of this was a circumcision ceremony which, contrary to traditional practice up to now, took place at the beginning of August—that is, still in the middle of winter—and its ritual completion was adapted to the *worgaia* schema. Only the circumcisional operation itself and all that immediately followed was carried out in the customary manner, substantiated by the tradition of the Dreamtime creator and hero pairs recognized by many groups of the Western Desert (Petri 1956:152 *et seq.*). Like many circumcision ceremonies, today as before, this is an intertribal event which in our fieldwork area brought together guests from Anna Plains, Marble Bar, Jigalong and Myroodah. Myroodah people took a leading role in its performance. A noteworthy indication of ongoing change was the fact that all the novices were seized by men who had settled down at La Grange, within the old tribal area of the Garadjeri: that is, they were 'foreigners'. Those regarded as being indigenous, among whom were Njangomada and Mangala (the novices were Mangala), conducted themselves more or less passively. In our opinion, this is an unusual picture within the framework of Australian circumcisional rituals, and should be viewed within the context of ethnic migratory processes of which we shall speak later.

All *worgaia* experts whom we met at La Grange and in Broome emphasized that they were dealing initially only with 'what came first'. That is, they were concerned with the primary forms of the total complex. It was often said: 'More will come, maybe this year, maybe next.' We were thus able to determine that the taking over of a new, or rather, a 'foreign' cult and tradition by a particular local community can be a lengthy process, protracted over the years, and taken stage by stage. We had a similar experience in 1954 and again in 1960. It would be wrong, though, to deduce from these examples that this must always be the case. For example, in 1963 two new mythically sanctioned ritual performances were practised and rehearsed within a few weeks and were then incorporated within a circumcision ceremony in October of the same year. These were imported from the south and south-west, and normally preceded the circumcisional operation: they are known as *garbina* and *milgo* rituals. It is difficult to say why the acceptance of certain culture elements, including cult and tradition complexes, but also the so-called *jinma* (song and dance compositions on varied themes, serving primarily as entertainment), takes more time, while others take less. There seem to be no general rules regarding this, as far as can be discovered.

Aspects of the *worgaia* 'Law' with its song sequences, ritual activities and sacred objects, which the initiated and particularly Udialla men of all age levels took for their own, were in 1966 termed *ngaru-ngaru*. To repeat, this was not interpreted as being the actual *worgaia*, but rather a preliminary stage of it. In the limited space of this contribution only a short description of this form can be given. According to its content, the *ngaru-ngaru* proves to be one of the numerous *dingari-kuranggara* (*gurangara*) traditions, which we find widely distributed among the central and western Australian groups. These provide accounts of Dreamtime beings who, in groups and under the guidance of mythical leaders, criss-crossed the countryside in all directions. At that time all was dark and the country unformed. They wandered, opening up the country, exploring it. Finally, they united so that they could all reach the 'Dingari', a mythical country at the eastern fringe. The oral traditions illustrated by these events are expressed in thousands of song verses, containing exact topographical information and referring in a matter-of-fact way to many details, among them accounts of difficulties, dangers and hardships experienced by these beings during their Dreamtime migrations. It could be assumed that these *dingari-kuranggara* traditions reflect the 'remembrance' of early Aboriginal settlement in Australia from south-east Asia (a somewhat daring thought!). (See Petri 1956:152 *et seq.*, 1966:331 *et seq.*, 1967:1 *et seq.*; Berndt and Berndt 1964:224, 242 *et seq.*, 442.) At the very least, they reflect ethnic dynamics within the continent's interior, which probably occurred during more recent periods of Australia's unwritten history, and which (as will be shown below) still occur today.

Of late—and we heard about this for the first time in 1963—these epics of the Dreamtime wanderings toward the mythical land called Dingari (where, according to local views, the spirit beings are believed to have ended their 'physical existence' by 'going into' the earth), have undergone reinterpretation. All *dingari-kuranggara* experts state that, in present times, these Dreamtime groups are returning, travelling as spirit beings on the very same tracks as before to their different points of origin—to the north, south, and 'middle'. This time, however, they no longer travel on the surface of the earth but go underneath. That is, to be more precise, it retains the essence of the first and basic *worgaia* tradition, celebrated at La Grange in 1966 under the name *ngaru-ngaru*. However, it has become a system which has fused old Australian religious concepts and thought categories with ideas and doctrines originating in the dogmatic Old Testament teachings of Protestant missionaries. The *dingari-kuranggara* complex in its original form was studied by us between 1954 and 1963. At that time we tried to record by means of tape-recorder, photographs and written notes as much as we could, since this was one of the main expressions of Australian traditionalism in this area. At this stage, as I have said, it presented itself as a new syncretistic religion, grown out of the influence of the nativistic millenarian Jinimin-Jesus movement of the Wonajagu. *Ngaru-ngaru*, as a preliminary stage of the *worgaia*, became a reservoir of anti-European feelings for the Udiallas under the influence of either the Jigalong or Myroodah people. A few examples will suffice to describe this new order which, although oriented to old traditional and cult models, incorporated Christian concepts. *Ngaru-ngaru* (*worgaia*) is, as noted, the 'Law' of God—that is, of the Old Testament God. The return of the Dreamtime beings from the mythical land of Dingari to their original territories took place expressly on the orders of Jinimin-Jesus (or Our Lord Himself). They march on the underground routes, using camels which carry their belongings including the *darogo* (the cult objects).

The Preliminary Ngaru-ngaru

The preliminary stage, *ngaru-ngaru*, of the *worgaia* traditional cult complex developed a ritual formalism, which stood in striking contrast to all formerly observed cult customs of these particular Aborigines. Most cult activities supported by mythic religious or mythic historic belief were performed (within the area under consideration) in a relaxed and unconstrained atmosphere. Humorous remarks as well as laughter, all appropriate to such an occasion, contributed to a sense of well being. The event itself was serious and was actually taken seriously by the participants. A kind of cultic seriousness and a distant respectfulness full of humour for the occurrence were not mutually exclusive. A key to understanding this viewpoint is expressed in the Njangomada word *widu widi* (great play or 'big fun'), which is used to refer to a ritual cult event. However, this can no longer be said to be the case with the *ngaru-ngaru*. All these ritual activities prove to be of an abstract nature, executed partially within the framework of church services held by the United Aborigines Mission. For example: a group of people approach the *ngaru-ngaru* ceremonial ground yodelling and waving their hands. Bells are rung to set off the different ritual acts sharply from each other. This *ngaru-ngaru* ground, incidentally, resembles strikingly in its formal lay-out the *bora* grounds – the initiation centres of south-eastern Aboriginal groups around the middle of the last century. Late arrival or early departure from such cult observances can, under certain circumstances, bring harsh penalties. During the course of the performance, which is limited essentially to an exhibition of the sacra, reverent earnestness and absolute silence are expected of everyone. These sacra, aside from the sacred boards of varying size, are called *djabanda* and *gurabuga*, and are coloured with ochre; there are also strings of human hair, and specially shaped boomerangs called *woraga*. All are objects of eastern origin. These are touched by participants with their hands while singing the *ngaru-ngaru* songs. The main punishment for violating the rules of proper conduct at such rituals, in having scorned God's 'Law', is to stand for a whole day, from sunrise to sunset, under supervision in a shadowless place with hands raised and without food or water. But such punishments are exacted for a whole range of what is regarded as wrong behaviour, outside the specific ritual field.

These new and strict rules have led to an interesting secondary phenomenon, which has been unpleasant for some Aborigines. The *ngaru-ngaru* experts have developed, as a new way of passing the time, a delight in exacting punishment to an extent which had not been known up to now. For instance, members of the Gularabulu (coastal group), among others, were punished anew according to the *worgaia* 'Law' for offences for which they had been already punished years before. In 1966 (and only one example will be noted here), *worgaia* experts of La Grange punished for the second time a young Njangomada man and his wife who had been married illegally two years previously. At that time they were soundly beaten. In the second instance, the husband was made to stand in the sun in the same way as mentioned above. A number of other examples of re-punishment for offences of this or of a similar kind, could be given. It is probable that the wave of punishments (first introduced in 1966 by the *worgaia* or *ngaru-ngaru* believers of the Udialla group) for past and present transgressions has since decreased. But two years ago it offered a rare opportunity to study in detail common-law regulations, as yet unrecorded, and their modern transformations.

The following may be added concerning the concepts and beliefs essential to the *ngaru-ngaru*. Besides Tommy Djilamanga at Myroodah, a second and perhaps an even more influential leader (or prophet) was 'nominated' in 1966. He is Lulidj, a Walmadjeri man living at Fitzroy Crossing, who identifies himself with the patriarch Noah and is said to have at his disposal an ark filled with crystal and gold. Jinimin-Jesus as the safe-keeper and preserver of the old 'Law' in the *bugari-gara*, or Dreamtime, had placed this in his keeping, sending it directly to him from heaven. According to the alleged statements of this new Noah, and this is said to be set out in the so-called 'Holy Book' (a kind of Aboriginal Bible kept in Myroodah), this ark serves two purposes. First, it is to be a place of refuge for those loyal to the 'Law' after the destruction of Europeans and of those Aborigines who have fallen away from the 'Law', by the 'pouring down of Holy Water'—that is, in an expected flood. Second, the ark is intended for the storage of gold and glittering crystal, the basis of the wealth of a future and more powerful Aboriginal society, no longer knowing any kind of economic difficulties. This fusion of the Christian story of Noah's Ark with the Melanesian idea of a cargo ship laden with riches was already present in this area in 1963. It was then part of the expectancy of salvation in the Jinimin religion. At that time, Tommy Djilamanga from Myroodah was considered responsible for the stone boat, while the Noah patriarch had probably not been reincarnated in Lulidj. It was Lulidj who embarked on this charismatic task in 1966. (See Petri and Petri-Odermann 1964:465; Worms and Petri 1968.)

The content of other aspects of the *ngaru-ngaru* and the views held by such experts suggest that attempts are being made to reinterpret it further in terms of Christian belief. For instance, it was maintained that deceased Aborigines who had been buried at the station of a 'mission-missionary' (that is, those associated with the Australian Inland Mission or the United Aborigines Mission) rose from the dead after three days and ascended into heaven. One informant, Moko, a Njanidjara, asserted that he had personally witnessed such an event at Fitzroy Crossing.

Readiness to believe in resurrection, within the Christian context, is not unusual. It is an idea which is present in some Aboriginal mythic systems. Dreamtime creators and heroes are on occasion believed to enter the sky world after the completion of their earthly activities, there to reside as heavenly constellations for all time. Singular, and in a way suspect, is the idea, taken seriously by only a few Aborigines, that those resurrected have white skin-colour, returning to wander across the land proclaiming God's 'Law'. For the first time in 1963 we heard from different sources the story of two such travelling preachers in the

Fitzroy River area. These two men, speaking Djualin and Walmadjeri, obtained many followers simply by claiming to have returned from the dead. It was not possible for us to check this story. It could have been a rumour planned and spread for the benefit of missionary proselytism.

Data also show that the *ngaru-ngaru*, as a partial or preliminary stage of the traditional cult complex *worgaia*, is being gradually diffused from the east. This seems, in our opinion, to justify the conclusion that in a widespread area of Australia's north the beginnings of a new syncretistic religiosity are taking form, encouraged by missionary activities. Be this as it may, the material from our area suggests (if we apply W. E. Mühlmann's 1961 definition) that we could be faced with a synthetization of revivalistic, millenarian, xenophobic-nativistic trends, and even an element of social revolution. With the last, the 'Don McLeod Law' represents a kind of secularized social utopianism.

In another context, it has been pointed out that it is in fact the Catholic mission at La Grange which has of late become a centre of this new syncretistic religiosity. Its carriers are to be found mainly among the immigrant Udiallas, desert Aborigines who have had little contact with Europeans. One interesting fact is that none of these people had personally come into close association with 'mission-missionaries', who are concentrated at Jigalong, at Fitzroy Crossing, and in other areas. Indoctrination appears to have come in a more indirect way through the close relations existing between La Grange and Myroodah since 1963.

Two years ago, the actual *worgaia* complex was supposed to 'come behind' the *ngaru-ngaru*, in the sense of a ritual fulfilment. On the nature of this 'true *worgaia*', or *Gadjeri*, there was no clear view, and people did not wish to speak of it. Such reservation is by no means unusual. It conforms to widespread behavioural patterns in Aboriginal Australia. Traditional cult activity is often subject to tabus and obligations. And this is so, particularly, when certain rites and ceremonies have not been 'officially' accepted by initiated men, for instance, a local group. This was the case with the *ngaru-ngaru* in 1966. For example, several men, in one way or another, have come to learn about a new and expected 'Law' along with its esoteric content. Under such circumstances they have found it necessary to keep it to themselves until an opportune time when it can be revealed. During our periods of fieldwork we have recorded examples of this kind. One case is that of Butcher Joe, a Njigina man about sixty-five years of age living in Broome. (One of us has maintained close ties with him since 1938.) This man was initiated into the 'true *worgaia*' about three years ago at Fitzroy Crossing. In contrast to his usual willingness to provide information, he refused to speak of it—the *worgaia* had not yet come to Broome, and probably never would. The only thing he hinted at was the mythology of two

Dreamtime women, who brought with them sacred stone *darogo* on their wanderings from east to west. In this way he confirmed to a certain extent the basic framework of a *worgaia* tradition which a young Gidja or Lunga Aboriginal from the eastern Kimberley had confided to us at Anna Plains in 1954.

It is obvious that we are dealing here with the concept of the so-called 'fertility mothers', or creative female Dreamtime beings, which is central to the *dingari-kuranggara*. This system has spread during the last few decades over much of the Northern Territory and into the neighbouring regions of Western and Central Australia and has been studied particularly by R. M. and C. H. Berndt (see, for instance, 1964:234 *et seq.*). It would be idle to list here all the designations under which this tradition and cult system has been accepted by different groups and units within that region. The names *Worgaia* (there is a tribe of this name in Central Australia; see Meggitt 1962:37) or *Gadjeri* seem to have prevailed in parts of the eastern, central and western Kimberleys and are also relevant farther west at the northern edge of the Western Desert. In this connection Meggitt (1966) refers to the *Gadjeri* complex (spelt 'Gadjari' by him) of the Walbiri. There the mythology refers to the Dreamtime hero pair, named *Mamandabari*, who act as culture heroes in the pattern of the Western Desert 'Two Men' tradition, and have introduced the ritual operation of subincision. That is to say, the emphasis is placed on these two men and not on the fertility mothers, frequently referred to by the term *Gadjeri*. Meggitt (1966:23) expresses his belief that the Walbiri have kept themselves aloof from the ritual importance of the female principle as found among their northern and western neighbours. This point should be kept in mind when considering the introduction of *Gadjeri-worgaia* in the western area. There too, at least until now, there has been the tendency to minimize the share women play in the Dreamtime, especially in the context of creation. It is thus conceivable that the so-called 'true' *worgaia* or *Gadjeri* complex, that which is to follow the *ngaru-ngaru*, has an appearance different from what is theoretically expected. Supplementary field studies are, therefore, necessary. It should also be possible to establish to what degree this enlarged tradition and cult system has become amalgamated with Christian beliefs, which are apparent in the *ngaru-ngaru*. This would mean an extended period of fieldwork.

The Migrations

A better understanding of all such movements, of the kind we have been discussing, can be gained by considering the problem of the migrations of three Western Desert groups: the Julbari-dja, the

Djualin-Walmadjeri and the Gogadja. (See Petri 1956:152 *et seq.*) These took place in the first half of this century. The term 'Julbari-dja' means 'south-from'. In northern coastal areas it is used to refer to those people whose home territories were in the region of the Canning Stock Route or south of it, and who during the past three or four decades have migrated at irregular intervals to the European coastal settlements between Port Hedland and Derby. They have come as isolated persons or in family groups, and for various reasons they have sought the new types of community which have been growing in these areas.

Tindale and Worms have mentioned the Julbari-dja as a tribal unit, supposed to have come originally from the Canning Basin. According to our information, this can be only partially true. Tindale's tribal map (1940) shows the name Julbre (or Julbari) located in the Sturt Creek area (south-eastern Kimberley). However, it is doubtful whether this is associated with the Julbari-dja now settled at the northern edge of the Western Desert. These are clearly migrants from the south and south-west, who speak dialects of what has been called the Western Desert language (Douglas 1958). Among them are Njanidjara, Mandjildjara, Wanman, Geadjara, Gadudjara and Budidjara. 'Julbari-dja' seems to be a collective appellation for all 'strangers' who have come in from the *Warmala*, as the regions to the far south and south-west are called. At Anna Plains, La Grange and Broome we recorded a large number of Julbari-dja case histories. None of these indicates that the people involved have left their home countries through European pressure. Almost all informants noted that the decision to leave their Desert areas had been made on their own initiative, or that they had been persuaded by their relatives to leave their old waterholes and cult centres to seek new possibilities of making a living. Reasons for such decisions varied considerably. In some cases it was long periods of drought which were responsible: waterholes dried up, game disappeared and vegetable foods became scarce. In others, informants said they had felt the need to undertake a long trip; the idea of getting to know new regions had attracted them. Or, they wished to visit friends or relatives, attend cult ceremonies, and so on. Most Julbari-dja migrants whom we met in Wallal, Mandoorah, Anna Plains, La Grange and Broome in 1954, seemed to consider their stay in the north-west and their not always so friendly contacts with the coastal Garadjeri and Njangomada Aborigines as being only temporary. In general, they enjoyed repeating that they wanted to return to their home countries—if not immediately, at least later. But this did not happen, for with the exception of those who had died in the meanwhile, they were still there in 1966, gradually being integrated into the La Grange Udialla group. The once-planned return did not take place: instead, during the past twelve years other

Julbari-dja have joined them. Nothing seems to be able to disturb their sense of spiritual equilibrium more than the threat to punish them for being agitators by loading them on trucks and sending them back to their regions of origin. There can be no doubt, therefore, as to their desire to remain. Even if a large percentage of them have joined the anti-European-nativistic cults mentioned before, their immediate contacts with Europeans remain attractive, even for the traditionally oriented — motor vehicles, firearms, transistor radios, tinned food, tools and alcohol are only a few of these attractions.

According to our Garadjeri, Mangala, Njangomada and Njigina informants, these Julbari-dja were unknown in northern coastal districts forty to forty-five years ago. This seems to be even more true for the Djualin or Walmadjeri, who, in contrast to the more loosely organized Julbari-dja, represent a definite tribal and linguistic unit. Worms, to whom we owe our earliest information about these people (personal communication), mentions that their original habitat was located between Christmas Creek and Sturt Creek. That is, their territories coincided roughly with what Tindale called the Julbre or Julbari. Worms also notes that several Aborigines at the old Balgo mission, situated near Gregory Salt Lake, told him the Djualin-Walmadjeri had already begun to migrate in a westerly direction at the turn of the century. The Kukatja, or Gogadja (Meggitt 1962:43-4), on the other hand, have been pushing their way out of the south, occupying the others' territory. We can only conjecture as to the real reasons for this movement of the Walmadjeri or Djualin (as they are called by their neighbours). Historically, it is known that they actually left for the west at a particular time. Aborigines who today live near La Grange, Nita Downs, Frazier Downs and Anna Plains affirm this.

In the east, small as well as large Walmadjeri units continue to reside in or around the edge of their former home countries — that is, at Hall's Creek, and on certain cattle stations within that area. Besides this, they have become the predominating Aboriginal population element at Fitzroy River — that is, from Margaret River in the east to Myroodah, Liveringa and Derby in the west. This means that they have set themselves up in territories which formerly were the hunting grounds of south-central Kimberley tribes such as the Guneada, Bunapa and Njigina. In September 1966 we heard from a police officer passing through Derby that during a just-completed desert patrol he had met a small Djualin-Walmadjeri extended family group. These people were leading a traditional existence of hunters and food gatherers near Joanna Springs — a well-watered oasis in the Great Sandy Desert, about 200 miles south-east of La Grange. This report was verified by a prospector who had also visited Joanna Springs. The leader of this small unit was the father of a thirty-year old Walmadjeri man who had lived intermittently at La Grange. These circumstances led us to reflect on the relatively strong Djualin-Walmadjeri group now living at La Grange, within the heart of the former tribal territory of the northern Garadjeri. They have their own story, which is not lacking in dramatic incidents. Shortly after the last war they were allegedly settled at La Grange. The older people told us how they were brought there in a 'big government truck' from Udialla. Udialla was a resettlement camp situated on the middle Fitzroy River. It is from this place that the name Udiallas is derived, and is now used for all those Aborigines of the Western Desert, originally strangers in the north. At that time there was no Catholic mission at La Grange, only a government Ration Depot. Its task was to settle these Aborigines in a permanent place and to make them economically productive. What happened in this direction is not relevant to our main theme and will not be enlarged upon. However, it is said that shortly after their transfer from Udialla to La Grange, a large group decided to return to their old hunting grounds about 200 miles south of Fitzroy Crossing. For several years they resumed their semi-nomadic life. In the salt marshes of Budidjara a powerful mythical watersnake lived and provided for the fertility of the land: because of this, they were to find everything necessary for an untroubled existence. But this life did not turn out to be quite like they had anticipated. They finally came to the decision to return once more to the fringe areas, and to the advantages they had learned about during their stay at Udialla and La Grange. This occurred during the winter months of 1954, when we had the opportunity to get to know these people personally as they made their way from the Canning Stock Route to La Grange via Anna Plains, where we were then carrying out fieldwork (Petri 1962:301 *et seq.*).

The Dominance of Desert People

Together with the Julbari-dja, they formed at that time (1954) the Udialla group at La Grange. The tensions between them and the Gularabulu (that is, the group made up of members of the Garadjeri, Njangomada and Mangala tribal units) were intensified. Those strangers who profited the most from their critical situation were the Djualin-Walmadjeri who, from the beginning, appeared in their new surroundings with definite claims to power. As a group aware of its own importance, its members continually invoking the old 'Law', they were able to secure all key positions both in spiritual-religious sectors and also in the other social ones of a traditional nature. Gradually, they laid claim to being competent judges on all traditional matters, especially in relation to traditional values. In 1966 the Djualin-Walmadjeri was in every way the dominating group at La Grange. Partly in collaboration with the Julbari-dja, partly in opposition to them, but always opposed to the numerically weaker Gularabulu, they devised an almost dictatorial system. Also, they let no opportunity pass in getting the *worgaia* tradition and cult complex accepted as God's 'Law'—as, in their opinion, a final revelation. This development is anthropologically interesting. But it became almost a nightmare to other Aborigines who rejected the *ngaru-ngaru* innovation. This was particularly true of the Gularabulu community; but there were also people among the Udiallas who were suspicious of this new 'Law of God'. The spokesman of the 'anti-*ngaru-ngaru*' group was Jack Muladi, a fifty-five year old Garadjeri who, with the support of the mission, claimed to be the leader of all those Aborigines settling near La Grange. His position was not upheld by public opinion; in actuality he was unable to count on any following. Moreover, he was aware of this embarrassing situation, since he often complained that nobody turned up at the meetings which he called from time to time to discuss questions of local policy and problems of the social and cult life. As an Aboriginal who was not only Christianized, but also an advocate of his people's traditional value systems, he constantly tried to come to a compromise whenever the interests of the mission administration were in conflict with the concepts and wishes of the Aborigines. But Muladi's diplomatic attempts, combined with his undoubtedly weak personality, made him suspect of double-dealing. That is, he was said to be a man who carried water on both shoulders. His opponent in 1966 was Jimmy Bango, a Walmadjeri or Djualin of about forty years of age. This man was obviously a more successful leader. Although not a baptised Christian, he stood firmly as one of the most influential *ngaru-ngaru* experts of the new syncretistic religion. He occasionally expressed anti-European feelings, particularly anti-Catholic ones, and these fitted well into the utopian framework. His aim was—and this made personal relations with him always most difficult—the complete revival of the old 'Law' and, subsequently, the disappearance of Europeans from what he regarded as Aboriginal Australia. Bango's uncompromising nativistic anti-European attitude and behaviour as well as his *ngaru-ngaru* or *worgaia* belief in a future Aboriginal society free of European domination would have been bearable had he not constantly used Europeans for his own ends. He sought us out only when he wanted to complain about the mission's lack of interest, or when he was in some trouble and thought we could help him. Occasional work with Bango was certainly relevant to our anthropological research, but only rarely was it a real pleasure. He had a distinctive personality of his own: he knew what he wanted, and was able to formulate his ideas clearly. Probably, for these reasons alone, he is one of the most influential men in this area today. In contrast to Muladi, he organized no meetings but employed a man-to-man approach. As far as we have been able to ascertain, this seems to be the more successful method. Without any doubt, Jimmy Bango understood better than Jack Muladi how to make himself heard. However, Jimmy Bango's intellectual capacity did not measure up to what it takes to be a political leader or prophet of a more widely diffused religious revitalization movement. Up to now, he has not been able to overcome his Walmadjeri ethnocentricity and move more widely afield, as is implied for instance in the case of 'Don McLeod Law'.

Perhaps for the first time in the history of the Aborigines in this area, Bango, together with several other Walmadjeri, went to Port Hedland in 1966. This place is more than 1,000 miles west of the original home countries of the Walmadjeri. They took an active part in two *jona* (circumcisional performances), and then visited Jigalong. This journey seems to fit into certain visions of the future held by some of the Djualin-Walmadjeri people. As Bango once expressed it, 'It is the destiny of the Djualin-Walmadjeri, already prescribed in the Dreamtime, to push continually westward.' As a supplement to this, Wili-Guda, who was responsible for introducing the preliminary stages of the *ngarungaru* to La Grange, gave the following details three years later: Tommy Djilamanga, one of the *worgaia* leaders, stated that it was God's will that the mythical groups, returning as spirits underground from Dingari in the far east, with their human descendants (that is, all those Walmadjeri initiated into the *worgaia* 'Law') must continue their migration as far as *Garbadi* and *Winba*, the centre of the world. This supposed 'centre of the world', where an anticipated future realm of salvation is to exist, and to which the millenarian expectations of various Aborigines were also linked, is believed to be situated in the Lake Disappointment area. *Garbadi* and *Winba* are two *djila* or waterholes which, together with their two *wona* (mythical rain-snakes), are part of the traditional belief system of the Western Desert people. (See Worms and Petri 1968.)

Conclusion

This westward advance of many of the Walmadjeri is to be viewed only in connection with that part of the Western Desert which is adjacent to the areas discussed in this paper. It has taken place in the distant as well as in the immediate past and is relevant today. It is not possible to treat this problem extensively, since it would require further research in other areas. But we consider it is both historically and sociologically important.

We turn once more to the question of migrations in relation to the Kukatja or Gogadja. It is to be remembered that they migrated northward in sections at the beginning of this century, and some had settled in the Sturt Creek and Gregory Salt Lake areas—that is, in the former habitat of the Djualin-Walmadjeri. It is conceivable that the Gogadja forced the Djualin-Walmadjeri to move westward, but it is not possible to make a conclusive statement in this respect. Other Gogadja groups (personal communication, N. B. Tindale) are said to have abandoned their hunting grounds around the same time and moved to the south. It has been thought that they eventually settled on the Eyre Peninsula, south of Port Augusta, in the former territory of the now extinct Parnkalla tribe.

Naturally, we are unable to consider these migrations, and their associated religious cults, without taking into account the pressures of European contact. These pressures have been significant in stimulating such movements as we have spoken about here. Nevertheless it is to be remembered that such migrations must also have taken place frequently in pre-European times. One only has to consider the differing traditions, on a continent-wide basis, dealing with the migrations of Dreamtime ancestral groups (for instance, the *dingari-kuranggara*).

A total assessment of Australian Aboriginal cultures within the perspective of the present, with the pressures toward assimilation, does not permit us at this time to a general prognosis. The two polar concepts of 'stability' and 'change' stand in a relationship to each other which does not conform with certain theoretical expectations of the social sciences. Numerous changes have certainly taken place within the context of Aboriginal Australian society—and there is no question of these. However, not all have led to a break with the past, to a complete turning toward Australian-European life. And it is this which we have demonstrated in this paper.

Finally, we shall mention two examples which are particularly informative about the present-day situation of the Aborigines of the Western Desert. We received a letter dated 18 February 1969 from Father K. McKelsen, the acting-missionary at La Grange. In this he noted the arrival, in the middle of April of the previous year (1967), of Djualin people who had come from Joanna Springs and who were considered to be still 'traditionally oriented'. They intended to remain at La Grange. Two of the leading men of the Udialla group, Bulun and Jimmy Bango, took them under their care and (as McKelsen says) they are believed, with one exception, to have adjusted themselves to the conditions prescribed by the mission. Doubtless, this is the same group contacted by the Derby policeman and the prospector in 1966. This case throws some light on the migratory pattern of the Djualin-Walmadjeri.

It also leads us to the conclusion that the numerically stronger group of these people formed an even more absolute majority in an area which formerly represented the heart of Garadjeri country. It is a further chapter, too, in the movement of the Walmadjeri toward the west and south-west, toward reaching a supposed 'centre of the world'. Into this phenomenon fits the fatalistic vision of the past and the present, as well as of the future, as conceived by Muladi, the so-called 'chief' of the La Grange Aborigines including the Gularabulu as well as the Udiallas. As a tribally conscious Garadjeri, who has carefully observed the gradual disintegration of his people and their culture for several decades, Muladi made the following statement in 1966. Originally, he said, the coastal area from Thangoo in the north-west to Wallal in the south-west was the territory of the Nada-Nada (the northern Garadjeri). Later (an exact date is not mentioned), the Njangomada came from the south out of the desert and occupied a large part of that area, in particular, the territory between Wallal and Djinmanguru (Chinaman's Mangrove), approximately 12 miles north of Anna Plains. At that time many of the Nada-Nada migrated northward to form new-type local groupings with survivors of the Jaoro and Njigina. These continue to exist. About thirty to forty years ago, the first Julbari-dja came from the 'Warmala'—that is, out of the south and south-west, like the Njangomada before them. They too established themselves firmly in the northern coastal regions. This in turn led to a larger migration of the Njangomada, who settled partly near Broome but mostly near and south of Port Hedland. This statement tallies with our own findings during the past twelve years. The Njangomada are at present the predominant element in the Pilbara District: that is, they occupy the former territories of the Ngala, Njamal, and Kariera, west of the De Grey River and south of Port Hedland. Following World War II, Muladi added, the Djualin-Walmadjeri (originally from Waringari and Wonajagu) began to trickle in, with the help of Europeans. This started the dislodgement of the Julbari-dja. But their role as the new 'masters' of this country, so Muladi said, is not to last. New tribes out of the east, the Gogadja or Kukatja, have already begun to march westward. Whether this will happen or not is another matter. Probably Muladi simply wished to express his personal pessimism in this respect. He was certainly depressed in 1966 by Djualin-Walmadjeri claims of domination which had been expressed in the *ngaru-ngaru* and *worgaia* cults. He recognized that his own tribe, the Garadjeri, had been virtually submerged culturally and territorially. Resigned to this fact, he left La Grange at the end of 1966 or the beginning of 1967 and settled in Derby after his wife, Lilly Limby, had contracted leprosy and been admitted into the leprosarium. When we saw him in October 1966 he remarked that, despite his wife's condition, he would not have considered leaving La Grange if the Walmadjeri had not constantly given him so many difficulties. Whether there are at present any Gularabulu remaining at La Grange is not known. In 1966 there were fewer than ten.

A second point, which we should not overlook, is that in the northern fringe areas of the Western Desert there is at least one other enclave which has not yet been affected by what we have described above. In October 1966 we stayed for four weeks near Lombadina, originally part of the tribal territory of the Bād of northern Dampierland Peninsula. The reason for this visit lay in one of us having carried out research there in November and December 1938, in conjunction with D. C. Fox. Now we wished to see what changes had taken place within that period. Generally speaking, the result was negative. In spite of Catholic missionary activity since the beginning of this century, the 'traditional orientation' of these Aborigines had remained more or less the same. Their adherence to Christianity had not, as far as we could see, detracted from their belief in the values of the 'old Law'. This was centred on the myth of the Dreamtime creator, *Djamar*. Syncretistic and utopian ideas such as we have already described gained little or no foothold in this region. Christianity and the Dreamtime tradition seem to co-exist harmoniously. The new-type local group at Lombadina is formed from an amalgamation of the Bād and Djaui (from Sunday Island, north of Cape Leveque). These people have, of course, been aware of what has been going on at La Grange and elsewhere in the region discussed, but they appear not to have felt the repercussions. Most of the fully initiated men who visit Broome and Derby have a relatively clear idea of the newer cults, but they are not prepared to accept these for themselves and for their society. Now, as before, the *Djamar* 'Law' remains in force and the values of the people living farther south are viewed with suspicion. A similar situation existed at Lombadina in 1938. It would be interesting to know if a similar state of affairs exists in other parts of Australia: if there are other people who have shown themselves to be conservative and have resisted the influences and pressures of Australian-European society—who have, in fact, considered adjustment to the wider world outside to be of secondary importance.

Notes

1. This contribution has been substantially edited, in places where it appeared to present difficulties to English-speaking readers. However, in doing this great care has been taken to retain the authors' content, in their specific points as well as in their more general themes. (Editor.)

2. We were able to spend a further period of field research in this area in 1969. Since 1966, the Aboriginal population has increased appreciably in the La Grange area, and this has meant the regrouping of sections of the earlier tribal and linguistic units. Whereas in 1966 the Walmadjeri seemed to be the dominant unit, in 1969 the Julbari-dja had taken their place. These changes, however, have not affected the traditional patterns of the two La Grange communities discussed in this paper. (H. Petri and G. Petri-Odermann.)

REFERENCES

BERNDT, R. M. 1959 The Concept of 'the Tribe' in the Western Desert of Australia, *Oceania*, Vol. XXX, No. 2.
BERNDT, R. M. and C. H. 1964 *The World of the First Australians*. University of Chicago Press, Chicago, and Ure Smith, Sydney.
——— (eds) 1965 *Aboriginal Man in Australia*. Angus and Robertson, Sydney.
DOUGLAS, W. H. 1958 An Introduction to the Western Desert Language. *Oceania Linguistic Monographs* No. 4, Sydney.
MEGGITT, M. J. 1962 *Desert People*. Angus and Robertson, Sydney.
——— 1966 Gadjari among the Walbiri Aborigines of Central Australia. *Oceania Monographs* No. 14, Sydney.
MICHA, F. J. 1965 Zur Geschichte der australischen Eingeborenen, *Saeculum*, Vol. 16 (Munich-Freiburg).
MÜHLMANN, W. E. 1961 *Chiliasmus und Nativismus*. Berlin.
PETRI, H. 1956 Dynamik im Stammesleben Nordwest-Australiens, *Paideuma*, Vol. VI (Wiesbaden).
——— 1962 Gibt es noch 'unberührte' Wildbeuter im heutigen Australien? *Baessler-Archiv* (new series), Vol. X (Berlin).
——— 1963 and 1966 Berichte an die Deutsche Forschungsgemeinschaft. *Reports to the German Research Association*.
——— 1966 Badur (Parda Hills), ein Felsbilder- und Kultzentrum im Norden der Westlichen Wüste Australiens, *Baessler-Archiv* (new series), Vol. XIV (Berlin).
——— 1967 'Wandji-Kuran-gara', ein mythischer Traditionskomplex aus der Westlichen Wüste Australiens, *Baessler-Archiv* (new series), Vol. XV (Berlin).
PETRI, H. and G. PETRI-ODERMANN 1964 Nativismus und Millenarismus im gegenwärtigen Australien, in *Festschrift für A. E. Jensen*, Munich.
TINDALE, N. B. 1940 Distribution of Australian Aboriginal Tribes: a field survey, *Transactions of the Royal Society of South Australia*, Vol. 64, No. 1.
WORMS, E. A. and H. PETRI 1968 Australische Eingeborenen–Religionen. In *Die Religionen der Südsee und Australiens* (H. Nevermann, E. A. Worms and H. Petri, eds). W. Kohlhammer, Stuttgart.

ROBERT TONKINSON

Aboriginal Dream-Spirit Beliefs in a Contact Situation: Jigalong, Western Australia

INTRODUCTION

A striking feature of traditional Aboriginal culture was the intimate bond that linked the Aborigines to their home territories. Although they had adapted to their environment as semi-nomadic hunters and foragers, every Aboriginal group had an attachment to its own stretch of territory which was fundamental to its continuing existence. The home area of a given group was the source and repository of spirit children from whom its members believed they grew, the source of the natural species upon which their subsistence depended, and its physical features were for them convincing proof of the wanderings of the great ancestral beings who had created their world and their culture.

Most writers concerned with the Aborigines have stressed the basic importance of their ties to their land, but few attempts have been made to reconcile this strong attachment with the fact that in many interior areas of Australia, particularly the Western Desert region, Aborigines voluntarily left their home territories and migrated to fringe settlements where they contacted and eventually settled near Europeans. Almost all Western Desert Aborigines, although predominantly still tradition-oriented, are now living in settlements scattered in and around the edges of the desert proper. Most live in communities made up of members of different linguistic and tribal groups, far from their original homelands, which for many reasons they find they are no longer able to revisit.

What has become of their once intimate and life-giving link to their home territories, if they are no longer able, or motivated, to return to their sacred ancestral sites, increase centres, spirit homes and hunting areas? Research at a mission settlement in Western Australia[1] reveals that the sentiment and attachment remain strong: the Aborigines claim to maintain continuous contact by making journeys to and from their home territories in dream-spirit form.

The Setting

Jigalong is an Apostolic Church mission station on the western edge of the Gibson Desert (see map),[2] about 800 miles north-east of Perth. About 55 per cent of its Aboriginal inhabitants belong to the Mandjildjara dialect group, whose original home area is north-east and east of Lake Disappointment, and 35 per cent are Gaḍudjara speakers who come from the area surrounding the lake. Although the Mandjildjara were the more recent immigrants, about 90 per cent of all adults had been born in the desert and had never encountered Europeans until their migration to the west. Remnant desert groups were still arriving at the mission as recently as 1966, but only 15 per cent of children under sixteen were born in the desert.[3]

The mission has a relatively stable core population of about 160, consisting of school-children and their mothers, pensioners and mission employees. From a midwinter low, when most able-bodied men are away working as cattle-station labourers, the population rises each year to a midsummer peak of over 300 during the ceremonial season, when the demand for station labour is at its lowest. The mission was established comparatively recently, in 1946, and after two decades of strong resistance on the part of the Aborigines, it has been unsuccessful in its attempts to convert them to its version of Christianity. The Aborigines continue to participate actively in traditional religious activities without outside interference. In fact, their migration to Jigalong has for various reasons led to an intensification of this religious life.

In summary, Aboriginal social organization at Jigalong is characterized by:[4]

1. A classificatory kinship system that is a variant of the Kariera type, based on the rule of preferred marriage with either cross-cousin, except that certain cross-cousins are classed as 'siblings' and therefore unmarriageable. About 92 per cent of extant marriages are between persons in the correct 'spouse' categories.

2. Despite a stated preference by married men for more than one wife, only 27 per cent of current marriages are polygynous.

3. A distinctive feature of the family has been the partial separation of school-age children through the operation of the school and mission dormitory system.

4. A section system operates, but with neither explicit, named patri- or matrimoieties, nor social entities or corporate groupings based on them. There are, however, reciprocally named alternate generation level categories that have ceremonial significance.

5. Traditional local groups, long since defunct, were patrilineal in descent emphasis and territorially anchored.

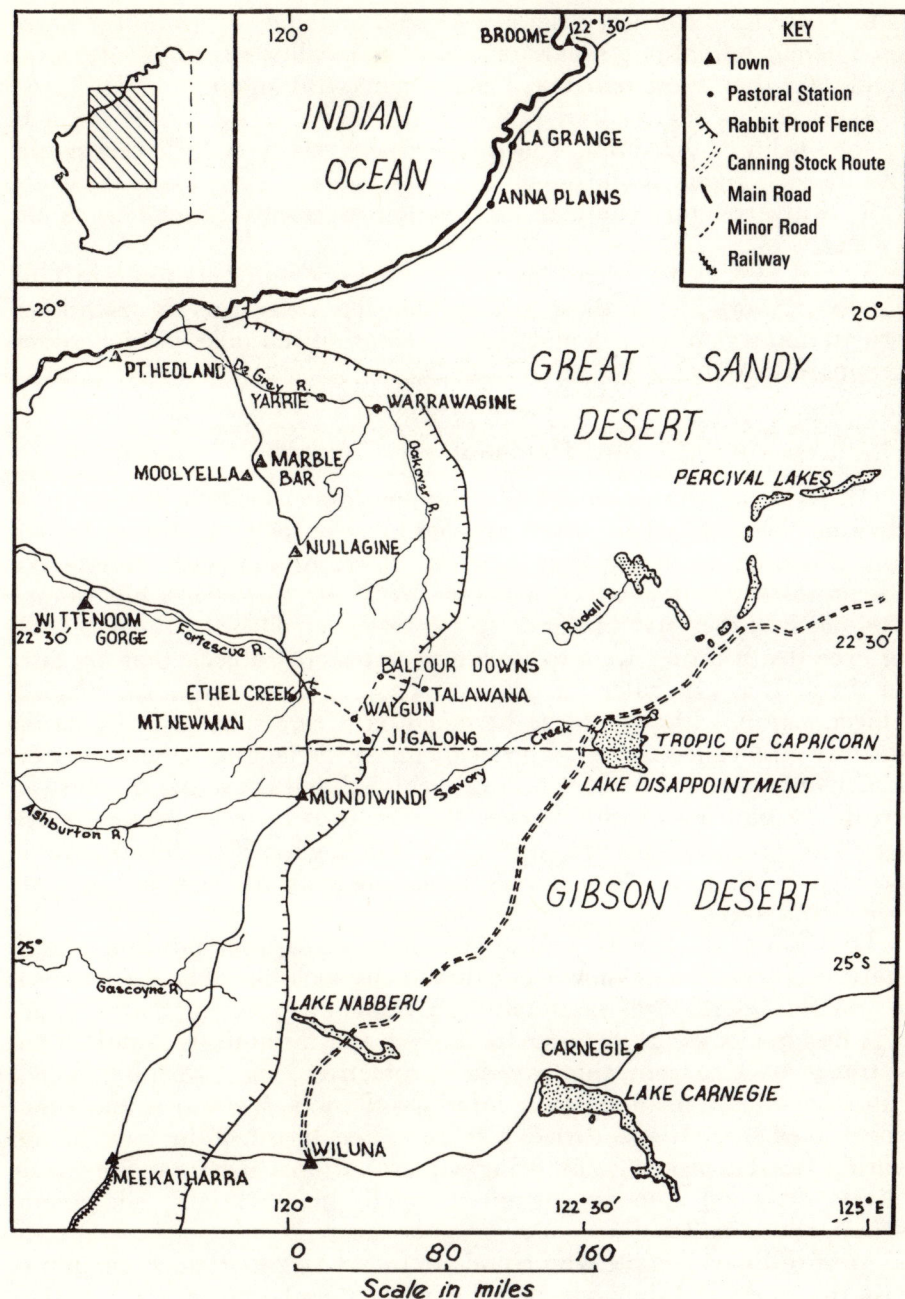

Fig. 1 North central area of Western Australia

6. There is no cult totemism as such and no lodges or groupings based on totemic affiliation; bonds of common locality or origin are more important than those based on a shared ancestral totem.

7. As among the Walbiri (for example, Meggitt 1962), the status of women is lower than that of men, they have relatively little ceremonial life, and few rights in marriage.

8. Native doctors continue to function as essential members of the society.

9. Ties of kinship, friendship and a shared culture continue to bind Jigalong Aborigines to those in neighbouring areas where a traditional orientation is maintained, and cultural transmission takes place between groups so linked.

The Dream-Spirit Concept

All Jigalong Aborigines share an unquestioning belief in the reality of dream-spirits, *baḍundjari*, which are said to leave the body during dreams and travel about, flying from place to place. Anyone can undertake a dream-spirit journey, which is known as 'going *baḍundjari*', but women are told that they should not do so because it could bring them sickness or even death if they were to see any secret-sacred objects that are tabu to them. It is also safer for ordinary people, those without a magical object, *mabaṇ*, within them, to be taken on dream-spirit trips by native doctors (also called *mabaṇ*), who sit them astride lengths of hairstring or, if men only, astride sacred boards or 'vehicles' that the native doctors can create by blowing on their *mabaṇ* stones.[5] In dreams, a person's spirit (*gu:ḍi*) accompanies his dream-spirit, which is why—if he meets with an accident while away, for example by falling from the vehicle—his body will sicken and die.

Only native doctors are said to be able to see *baḍundjari* during dream-spirit journeys and to know what they really look like. The dream-spirit is usually described as resembling an eaglehawk, except that a man's legs become its wings, his testicles its eyes and his anus its mouth. Thus it travels back to front, they say, as a protective device when it descends into the sometimes dangerous interiors of increase centres and other spirit-filled sites. It also carries a small sacred board of the pointed-end variety (used in projecting or 'firing' sorcery), from which it can fire deadly slivers of wood into its enemies, which are invariably malignant spirits, called *maḷbu*.

Most ordinary people who go or are taken *baḍundjari* do so mainly to visit the desert and sight-see, particularly in their home areas where they know the spirits to be generally friendly. During such journeys, they may visit increase sites and see the different species in animal or malignant spirit form, and mischievous spirit children (*djidjigargal*) who are said to live nearby. They may also see anthropomorphic ancestral beings at or near important sites with which they are associated, and may witness some of the exploits of their ancestral heroes, such as fights or ritual performances. It is conceded, however, that native doctors are usually the only ones fortunate enough actually to see or encounter ancestral heroes (*djugudani*) during dream-spirit trips.

Aborigines who awake after dreams in which they saw themselves elsewhere are convinced that they travelled there in dream-spirit form. Sometimes a man whose dream took him to a far distant place, for example beyond the Canning Stock Route or up into the Kimberleys, may complain the next morning of being exhausted by the distance he has travelled. 'Bad trips' are fairly common; and should two or three men dream, on the same night, of frightening encounters with malignant spirits in the Jigalong area, an entire ritual performance may be postponed until local native doctors have searched the mission area for signs of spirit intruders. It is during ceremonial times that people are thought to be most susceptible to attack, from both human and non-human beings. Men frequently discuss their dreams and compare experiences, and in this way discover who travelled together and in what areas. Sometimes a man will relate how, during a *baḍundjari* trip, he encountered a band of malignant spirits which tried to kill him, and how he managed to dodge all but one of the missiles hurled at him. When he woke up, he found himself unable to move, so he called in a native doctor to locate the cause of the trouble. Sure enough, the *maban̄* discovered and 'withdrew', by manipulation or sucking, a small wooden or stone sliver, and thus cured the victim. No one doubts the authenticity of such dream experiences, which are often shared by several people who can corroborate the encounter and fill in extra details.

The Dream-Spirit in Curative Magic

There is still strong belief in the magical powers of the fifteen or so Jigalong men who are regarded as native doctors by virtue of their ownership and use of magical objects and spirit familiars that they are said to keep inside their stomachs and may withdraw at will. Their curative powers depend to a large extent on the effectiveness of their communication with the ancestral beings from whom they receive their power, and with the spirits of their dead patrilineal forbears. Every person has a conception totem (the animal, mineral or vegetable form in which he pre-existed as a spirit child) and what I have called an ancestral totem (the ancestral hero or heroes who left behind certain objects whose life essence later activated them in conception spirit form). This last is not a cult totem, in that no social or ceremonial groupings arise through possession of a common ancestral totem, and no special bond need be felt by two or more people so related.

It is believed that a native doctor can safely go *baḍundjari* to the home or homes of the ancestral beings with whom he is associated and can enlist their help in curing sickness; or he can send his spirit familiar, which is an even safer way of dealing with his totemic affiliates. Jigalong's most reputable native doctors have the Ŋajunaŋalgu man-eating beings (see Mountford and Tonkinson 1969), who are said to live in a world of their own under Lake Disappointment, as their ancestral totems. The magical powers of the Ŋajunaŋalgu know no bounds, so native doctors who 'have Ŋajunaŋalgu in them' are thus very fortunate in the eyes of the Aborigines. Even men who are not native doctors but have Ŋajunaŋalgu as their ancestral totem may sometimes be able to get the beings to cure sickness for them, by going *baḍundjari* to the lake. The spirit familiar of native doctors who have Ŋajunaŋalgu as their ancestral totem is a small bird, *bibiṟuwar*, which is often linked with the Ŋajunaŋalgu in the mythology.

After a native doctor has examined his patient, he may decide that the trouble lies in a defective organ, usually the heart, which may look 'like ashes' or have a hole in it. When the patient is asleep, the native doctor removes the heart and either goes *baḍundjari* himself or sends his spirit familiar with the heart to Lake Disappointment, where it is left. The Ŋajunaŋalgu native doctors take the heart, clean it, wash it in special 'Dream-time' hot water, then cover it with eaglehawk down (*ɲuḍala*). The heart is then left out for the spirit familiar or *baḍundjari* to take back to its owner. The native doctor replaces the heart, by pushing it down through the top of the sleeping patient's head without marking him, and he is thus cured.[6]

Native doctors are said to be able to go *baḍundjari* or send their spirit familiars to locate lost or stolen objects, find out about the health of relatives in distant places and sometimes to foretell coming events or forewarn their human counterparts of impending danger or death. A spirit familiar may act independently to save its owner from danger. One informant told of how, on his return from a dream-spirit journey down into the Wiluna area, he saw another Jigalong man 'put a *mabaṇ* on' (i.e. work magic on) an influenza egg as it passed over the mission, causing it to burst and drop influenza 'mist' everywhere. However, his *bibiṟuwar* spirit familiar lifted the returning man above the swirling mist and also managed to shield the south side of the camp area from infection, so that few people there contracted the virus. These 'flu eggs', as the Aborigines call them, are said to be periodically fired into the mission area by malignant spirits associated with this sickness, and unless the native doctors are able to locate and deal with the egg, everyone gets influenza.

At times, the blame for an influenza epidemic or for an individual's illness is laid by local native doctors on spirits of the dead from a particular locality. These spirits can be either benign or malevolent, depending on such factors as the personalities of the humans they were formerly part of, and whether or not they approve of the activities of their Aboriginal descendants. One influenza outbreak, which affected Jigalong, Nullagine and Marble Bar (see map), was finally attributed to a malevolent and powerful old ancestral man whose home is said to be next to a salt lake in the desert north-east of Jigalong. The man who went *baḏundjari* to put a stop to the outbreak was an old native doctor whose father's spirit was believed to live in the lake with other spirits of the dead and its ancestral totem, the old man Gambalguṟa. The elder, during his dream-spirit journey, discovered that it was his father's spirit that released the influenza mist and spread it westward, in a fit of bad temper. The elder, in *baḏundjari* form, went into the lake and picked up his father's spirit, which he upbraided for sending influenza into an area which contained many of his children (i.e. people of the same linguistic group, Wanman), some of whom could even die from it. After extracting a promise of good behaviour and a guarantee that the influenza mist would be kept shut up inside the lake, the old man returned to the mission. This man says that he sometimes uses his father's spirit and the old man Gambalguṟa to cure sickness in the same way as the *baḏundjari* of the Ŋajunaŋalgu native doctors. It is believed that the only people who can safely go *baḏundjari* into ancestral sites are those who are totemic descendants of the ancestral beings who inhabit them, though other people, such as native doctors whose magic is strong, may also travel widely in dream-spirit form with little danger.

The Dream-Spirit in Ritual

The Aborigines of Jigalong still engage actively in many different types of religious activity that is traditional in orientation. (See Tonkinson 1966.) Their most important rituals centre on the journeys and exploits of certain major ancestral beings, the institutors of what is known as the Aboriginal 'Law'. These long and elaborate song-cycles and associated rituals are said to have originated in the creative period and to have been handed down to present-day Aborigines; they are termed *maŋundjanu*, 'from the creative period', and many are widely known and performed throughout the Western Desert area.

At Jigalong there is a second type of ritual, called *baḏundjaridjanu*, 'from the dream-spirit', which is based on the dream-spirit journeys of local Aboriginal men. This type of ritual plays an important role in the religious life of Jigalong Aborigines, and though it is performed in the main camp area and is attended by women and children, some of its songs concern ancestral heroes and it has a secret-sacred section during which certain exploits of these heroes (witnessed during dream-spirit journeys) are depicted in dance, and elaborate sacred objects are exhibited to an audience of initiated men.

Every few years, a new *baḍundjari* song-line is composed. It originates when one of the elders, most often a native doctor who is known to undertake dream-spirit journeys frequently, goes *baḍundjari* and in the course of his trip is taken by spirit children (*djidjigargal*) who show him songs and dances generally involving spirit beings or creatures in totemic form. He may also see a fight or some spectacular magical happening, which he remembers when he wakes up. If he is sufficiently impressed with what he has experienced, he will relate the events to other men, gain their views and possible interpretations, and he will sing the song that he was given during his *baḍundjari* journey. In this way a theme is established, centring usually on a known group of ancestral or spirit beings who are already embodied in myths, and whose characteristics are well known. Later, other men report their dream-spirit journeys and experiences to an informal group, among whom there are native doctors who usually compose the bulk of the songs that will form the series for the ritual. More and more songs are added to the original one, and men describe the dances and sacred objects that they have seen. Rough sketches of the objects are made in the sand or on paper, dance steps are demonstrated and copied, and the overall ritual sequence falls into shape. The songs, similar in structure to the *maŋundjanu* songs, consist of only a few words each, repeated over and over again, and are thus easy to learn. They seem disjointed, with many words that are not heard in ordinary conversation, and the meaning they convey is often so esoteric that only the composer can adequately explain the experience to which they allude. Between six and twelve performances make up a complete series, which may contain from eighty to 140 different songs. Sometimes the ritual is performed for only a few nights at a time—and some songs, particularly those that are accompanied by dancing, may be repeated on different nights. Women and children quickly learn individual songs, and often sing them while in camp, but during the actual performance they take their lead from the men who make up the chorus and orchestra.

In overall form and procedure, all dream-spirit rituals are similar, but each has its own distinctive theme, songs, tune, dances, body decorations and constructed sacred objects. In terms of the personnel involved, these rituals can be classed as general-sacred, because men and women, uninitiated youths and children all attend the same place at the same time. All those present may sing, and sometimes a few women dance near the male dancers. However, the concluding section is secret-sacred to initiated men and at this time they alone sing and watch the dances.

During the fieldwork period, three different series of dream-spirit rituals were witnessed at Jigalong. The current locally composed series was called *winba* or *djaṟamara*, with a theme of lightning, rain, clouds and thunder, and ancestral beings and natural species associated with the rain-making ancestor by whose names the ritual is known. It replaced an imported dream-spirit ritual, from Yarrie Station (see map), which had a rainmaking theme and had itself followed a large locally composed ritual which centred on the exploits of the Ŋajunaŋalgu. The *winba* series was composed early in 1962 at Jigalong, and consists of over 120 songs, contributed by nineteen middle-aged and old men representing several different linguistic groups and ancestral totemic affiliations, and widely scattered home territories. Nine of them contributed only one or two songs; three others, all native doctors, composed a total of about sixty-five songs. Several songs were composed jointly by two or more men. A few songs concerned events (usually lightning strikes) seen during waking hours.

Jigalong is a centre for the performance of a body of interesting and elaborate rainmaking rituals, called *ŋa:wajil*, that propitiate Djaṟamara, the ancestral man from whose home waterhole, Winba (in the Percival Lakes region north-east of Jigalong),[7] all precipitation is said to emanate and whose control over weather phenomena is said to be absolute. Although only two of the men who contributed songs have Djaṟamara as their ancestral totem, the various exploits of the old rainmaker, said to be the 'last man' of the creative period, are well known to Jigalong men, some of whom used to make long journeys away from their home territories to participate in rainmaking rituals at Winba. In the *winba* dream-spirit songs, Djaṟamara himself is only mentioned a few times, as are the spirit beings, water birds and snakes that are closely associated with him, but almost all the secret-sacred dances and accompanying objects depict the activities of these beings as seen during dream-spirit journeys. Most songs mention place names that are well south of the Percival Lakes area, but they are the places where the composers witnessed unusual weather phenomena, occurrences or sacred objects. The wording of the songs reflects the Aborigines' detailed vocabulary to describe different types of clouds, rain and lightning.

During a twenty-seven-day period in 1963 there were ten performances of the *winba* ritual, separated first by a twelve-day period when two daytime ritual sequences took precedence, and then by a five-day period of mourning after a death. The overall structure of the rituals can be summarized as follows:

1. The afternoon before the performance, otherwise unoccupied men assemble in a creek bed (in 'men's country'—that is, in a secret-sacred area) to decide who will dance that evening, and to make the necessary

sacred objects, which are all of the thread-cross (*wanigi*) variety. These are of wool and hairstring which is threaded around cross-pieces bound on to objects ranging from boomerangs and shields to spears and long sacred boards. As the series continues, the objects are made larger and larger (by binding spears and boards together with lengths of rag) until they resemble fences, over 30 feet long and 8 feet high. As with all thread-crosses, they can be used only once, after which they must be dismantled. Any man, composer or not, can elect to dance on any night, and considerations of kinship, linguistic or totemic affiliation are irrelevant in this context.

2. In the early evening, women and children assemble at the dancing ground, and sit in a semi-circle behind the male chorus and orchestra. The women separate into two groups, according to generation level, and during the early part of the ritual both male and female members of alternate generation levels poke fun at one another. The women sing and beat on their laps in accompaniment to the clicking of boomerangs.

3. The dancers, who vary in number from four to ten, make between six and nine appearances in non-secret dances, repeating the same steps each time they dance from behind their bush windbreak, around two fires in front of the audience, then back to the windbreak where they sit for several minutes before their next appearance. Each is painted with a charcoal and white ochre Y-shaped lightning motif, and wears woollen head- and armbands, feather headdress, hairbelt, pearlshell pubic pendant and perhaps a pearlshell rainmaking-ornament in his armband.

4. Usually two decorated women, one from each alternate generation level, dance at the same time as the men, but stay close to their respective groups.

5. At a given signal toward the end of the ritual, women and children hide their heads under blankets, and the dancers go to collect the sacred objects they have prepared.

6. The secret-sacred dance lasts for four or five minutes, and is characterized by a different song rhythm and style of singing, and much more expressive and exciting dance-steps, as the performers manipulate the thread-crosses they are carrying and re-enact the incident embodied in the song. The secret-sacred performance, unlike the non-secret dances, is a different one each night.

7. After the thread-crosses have been returned to the creek bed, the women and children are told to sit up and the singing recommences, with the dancers joining the audience. After several songs have been sung, the women and children are sent to bed, but the men stay on for a short while longer to sing a few of the dancing songs that women are not permitted to sing.

8. For the *winba* dream-spirit series, each night's performance lasts

seventy-five to ninety minutes, and between twelve and twenty-three different songs are sung. The dancing songs are repeated several times, and a few songs each night are repeated from earlier performances.

Although the other two dream-spirit rituals performed at Jigalong during fieldwork were both composed elsewhere, their structure closely resembled that of the *winba* ritual. This in turn conforms in its overall configuration to the type of historical *maŋundjanu* ritual, part of which is performed in the main camp area at night, with women and children attending and watching most of the dancing. A casual observer could not distinguish between the two types of ritual—that is, in translating their compositions into ritual, the local men work within a pre-existing framework and make no radical departures from tradition. Although the dream-spirit rituals involve new songs and new dances, the final men-only dance each night is not held to be any less sacred than those of the big historical rituals and, as in all of the important dances, the performers believe themselves to embody the characters they are dramatizing.

The Role of Dream-Spirit Beliefs at Jigalong

Despite many years of contact and the acceptance of a wide range of material goods, the Aborigines of Jigalong have remained largely tradition-oriented in their social organization, religious life and value system. They frequently reveal, through both words and actions, the very strong spiritual and emotional bond that they feel with their countries of origin. A person's home territory, with its associated ancestral beings, spirit homes, etc., is the source of his being and the ultimate home of his spirit after death. It is also the focus of his religious beliefs and mythological knowledge, and its physiographic features are his proof of the reality of the creative period and of the exploits of its inhabitants. The home country also contains increase sites, believed to be the source of certain plant or animal species. At these sites, local group members traditionally performed simple rites at certain seasons each year to ensure a continued supply of the species concerned.

The Jigalong people, now far from their homelands, say that they are unable to return because they have lost the skills necessary for prolonged survival in the desert and have grown too used to European food. The dream-spirit has thus assumed a vital role in their lives by providing the only convenient means of communication with their homeland, and has enabled them to maintain contact and identity with ancestral and other spirit beings, totemic creatures and so on. Dream-spirit journeys supply them with proof that these beings are still active inhabitants of the Aboriginal cosmic order and remain interested in the affairs of their human counterparts, whose lives may still be affected by their actions.

Predictably, then, the older men whose responsibility it had been to perform increase rites at certain sites in their home territories, can go *baḍundjari* in the right season and visit the increase centres. The men, who may go singly or take others with them for educational purposes, are said to be able to fly right inside an increase centre, bring out its plants or animals and scatter them about near the mission or in other areas where they are known to be in short supply. If the centre is for an animal species, the men in their dream-spirit form carry away the 'boss' and the rest automatically follow. Some 'owners', particularly of kangaroo increase centres, are believed to be able to carry away hundreds of baby animals in their stomachs. Admittedly, the Aborigines are now largely dependent on European food, but they continue to make hunting and gathering trips away from the mission, and animals such as kangaroos and emus are still major items of diet and ritual payment. It is therefore important that they keep up the supply by means of dream-spirit journeys and the performance of certain rituals believed to have an increase function.

Cultural transmission was an integral part of Western Desert traditional life. When large groups of Aborigines congregated for short periods each year, part of the essential business involved was the handing on of songlines and associated rituals and sacred objects from one group to the next. In this way a ritual could travel 2,000 miles or more, from group to group. This practice was so basic a part of desert culture that it continued after their migration to the desert fringes, and still goes on today from place to place around the edge of the Western Desert, where big inter-area meetings are held at some centres, such as Jigalong, Wiluna and Laverton. Although most lines of transmission are still open, the volume of material being transferred appears to be steadily diminishing from areas of strong European influence, such as the Kimberleys and Port Hedland area, where cultural disintegration stems the supply. Currently there is much cultural transmission between Jigalong and the neighbouring centres to the south; but the Jigalong people are aware that the Aboriginal 'Law' is in difficulties in the north, and are dissociating themselves from outside influences that would weaken tradition. They can do this successfully because of the mission's isolation and their intelligent adaptation to the contact situation there. They are still able to affirm and strengthen their belief in the traditional religion and maintain its continuity through the performance of initiation and other rituals; by the finding and contemplation of objects believed to have been left behind by the creative ancestors; by the continuing practice of cultural transmission; by their belief in the reality of dream-spirit journeys and by their ability to create important new rituals every few years. It thus seems that, as Jigalong's cultural isolation increases, the composing of dream-spirit rituals could assume greater importance, with innovation at the local level providing new and acceptable ritual forms in the face of lessening reliance on imported cultural elements.

The composing of the rituals, involving as it does co-operation and collaboration among men of several different linguistic groups and of widely separated home countries, facilitates the social integration of the new type of group that has arisen since relocation. This larger group is a manifestation of the altered physical and social environment in which the Aborigines find themselves. Belief in dream-spirits is only one of innumerable shared beliefs, but the co-operation involved in creating and performing these and other rituals reaffirms the growing ethnocentrism and in-group solidarity of the Jigalong 'mob' (the name they give to this entity) as a new kind of social group that is much larger than traditional social groupings such as hordes and territorially anchored descent groups. In hierarchical societies, leadership structure is a primary mechanism of integration. In relatively egalitarian Aboriginal society with its absence of a clearly defined leadership structure, the new entity emphasizes ritual activities, a traditional element of social organization, as its primary mechanism of integration.

Aboriginal conceptions of the dream-spirit have been influenced by contact with 'whites'. Crayon drawings made by Aborigines of *baḍundjari* sometimes resemble aircraft, and vehicles said to be used by *baḍundjari* to transport others are depicted as aeroplanes, complete with wings, tail, windows and headlights, but with sacred boards, not propellors or jets, supplying the power source. The Aborigines usually insist that the dream-spirits had these types of vehicle before the Europeans invented them.

The Aborigines do not question the alien origin of the great majority of objects they utilize, and they tend to take the technological achievements of European culture very much for granted. However, there are certain secret-sacred objects associated with dream-spirit beliefs, the alien origin of which is denied by the Aborigines, when in fact it is obvious to an observer that they are of alien manufacture. The objects, owned and allegedly used by several native doctors, are of two types: cut-glass decanter stoppers, and radio valves or globes of an uncommon type. Each is connected to a length of hair-string by a wad of spinifex gum. The objects are all known as *guṟu* ('eyes') which are said to light up the night sky for the native doctors as they go *baḍundjari*, with their passengers sitting astride the hairstring. Falling stars are cited as proof of the existence of *guṟu*. When the objects were first shown to me, the men stressed that they had been left for them by ancestral beings and were definitely not of alien manufacture. It appears that the men had never seen such objects in use by Europeans, so they could confidently deny their alien origin: they had acquired them from northerners, and with them an explanation that validated their mythological origin. Although the men were obviously aware that the objects looked manufactured, their belief in the magical power of their ancestral heroes is so strong that they did not doubt the truth of the accompanying validation.

It seems clear that, since their migration from the desert and subsequent contact with Europeans, Jigalong's Aborigines have made many adjustments to ensure the maintenance of their traditional religious life. Their belief in the reality of dream-spirit journeys has provided the inspiration necessary for the creation of new and meaningful rituals, and has assumed a role of considerable importance in maintaining their links with both their countries of origin and their ancestral heroes, thus ensuring continuity with the past and a measure of confidence in the future.

Notes

1. The fieldwork on which this paper is based was carried out under the auspices of the Department of Anthropology, University of Western Australia, in three periods totalling eleven months, between June 1963 and January 1965. Further brief visits were made in 1966 and 1967, and for three months in 1969-70. I worked at Jigalong under a grant from the Australian Institute of Aboriginal Studies.

2. The mission at Jigalong has now been closed (1969), but the settlement is operated as an experimental pastoral station by the Native Welfare Department of Western Australia.

3. Reference is made to the distribution of dialectal units in R. M. Berndt (1959). See also Tonkinson (1966).

4. In my Master's thesis (submitted in Anthropology at the University of Western Australia, 1966), I provide full details on the social organization and structure of this area.

5. Concerning this term *maban*. It has wide currency in the Western Desert: see Berndt and Berndt 1945:158 (1943, Vol. XIV, No. 1:56), who call it a shell disc while recognizing that the same word is used for other magical objects. It should be noted that the roles of native doctor (who is primarily concerned with curative forms of magic) and sorcerer often coincide. Elkin (1944) gives examples of native doctors flying.

6. Especially significant here is the removal of an internal organ for curative purposes. In most references to magical operations (excluding those relevant to the initiation of native doctors and sorcerers), the alleged removal of internal organs and their replacement by other substances is for sorcery purposes. An example is discussed in Berndt and Berndt 1945:177-80 (1943, Vol. XIV, No. 2:129-32). See also Elkin (1944).

7. It is interesting to note that R. M. Berndt collected songs concerning this ritual and its mythology from Winba while at Balgo in the southern Kimberleys (most recently in 1969). The names 'Winba' and 'Djaramara' are used interchangeably.

References

BERNDT, R. M. and C. H. 1945 A preliminary report of field work in the Ooldea Region, Western South Australia. *Oceania Bound Offprint*, Sydney.
BERNDT, R. M. 1959 The concept of 'the tribe' in the Western Desert of Australia. *Oceania*, Vol. XXX, No. 2.
ELKIN, A. P. 1944 *Aboriginal Men of High Degree*. Australasian Publishing Co., Sydney.

MEGGITT, M. J. 1962 *Desert People*. Angus and Robertson, Sydney.
MOUNTFORD, C. P. and R. TONKINSON 1969 Carved and engraved human figures from North Western Australia, *Anthropological Forum*, Vol. II, No. 3.
TONKINSON, R. 1966 Social Structure and Acculturation of Aborigines in the Western Desert. M.A. thesis in Anthropology, University of Western Australia.

ACKNOWLEDGEMENTS

For their comments on an earlier draft of this chapter, my thanks to Professor R. M. Berndt, Dr C. H. Berndt, Professor K. O. L. Burridge (University of British Columbia), and Dr Peter M. Weil (University of Delaware).

JEREMY LONG

Polygyny, Acculturation and Contact:
Aspects of Aboriginal Marriage in Central Australia

> Polygyny seems to be restricted to the old and influential men, and to be rather an exception, although it seems to be found in all tribes.
>
> B. Malinowski (1913:307)

In 1962, after reading Rose's study of the Aborigines of Groote Eylandt (1960), I compiled tables, modelled on his, showing the incidence of polygyny in three Aboriginal communities west of Alice Springs: Areyonga, Haasts Bluff-Papunya and Yuendumu (see Table 1). These tables were based on census data I had gathered for studies of population growth in various Aboriginal communities.[1] The tables showed that the incidence of polygyny varied considerably from one community to another, and that:

(*a*) the situation at Yuendumu in 1961 was roughly similar to that at Groote Eylandt in 1941, at least in the proportion of husbands who had only one wife and the proportion of women who were married to monogamous men; and

(*b*) the incidence of polygyny was lower at Papunya than at Yuendumu and lower at Areyonga than at Papunya.

I assumed, as did others working in the area, that polygynous unions were few in the Areyonga community because the Petermann Range people who made up the bulk of the population were traditionally more monogamous than some, perhaps most, other Aboriginal groups. The Areyonga people were generally regarded as conservative and strongly 'tradition-oriented': initiation and other ceremonies were maintained and a ritual murder had occurred there as recently as 1953. Young women were generally older when they married than in other communities and they often married men not a great deal older than themselves.

TABLE 1
Polygyny and Monogamy in Some Aboriginal Populations, I

A. Groote Eylandt, 1940*

Husband's Age Group	Number of Wives						Total Husbands	Total Wives	Mean Wives per Man
	1	2	3	4	5	6			
16-20	—	—	—	—	—	—	—	—	—
21-30	6	3	—	—	—	—	9	12	1·3
31-40	11	5	1	2	1	—	20	37	1·9
41-50	3	4	—	1	1	2	11	32	2·9
51-60	2	2	1	—	—	—	5	9	1·8
61 and over	3	1	—	—	—	—	4	5	1·3
Totals	25	15	2	3	2	2	49	95	1·94
Percentage Husbands	51	31	4	6	4	4	100	—	—
Percentage Wives	26	31	6	13	10	13	—	99	—

Range: 1 to 6.   * After Rose (1960), Table 27, p. 69

B. Yuendumu, 1962

Husband's Age Group	Number of Wives						Total Husbands	Total Wives	Mean Wives per Man
	1	2	3	4	5	6			
16-20	—	—	—	—	—	—	—	—	—
21-30	7	—	—	—	—	—	7	7	1·0
31-40	10	7	1	—	—	—	18	27	1·5
41-50	9	8	4	1	—	—	22	41	1·9
51-60	6	6	2	2	1	—	17	37	2·2
61 and over	10	5	—	—	—	—	15	20	1·3
Totals	42	26	7	3	1	—	79	132	1·67
Percentage Husbands	53	33	9	4	1	—	100	—	—
Percentage Wives	32	39	16	9	4	—	—	100	—

Range: 1 to 5

C. Desert Groups, 1956-62

Husband's Age Group	Number of Wives						Total Husbands	Total Wives	Mean Wives per Man
	1	2	3	4	5	6			
16-20	1	—	—	—	—	—	1	1	1·0
21-30	6	3	—	—	—	—	9	12	1·3
31-40	3	2	—	—	—	—	5	7	1·4
41-50	3	1	—	—	—	—	4	5	1·3
51-60	3	—	—	—	—	—	3	3	1·0
61 and over	2	1	1	—	—	—	4	7	1·8
Totals	18	7	1	—	—	—	26	35	1·34
Percentage Husbands	69	27	4	—	—	—	100	—	—
Percentage Wives	51	40	9	—	—	—	—	100	—

Range: 1 to 3

Table 1 (continued)
D. HAASTS BLUFF—PAPUNYA, 1962

Husband's Age Group	Number of Wives						Total Husbands	Total Wives	Mean Wives per Man
	1	2	3	4	5	6			
16-20	4	—	—	—	—	—	4	4	1·0
21-30	18	—	—	—	—	—	18	18	1·0
31-40	19	6	1	—	—	—	26	34	1·3
41-50	16	6	1	—	—	—	23	31	1·3
51-60	6	1	1	—	—	—	8	11	1·4
60 and over	4	1	1	—	—	—	6	9	1·5
Totals	67	14	4	—	—	—	85	108	1·26
Percentage Husbands	79	16	5	—	—	—	100	—	—
Percentage Wives	63	26	11	—	—	—	—	100	—

Range: 1 to 3

E. AREYONGA, 1961

Husband's Age Group	Number of Wives						Total Husbands	Total Wives	Mean Wives per Man
	1	2	3	4	5	6			
16-20	—	—	—	—	—	—	—	—	—
21-30	11	—	—	—	—	—	11	11	1·0
31-40	14	—	—	—	—	—	14	14	1·0
41-50	8	—	—	—	—	—	8	8	1·0
51-60	6	1	—	—	—	—	7	8	1·1
61 and over	4	1	—	—	—	—	5	6	1·2
Totals	43	2	—	—	—	—	45	47	1·04
Percentage Husbands	96	4	—	—	—	—	100	—	—
Percentage Wives	91·5	8·5	—	—	—	—	—	100	—

Range: 1 to 2

I

In hopes of providing some evidence on whether these differences reflected traditional regional differences in behaviour and social organization, I compiled another table showing the incidence of polygyny among groups of Aborigines who were or had been living in the area near the Western Australian border. These groups had had no contact with non-Aborigines until they met (Northern Territory) Welfare Branch patrols (between 1957 and 1962) or themselves had walked in to the settlement at Haasts Bluff (as groups did in 1956 and 1958). The 'desert groups' table (1, C), unlike the others, does not indicate the marriage situation in a population at a single point in time but the distribution of wives among men at the time they were first met by non-Aborigines. Some of the husbands and wives whose marriages were recorded in 1956 or 1957 had died, separated or taken another spouse before 1962. The incidence of polygyny in the desert groups was similar to that in the Papunya population (Table 1, D). This tended to suggest that the differences in the incidence of polygyny between the three communities reflected traditional regional differences (Table 1, B, D and E). More than half of the Papunya population were identified at Pintupi and derived from roughly the same area as the 'desert groups' population. The more acculturated, mission-influenced element in the Papunya population was more monogamous than the Pintupi and a Walbiri (Ngalia) group was more polygynous than the Pintupi.

Examination of the tables (1, B, C, D and E) suggested that contact over a period of up to about thirty years and some fifteen to thirty years of settlement life had had some, but probably not a very marked effect on polygyny rates in these populations. Ration depots had been established at Areyonga and Haasts Bluff in the early 1940s and many of the people attracted to these depots had had contact with Lutheran mission evangelists and with cattle stations during the 1930s. Many of the Walbiri had had contact with cattle stations and with the mining camps at the Granites and Tanami in the 1930s or earlier. The ration depot at Yuendumu was established in 1946. It seemed safe to conclude that the Walbiri (living at Yuendumu and at Papunya) had been, and remained rather more polygynous than their south-western neighbours (the Pintupi) and conspicuously more polygynous than the people of the Petermann Ranges (Pitjantjara). Areyonga was evidently a community in which the accumulation of wives was not an engrossing pursuit and there was no apparent reason to suppose that it had ever been so for the people who were living there.

In 1965 Meggitt published (1965:148) a statistical paper on aspects of marriage among the Walbiri, in which he argued that the three Walbiri settlement communities—Yuendumu, Hooker Creek and Warrabri—are apparently to various degrees acculturated and that 'the variable of acculturation is *prima facie* a significant determinant of rates of, and ages at, marriage'. His data show that the three Walbiri communities have different polygyny rates and the least polygynous of the three communities is evidently the most acculturated one. He argues (*ibid.*: 165) that 'quantifiable changes in several features of the marriage system of inland Aborigines provide fairly sensitive indices of degrees of increasing acculturation (or detribalization)', one of these changes being a decline in the incidence of polygyny.

Meggitt's table (*ibid.*) showing the incidence of polygyny at Yuendumu was reassuringly similar to my own and there is no necessary conflict between his hypothesis that a decline in polygyny indicates increasing acculturation and my own that variations in the incidence of polygyny in different communities may indicate differences in traditional behaviours rather than differences in degrees of acculturation. The difficulty lies in determining what changes have occurred or what the incidence of polygyny was before contact. The evidence for a causal connection between greater degrees of contact and lower polygyny rates is perhaps suggestive rather than conclusive. Conceivably, the eastern and northern Walbiri (now concentrated at Warrabri and Hooker Creek) may have been traditionally less polygynous than the southern groups now living mostly at Yuendumu. Acculturation is a process, one symptom of which may be a decline in polygyny, rather than a factor determining change in marriage behaviour. On the evidence of the Walbiri figures alone, one would clearly not be justified in assuming that any Aboriginal community with a lower incidence of polygyny than another was necessarily more acculturated than that other community.

TABLE 2
POLYGYNY AND MONOGAMY IN SOME ABORIGINAL POPULATIONS, II

A. YUENDUMU, 1967

Husband's Age Group	Number of Wives						Total Husbands	Total Wives	Mean Wives per Man
	1	2	3	4	5	6			
16-20	—	—	—	—	—	—	—	—	—
21-30	12	4	1	—	—	—	17	23	1·4
31-40	14	9	3	—	—	—	26	41	1·6
41-50	14	15	4	—	—	—	33	56	1·7
51-60	13	7	7	2	—	—	29	56	1·9
61 and over	12	6	1	—	—	—	19	27	1·4
Totals	65	41	16	2	—	—	124	203	1·63
Percentage Husbands	52	33	13	2	—	—	100	—	—
Percentage Wives	32	40	24	4	—	—	—	100	—

Range: 1 to 4

B. DESERT GROUPS, 1956-66

Husband's Age Group	Number of Wives						Total Husbands	Total Wives	Mean Wives per Man
	1	2	3	4	5	6			
16-20	1	—	—	—	—	—	1	1	1·0
21-30	6	4	—	—	—	—	10	14	1·4
31-40	7	3	2	—	—	—	12	19	1·6
41-50	3	2	—	—	—	—	5	7	1·4
51-60	3	—	—	1	—	—	4	7	1·8
61 and over	3	1	2	—	—	—	6	11	1·8
Totals	23	10	4	1	—	—	38	59	1·57
Percentage Husbands	60·5	26	10·5	3	—	—	100	—	—
Percentage Wives	39	34	20	7	—	—	—	100	—

Range: 1 to 4

C. HAASTS BLUFF – PAPUNYA, 1967

Husband's Age Group	Number of Wives						Total Husbands	Total Wives	Mean Wives per Man
	1	2	3	4	5	6			
16-20	4	—	—	—	—	—	4	4	1·0
21-30	36	3	—	—	—	—	39	42	1·1
31-40	27	8	1	—	—	—	36	46	1·3
41-50	25	7	1	1	—	—	34	46	1·4
51-60	12	4	1	—	—	—	17	23	1·4
61 and over	5	4	1	—	—	—	10	16	1·6
Totals	109	26	4	1	—	—	140	177	1·26
Percentage Husbands	78	19	2	1	—	—	100	—	—
Percentage Wives	62	29	7	2	—	—	—	100	—

Range: 1 to 4

II

Recently I compiled more tables of the incidence of polygyny at Yuendumu and Papunya, based on data collected in 1967 (Table 2, A and C). These show relatively little change from the 1962 data in what seem to be useful indices of the polygyny rate in any community: the proportion of monogamous husbands, the mean number of wives per husband and the range in numbers of wives per man. The addition to the 'desert groups' table of information about men met in the desert in the period 1963 to 1966 did, however, change the picture substantially (Table 2, B). Seven of the additional twelve men were polygynists and the revised table indicates a situation much more like the situation at Yuendumu in 1962 and 1967 than like the Papunya situation. But since the desert groups are not *more* polygynous than the Yuendumu groups are after some years of contact, the data suggest that the Yuendumu Walbiri may have been traditionally more polygynous than the Pintupi. The fact that there is little change in the situation at Yuendumu since 1962 might suggest also that settlement life does not necessarily lead to a rapid decline in polygyny rates.

The argument that a low incidence of polygyny in an Aboriginal population is an effect of contact and acculturation was taken further by Rose (1965) in his study of the Aborigines at Angas Downs, southwest of Alice Springs. Rose observed (*ibid.*: 6, 81) that few of these men had two wives and none more than two. He argues that polygyny has virtually disappeared in the space of about twenty years because it is a custom which has financial disadvantages in the contemporary situation. He suggests (*ibid.*: 54) that the literature shows that the southern Pitjantjara neighbours of the Angas Downs group (most of whom derived from the Petermann Ranges) were polygynous, and two genealogies he collected suggest that the Angas Downs people were formerly more polygynous. Rose's evidence that polygyny before contact was 'quantitatively pronounced' (*ibid.*) is perhaps unconvincing. As he acknowledges, the literature of the Aborigines of northern South Australia on which he relies indicates only that polygyny was practised, *not* how common it was.

III

The anthropological literature on the people of the southern parts of the Western Desert area tends to support the view that the people of that area were in fact conspicuously *less* polygynous than the Walbiri and Groote Eylandt people. At Ooldea in 1941 the Berndts noted (1945: 50) that no men had more than two wives:

OOLDEA, 1941 (western South Australia)

	One Wife	Two Wives	Three Wives	Total Husbands	Total Wives	Total Wives per Man
Number of Husbands	42	11	—	53	64	1·2
Percentage of Husbands	79	21	—	100		

They noted (*ibid.*: 51, 113) that 'no prestige is gained by having more than one wife' and that 'monogamy seemed to be the state generally preferred'. Their evidence also suggests that among these people the age differences between marriage partners might generally be less great than in some other areas and that women commonly married later, and men earlier, than elsewhere. They report (*ibid.*: 220, 112) that there were 'no unmarried women who have passed the age of about twenty-six years', that 'betrothed girls have to wait for their betrothed to pass his final initiation'. A girl's husband 'usually ... is a young man' and 'arrangements ... work out so that a girl's puberty is reached some little time after a youth's subincision or cicatrization, and marriage normally follows'. The Ooldea population then, derived from areas west of and north of Ooldea Soak, could not be considered a highly acculturated group.

Reporting on fieldwork at Areyonga in 1964-65, Munn noted (1965) the high percentage of monogamous unions among the 'western desert men' (as distinct from the Aranda) there, but observed that 'genealogical data indicate a higher proportion of polygynous marriages in the previous generation'.

Areyonga, 1964-65

	One Wife	Two Wives	Three Wives	Total Husbands	Total Wives	Mean Wives per Man
Number of Husbands	57	5	—	62	67	1·08
Percentage of Husbands	91	8	—	99		

Areyonga—genealogies

	One Wife	Two Wives	Three Wives	Total Husbands	Total Wives	Mean Wives per Man
Number of Husbands	28	13	4	45	66	1·46
Percentage of Husbands	62	29	9	100		

The genealogical data can be taken as no more than indicative of the pre-contact situation. For a number of reasons, information in genealogies may distort the picture, and in particular it seems likely that serial polygyny could inflate the numbers of apparent polygynists in genealogies. But it is interesting that Munn's data from Areyonga genealogies more closely resemble the data for the desert groups in my Tables 1 and 2 than the data for Yuendumu and Groote Eylandt.

Census material gathered at Amata, South Australia, by Yengoyan (1967) in 1966-67 shows a less marked but still striking predominance of monogamous unions in this population, which derives mainly from the country of the Mann and Tomkinson ranges to the west.

Amata, 1966-67

	One Wife	Two Wives	Three Wives	Four Wives	Total Husbands	Total Wives	Mean Wives per Man
Number of Husbands	48	15	—	1	64	82	1·28
Percentage of Husbands	75	23	—	2	100		

Yengoyan notes (*ibid.*:2) that eleven of the sixteen polygynists were forty years of age or over, and that 'the economic incentive behind polygynous unions has markedly decreased'.

The evidence suggests that, at least in the recent past, polygyny was much *less* common among the Western Desert people of the region now included in the large reserves in South Australia, Western Australia and the Northern Territory than it was at Groote Eylandt and among the Walbiri. In this area men with as many as four or even three wives were relatively few and far between. It appears that this relatively low incidence of polygyny was correlated with, and perhaps causally linked with, relatively late marriage of females and a less marked disparity in age between spouses than in some other Aboriginal societies.[2] There is certainly evidence that there has been some decline in polygyny rates, but it seems unnecessary to assume that there has been a very marked decline or to regard this as a direct effect of contact or acculturation. Why, one may ask, does polygyny remain common, among young men and old, at Yuendumu where economic conditions are not significantly different from conditions at Areyonga if, as Rose seems to argue, economic factors determine the incidence of polygyny?

Rose's hypothesis about how change in marriage behaviour has occurred in the population at Angas Downs, like Meggitt's correlation of declining polygyny with acculturation among the Walbiri, raises questions about the mechanisms of change when Aborigines are in contact with Europeans. Certainly polygyny generally seems to be abandoned or to decrease among Aborigines in contact. But *why* this should happen is not immediately obvious. In some places, of course, the change has been engineered or imposed, as it was by missionaries at Bathurst Island and more recently at Groote Eylandt. But in situations where, as at settlements and at some cattle stations, rations were provided for women and children and jobs were available to women, explanation of the disappearance of polygyny in terms of economic advantage does not seem plausible. And the persistence of polygyny even in places like eastern Arnhem Land where Europeans in positions of power and influence disapprove of it, and are interested enough in what Aborigines do to tell them so, suggests that an enthusiasm to adopt the customs of Europeans is unlikely to have been a major factor in the disappearance of polygyny elsewhere.

It seems possible that the mechanisms of change might be primarily demographic. It is common knowledge that Aboriginal populations in touch with European populations decline or have done so until quite recently. It is a widespread, if inadequately explained, characteristic of populations in decline that males outnumber females. Relative shortages of females in declining populations, it seems, may provide at least a partial explanation of a declining incidence of polygyny in Aboriginal populations in contact with Europeans.

IV

To test this hypothesis, at least in a preliminary way, I made rough counts of males and females in the three Walbiri communities and at Areyonga and Haasts Bluff—Papunya (Table 3). The ratios of males to females in the Walbiri communities correlate strikingly with Meggitt's data on the relative incidence of polygyny in these communities. And

Table 3

Adult Sex Ratios in Some Northern Territory Aboriginal Populations (1956*)

	Males 20 Years and Over	Females 20 Years and Over	Females 15 Years and Over	Females per 100 Males 20 Years and Over	Females 15 and Over per 100 Males 20 Years and Over
Yuendumu	107	178	193	166	180
Hooker Creek	34	47	52	138	153
Warrabri	81	93	108	114	133
Haasts Bluff–Papunya	104	117	137	112	190
Areyonga	80	73	97	91	121
Yirrkalla	77	115	146	149	193
Groote Eylandt	110	96	125	87	114
Barkly Tableland District	293	250	281	85	97
Kimberley District	370	315	345	85	93

* Figures derived from counts of persons listed in relevant sections of the Register of Wards (*N.T. Government Gazette*, No. 19B, 13 May 1957).

the contrast between the ratios in the communities where polygyny rates are relatively high and the ratio at Areyonga is marked. I also made similar counts of adult males and females in some Northern Territory populations which have had long and relatively intensive contact (the Barkly Tableland and Kimberley districts) and in two communities (Yirrkalla and Groote Eylandt) where contact began much more recently and has been controlled (see Table 3). The two areas of pastoral settlement show the expected high masculinity, and Yirrkalla the expected high proportion of females.

Groote Eylandt is an interesting anomaly, which may only indicate the dangers of theorizing on the basis of data from such small populations. It is interesting that a ban on new polygynous marriages has been enforced there since 1942, but with considerable opposition latterly both from men who would take more than one wife and from others involved in marriage arrangements. Figures of the gross numbers of adult males and females are by no means adequate for a proper analysis of the effects of demographic factors on polygyny rates. At Groote Eylandt, there have been more single females of marriageable age than single males of marriageable age and the ratio of males over twenty-one years of age to females over fifteen may be a more significant measure than the ratio of males to females over twenty years old.

The fact that adult males outnumber females in the Areyonga

populations seems to need explanation. I have argued that the Areyonga people have apparently had a history of contact not significantly different in kind from that of the people of Papunya and Yuendumu. It is possible that these people were affected by introduced diseases earlier and more drastically than their northern neighbours, but the evidence that polygyny was rarer among the Pitjantjara suggests that other factors—possibly related to the problems of survival in a low-rainfall area—may have been at work in pre-contact times. One possible hypothesis might be that, in areas of extremely sparse population, fighting may have been less frequent and the male mortality rate may have therefore been lower than in areas of relatively dense population. But other explanations, including the possibility of selective infanticide, are equally plausible in the absence of any direct evidence.

Evidence from Arnhem Land as well as from central Australia suggests that factors other than length of contact with non-Aborigines must be considered in explanations of contemporary differences in polygyny rates. Maningrida is the most recently established community in Arnhem Land, yet the community is less polygynous that the longer established mission communities farther east. Some of the people now at Maningrida have had long contact but the majority had minimal contact with non-Aborigines before 1957. The mean number of wives per husband is lower at Maningrida than it is at Milingimbi (established in 1921) or at Elcho Island (first established for a few months in the 1920s but re-established only in 1942) or at Yirrkalla (established in 1934). (See Table 4.) Polygyny rates may well not have varied significantly in pre-contact times in the different parts of Arnhem Land, but it seems evident that the contact these populations have had has produced no really radical changes.

TABLE 4

POLYGYNY AND MONOGAMY IN SOME ARNHEM LAND POPULATIONS, 1966

MANINGRIDA	Number of Wives								Total Husbands	Total Wives
	1	2	3	4	5	6	7	10		
Number of Husbands	91	35	13	1	2	—	—	—	142	214
Percentage of Husbands	64·1	24·6	9·2	0·7	1·4	—	—	—	100	—
Percentage of Wives	42·5	32·7	18·2	1·9	4·7	—	—	—	—	100

Range: 1 to 5. Mean: 1·5

Milingimbi	Number of Wives								Total Husbands	Total Wives
	1	2	3	4	5	6	7	10		
Number of Husbands	41	18	19	4	1	1	1	—	75	138
Percentage of Husbands	54·7	24·0	12·0	5·3	1·3	1·3	1·3	—	99·9	—
Percentage of Wives	29·7	26·1	19·6	11·6	3·6	4·3	5·1	—	—	100

Range: 1 to 7. Mean: 1·84

Elcho Island	1	2	3	4	5	6	7	10	Total Husbands	Total Wives
Number of Husbands	66	17	10	7	3	—	—	—	103	173
Percentage of Husbands	64·1	16·5	9·7	6·8	2·9	—	—	—	100	—
Percentage of Wives	38·2	19·6	17·3	16·2	8·7	—	—	—	—	100

Range: 1 to 5. Mean: 1·68

Yirrkalla	1	2	3	4	5	6	7	10	Total Husbands	Total Wives
Number of Husbands	36	19	5	1	—	1	—	2	64	119
Percentage of Husbands	56·2	29·6	7·8	1·6	—	1·6	—	3·1	99·9	—
Percentage of Wives	30·2	31·9	12·6	3·4	—	5·0	—	16·8	—	99·9

Range: 1 to 10. Mean: 1·86

There were polygynists in all Aboriginal societies and there are still polygynists in most areas of the Northern Territory today. Where polygyny is a permissible practice and no women remain unmarried, a number of factors can influence whether a man has one wife, several wives or no wives. In some contact situations there have been demographic changes which have reduced the scope for accumulating a number of wives. A man may have, and might have had, several wives while other men have had none; but it seems that one important factor influencing the overall polygyny rates in any population of Aborigines was and is the overall ratio of males to females of marriageable age in the population. Some polygynously married Aborigines have had more contact with, and have been more changed by contact with, non-Aboriginal society than some monogamous Aborigines. Just as the marital situation of an individual is an unreliable guide to his degree of acculturation, so the incidence of polygyny in any community is evidently an unreliable index of the relative degree of acculturation of that community.

Notes

1. These and later studies on which this article is based were made while I was an Investigation Officer with the Welfare Branch, Northern Territory Administration.

2. Further evidence for later marriage of females in Pitjandjara society is given in a recently published book by Hilliard (1968:112) on the mission at Ernabella: '... early marriage is not acceptable in Pitjantjara society. A man is not considered to be of marriageable age until he has passed through several degrees of initiation which could make him at least twenty-five. Girls marry younger, but some are over twenty, or even thirty, before marriage, though all marry eventually. There is a word to describe an older girl, of about twenty-seven or more, indicating that this late marriage was by no means a rare occurrence.'

References

BERNDT, R. M. and C. H. 1945 A preliminary report of field work in the Ooldea Region, Western South Australia. *Oceania Bound Offprint*, Sydney. (References to *Oceania*, Vol. XIII, No. 2, 1942; Vol. XIII, No. 3, 1943; Vol. XIV, No. 3, 1944.)

——— (eds) 1965 *Aboriginal Man in Australia*. Angus and Robertson, Sydney.

HILLIARD, W. M. 1968 *The People in Between*. Hodder and Stoughton, London.

MALINOWSKI, B. 1913 *The Family Among the Australian Aborigines*. University of London Press, London.

MEGGITT, M. J. 1965 Marriage among the Walbiri of Central Australia, a Statistical Examination. In *Aboriginal Man in Australia* (R. M. and C. H. Berndt, eds).

MUNN, N. D. 1965 A Report on Field Research at Areyonga, 1964-5, Australian Institute of Aboriginal Studies, Canberra.

ROSE, F. G. G. 1960 *Classification of Kin, Age Structure and Marriage amongst the Groote Eylandt*. Akademie-Verlag, Berlin.

——— 1965 *The Wind of Change in Central Australia*. Akademie-Verlag, Berlin.

YENGOYAN, A. A. 1967 Field Report No. 2, Australian Institute of Aboriginal Studies, Doc. 67/556, Canberra.

FAY GALE

The Impact of Urbanization on Aboriginal Marriage Patterns[1]

Cities, because of their opportunities and interest, exert a strong pull on rural populations. This is particularly true in Australia, where the size and nature of the country makes centralization of industry and tertiary services almost inevitable. Contrary to popular opinion, Australians are largely city dwellers. According to the 1966 census, 83 per cent of Australians were living in urban areas.

In contrast to this general Australian pattern of population distribution the Australian Aborigines, until the last decade, were almost exclusively rural dwellers. Several factors accounted for this. The dark skin-colour made them very distinct from other Australians. In the outback areas where Aborigines retained some of their traditional way of life, they were culturally quite separate from the general Australian population. Even those who had adopted a European form of life remained for the most part in scattered rural communities or on reserves or missions. Government policy had fostered their isolation from the bulk of the population and had encouraged their withdrawal into separate communities. It is in the context of this previous rural isolation that the emergence of Aborigines as a city group during the last decade appears as such a startling contrast. As Aborigines become urbanized, their way of life is altered and many of their traditional patterns of behaviour are changed. But the old ways are not completely obliterated. Kinship and group identification are still of fundamental importance to urban Aborigines though these have been changed considerably from the traditional pattern.

I

In this paper the city of Adelaide is taken as a case study to show some of the changes which urbanization is causing in the Aboriginal way of life. Adelaide is the capital of the state of South Australia and contains a major proportion of the population of that state. In 1966, 66·67 per cent of the population of South Australia was living in Metropolitan Adelaide as defined by the census. The aridity of some two-thirds[2] of the state together with the isolating effect of the coastline's shape have meant that most secondary and tertiary facilities have developed almost exclusively in Adelaide. Only one country town, Whyalla, has more than 20,000 people.[3] It is thus inevitable that Adelaide has become the main centre to which the Aborigines of this state are moving. But Adelaide is also largely the functional capital for the Northern Territory, particularly in such services as health and education. Thus Adelaide is also the city to which many of the Aborigines from the Northern Territory are being attracted.

I collected data on 2,039 Aborigines who lived in Adelaide for a minimum of six consecutive months between January 1963 and January 1966. This number represents approximately one-quarter of the total Aboriginal population of South Australia. Not all of these people were resident in Adelaide at any one time during the three-year period. Some came, settled in the city, but later moved back to the country again. In many cases they returned to the city again later. But only if they stayed for at least six months at any one time were they counted in this survey of city dwellers. Many others came to the city for shorter visits of less than six months' duration, and they were not included. The study thus excluded the more transient people. It also excluded many Aborigines who have been totally absorbed into the general community. Only people who call themselves Aboriginal and identify themselves with the Aboriginal community in Adelaide were counted. Some of these are quite fair in colouring and are fully integrated into the life of the city. But they were included if they call themselves Aborigines and still associate with Aboriginal kinsfolk. Those excluded do not consider themselves to be Aboriginal and do not participate in any Aboriginal group activities in the city. Indeed it would have been impossible to include such people because they have completely or almost completely merged with the general Australian community.

When one is working with Aborigines in the city it is not hard to draw the line between Aborigines and non-Aborigines on this basis. The distinction is not made on the basis of skin colour or economic independence although these are quite significant factors influencing the absorption of Aborigines into the community. The distinction is made by the people themselves. For example an Aboriginal informant said on one occasion: 'Now there's my niece. You ought to have her down on your list. I've got another niece too, but you can't include her; she's married a white man and we never see them now.'

Detailed records were built up for each of these individuals who chose to call themselves Aborigines in Adelaide. Computer cards containing a range of personal data including vital statistics and life histories were punched for each person. It was possible then to obtain a very comprehensive cross-correlation of the way of the life of these 2,039 urban Aborigines by computer analysis of their individual case studies. The results were tabulated in 180 sets of correlations. This paper deals with the information obtained from three of these 180 tables: the three tables dealing with marriage in relation to age and regional affiliation.

All of the Aboriginal data was corrected to the year 1966. No information obtained after that year was added. The year 1966 was taken as the base line to make possible a comparison between the Aboriginal population and the general population of Adelaide, recorded at the 1966 census. It was necessary to draw the same boundaries not only in point of time but also in area for both the Aboriginal study and the census material to make comparisons valid. There were several Aborigines who had moved to the towns on the outskirts of Adelaide such as Port Noarlunga and Gawler. These places were included in the Adelaide study because such Aborigines considered that they had moved to the city. Adelaide for the Aboriginal study was thus a slightly larger area than Metropolitan Adelaide as defined by the 1966 census. Thus it was necessary to add certain peripheral areas to the Adelaide census figures to obtain a comparative area in both populations. Through doing this, 'greater Adelaide' for the purposes of this study registered a total population of 764,905 individuals at the 1966 census instead of 727,916 persons as specified in the *Census Bulletin* No. 41 for Metropolitan Adelaide. In this way the same boundaries were drawn for urban Adelaide in both the Aboriginal and the general population.

The two populations are compared in graphic form in the following figures to give a clear picture of the relationship of the Aboriginal group to the total population of the city. There is a vast difference in size between the two populations (Aboriginal 2,039; and total 764,905) but comparisons can be made by using a percentage relationship within each group. We are not comparing actual numbers but relative numbers. Thus we are not comparing the actual number of Aborigines and non-Aborigines who are single, married, divorced or in the 'other' category. We are comparing the percentage number of Aboriginal people in a particular category with the percentage number of non-Aborigines in the same category. It is a comparison of relative distributions within two separate populations.

II

This paper attempts to do two things. First, a comparison is made between the marriage patterns of the urban Aboriginal community and those of the total urban community in Adelaide. Second, it analyses the difference in marriage patterns between the various Aboriginal kin groups living in the city. However, before the marriage figures are studied it is necessary to have some understanding of the demographic composition of both the Aboriginal and the non-Aboriginal population in Adelaide.

In Figure 1 two age pyramids have been drawn, one of the Aboriginal population of Adelaide in 1966 and the other of the general, non-Aboriginal population in Adelaide at the 1966 census. These pyramids show significant differences between the composition of the two populations. Two contrasts are immediately obvious. The Aboriginal population is a very youthful one. Indeed, 60 per cent of Adelaide's Aboriginal population is under twenty years of age, whereas only 39 per cent of the general Adelaide population is under twenty years of age. There are considerably more older people in the general population than there are in the Aboriginal group. Nearly 13 per cent of the non-Aboriginal population is over the age of sixty years but only 3 per cent of the Aboriginal population in Adelaide is more than sixty years of age.

At first glance one might be tempted to say that a young, urban Aboriginal population could be expected since only young people tend to migrate. The graph could thus be explained by saying that the older people have remained on the reserves or in the country. This is not the case. Age pyramids constructed for country Aborigines show similar features. Aborigines have strong kinship ties and, much like some of the southern European families in Australia, have brought parents and grandparents with them in their move to the city. There are many inducements to encourage older Aborigines to move to the city with their families. Medical services and other social services are available more readily in the city and houses are offered at reduced rates for pensioners.

Actually the general shape of the pyramid is due to two factors which are common throughout the Aboriginal population in Australia and do not occur only in the case of city people. First, a higher birth rate among Aborigines during much of this century has meant that a higher percentage of young people is found among the Aborigines. Second, a much higher death rate, especially in the past, has led to a lower life expectancy and therefore a smaller percentage of Aborigines who survive to the older age groups, a factor which has already been commented upon by one life insurance firm in Adelaide. A third, though less immediately obvious, contrast can be seen in the different distribution of the sexes in the two populations. The pyramids drawn in Figure 1 show that the overall masculinity is higher in the Aboriginal urban population than in the general urban population. In the general population there is a marked predominance of female numbers over

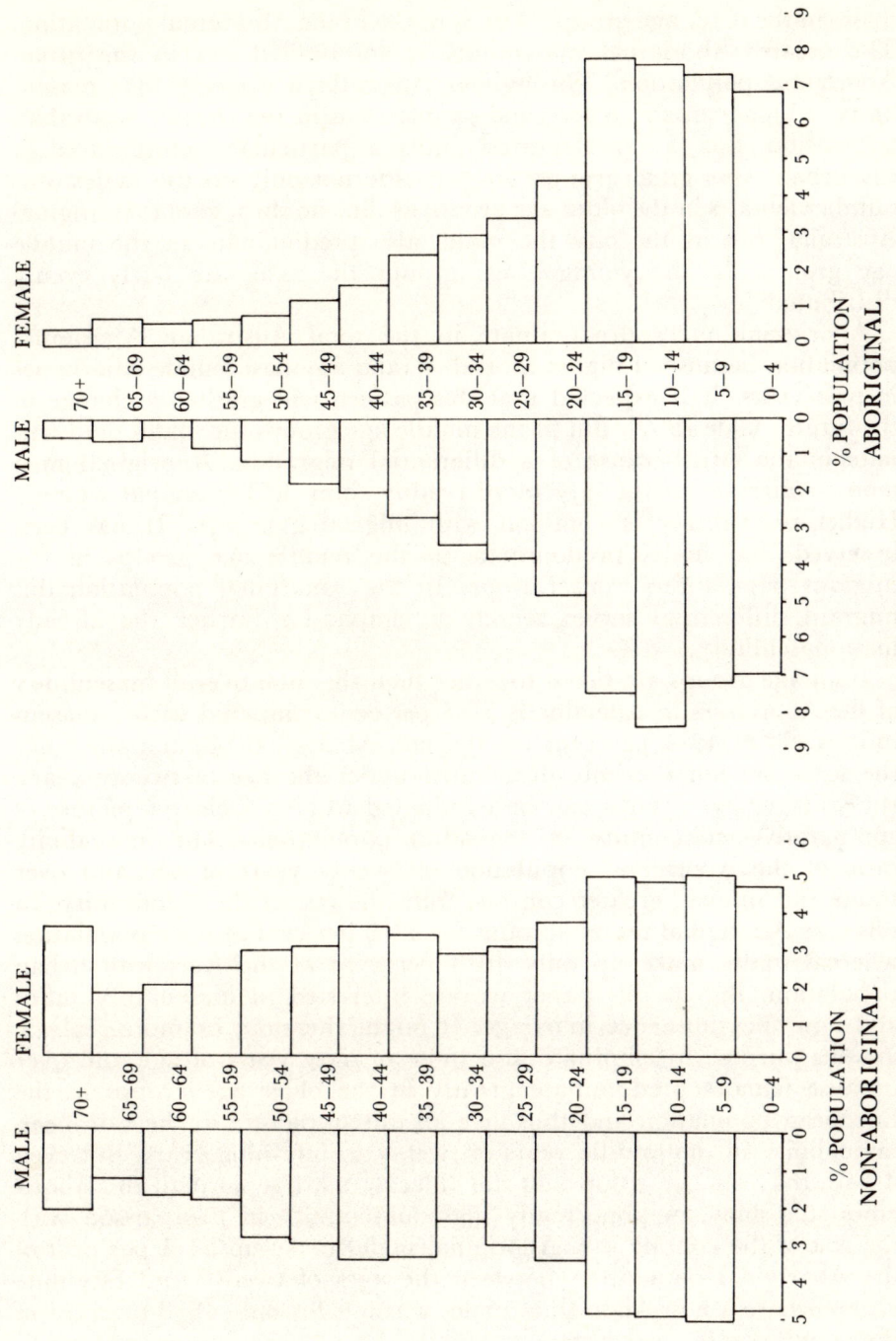

Fig. 1 Age pyramids of the Aboriginal and non-Aboriginal population, Adelaide, 1966

males in the older age groups. This is not so in the Aboriginal population. The greater Aboriginal masculinity is not limited just to the urban Aboriginal population. Throughout Australia it appears that masculinity is higher in the Aboriginal people than in the overall Australian population. But the greater masculinity is particularly emphasized in the urban Aboriginal groups. In Adelaide not only do the males outnumber females in the older age groups as they do throughout Aboriginal Australia, but in the city the males also predominate in the middle age groups. In the younger age groups the sexes are fairly evenly distributed.

Aboriginal males predominate in the total Australian Aboriginal population because of higher mortality rates amongst female Aborigines in past years. It is expected that this pattern will gradually change in the future (Gale 1969). But in the middle age groups the males predominate in the city because of a differential migration. Aboriginal men tend to migrate to the city more readily than do Aboriginal women. Higher masculinity is common with migrating groups. It has been observed that males predominate in the middle age groups in the migrant populations from Europe. In the Aboriginal population this migrant differential serves merely to emphasize further the already high masculinity.

If all age groups are taken together then the total overall masculinity of the Aborigines in Adelaide is 51·7 per cent compared with a masculinity ratio of 49·4 per cent for the non-Aboriginal population. Since the sexes are fairly evenly distributed under the age of twenty years, the younger age groups can be eliminated to give a clearer picture of comparative masculinity in the adult populations. The masculinity ratio of the Aboriginal population of twenty years of age and over stands out in even greater contrast from the rest of the community. In this case Aboriginal males account for 52·8 per cent of their population whereas males make up only 46·3 per cent of the European urban population. But in this paper we are interested in masculinity ratios and how they influence marriage. It might therefore be more realistic for this purpose to eliminate also those of sixty years of age and over because females predominate greatly in the older age groups in the European population and thus give an unreal picture to the European masculinity in the middle years of twenty to fifty-nine years. But even if both the younger group and the older ages are separated, the Aborigines still show an abnormally high masculinity in comparison with the rest of the community. Aboriginal males make up 53·1 per cent of the Aboriginal population between the ages of twenty and fifty-nine years—whereas non-Aboriginal males account for only 48·8 per cent of the population in these ages.

The city has a differential attraction to migrant Aborigines. More males than females come to the city and this is significant in the marriage patterns which emerge in the city. Urbanization has other strong influences on the demographic and marital structure of the city people in comparison with country Aborigines. It not only increases the masculinity ratio but it also influences the general shape of the age pyramid at the younger age levels, especially below the age of ten years.

There is a decline in the birth rate of the Aborigines who move to the city. Figure 1 shows that the age pyramid of Aborigines is contracting at the base. The pyramid no longer has the true triangular shape of rapidly increasing populations: the kind of pyramid drawn for many of the underdeveloped countries. The great bulge in the city Aboriginal groups is not in the nought to five age groups but in the ten to nineteen age groups. These were children born before the Aboriginal migration to the city began. But in the city the birth rate declines and thus the age pyramid contracts at the base. This is not so for country Aborigines. The influence of urban life on the Aboriginal fertility is discussed in more detail in Gale (1969). Suffice it here to say that the Aboriginal population structure in Adelaide is different from that of the general Adelaide population, but it is also different in some aspects from that of the Aboriginal communities in country areas. Urbanization is having a strong influence on Aboriginal demographic structure.

III

There are certainly very real differences between the age and sex composition of the Aboriginal population in Adelaide and the age and sex composition of the non-Aboriginal population in Adelaide. These demographic differences are reflected in the marriage patterns of the two groups. But there are additional factors at work in the Aboriginal community and these further separate their marriage patterns from those of the non-Aboriginal population.

The following figures deal with marriage. Figure 2 is a composite bar diagram showing the marital status of male and female Aborigines at various ages in Adelaide in 1966 compared with the marital status of the general population as described by the 1966 census for Adelaide. The diagram commences at the age of fifteen years for both population groups. The number of married people in either the Aboriginal or the European population under fifteen years of age was too insignificant to appear on such a diagram and has therefore been omitted in this instance.

From Figure 2, a comparison can be made of the relative numbers of Aborigines and Europeans who are single, married, widowed and

312 AUSTRALIAN ABORIGINAL ANTHROPOLOGY

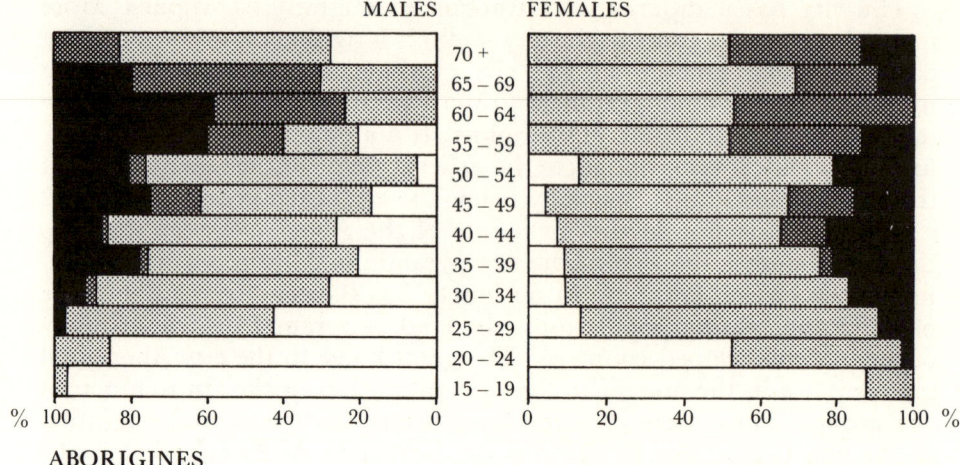

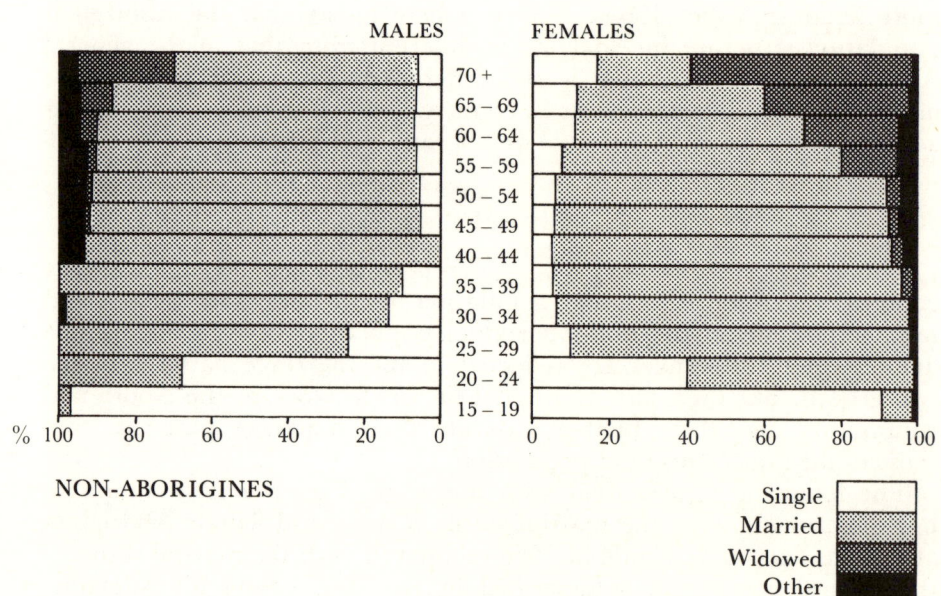

Fig. 2 A comparison of the marital status of Aborigines and non-Aborigines Adelaide, 1966

'other' in each five-year age group. As was evident in Figure 1, the age structure of the two populations is very different. To make a clear comparison of marital status in any one age group, it is therefore necessary to eliminate the overshadowing effect of this basic demographic difference. Thus, the age groups in Figure 2 are all brought to the same value—that is, the same length of bar. Separate bars are drawn for male and female Aborigines and non-Aborigines in each five-year age group. Each age bar is then divided purely on the percentage number of male or female, Aboriginal or non-Aboriginal persons in each marital category. There are thus four bars of equal length for each age group. By eliminating, in this way, the differences in both the total numbers and the relative age variations, it is possible to compare only the marriage differences between the Aboriginal and non-Aboriginal males and females.

There are 1,190 Aborigines and 540,057 non-Aborigines of fifteen years of age and over represented in Figure 2. They are divided into four marital categories of single, married, widowed and 'other'. The category 'single', of course, means those who have never married in both the Aboriginal and the non-Aboriginal groups. The terms 'married' and 'widowed' are also equally clear for both populations. But the category 'other' is not strictly comparable in the two population groups. Separated and divorced persons are included in the category 'other' in both populations as they are clearly defined in the census data. But since the Aboriginal data were obtained from first-hand information and interviews, the material is more precise than that obtained for the general population from the census data. Aborigines living in *de facto* relationships, whether short or long term, have been included in the category 'other'. It is not possible to say where such people in the general population would list themselves on the census forms. Probably the long standing *de facto* relationships would be entered as married, and the short-term or more casual liaisons would be entered as single or separated or whatever the actual legal status might be. For the purpose of this paper, I have placed all Aboriginal extra-marital relationships in the category 'other'. This decision was made because there are few long-term *de facto* relationships among Aborigines in Adelaide. The longest recorded relationship of this kind was between an Aboriginal woman and a European. They had lived together in the city for seven years. But they were an exception. Most extra-marital relationships among Aborigines in the city are of a temporary nature. It is not possible to say where comparable Europeans would class themselves on a census form.

Nevertheless, in spite of this anomaly in classification between the two populations, very significant contrasts can still be seen between the Aboriginal and the general population in Adelaide in 1966.

The first obvious difference between Aborigines and Europeans is in the percentage numbers of normal marriages. Whereas in the general population the majority of people over the age of twenty years is married, this is barely so in the Aboriginal population. In the general population 75 per cent of the individuals over the age of twenty years is married, but only 52 per cent of the Aborigines over the age of twenty years is married. A further 9 per cent of the general population over the age of twenty years is widowed, but only 6 per cent of the Aboriginal population over this age is widowed. Thus the percentage marriage rate among adult Aborigines in the city is considerably less than that among the rest of the community. No anomaly in classification could account for such a difference. Marriage is the expected norm for adult urban Europeans, but it is not so for adult urban Aborigines. It is considerably more difficult for an Aboriginal in the city to find a marriage partner than it is for anyone else. This is the first important influence of urbanization on Aboriginal social structure. It breaks traditional patterns of marriage normality and does not provide for the development of other marriage possibilities.

It follows therefore that there must be a high percentage of single Aborigines in the city. Only 14 per cent of the general population over the age of twenty years is single, but 30 per cent of the Aboriginal population over the age of twenty years is single. Actually the contrast is probably even greater than this. Aborigines who are legally single but who in 1966 were living in a *de facto* relationship or temporary liaison were counted as 'other'. Such persons in the general population would probably count themselves as single for the purpose of the census. Thus in this case the anomaly of the classification only serves to underestimate the contrast rather than to accentuate it.

There is a significantly high percentage, 12 per cent of Aborigines, in the 'other' category of separated, divorced or broken marriages or people constantly changing sexual partners. Only 3 per cent of the general population appears as separated or divorced according to the 1966 census data. This is not a valid comparison because of the different methods used in collecting the data for the two populations. Nevertheless, if complete figures were available for the general population, it is doubtful whether the percentage of aberrant marriage relationships of people over the age of twenty years would be as significantly high as 12 per cent in the general community.

The Aboriginal population of the city is definitely an unstable one from a marital point of view and consequently exhibits a marital pattern quite different from that of the rest of the city population. The relatively low number of 'normal' Aboriginal families in the city is highly significant and is related to the breakdown in the traditional patterns of kinship ties that occurs so abruptly when Aborigines move to the city.

This is in stark contrast to the structure of traditional Aboriginal society where marriage, not necessarily monogamous, but marriage nevertheless, is the rule and single or separated individuals living alone are rare indeed. Even in the decultured groups of Aborigines living in country areas or on reserves, marriage is still the norm. Many of Adelaide's Aborigines have come from old reserves where most other traditional practices are no longer in use. But the arrangement of marriages by older kinsfolk remained a common practice on these reserves even after many other traditional forces had died out.

In the urban environment there are strong forces which break even these residual traditional patterns. The fact that Aborigines can now move so readily away from the reserves to the city lessens the influences of the older people. Young people for whom a marriage is planned may leave the group and 'try their luck in the city', rather than abide by the decisions of their older kinspeople. Furthermore, under the policy of assimilation young people have been actively encouraged to leave rather than stay and marry a tribally chosen partner. Government and mission policies, in encouraging disobedience to tribal elders on marriage laws, have assisted in the breakdown of traditional marriage without giving any replacement. For what alternative does 'assimilation' really offer Aborigines in the city? Often, only the chance to be single or amoral.

The males are particularly affected by these changing social forces. In Adelaide, 41 per cent of Aboriginal males over the age of twenty years is single, whereas only 17 per cent of European males over this age is single. It is much harder for Aboriginal males to find spouses in the city than it is for other males. It is also more difficult for Aboriginal males to find partners than it is for Aboriginal females. But it is also more difficult for Aboriginal girls to find husbands than it is for European girls. Figure 2 shows that in 1966 some 19 per cent of the Aboriginal females over the age of twenty years in Adelaide was single whereas only 11 per cent of other females over the age of twenty years was single.

Thus, all Aborigines in the city find difficulty in acquiring a marriage partner but it is considerably more difficult for Aboriginal males than it is for Aboriginal females. Many Aboriginal girls in the city prefer to marry European men. Indeed this has been their main reason for migrating to the city. One of the probable factors in this situation is that Aboriginal girls in the city have often been better educated than have Aboriginal males. The girls thus seek marriage partners in higher social and economic groups than most Aboriginal males can offer. This factor is not uncommon with depressed cultural groups and has been associated with the rise of 'matriarchy' among the people on the social fringes. The Aboriginal male is thus doubly handicapped in finding a spouse. He is coloured and uneducated. He is socially and often economically unattractive even to Aboriginal girls. Aboriginal girls prefer to marry European men and frequently do so but only occasionally do European girls marry Aboriginal men.

The same pattern, of course, emerges if we look at the marriage statistics. In 1966 some 80 per cent of Adelaide's male population over the age of twenty years was married but only 44 per cent of the Aboriginal male population over this age was married.

Urbanization breaks traditional kin ties for Aborigines with the result that family structures are changed significantly. Many adult Aboriginal males in the city have no home. This is reflected in the high and increasing crime rate among single Aboriginal males. I have heard such an adult Aboriginal say, with a wide grin, he is in gaol because 'Her Majesty's boarding house is the best accommodation available in Adelaide'.

The marriage differential between European and Aboriginal females is not so great. This is partly because Aboriginal girls find spouses more readily than do Aboriginal males and partly because there is a high percentage of widowed European women in the city population. In 1966, some 71 per cent of the European females in Adelaide over the age of twenty years was married and 61 per cent of the Aboriginal females over the age of twenty years was married.

IV

The contrast between the male and female Aboriginal marriage opportunities is shown more clearly in Figure 3 which deals just with Aborigines. Figure 3 is a bar diagram showing a comparison between male and female marriage choices of Aborigines in Adelaide. It depicts the actual unions of Aborigines either legally married or living in *de facto* marriages in 1966. There are 354 married Aborigines and forty-five *de facto* Aborigines shown in this diagram, thus making 100 per cent represent 399 persons.

Certain factors are immediately obvious when examining Figure 3. First, the largest married group in Adelaide consists of Aboriginal females who have married non-Aborigines, either Australian or European 'white' men (i.e. Figure 3, C). Indeed, in 1966 nearly one-quarter of the married Aborigines in Adelaide were females married to European men. A further 5 per cent of the total number of individuals shown on this diagram were Aboriginal females who were living in a marital relationship with European men although not legally married to their partners. Thus some 30 per cent of all the Aborigines who were married or living in *de facto* marriages in Adelaide in 1966 were Aboriginal women with 'white' male partners.

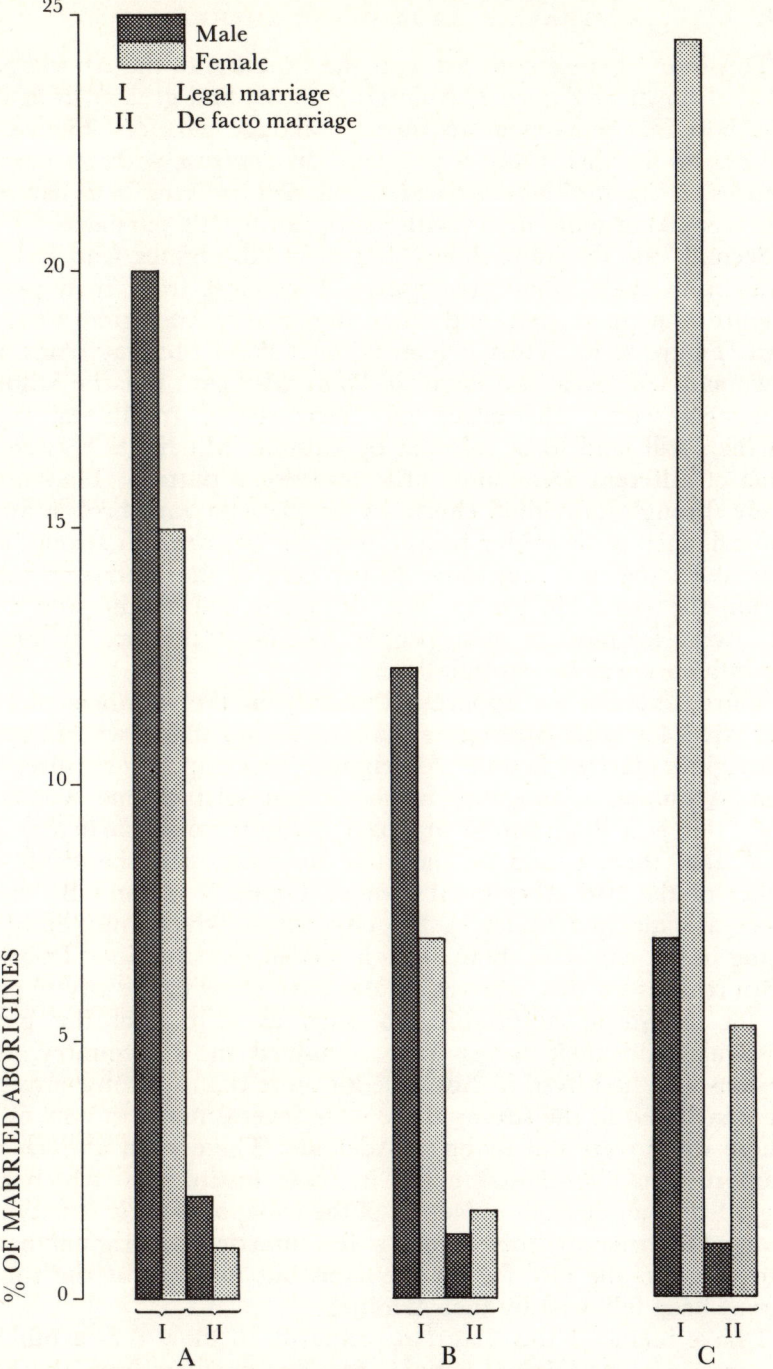

Fig. 3 A comparison of Aboriginal male and female marriage choices in Adelaide

A – Unions in own Aboriginal group
B – Unions with members of other Aboriginal groups
C – Unions with non-Aborigines

This is an obvious contrast with the situation of the Aboriginal male. As was shown in Figure 2, Aboriginal males find greater difficulty than do Aboriginal females in acquiring marriage partners. Figure 3 shows the reason for this. Only 8 per cent (in contrast with 30 per cent for females) of the individuals listed as married or living in *de facto* relationship were Aboriginal males with European female partners.

Second, the diagram shows that even Aborigines who have moved away from their home area marry Aborigines from their own group (Figure 3, A) more frequently than they marry Aborigines from another area (Figure 3, B). Thus, a man born at Point McLeay tends to marry a woman who was also born at Point McLeay. On the whole, these marriages within the group still bear strong traditional influences. Partners still tend to be selected by kinsfolk. Marriages between Aborigines of different areas show little traditional pattern. They tend to be made through individual choice by people who have broken away from the influence of the older people. But kin ties are still strong, as is evidenced by the fact that some 35 per cent of the marriages take place within the same kin group. But, of course, this is the first decade of city living for most of these people. Maybe in the next generation the kin influence will be less significant.

Third, there is an apparent disparity in the numbers of husbands and wives for both Aborigines married within their own kin group and Aborigines married to other Aborigines. This disparity requires explanation. Assuming monogamy in the urban setting, one would expect, since this is a diagram of marriage patterns at a particular point of time, that there would be the same numbers of husbands as wives in either of the two Aboriginal groups. Figure 3 (A and B) shows that there are married males in the city whose wives apparently are not living in the city with them. This is indeed the situation. There are two main reasons for this. Married males have come to the city to go to gaol or for long-term hospitalization—such as to one of the psychiatric hospitals—and their wives have remained in the country. Since all persons who had lived in Adelaide for more than six consecutive months were included in the survey there were several males in gaol or hospital whose wives were not living in Adelaide. There is an abnormally high proportion of Aboriginal males in these institutions—which could be regarded as an obvious reflection of the collapse of their society in recent years. Furthermore there were a few married Aboriginal males who had come to the city for employment but had not at the time of the survey been followed by their families.

I have included this diagram primarily to show that a much higher proportion of Aboriginal females acquires partners from the European community than is possible for Aboriginal males. Intermarriage has

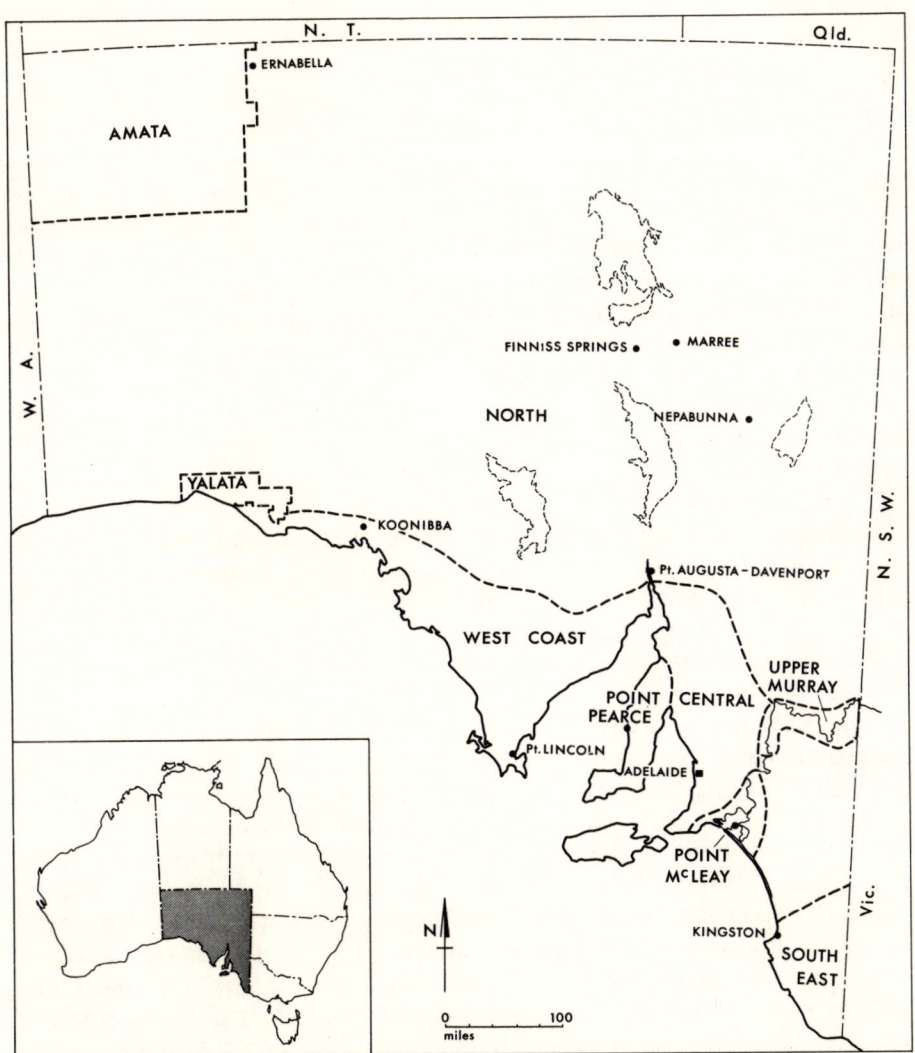

Fig. 4 Regional origins of Adelaide Aborigines

been praised by some administrators as one of the evident successes of the policy of assimilation and the movement of people to the city. But it has been a very one-sided success leading to greater social problems in the long run.

V

Figure 4 is a map of the regional distribution of Aborigines in South Australia. It is drawn on the basis of recognized group identification. Aborigines in Adelaide see themselves as having originated in one or other of the groups shown on the map. There are strong kin feelings within the groups, and certainly in the city, intergroup animosities are evident. Even in Adelaide, Aborigines mix most commonly with members of their own kin group. Social dealings with Aborigines from other areas are less common. Indeed at present Aborigines in the city mix with Europeans as frequently as they mix with Aborigines outside their kin group. But there are signs that this social pattern is changing in Adelaide and that an Aboriginal community which goes beyond kin groupings is now forming.

Figure 5 shows marriage choice on the basis of this group identification. Each column represents one of the main areas outlined in Figure 4. The height of the columns depicts the relative numbers of married Aborigines who have come to Adelaide from each of these areas. It is evident that the greatest numbers of married Aborigines have come from the two oldest reserves of Point McLeay, 29 per cent, and Point Pearce, 22 per cent.

The patterns of marriage choice vary from group to group. The variation is shown by a differential shading in each column. It can be seen that Aborigines from Point McLeay not only form the largest group of married Aborigines in Adelaide but also they choose spouses more frequently from their own group than from the remainder of the Aboriginal community in Adelaide. There are probably two reasons for this. Where the numbers are greatest there is less necessity for people to move out of their own group in search of friendship or marriage partners. Thus from the mere point of larger numbers it is likely that people of Point McLeay origin will form a more tightly knit group within the city than any other Aboriginal group. The Point McLeay people are said, by the other Aborigines in Adelaide, 'to stick together'. But also people from Point McLeay have come from a very old reserve. It was first established in 1859.[4] The people there have had time to become welded together into a definite mixed-blood cultural group, distinct from the old traditional Aboriginal culture of the area but also quite culturally and socially distinct from the European population. Certain

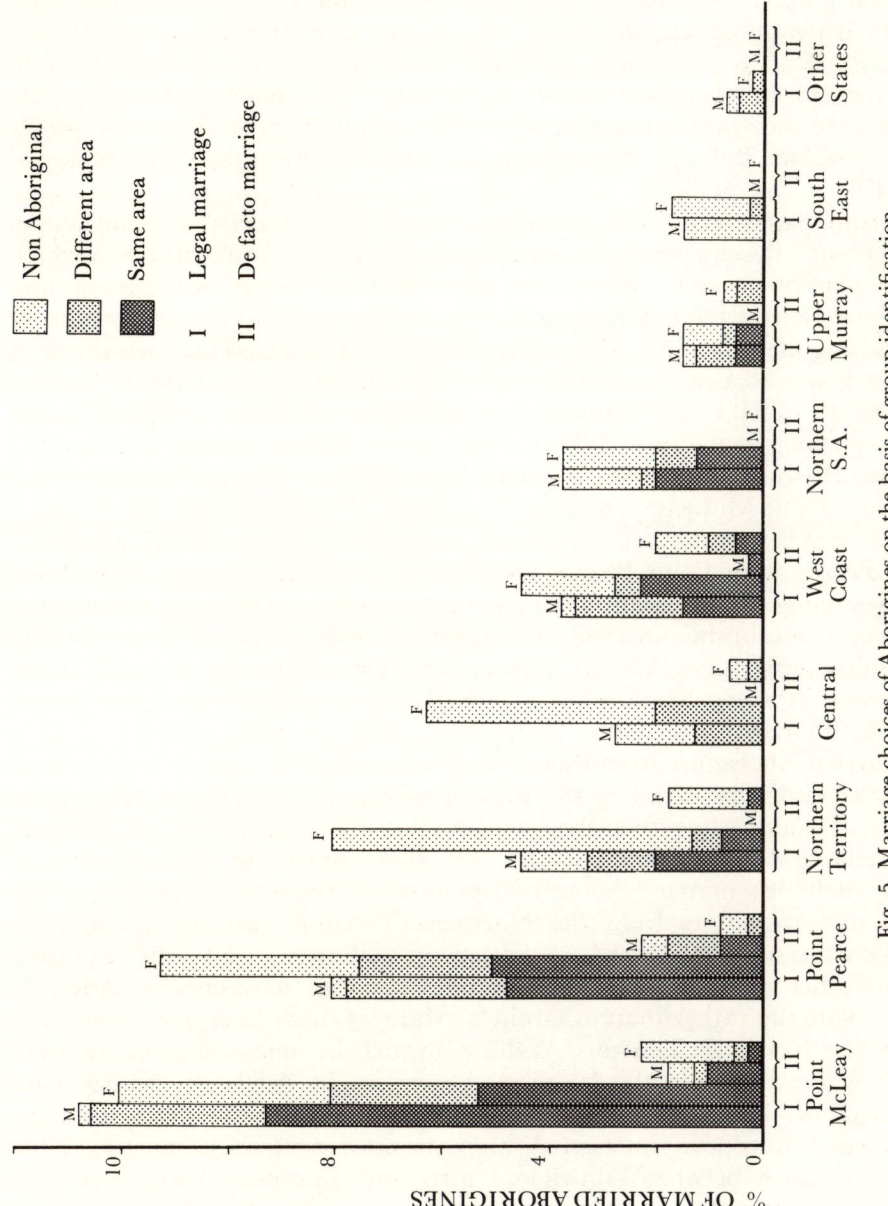

Fig. 5. Marriage choices of Aborigines on the basis of group identification

traditional remnants, such as marriage choice made by the group, have remained and been moulded to their own particular mixed cultural pattern. Though neither truly Aboriginal in the traditional sense nor truly European, the group has formed a distinct culture of its own with elements from both societies. These elements have remained to some extent when they move to the city. They have remained partly because they have moved in large enough numbers to keep alive group association. But they have remained also because they had developed fairly strong patterns already adjusted to European ways of life to a certain extent and therefore adjustable to life in the city. Certain homes of Point McLeay people in Adelaide have become focal centres to which all newcomers and visitors can come and be sure of accommodation. These centres tend to become the heart of the group and the means of keeping members informed of the activities of others. Thus two-thirds of the Point McLeay married people in Adelaide are married to spouses from Point McLeay. Many of these marriages of course took place before they came to the city. Whether this strong group pattern will remain with the next generation is yet to be seen. It is evident, however, that when Point McLeay people marry outside their own group, they marry Europeans slightly more frequently than they marry other Aborigines.

People from Point Pearce form the second largest group of married Aborigines in Adelaide. Though they too have come from a fairly old reserve, established in 1868, they have never developed the same strong, traditionally based kin ties that are evident among the Point McLeay people. It is not therefore surprising that more people from Point Pearce have married Aborigines from other areas or Europeans than have married Aborigines from their own group.

'Territorians' make up the third largest group of married Aborigines in Adelaide. Altogether they account for almost a quarter of the total Adelaide Aboriginal population, but they contribute only 14 per cent of Adelaide's married Aboriginal population because a high proportion of the Aborigines from the Northern Territory are young children. 'Territorian' Aborigines have less group affiliation and kinship ties than any other group in Adelaide. On the whole they have come to Adelaide individually rather than in families. Many of them have been sent south by the Northern Territory Welfare Branch for one reason or another. They are certainly the loneliest Aborigines in Adelaide. Nearly two-thirds of the married Aborigines from the Northern Territory have married European spouses. A high proportion of these marriages has taken place between Aboriginal girls and European men, leaving a large number of single Aboriginal males without potential spouses.

Aborigines born in Adelaide form as large a part of the total Aboriginal population as do those from the Northern Territory but the majority is not yet old enough to be married and therefore does not appear in this diagram. In 1966, some 24 per cent of the total Adelaide Aboriginal population had been born in Adelaide, but a high proportion of these were children under ten years of age born to parents who had migrated to the city in this present decade. Only 9·5 per cent of the married Aborigines had been born in Adelaide. Thus although Aborigines born in the Northern Territory and in Adelaide itself account for almost one-half of the total Adelaide Aboriginal population, they have such a high proportion of children in their midst that together they account for just under one-quarter of the married Aboriginal population.

Aborigines born in Adelaide have little group or kinship identity. Those now old enough to be married, grew up in a period when there were few other Aborigines in the city and they were forced to become assimilated into the general community. Therefore most of the adult Aborigines who were born in Adelaide have now married Europeans. Whether this will happen in the next generation is not so certain. It may well be that in the future there will be sufficient numbers of Aborigines living in strong enough social groupings to enable marriage to take place within the Aboriginal community rather than outside of it. The Aboriginal population is growing rapidly both in numbers and in group solidarity. Aborigines in the city are becoming increasingly conscious of an identity separate from that of the white community. Aborigines who once considered themselves to be completely assimilated are now beginning to identify with other Aborigines. Now that it has become socially acceptable to be known as an Aboriginal and there is a sufficiently large community to identify with, people who once 'passed' as European are now referring to themselves as Aborigines. If this process of group identification continues it is likely that the amount of intermarriage with Europeans will diminish and more Aborigines will marry within their own community in the future. It also means that new Aboriginal social groups are forming which are no longer based on kin affiliation. Furthermore, the population in Adelaide is increasing, not just because of the increasing rate of immigration to the city but also because of the people who were once 'white' but now call themselves Aboriginal. There is thus a social as well as a natural increase in population taking place in the city.

The West Coast people who have come chiefly from Koonibba form the only other significant group in Adelaide. They are a fairly definite group and have closer ties with each other in the city than do any Aborigines other than those from Point McLeay. Certainly they form a closer kin structure than people from Point Pearce and, of course, those from the Northern Territory or Adelaide itself have very little kin identification. This tightness of the kin grouping, in spite of the relatively small numbers, is seen in the fact that a high proportion of the West Coast Aborigines have married within their own group.

The people from the northern part of South Australia have been classified in one group. They do not show as much social cohesion within themselves as do the people from Point McLeay, the West Coast or even the less cohesive Point Pearce Aborigines. They have come from many different areas from Port Augusta north to the Northern Territory border. In actual fact they see themselves as belonging to at least two different groups but other Aborigines in Adelaide refer to them all as the 'northerners'. They have not come from any one area in particular and apart from those who were married before they came to Adelaide they tend to have married either Aborigines from other areas or Europeans.

The remaining groups are quite small. Aborigines in the Upper Murray have quite a definite community and have not felt the economic pressure in that growing part of the state to move out to the city. The same is partly true of the south-east, although there have never been any large concentrations of Aborigines in the south-east since European settlement.

VI

During the 1950s an Aboriginal migration to the cities began. The rate of this migration is now increasing annually. At the present rate, more than half of South Australia's Aborigines will be living in urban areas by the next decade. The number of children being born in the cities is increasing. These children are growing up without a knowledge of the patterns of behaviour or social organization which their parents knew on the reserves. City living tends to break down existing patterns of social behaviour. The Aborigines who have moved into Adelaide in the largest numbers have been more able to retain some of their kin ties. Whether they will be able to maintain these ties in the future is not yet clear. They may in time come to identify with the larger but not necessarily kin-related Aboriginal community which is developing in the city in spite of a large number of intergroup conflicts.

Urbanization has precipitated a definite change in social structure and therefore in marriage patterns. There have been a number of social consequences resulting from this breakdown in past patterns. Not all of these have been to the good. The city speeds up the rate of assimilation of Aboriginal girls into the general community, but, at the same time, it increases the number of single males.

NOTES

1. For earlier material on South Australia and on Adelaide in relation to Aborigines and those of Aboriginal descent, see Berndt and Berndt (1951). But also see the following for background material to this study: Gale (1963:414-22, 1964:101-14) and Inglis (1963:423-8, 1964:115-32).

I wish to acknowledge the help of Mrs Alison Brookman who assisted with the collection and tabulation of data, and Max Foale who did all the cartographic work. The Australian Institute of Aboriginal Studies gave financial support for the original fieldwork.

2. Eighty-three per cent of South Australia has less than 10 inches rainfall per annum (*Commonwealth Year Book*, No. 51, 1965).

3. Whyalla population, 22,126 (1966 census).

4. Early material on Point McLeay is noted in Berndt and Berndt (1951): their combined research in this area was carried out between 1941 and 1944, although R. M. Berndt commenced work there in 1939.

REFERENCES

BERNDT, R. M. and C. H. 1951 *From Black to White in South Australia*. Cheshire, Melbourne.

GALE, F. 1963 Aborigines in South Australia. In *Australian Aboriginal Studies* (H. Sheils, ed.). Oxford University Press, Melbourne.

——— 1964 Administration as Guided Assimilation (South Australia). In *Aborigines Now* (M. Reay, ed.). Angus and Robertson, Sydney.

——— 1969 A Changing Aboriginal Population. In *Settlement and Encounter* (F. Gale and G. H. Lawton, eds). Oxford University Press, Melbourne.

INGLIS, J. 1963 Aborigines in Adelaide. In *Australian Aboriginal Studies* (H. Sheils, ed.). Oxford University Press, Melbourne.

——— 1964 Dispersal of Aboriginal Families in South Australia (1860-1960). In *Aborigines Now* (M. Reay, ed.). Angus and Robertson, Sydney.

The Contributors

The Editor

RONALD M. BERNDT, Foundation Professor of Anthropology in the University of Western Australia, was appointed to this Chair in 1963. Having come from the Department of Anthropology, University of Sydney, he was appointed, first as a Senior Lecturer in 1956 and then as a Reader, to develop anthropological teaching and research in Western Australia. He studied at the University of Sydney (under Professor A. P. Elkin), and at the London School of Economics and Political Science (under Professor Raymond Firth) where he obtained his doctorate in 1955.

He has carried out extensive field research in Aboriginal Australia since 1939, and has also worked in New Guinea between 1951 and 1953. He is a member of, and has held office in, a number of professional associations. He was President of Section F (Anthropology) during the 1962 A.N.Z.A.A.S. Congress; President of the Australian Branch of the Association of Social Anthropologists, 1962-64, and first Chairman of the Australian Association of Social Anthropologists (1969-71); and past-President and Vice-President of the Anthropological Society of Western Australia. He has been a member of the Interim Council and then of the Council of the Australian Institute of Aboriginal Studies and currently of its Executive Committee, and Chairman of its Social Anthropology Advisory Committee, and a member of the Social Science Research Council of Australia. He is also a member of the newly set up research committee of the Commonwealth Office of Aboriginal Affairs, a member of the Aboriginal Arts Advisory Committee of the Australian Council for the Arts, an Honorary Associate of the Western Australian Museum and a Vice-President of the Royal Society of Western Australia, etc. He has also held a number of fellowships: e.g. as a Nuffield Fellow in 1953-54, a Carnegie Corporation Travelling Fellow in 1955-56, also a Leverhulme award in 1955, etc. He has been a recipient (jointly with his wife) of the Edgeworth David Medal for Anthropology (Royal Society of New South Wales) in 1950, and of the Wellcome Medal (Royal Anthropological Institute) for 1958, and has participated in a Wenner-Gren symposium at Burg Wartenstein. He has published a number of volumes and scientific articles, both jointly with his wife, and separately, and is general editor of *Anthropological Forum*.

CONTRIBUTORS
(as they appear in this volume)

A. P. ELKIN, C.M.G., Ph.D., M.A., D.Litt. (Hon.) (Sydney), is Emeritus Professor of Anthropology in the University of Sydney. Professor Elkin became lecturer-in-charge at the Department of Anthropology, University of Sydney in 1933; it had been established in 1926. He was appointed to the Chair in 1934 and retired in 1956. A measure of the tremendous impact Elkin has had on Australian Anthropology is indicated in his *Festschrift* volume (*Aboriginal Man in Australia*, edited by R. M. and C. H. Berndt, 1965); reference should be made, especially, to Chapter 1, entitled 'A. P. Elkin—the man and the anthropologist'.

Professor Elkin has held office in, and been a member of, a large number of professional bodies: to mention only a few, the Australian National Research Council, the Royal Society of New South Wales, the Australian Branch of the Association of Social Anthropologists, the Social Science Research Council of Australia, the Australian Institute of Aboriginal Studies, A.N.Z.A.A.S., the Pacific Science Council, etc. He has been editor of the journal *Oceania* since 1933, and founder of *Archaeology and Physical Anthropology in Oceania* (1966); a Trustee of the Australian Museum, since 1946, and President (1961-68).

Professor Elkin has carried out intensive research in many parts of Aboriginal Australia and in the Western Highlands of New Guinea. He has published a large number of articles and monographs, but is probably best known for *The Australian Aborigines: How to Understand Them* (first published in 1938), *Studies in Australian Totemism* (*Oceania* Monograph, No. 2, 1933), and *Aboriginal Men of High Degree* (1945). He has been the recipient of many honours: e.g. the Medal of the Royal Society of New South Wales (1949) and that Society's James Cook Medal (1955), the Mueller Medal of A.N.Z.A.A.S. (1957) and the Herbert E. Gregory Medal of the Bernice P. Bishop Museum (1957).

CATHERINE H. BERNDT did her initial training in Anthropology in New Zealand and later took her Master's degree at the Department of Anthropology, University of Sydney, where (with her husband) she taught and carried out research. She studied for her doctorate at the London

School of Economics and Political Science, and eventually came to Perth in Western Australia where her husband was appointed in 1956. Since then she has held various teaching and research appointments, through the University of Western Australia and the Australian Research Grants Committee (as Senior and Junior Fellow).

With her husband, she has carried out extensive field research in Aboriginal Australia since 1941, and has also worked in the Eastern Highlands of New Guinea. She has held office in and/or been a member of various associations, particularly, Section F (Anthropology) of A.N.Z.A.A.S., the Australian Institute of Aboriginal Studies, the Anthropological Society of Western Australia, the Australian Branch of the Association of Social Anthropologists and the newly established Australian Association of Social Anthropologists, and is an Hon. Associate of the Western Australian Museum, etc.

Dr Berndt has held several awards, most notably a British Council Grant (1953-54), and an Ohio State Fellowship (1951-52), and a Winifred Cullis Award (1954), both from the International Federation of University Women. With her husband, she has been a recipient of the Edgeworth David Medal for Anthropology (Royal Society of New South Wales) in 1950; and she was awarded the Percy Smith Medal, University of Otago, New Zealand, in 1950.

She has published a number of books and articles, both jointly with her husband and separately.

WARREN SHAPIRO, currently Assistant Professor of Anthropology at Livingston College in Rutgers University at New Jersey, took his Ph.D. degree at the Australian National University, Canberra, in 1969. Prior to that Professor Shapiro carried out eighteen months of field research in north-eastern Arnhem Land, mainly on Elcho Island and at associated bush camps, during the period 1965-67. His contribution in this volume is based on that research. Commencing to publish in 1966, he has now produced a dozen contributions in major anthropological journals. His primary focus in theoretical terms is on kinship and marriage. He is planning to carry out further research in Aboriginal Australia.

ARAM A. YENGOYAN is an Associate Professor of Anthropology in the University of Michigan, Ann Arbor. He took his Ph.D. at the University of Chicago.

During 1960-62, and in 1965 Professor Yengoyan carried out field research among the Mandaya of eastern Mindanao, in the Philippines, and during 1970-71 is continuing research in Capiz, Western Visayas. In 1966-67, under a grant from the Australian Institute of Aboriginal Studies, Yengoyan worked among the Bidjandjara (Pitjandjara) of the Western Desert of Australia, and part of the material collected then provides the basis of his contribution to this volume. During late 1970 he made a further supplementary field trip to the same area.

Professor Yengoyan's anthropological interests focus primarily on problems relevant to demography, ecology and social structure. Among his various papers is his contribution to *Man The Hunter* (Lee and DeVore, eds).

T. G. H. STREHLOW is Professor in Australian Linguistics at the University of Adelaide. Born at Hermannsburg, Central Australia, he later studied at the University of Adelaide where he gained his M.A. degree. Between 1931 and 1934 he carried out linguistic and cultural research in Central Australia under the auspices of the (then) Australian National Research Council. Later he worked among Aborigines in the Commonwealth administration from 1936-42, first as a patrol officer and later as a Deputy Director of Native Affairs for Central Australia. He was an instructor in the School of Civil Affairs, Duntroon. Returning to academic life in 1946 at the University of Adelaide, he also held the position of a Research Fellow at the Australian National University (1949-51), did post-graduate study in the University of London, and lectured extensively in England and on the Continent. Since then, Strehlow has carried out long periods of field research among the Aranda and adjacent groups, and has held grants from the Australian Institute of Aboriginal Studies. He is also a member of the Australian Institute of Aboriginal Studies' Advisory Committees on Social Anthropology and Linguistics.

He has published a number of scientific papers on the Australian Aborigines, especially on the Aranda. His *Aranda Phonetics and Grammar* (*Oceania* monograph series, 1944) and *Aranda Traditions* (1947) are well known. But he has also worked on and published *Testamenta Ljaṭinja, Aŋkatja Araṇḍauṇa Kṇaṭiwumala* (1956) and *Ljelintjamea-Pepa Lutherarinja* (with P. A. Scherer, 1964). His large volume *Songs of Central Australia* is in the course of publication, and his *Journey to Horseshoe Bend* (1969) records the last journey of his father, Carl Strehlow of *Die Aranda- und Loritja-Stämme* fame.

NANCY D. MUNN is currently on the staff of the Department of Sociology and Anthropology, the Commonwealth of Massachusetts, University of Massachusetts, Amherst. She took her M.A. degree at Indiana and her doctorate at the Australian National University. Her initial field research was carried out in 1956-58 among the Wailbri (Walbiri) and was supported by a Fulbright award and by the Australian National University. Later, in 1964-65, Dr Munn worked at Areyonga in Central Australia under a grant from the Australian Institute of Aboriginal

Studies. Her present contribution is based on these two periods. She has published several scientific papers in, for example, *Aborigines Now* (M. Reay, ed.), and in various journals, focusing primarily on symbolism, and participated in a Wenner-Gren symposium at Burg Wartenstein on that topic.

MARIE REAY is a Senior Fellow in the Department of Anthropology and Sociology, Australian National University. For some years she was associated with the Department of Anthropology, University of Sydney, where she took her Master's degree. She also carried out field research among part-Aborigines in New South Wales, and then went to Papua to study the Orokaiva. Later, under the auspices of the Australian National University, she again went to New Guinea to work among the Kuma of the Central Highlands. One of the publications resulting from this research was *The Kuma: freedom and conformity in the New Guinea Highlands* (1959); and she was awarded the Ph.D. degree from the Australian National University. She has published a number of scientific papers on New Guinea and on Aboriginal Australia. Since the publication of *The Kuma*, she has made many field excursions to New Guinea. In 1964 she edited *Aborigines Now;* and the fieldwork on which her present contribution (to this volume) is based covered twenty months during 1959-62 and was sponsored by the Australian National University. She is a member of the Advisory Committee on Social Anthropology for the Australian Institute of Aboriginal Studies.

KENNETH MADDOCK was appointed Lecturer in Anthropology at the Macquarie University (N.S.W.) in 1969; before that, he was a Junior Lecturer in Anthropology at the University of Auckland (1963) and a Research Student at the Department of Anthropology, University of Sydney (1964-68). He holds the degree of LL.B. from the University of New Zealand, a Master's from Auckland and a Ph.D. from Sydney.

His field research, extending from 1964 to 1970, has been focused on the Beswick Reserve and neighbouring areas of the Northern Territory, and has been supported by the Australian Institute of Aboriginal Studies. He has published several papers on Aboriginal kinship and ritual in the journals *Mankind, Oceania* and *Anthropological Forum*, and took part in a Wenner-Gren Symposium at Burg Wartenstein in 1968.

NICOLAS PETERSON read Anthropology and Archaeology at King's College, Cambridge. At present he is a post-graduate research student in the Department of Anthropology, University of Sydney, where he is preparing a Ph.D. thesis based on his Australian Aboriginal fieldwork. His anthropological research, for several years now, has been focused on the mainland opposite Elcho Island in north coastal Arnhem Land, under the auspices of the Australian Institute of Aboriginal Studies. Also, under this same body, he has worked at Yuendumu (on which his present contribution is based); he has served as an anthropological adviser to the Australian Institute of Aboriginal Studies' Film Unit, and to the Commonwealth Office of Aboriginal Studies in a Western Desert survey. He is commencing to publish his field material.

RONALD M. BERNDT. See under entry for editor of this volume.

HELMUT PETRI and GISELA PETRI-ODERMANN. Dr Petri is Professor and Director of the Institut für Völkerkunde, Universität zu Köln, and with his wife (Dr Petri-Odermann) was for some time associated with the Frankfurt Museum. In 1938-39, Professor Petri accompanied the Leo Frobenius expedition to north-west Australia, and one outcome of that research was his volume *Sterbende Welt in Nordwestaustralien* (1954). After World War II, Professor Petri and his wife began a series of revisits to the north-west Kimberleys, concentrating primarily in the Anna Plains-La Grange-Broome area, in 1954-55, 1960, 1963, 1966 and 1969. Both have published a number of scientific papers and other works. Professor Petri has concentrated on mythology and ritual, as well as on social and cultural change. He has been responsible, as one of the contributors, for Nevermann, Worms and Petri, *Die Religionen der Südsee und Australiens* (Kohlhammer, 1968). His section, which constitutes over half of that volume, is under the authorship of himself and Father Ernest Worms. In fact, the full responsibility of writing fell on his shoulders on the death of Fr Worms in 1963. With Dr Petri-Odermann, he has published (in 1964) 'Nativismus und Millenarismus im gegenwärtigen Australien' in the E. Jensen *Festschrift*.

ROBERT TONKINSON obtained his Bachelor's degree with Honours in 1962 and his Master's in 1966. His main field research in Aboriginal Australia was carried out under the auspices of the Department of Anthropology, University of Western Australia, while holding various grants. After earlier work among part-Aborigines in the South-West, he commenced work at Jigalong; he had three field periods there between 1963 and 1965, and was also able to visit other sections of the Western Desert. In 1969-70 he returned to this area under a grant from the Australian Institute of Aboriginal Studies.

He also carried out field research in the New Hebrides (between 1966-67) in the re-location programme of Professor Homer Barnett, and was subsequently a Research Assistant at the University of Oregon (1966-68) and a Visiting Instructor in the same institution (1968-69). Currently, he is a graduate fellow at the University of British Columbia, Vancouver, where he is working on Aboriginal material to prepare a

Ph.D. thesis. He is commencing to publish his field results: a detailed monograph on his New Hebrides research has appeared (1968), and an article (with C. P. Mountford) in *Anthropological Forum* (1969).

JEREMY P. M. LONG is an Assistant Director of Research with the Commonwealth Office of Aboriginal Affairs, Canberra. He holds the degree of B.A. (Hons) from Sydney, and was primarily employed, for some years, with the Welfare Branch of the Northern Territory Administration—initially as a Patrol Officer and Settlement Superintendent, and later as a Research and Investigation Officer. In 1965-66, as a Research Fellow under the auspices of the Social Science Research Council's research project on Aborigines (under the direction of Professor Charles Rowley), he made a survey of Aboriginal settlements in eastern Australia (this report was published by the Australian National University Press in 1970). He has also published articles dealing with aspects of Aboriginal traditional life and current problems in *Oceania* and in other journals, and was a contributor to *Aborigines Now* (edited by Marie Reay).

FAY GALE is a Lecturer in Geography at the University of Adelaide. She took an Honours degree in Geography in 1954 and was the first Ph.D. student to graduate from that Department (under the supervision of Sir Grenfell Price), in 1962. During 1957-60 she carried out research among people of Aboriginal descent in rural areas of South Australia, and in 1964 was appointed a post-doctoral research fellow at the University of Adelaide and commenced her study of urban Aborigines: she became a Lecturer in 1966.

She has contributed to several volumes: for example, *Aborigines Now* (M. Reay, ed.), *Australian Aboriginal Studies* (H. Sheils, ed.), and *Settlement and Encounter* (which she also edited with Professor Graham Lawton). Currently, she has just completed her volume on urban Aborigines, based on her South Australian research.

Index

Anthropology: and research 3, 4, 70, 92, 248; past 19-26; publication of field notes 7, 22, 23, 25, 26, 30
Assimilation policies 5, 106, 255, 273
Australian Institute of Aboriginal Studies 1, 2, 4, 21, 22, 26n, 29, 91n, 160n, 198n, 214n, 290n, 325n; 1961 Conference 2, 5, 19; General Meeting, *1968* 29
Australian National Research Council 20, 22
Australian School of Pacific Administration 23
Authority: and leadership 10, 26, 105, 107-138, 135, 152, 289; and local groups 99, 110, 111-112, 113-115, 122; and social control 10, 11, 39-40, 49, 86, 92, 93, 101, 126, 130, 132-133, 138n, 146, 151, 158-159, 212, 213, 214n, 216-246; based on religious foundations 13, 92-140, 151, 152, 153, 157-160, 216-218, 219, 220, 221, 222, 229, 239, 242, 243, 264, 265, 270-271; change in punishment due to contact 264, 266; councils 48, 109, 111, 112, 118; infliction of capital punishment by 105, 111-114, 117-127, 130, 137n, 138n; weakened in contact situation 41, 106, 107, 113, 125-126, 135, 136n, 137n, 138n, 238, 239. *See also* Leaders; Social control; Rituals

Barnes, J. A. 25, 31, 67n
Barrett, M. J. 211
Basedow, H. 20, 26n, 71, 137n
Beckett, J. 1, 56
Beings, creative/mythical/totemic 11-13, 16, 94-95, 174-198, 222-227, 262, 263, 280, 281; and contemporary behaviour 11, 130, 132, 133, 168, 216, 219; and establishment of moral order 95, 123, 126, 127, 128, 132-133, 150-152, 156, 216-246; and sacred sites 94, 95, 97, 98, 102, 103, 113, 114, 115, 116, 117, 130, 133, 134, 137n, 138n, 139n, 141, 143, 144, 146, 147, 148, 149, 150, 151, 152, 160n, 201, 202, 204, 216, 217, 227, 277, 280, 285; and symbolism 117, 133-134, 141-163, 217, 218, 223-232, 235; as creators of fire 174-198, of life 132, 134, 142, 149, 216, 217, 277, 281, of natural environment 98, 141, 142, 143, 145, 147, 148, 150, 151, 216, 262, 263, 272; associated with women's ceremonies 154, 166-172; personal identification with 110-111, 114, 127, 139n, 144, 146-159, 217, 238, 283; sickness due to 281, 282, 283; transmutation of 11, 141-163, 176, 202, 217, 218; travelling 12, 16, 94, 95, 103, 104, 134, 143, 147, 148, 149, 151, 154, 155, 201, 202, 222-232, 259, 262, 263, 265, 267, 272, 277. *See also* Dream-spirits; Myth
Berndt, R. M. and/or C. H. 1, 5, 7-11, 13, 14, 17, 18, 25, 26n, 30, 36, 39, 48, 63, 67n, 68n, 71, 85, 99, 112, 160n, 161n, 166, 167, 170, 171, 172n, 197, 217-219, 222-224, 226, 227, 231, 235, 243, 248, 249, 267, 290n, 291n, 298, 325n; chapter by C. H. B. 29-50; chapter by R. M. B. 216-247
Betrothal 7, 8, 9, 34, 39-49, 53, 61, 63, 126, 209-213; and kinship 39, 40, 200, 211-213; bestowal ritual 8, 62, 63, 200-214; blocking/cancellation of 40, 43, 212; changes in, following outside contact 41,

48; mother-in-law bestowal 8, 9, 52, 62-66, 68n, 214n; role of individual women in 49. *See also* Marriage
Birdsell, J. 84
British Association for the Advancement of Science 20
Brookman, A. 325n
Brown, A. R. *see* Radcliffe-Brown, A. R.
Burridge, K. O. L. 291n

Calley, M. J. C. 1
Capell, A. 23
Ceremonies *see* Rites
Chaseling, W. 62
Circumcision *see* Rites: initiation
Clan(s) and linguistic units, north-eastern Arnhem Land 8, 25, 33, 34-39, 42, 43, 54, 99; totemic *see* Totemism. *See also* Local groups
Coate, H. H. 24
Conflict: and marriage 40-42, 48, 49, 200, 211-213; resolution of, in ritual 200-214; with Europeans 107, 108, 125, 135. *See also* Authority; Disputes; Fighting
Councils *see* Authority
Curr, E. M. 19, 192

Davies, H. Whitridge 136n
Dawson, J. 197
Demography 9, 29, 31, 32, 71-91, 96, 97, 98, 107, 130, 136n, 172, 202, 278, 307; and polygyny *see* Polygyny; birth rates 73, 74, 77, 78, 308, 311; census 29, 72, 73, 76, 77, 90, 99, 100, 136n, 307; death rates 74, 75, 78-81, 308, 310; growth in population 30, 32, 74, 78, 79, 80, 90; infant mortality 30, 73-75, 78-81, 90; marriage rates 73, 76, 77, 87-90, 98, 278, 311, 312, 314, 316; sex ratios 73-74, 76, 88, 300, 301, 308-312
Disputes 119, 121-127, 133, 136n-137n, 138n, 166, 234, 240; about women 121-122, 211, 213, 214. *See also* Authority; Conflict; Fighting
Dogs 38-39
Douglas, M. 162n
Douglas, W. 268
Dream-spirits: and contact with home territory 280-290; change in concept of 289; in ritual 283-288. *See also* Beings
Dreaming/Dreamtime 10, 11, 16, 84, 144, 145, 177, 216, 221, 223, 244, 251, 259, 262, 263, 265-267, 272

Dreams 11, 16, 145, 166, 169, 170, 171; and dream-spirits 280-290; and revelation of sacred objects 280, 281, 284; ancestral 11, 144, 145; as source of songs 171, 284
Dunning, R. W. 67n
Durkheim, E. 3, 157, 165, 246n

Economy: and availability of water 72, 83, 84-85, 93-97, 99, 101, 104, 111, 228-229, 233-234, 268; changes following outside contact 5-6, 72, 76, 83-84, 89, 90, 111, 130, 134, 165-166, 249-250, 253, 254, 255, 256, 269, 270. *See also* Payments
Eliade, M. 132, 139n
Elkin, A. P. 1, 7, 8, 19, 53, 55-58, 62, 71, 85, 86, 251, 290n; chapter by 19-28
Elopement 34, 35, 44, 48, 49, 86, 88, 172. *See also* Betrothal; Marriage
English, H. B. and Ava C. 55
Epstein, A. L. 67n

Fighting/Feuding, traditional 31, 36, 40, 42, 49, 103, 108, 110, 116, 117, 118, 119, 120, 121, 123, 124-126, 130, 132, 138n, 170. *See also* Authority; Conflict; Disputes
Fire: mythically linked with death 197, 198; myths re acquisition of 11, 12, 174-198, 224
Foale, M. 325n
Fox, D. C. 275
Frazer, J. G. 192-194
Freud, S. 174
Fry, H. K. 139n

Gale, F. 1, 17, 325n; chapter by 305-325
Geddes, W. R. 1
Genealogies, collection of 7, 23-25, 29-49, 59, 60, 65, 66, 88, 97, 98, 101, 298, 299
Gifts *see* Payments
Goodale, J. 53, 61-63, 67n, 214
Gould, R. A. 1, 160n, 161n, 245n

Hallowell, A. I. 162n
Hamilton, A. 63
Hart, C. W. M. 63, 214
Hiatt, L. 1, 9, 10, 53, 57, 61, 63, 70, 84, 128, 161n, 213, 214
Hilliard, W. M. 304n
Horde (Band) 10, 16, 56. *See also* Local groups
Howitt, A. W. 19, 20, 26n, 190, 191, 197

Inglis, J. 325n

Jolly, A. H. 24
Jones, F. L. 74
Josselin de Jong, P. E. de 59

Kaberry, P. 23
Kinship 7-8, 23-26, 30, 34-49, 51-68, 75, 82-88, 90, 97, 98, 99, 100, 101, 108, 109, 118, 149, 152-153, 155, 156, 161n, 167, 169, 170, 182, 200, 202, 209-214, 280; and betrothal 7, 34, 39-49, 98, 200, 210-214; and establishing relationship with strangers 11, 84, 86, 164-172; avoidance or constraint in 56-58, 62, 63, 121, 126, 221, 224, 230, 241; effects of urbanization on 318-324; in contact situation 25, 84, 136n; systems 7, 25, 26, 30-31, 39, 135n, 278; terms, terminology 23, 24, 37, 54, 55, 58, 59, 65, 66, 85, 87
Klaatsch, H. 20

Land: and group mobility 96, 97; and natural resources 6-7, 82-84, 92-94, 95-97, 99, 103, 111, 124, 134, 136n, 146, 233-234, 245, 246n, 268, 287-288; attachment to 6, 11, 16, 133-135, 145, 146, 277; influence of Indonesian traders 32; loss of, in contact situation 6, 7, 17, 97, 135, 152; maintaining contact with, through dream-spirits 16, 277, 287; ownership/inheritance of 6, 16, 18, 83, 84, 97, 130, 145, 146, 147, 148, 149, 150, 151, 157, 161n, 233, 258; personal identification with 11, 134-135, 146-148; social and religious links with 6-7, 16, 53, 82-84, 92-98, 103, 109, 110, 130, 132, 134, 145, 146, 147, 148, 161n, 233, 277, 287. *See also* Economy; Myth; Ritual/ceremonial centres; Territories; Totemism
Leach, E. R. 57, 61
Leaders/leadership: camp, clan, local group 99, 101, 106, 108, 109-112, 116, 119, 128, 129; geographical range of 109, 110, 114-115, 119, 122, 124, 129, 138n; in contact situation 106-108, 135, 136n-137n, 256-258, 260, 265-266, 270-272; in women's ceremonies 167; personal qualities of 108, 109, 115, 116, 123; punishment of 116-118, 120, 123-127; religious/ritual 26, 105-120, 123, 127, 129, 135, 167, 204, 206, 229, 236, 238, 251, 260, 265, 270-274, 288, 289; status of 111, 118, 119. *See also* Authority
Lévi-Strauss, C. 3, 11-13, 165, 174, 177, 178, 189, 235
Livingstone, F. B. 24
Local groups 10, 16, 53, 56, 57, 64, 65, 79, 82-85, 98, 101, 102, 103, 110, 249, 252, 254, 261, 274, 278; and economy 101, 102; and residence patterns 9, 82-85, 97, 100, 146, 147, 157, 218; effect of contact on 249, 251, 254, 261, 274, 289; structure/size of 81, 83, 90, 146
Local organization: breakdown of 9, 10, 72, 81, 83, 289; traditional pattern of 9, 10, 81-85
Localities: Adelaide 6, 17, 305-325; Amata (Musgrave Park) 70-91, 299; Amoonguna 105; Angas Downs 71, 75, 297, 298, 300; Anna Plains 250, 254, 261, 267-269; Areyonga 71, 82, 160n, 292-304; Arnhem Land 5, 6, 7, 8, 12, 17, 29-49, 52-67, 174-189, 302; Balgo 13, 14, 15, 16, 222, 224, 239, 245n; Beagle Bay 23, 253; Beswick 23, 174-199; Birrundudu 14, 223, 245n; Borroloola 17, 164-173; Broome 24, 245n, 250, 254, 260, 261, 266, 268; Central Australia 10, 11, 20, 93-140; Daly River 12; Derby 14, 24, 268, 269; Elcho Island 7, 32-36, 38, 43, 44n, 48, 51-69, 302, 303; Ernabella 15, 70-91, 160n, 161n, 304n; Gove 30, 32; Groote Eylandt 16, 60, 67n, 70, 292, 298-301; Haasts Bluff 292-304; Halls Creek 239, 245n; Hermannsburg 125, 135; Hooker Creek 106, 107, 201-215, 295, 296; Jay Creek 109, 110; Jigalong 10, 13, 14, 16, 245n, 256, 261, 263, 266, 272, 278-291; La Grange 13-17, 23, 224, 245n, 250-276; Laverton 23, 288; Lombadina 260, 275; Maningrida 33, 34, 302; Marble Bar 255, 257, 261, 283; Milingimbi 30, 31, 33, 35, 38, 302, 303; Mt Davies 82-84; Mt Margaret 24, 86; Mulga Park 70-91; Musgrave Ranges 26n, 72, 86, 87, 89; Myroodah 260, 261, 263, 265, 266; Oenpelli 11, 12, 20, 33, 180, 183; Ooldea 9, 71, 298; Papunya 292-304; Petermann Ranges 82, 83, 100, 104, 292; Point McLeay 320, 322-324; Point Pearce 320, 322-324; Port Augusta 93, 94; Port Hedland 255, 257, 260, 268,

272, 288; Rawlinson Range 82, 83, 100; Roper River 23, 33, 187; Simpson Desert 93-95, 101; Wallal 250, 254, 268; Warburton Range 71, 82, 245n; Warrabri 107, 295, 296; Wave Hill 12, 223, 245n; Yirrkalla 24, 29, 30, 32, 33, 35-38, 41, 43, 48, 301-303; Yuendumu 15, 106, 107, 160n, 200-215, 292-304

Long, J. P. M. 1, 16, 17; chapter by 292-304

Lucich, P. 26n

Luckmann, T. 159

McConnel, U. 57, 187

McKelsen, K. 273

McLeod, D. 14, 255, 256, 258, 266, 272

Maddock, K. 1, 11, 12; chapter by 174-199

Malinowski, B. 214, 292

Marriage: acceptable, 25, 39, 41, 42, 54, 85, 87, 88, 98, 100, 101, 118; advantageous alliances in 39, 41, 43, 49; age at 60, 61, 66, 86, 89, 118, 293, 294, 296-299, 312, 313; age differences between spouses 8, 26, 42, 43, 59-61, 87, 89, 168, 224, 241, 298, 300, 304n; alternative unions 25, 86, 87, 88; and conflict 40-42, 48, 49, 126, 210-213; and kinship 8, 24-26, 39-48, 52-68n, 86, 87-88, 90, 121, 122, 126, 200, 202, 210-213, 214n; changes in, due to contact 17, 38, 40, 41, 48, 49, 86, 87, 89, 90, 310-323; data needed in study of 25; extra-marital relations 33, 34, 38, 41, 43, 121, 165, 168, 170, 172, 239; ideal 24, 25, 35, 39, 41, 42, 48, 49, 53, 54, 61, 67n, 79, 80, 85, 87, 88, 90, 214n, 278; in urban situation 305-325; inheritance or taking of widows 35, 39, 40, 41, 42, 232, 239; mother-in-law avoidance 56, 57, 121, 210, 224, 231, 241; variability in relationships 7, 24, 43, 58; wife-stealing 54, 66; wrong 31, 34, 41-43, 44, 48, 49, 55, 58, 86-88, 118, 121, 122, 138n, 264. See also Betrothal; Elopement

Marriage rates see Demography

Marx, K. 130

Massola, A. 198n

Mathew, J. 20

Mathews, R. H. 19, 20, 191

Mauss, M. 141

Maybury-Lewis, D. H. P. 67n

Meggitt, M. 10, 15, 16, 61, 67n, 70, 79, 90, 99, 105-107, 128, 139n, 209, 211, 214, 221, 223, 224, 248, 259, 261, 267, 269, 280

Micha, F. J. 259

Migration/movement of groups and individuals 9, 14-16, 24, 31-33, 71, 72, 77, 83, 84, 85, 87, 90, 91n, 96-97, 107, 110, 121, 136n, 146, 148, 222, 249n, 251-257, 261, 267-275, 277, 278-290; religiously motivated 72, 96, 97, 272-274

Mission(s): and adaptation of teachings in Aboriginal religion 138n-139n, 258-275; attitudes 31, 165, 166, 171, 250, 252, 253; effects of 13, 14, 32, 88-89, 106, 135, 139n, 250-275, 278, 288

Moieties and/or semi-moieties 8, 33, 36, 38, 51-55, 64, 65, 101, 161n, 178, 187, 197, 201, 202, 203, 209, 210, 211, 212; and marriage 41, 42, 51-53, 101, 210; children's knowledge of 38; in ritual life 201-210

Morris, W. 130

Mother-in-law see Betrothal; Marriage

Mountford, C. P. 12, 71, 137n, 160n, 161n, 180, 185, 197, 282

Mühlmann, W. E. 266

Munn, N. D. 1, 11, 172n, 298; chapter by 141-163

Myth(s), mythology 3, 11-13, 16, 104, 153, 154, 164-172; and birth 154-156, 162n; and incorporation of investigator into subsection system 164-172; and territorial association 16, 94, 95, 98, 103, 110, 118, 124, 126, 129, 132-134, 137n, 141, 142, 143, 146, 160n, 188, 195, 197, 224-233, 263; as guide to social behaviour 164, 172, 219-246; diffusion of 104, 178-198; fire 11, 12, 151, 154, 174-198, 224, 230, 236; linking different areas 94, 95, 98, 102, 104, 124, 126, 129, 148, 181, 186, 224, 233; moral and ethical values in 118, 123, 179, 180-196, 219-246; punishment or conflict in 104, 134, 146, 176, 180, 181, 182, 183-184, 187-188, 189, 190, 191, 192, 193, 194, 195, 219-244; transformation as a process of inheritance 150; transmutation in 141-160, 176, 202; variation in 11-12, 104, 137n, 138n, 180-198, 201, 222-224. See also Religion; Rites

Mythical characters see Beings

INDEX

Names; personal 33, 35, 36, 38, 143, 145; of dead 36, 75, 138*n*
Native doctors 16, 260, 280-285; magical curative powers of 281-283
Needham, R. 24, 59
Nimkoff, M. F. 8

Ownership: of myths, rites, songs 38, 110, 113, 146-152. *See also* Land; Ritual centres

Pan-Pacific Congress, *1923* 20
Parker, C. S. 20, 191, 197
Payments: and betrothal 40, 42, 43, 126-127; and participation in ritual 115, 118, 123, 228, 236
Peterson, N. 1, 12, 13, 214*n*; chapter by 200-215
Petri, H. and/or Petri-Odermann, G. 1, 13-16, 224, 226, 245*n*, 248-252, 256-259, 261, 265, 270, 272; chapter by 248-276
Piddington, R. 23
Pilling, A. R. 63, 214
Pin-Hsiung Lin, 25
Polygyny 16, 17, 35, 88, 89, 278; and outside contact 292-304; decline in 16, 90, 295, 297, 299, 302; demographic factors 16, 17, 89, 294, 296-303; low incidence of, as effect of contact 292-300; regional differences in 295, 297, 298, 301-303
Proust, M. 165

Radcliffe-Brown, A. R. 20, 51, 99, 165, 178, 246*n*
Read, H. 164
Reay, M. 1, 11, 14, 61; chapter by 164-173
Reincarnation 97, 109, 110, 114, 115, 123, 132, 133, 134, 139*n*, 146-147
Religion: and land 6, 10, 13, 107, 217, 287; as system of morality 13, 216-246; directly related to everyday living 95, 107, 111, 139*n*-140*n*, 216, 217, 219, 221, 223; in contact situation 14, 111, 131, 133, 252, 254-276; inheritance 111, 152, 153, 157; mythical transformation and symbolic elements in 11, 13, 141-160, 176, 217; revivalistic cult incorporating Christian concepts 251-258. *See also* Authority; Land; Myth; Rites; Totemism
Reuther, J. G. 26*n*
Rites/ceremonies: and myths/mythical beings 95, 102, 103, 104, 217, 220, 222, 224, 225, 236-238, 252, 258, 259, 261, 263, 283, 284; as resolution of conflict 200-215; associated with dream-spirits 283-288; bestowal *see* Betrothal; changing perspective 13, 14, 16, 97, 103, 104, 115, 136*n*, 254-275; co-operation in 13, 71, 102, 104, 109, 114, 123, 162, 167, 171, 172, 201-213, 284, 285, 288, 289; cultural revival 15, 72, 83, 251-276; diffusion of 94-95, 104, 222, 223, 259, 262, 263, 266, 267, 271, 273; fire 12, 13, 116-117, 186, 200-215; initiation 82, 86, 88, 90, 103-105, 108-109, 116-118, 124, 126, 136*n*, 137*n*, 152, 153, 156, 159, 162*n*, 209, 211, 221, 236, 252, 253, 259, 261, 262, 267, 272, 288; missionaries and effects on 165, 166, 250-275; ownership of 95-96, 102, 110, 146-151, 171, 201-212, 262, 288; special obligations in 201-210; totemic/increase 95-97, 102-104, 109-118, 123, 127, 129-130, 132, 137*n*, 152, 159, 238, 285-288; transmission of 115, 116, 117, 118, 122, 127, 132, 152, 156, 260, 283, 288, 289. *See also* Land; Myth; Religion; Totemism
Ritual/ceremonial centres: associated with person's life cycle 36, 96, 146-149; mythical associations with 36, 94, 95, 109, 110, 113-116, 124, 143-149, 151, 161*n*, 197, 217, 225-232, 244, 287; ownership of 9, 97, 109, 110, 115-116, 122, 135, 136*n*, 146, 151, 152
Robinson, M. 14
Robinson, R. 180
Rockefeller Foundation 20
Rose, F. G. G. 1, 16, 24, 26, 59-62, 65, 67*n*, 70, 75, 292, 297, 298, 300
Roth, W. E. 188, 189, 197

Sacred objects 16, 94, 113, 114-117, 120, 122, 123, 130, 142-159, 161*n*, 202, 203, 220, 224-232, 235-242, 245*n*, 254, 260-264, 267, 280, 281, 284-289; changes in form of 289
Sacred sites *see* Ritual/ceremonial centres
Section(s), subsection(s) (systems) 8, 23, 24, 33, 39, 85, 86, 90, 102, 129, 135*n*-136*n*, 156, 161*n*, 172*n*, 200; 278; and establishing relationship with strangers 86, 164-172; and marriage 25, 39, 51, 85-86, 87, 90, 98-101, 202, 212, 214*n*; and

ritual 102-104, 110, 201-214n; and socio-cultural complex 96-110; changes following outside contact 23, 38, 86, 87; children's knowledge of 38; co-operation in rituals 13, 129, 162, 167, 171, 172, 201-210; diffusion of 8, 10, 23, 24, 38, 86-87, 100
Service, E. R. 67n
Shapiro, W. 1, 7, 8, 26n, 51, 53, 58, 61, 62, 213; chapter by 51-69
Sharp, L. 57
Siebert, O. 26n
Smyth, R. Brough 19, 192, 193, 195
Social control *see* Authority; Leaders/leadership; Marriage
Songs/song cycles: associated with rituals 94, 95, 103, 104, 105, 110, 111, 113, 114, 116, 127, 132, 146, 147, 154, 169, 170, 172, 178, 201, 202, 203, 204, 205, 211, 224, 233, 245n, 262, 283-287, 290n; embodying dream-spirit journeys 284-286; incorporation of personal names in 36; 'travelling' 94, 95, 288
Spencer, W. B./F. J. Gillen 12, 19, 20, 24, 51, 62, 96, 105, 114, 120, 129, 136n, 138n, 139n, 183, 187, 200, 201, 204
Spirit beings *see* Beings; Dream spirits
Stanner, W. E. H. 9, 12, 84, 132, 139n, 161n, 165, 183, 187, 219, 220, 223, 244
Stirling, E. C. 19, 120, 138n,
Strehlow, C. 20, 99, 138n
Strehlow, T. G. H. 1, 5, 10, 12, 15, 102, 103, 221, 223; chapter by 92-140
Subsection(s) *see* Section(s)

Taplin, G. 19
Territories 15, 71-72, 82, 91n, 93, 99-100, 268-270, 274, 275, 278; climate 94, 111; flexibility of 9, 97, 98, 146; mapping of 83, 92, 98; topography 92, 93, 134, 135n, 136n, 146, 148. *See also* Land
Thomas, N. W. 198
Thomson, D. F. 55, 68n
Time 11, 34, 82, 96, 102, 113, 116, 118, 131, 132, 134, 139n, 143, 144, 156, 159, 203, 204, 205, 206, 214n, 216, 274, 284, 285
Tindale, N. B. 14, 15, 71, 162n, 268, 269, 273
Tonkinson, R. 1, 10, 14, 16, 245n, 282, 290n; chapter by 277-291
Totemism: and authority 112, 115, 116, 139n-140; and social organization 23, 97-101, 129, 178, 281-282; and totemic clans 94, 99, 102, 109, 111-115, 130, 133; geographically based 10, 11, 92-112, 130, 132-134, 285. *See also* Religion; Rites; Ritual/ceremonial centres
Totems: ancestral 281-283
Traditional life: changes in 5, 6, 7, 9, 10, 13-16, 17, 18, 31, 81, 84, 97, 113, 121, 122, 135n, 138n, 165-166, 172, 305-325; mission effects on 165, 166, 171-172, 250-275, 278; retention of 5, 6, 72, 90, 111, 113, 130, 249-253, 255, 258-275, 277, 278, 283, 287-290; revival of 5, 15-17, 26, 251, 252, 254, 256; revivalistic movement 15, 251-276
Tribal groups/languages; clans/dialect units (north-eastern Arnhem Land): Amurag 12; Andekerinja 100, 104, 105, 108; Anula 187; Arabana 94, 101; Aranda 9, 10, 17, 20, 51, 52, 61, 62, 64, 65, 82, 83, 93-140, 213, 221, 298; Balamumu 38; Bard (Bad) 23, 275; Bidjandjara *see* Pitjandjara; Bilgana *see* Dagobabwi; Brabralung 192; Bralbral 43, 44n; Budidjara 268; Bunapa 269; Dagobabwi 37, 44n; Dalabon 11, 12, 175-178, 180; Dalwongu 38, 40, 42; Dangbon *see* Dalabon; Damalamiri 37; Dieri 94, 101; Djabu 37, 44n; Djambarbingu 40, 44; Djaru 15; Djauan 24, 176, 180; Djaui 275; Djiwalin (Djualin) 15; Durili 40, 44; Euahlayi 191; Gadudjara 268, 278-290; Galbu 37, 42-44n, 48; Garadjeri 251, 255, 261, 269-271, 274; Gawur (Malawur) 42, 44n; Geadjara 268; Gidja (Lunga) 267; Gidjingali 63; Gobubingu 40; Gogadja *see* Kukatja; Gudji'un 44n; Gugadja *see* Kukatja; Gularabalu 255, 270, 271, 274, 275; Gumaidj 42, 43, 44n, 48; Guneada 269; Gunia 15; Gunwinggu 8, 11, 12, 34; Gurindji 12; Gwiula 44n; Iliaura 95, 119, 120; Jankuntjatjara (Jankuntjatara) 77, 91n, 95, 97, 100, 104, 108, 136n; Jaoro 274; Jarwila 44n; Julbari-dja 14, 15, 260-275, 276n; Julbre *see* Wailbri; Juwalbri *see* Wailbri; Kabikabi 191; Kakadu 12, 183; Kapin 42, 44n; Karadjeri 23, 25, 26, 52, 55, 58, 61; Kariera 61, 65, 274, 278; Kokowara 188; Kukatja (Gugadja) 13, 15, 95, 99, 104, 109, 110, 120, 129, 137n,

138n, 222-247, 268, 273, 274; Kulin 198n, Kurnai 26n; Lialanmiri 40; Loritja 20; Malag see Miwuyt, Murngin, Wulamba; Malawur 43, 44n; Mandjigai 40; Mandjildjara 13, 222-247, 268, 278-290; Mangala 261, 269, 270; Mangarai 24; Mara 187; Maragulu 40; Mararba 37; Marangu 40; Matuntara 98, 100, 104, 108, 124-126, 138n; Miliwurur 44; Miwuyt (Miwoidj or Miwaidj) 8, 55, 58-60, 62, 64-67n (see also Murngin, Wulamba); Mudbara 12; Mungkan 187; Murinbata 12, 186, 187, 197, 223; Murngin 7, 8, 12, 25, 26n, 31, 58, 61, 67n, 182 (see also Miwuyt, Wulamba); Nargala 40, 44n; Ngadi 15, 222-247; Ngala 274; Ngaladar 44n; Ngalagan 180; Ngalgbun 24; Ngalia (Walbiri) 107-109, 295; Ngatadajara (Ngatatjara) 77, 160n, 161n; Ngeimil 42, 44n; Ngulugwongga 12; Njamal 274; Njangomada 254-256, 261, 264, 269, 270, 274; Njanidjara 265, 268; Njigina 266, 269, 274; Nungbulula 42, 44n; Nyul-Nyul 23; Pangkala (Parnkalla) 94, 273; Pintubi 95, 100, 108, 109, 139n, 161n, 295, 297; Pitjandjara 9, 10, 11, 71-90, 100, 104, 109, 110, 120, 122, 138n, 141-163, 295, 297, 304n; Pitjantjatjara see Pitjandjara; Raiung 42, 43, 44n, 48; Riradjingu 37, 44; Tiwi 62, 63, 75, 89; Udialla(s) 254-275; Ungarinyin 24; Unmatjera 94, 95, 107, 117, 129, 135n, 138n; Wailbri see Walbiri; Waka-Waka 191; Walbiri (Wailbri) 11-14, 16, 79-89, 90, 99, 105-109, 136n, 139n, 141-163, 200-215, 221-224, 226, 229, 261, 267, 280, 295-300 (see also Ngalia); Walmadjeri (Walmadjari) 15, 222-247, 260, 265, 266, 268-275, 276n; Wangkamala 93, 94; Wankanguru 93-95, 97, 101, 103, 135n; Wangkatjaka 93, 94; Wanindiljaugwa 89; Wanman 268, 283; Waramiri 43, 44n, 48, 49; Waramunga 12, 200, 201; Warramunga see Waramunga; Western Desert 93, 96, 99, 100, 104, 221-247, 248-276; Wikmunkan 57; Wonajagu see Woneiga; Woneiga 14, 229, 259, 263, 274; Wonggadjunggu 222-247; Wonguri 39, 40; Worgaia 15; Wotjobaluk 198; Wulamba 37, 44n, 67n, (see also Malag, Miwuyt, Murngin); Yir-Yoront 52, 57, 61

Turner, T. 160n

Urbanization: and marriage 305-325; and 'own group' identification 5, 320-325

von Fürer-Haimendorf, C. 244, 245

Warner, W. L. 8, 25, 30, 33, 42, 63, 67n, 68n, 182
Weil, P. M. 291n
Wells, T. A. 121
Wilson, J. and/or K. 14
Winnecke, C. 120, 138n
Women: as original owners of myths/objects/rites 155-156, 225, 235, 236, 240, 267; in contact situation 11, 165-169; in myth 6, 12, 103, 151, 154-156, 162n, 183-185, 187, 188, 189, 191, 192, 193-194, 221-236, 259, 266, 267, 280, 283, 284, 286; love magic, etc. rites and lore 11, 112, 154, 161n, 162n, 165-172, 204; role in performance of rituals etc. 113, 161n, 201-210, 225, 237, 283, 284, 286, 287; status of 105, 156, 160n, 161n, 162n, 225, 280. See also Betrothal; Marriage
World view 13, 140-145, 157-159, 177-178, 216-221, 243, 250-251, 256
Worms, E. A. 23, 268, 269

Yengoyan, A. A. 1, 9, 10, 100, 299; chapter by 70-91